#5

D1269634

SOCIAL SECURITY ADMINISTRATION
OPERATIONS RESEARCH

INTRODUCTION TO
ELECTRONIC DIGITAL COMPUTERS

INTRODUCTION TO ELECTRONIC DIGITAL COMPUTERS

WITH EMPHASIS ON THE SYSTEM/360, FORTRAN IV, AND PL/1

HERBERT MAISEL

Associate Professor and Director, Computation Center
Georgetown University

Written with the Assistance of
DONALD L. WRIGHT
The Mitre Corporation

McGraw-Hill Book Company
New York   St. Louis   San Francisco   Toronto   London   Sydney

INTRODUCTION TO ELECTRONIC DIGITAL COMPUTERS

Library of Congress Catalog Card Number 68-28417
39736

1234567890 MAMM 7543210698

TO
MY WIFE AND MY PARENTS

PREFACE

General Objectives. This book is intended to serve primarily as a text for a first course in electronic digital computers at the undergraduate level and secondarily as an introduction to the computer for interested, scientifically oriented laymen. Because it is being published soon after the System/360 and PL/1 language have become available, it may also serve as a reference for the user of this equipment and/or programming language.

The book is oriented toward the System/360 and the FORTRAN and PL/1 languages because:

1. It is believed that a first course in computers should deal with a specific computer and a specific programming language in some detail. It should not be a superficial survey course, nor should it deal with hypothetical, artificial equipment or programming languages.
2. The System/360 will soon be, if it is not already, one of the most widely used computers at universities and colleges.
3. FORTRAN and PL/1 are expected to be two of the most important programming languages.

This book is planned as a first-course text for the computer-science, mathematics, physical science, social science, or business major but not for the engineering student. The interrelated subjects of logic, Boolean algebra, and circuit design—of special interest to the engineering student —are not covered, nor is equipment discussed from the engineer's point of view. We recognize that the computer-science major is also interested in these subjects. However, in his case, a separate course on logic and, perhaps, on the engineering aspects of computer equipment is preferred.

Analog computers and hybrid systems are not discussed; this book is an introduction to digital computers. Those who are interested in obtaining an introduction to analog computers are referred to either of the following two McGraw-Hill books:

G. A. Korn and T. M. Korn, "Electronic Analog and Hybrid Computers," 1964.

C. L. Johnson, "Analog Computer Techniques," 2d ed., 1963.

Special attention has been given throughout to the importance of software as a computer component. For example, the history of the development of computer software is presented in Part 1 along with the history of the development of the hardware, and the System/360 is described in Part 5 as an integrated system of hardware and software components.

An Annotated Supplementary Bibliography is provided at the end of each chapter for the student, layman, or computer user seeking further information. Also, key words and phrases are italicized in the context in which they are defined, and boldface type is used in the index for the page reference corresponding to this italicized word or phrase. This is done in lieu of providing a glossary; all too often, definitions offered in glossaries are incomplete, inadequate, or not illustrated.

Outline of the Book. The book is divided into five major parts. Part 1 is intended both to place the computer in the American cultural milieu and to provide a history of its development. Part 2 covers a potpourri of fundamental subjects that must be mastered, including the representation of numbers and the construction of algorithms and flow charts. A broad discussion of how a computer works is offered, and brief descriptions are given of some of the more important computer components and the ways in which they are used. Part 2 concludes with an introduction to computer programming and a survey description of some of the more important programming languages.

A few of the applications that are being made of computers are described in Part 3 before any specific programming language or computer is covered in detail. Some authors discuss applications after these topics.

This was not done in this book for two reasons. First, the student, especially the non-scientifically oriented student, needs some motivation before wrestling with the details of a programming language or a computer. Second, it is believed that by avoiding the tedious and somewhat annoying programming detail included in some descriptions of applications, the reader is encouraged to digest the description given and gains a better understanding of the application itself and the contribution made to it by the computer.

Part 4 contains a description of FORTRAN IV, in Chap. 11, and PL/1, in Chap. 12. It is expected that most students will cover either Chap. 11 or Chap. 12, but not both, and these chapters were written to be independent of each other.

The System/360 is described in Part 5. Chapter 13, the first chapter in Part 5, discusses the representation of information in the System/360 and the way arithmetic processes are carried out. Chapter 14 serves to introduce the system and describe some of its highlights. Chapter 15 contains a discussion of the PSW (program-status word), interrupts, and the operating system.

Possible Course Content. The table below indicates the parts of the book that would be most appropriate for a first course oriented toward the indicated type of student. In many colleges and universities, it may be necessary to combine all the nonengineering students into a single course section. The last entry in the table, corresponding to the student category "General," indicates the parts of the book that are believed to be appropriate for such a course. Two entries are provided for the physical

Major	Duration of course (No. of semesters)	Parts of book that might be covered
Computer science	2	All
Physical sciences and mathematics (systems)	1	Chaps. 1–8, 10, 12–14, and 15 as time permits
Physical sciences and mathematics (applications)	1	Chaps. 1–9, 11, 13, and 14
Social science	1	Chaps. 1–7; Secs. 8.5, 9.1, 9.4, and 9.5; Chap. 11 or 12 and 13 and 14
Business	1	Chaps. 1–7, 9, and 12; Secs. 13.1–13.8; and Chap. 14
General	1	Chaps. 1–7; Secs. 8.3, 8.4, 8.5, and 9.4; Chap. 11 or 12; Secs. 13.1–13.8; and Chap. 14.

science and mathematics student, one entry for the student who is applications-oriented, and another entry for the systems-oriented student.

Acknowledgments. The author is especially indebted to Mr. Donald Wright for his editing assistance and substantial systems contributions. Thanks are due to Dr. T. N. E. Greville for introducing the author to spline functions and to Dr. R. Colwell for introducing the author to numerical taxonomy. Miss Ruth Lane helped edit most of the manuscript, and Misses Billie London and Christine De Bruyne generously contributed their typing and illustrating skills. Finally, my sincere appreciation to my wife Millie, who helped out with the typing, withstood my tantrums, and sacrificed her weekends.

Credits. Thanks are due the IBM Corporation, the California Computer Products Corporation, the Teletype Corporation, the United States of America Standards Institute, and Bert F. Green, Jr., for generously giving the author permission to publish the following material:

Source	Material Published
IBM Corporation	Figure 4.3
IBM Corporation	Figure 4.4
IBM Corporation	Figure 4.5
IBM Corporation	Figure 4.7
IBM Corporation	Figure 4.8
IBM Corporation	Figure 4.10
IBM Corporation	Figure 4.12
IBM Corporation	Figure 4.13
IBM Corporation	Figure 4.15
IBM Corporation	Figure 4.16
IBM Corporation	Appendixes D and E
California Computer Products	Figure 4.9
Teletype Corporation	Figure 4.14
USA Standards Inst.	Figure 6.1 and Appendix B
Bert F. Green, Jr.	The table in Section 8.5

Herbert Maisel

CONTENTS

part 1

THE CULTURAL IMPACT
AND HISTORY
OF COMPUTERS

INTRODUCTION

Recent history is necessarily controversial.   Questions such as:

Who was first?

What was the precise nature of this development?

What is the real contribution of this development?

cannot be answered without stirring up a series of claims and counter-claims by the participants.   Any history of the development of the computer must be read with the understanding that other versions exist and that the author is presenting the history as it appears from his own perspective.

The present and future cultural impact of computers is an even more controversial topic.   However, because the impact of computers is substantial, it should be discussed.   It is expected that many of the students will have formed an opinion on the computer's impact before taking the course.   These opinions should be expressed and openly discussed.

OUTLINE

chapter 1
THE CULTURAL IMPACT
OF COMPUTERS

1.1 INTRODUCTION

World War II was the catalyst in the development of two discoveries that have reshaped the modern world—atomic energy and computers. It is the computer rather than atomic energy that will probably be recognized as the most significant scientific product of that war because of its impact on our day-to-day activities. This impact is substantial even today; by 1980 it will directly affect almost everyone in the United States, and by 1990 it will probably be recognized by the layman as one of the most important tools man has ever developed.

Man has always sought aids to assist him in his menial tasks. One of these tasks is computation, the manipulation of numbers. The Chinese merchant flicking the beads on his abacus, the Western merchant operating a modern cash register, and the statistical clerk working a desk calculator are all using computational aids. However, each of these aids is being applied to one problem or a single class of problems. Each is only one or two orders of magnitude faster and more reliable than a human calculator. None of these aids is called upon to make decisions— much less to implement them. The electronic digital computer is not similarly bound with respect to application, speed, reliability, or function. That is why its application to man's computational and information-handling problems will be truly revolutionary.

1.2 THE SECOND INDUSTRIAL REVOLUTION

The second industrial revolution is now taking place. We can already see some of its effects, and we should be able to predict most of the remaining effects. Many of the most menial mental tasks of humans will be relegated to the computer. Record keeping, the control of manufacturing processes, and even some instructional and supervisory tasks will soon be routinely assigned to the computer.

Several more developments that will surely come are needed to complete the second industrial revolution. Among these developments are another sharp drop in the cost of computers, the ability to communicate with computers by handwriting, and a broadly based capability to write instructions for computers. The third of these developments may come last. We may have to wait until a new generation grows to adulthood, a generation that takes computers for granted because it learned about base 2 in elementary school and about algorithms and problem-oriented languages in high school. The first two developments are a natural consequence of technological effort now under way. They are, perhaps, less than a decade away.

1.3 PRESENT IMPACT ON OUR CULTURE

Computers today are recording airline reservations, maintaining customer accounts in a single central location for a bank with many branches, assisting in the analysis of electrocardiograms, helping to control traffic in a large city, assisting in the review of income tax returns, and controlling a network of interlocking electrical supply lines.

What effects has this had on our day-to-day nonworking activities? It is now easier to make airline reservations; we have access to all flights, and chances for error are very much smaller. We are now permitted to bank at any one of a large number of branches of a commerical bank, and it is done more efficiently and with fewer errors than if we were required to bank at just a single branch. More electrocardiograms can now be processed in less time. More factors can now be taken into account in their analysis because data from many electrocardiograms for both normal and diseased patients can be systematically and thoroughly analyzed. These results can be incorporated into the analysis of a single electrocardiogram. It now takes 20 minutes rather than 30 minutes to drive into Toronto from its suburbs via routes whose traffic lights are controlled by a computer. We have been convinced, in no uncertain terms, that we must be more thorough in reporting our income and more careful in claiming deductions because all our income will be reported to and summed by a computer and because this same computer will be able to detect idiosyncrasies in our deduction patterns. Last, and most dramatic, the Northeast United States was subjected to a blackout of electrical service in the fall of 1965 that would probably not have been so widespread if the electrical supply systems had not been computer-analyzed. However, it is also true that the computer-analyzed system has substantially reduced electrical costs by allowing certain localities and suppliers to avoid duplicating facilities and to rely on neighboring facilities—in fact, on a whole network of facilities—for reserve supplies of electricity.

1.4 FUTURE IMPACT ON OUR CULTURE

What of the future? The computer is now our tool and should always remain so. This means that it must be asked to do only what we could not or would not do for ourselves. The danger that the computer will become the controller rather than the tool, either by default or by design, is a real one. The user must continue to synthesize, test, guide, decide, and communicate with other human beings. It is reasonable to expect that the computer will take on more and more routine "creative" activities. However, the choice of the activity, the scope of the computer's contribution, and the impact of this activity on related activities must remain under the control of man.

For example, let us consider the business executive. It seems reasonable to expect that he will maintain control but will permit the computer to make more and more decisions. He will concentrate most of his efforts on what will happen in the future—not in terms of short-range decisions on pricing, marketing, and manufacture but rather by implementing major policy changes in a representation stored in the computer of that portion of the economy that is significant to his business. He will then be able to anticipate what the effects of these policies would be if they were implemented and to compare this with the extrapolated effects of his current policies. His competitors will also be doing this, and such terms as "strategies" and "optimization," which are now used by technicians, will become more widely used by executives.

We have been talking of the business executive. What of the scientist, the secretary, the office manager, the laboratory technician, the machinist, the barber? There will certainly be changes in the working activities of some of these people. The scientist will function more and more creatively, the secretary will become a kind of administrative assistant, and the office manager will become a computer specialist. The job of machinist will probably become obsolete, but the demand in other areas will increase—for example, guides in the National Park Service, technicians assisting conservationists in field activities, and technical assistants to college instructors. The barber will probably be around for quite a while.

In one vision of the future, we can ultimately become a society of teachers and students, philosophers and artists, writers and actors, gardeners and artisans, and scientists and executives. Many of us can become missionaries, following the example of the Peace Corps. This happy result can be achieved if we are alert to the potential of the computer and are realistic about its inevitable place as our most widely used tool. Also, we should seriously consider such things as guaranteed annual wages and schooling as an adult activity, and we should recognize and encourage the creative contribution to our culture that everyone can make.

We shall conclude this section by discussing three potential areas of application that should help to illustrate the impact that the computer will make on our culture. Consider first a computer system that contains the medical history of almost every person in the United States. If we were willing to expend the necessary resources, we could, even today, begin to develop such a system; present computer technology would permit it. We shall very likely have such a system in operation within two or three decades. Let us consider this system from two points of view: the support it could offer the diagnostician and the information it could provide the medical researcher. Complete medical histories would be available to assist in diagnosis even though the patient might have had several different doctors and have resided in different areas. Once the diagnosis was established, information on the effectiveness of alternative methods of treatment would also be available. The medical researcher would be able to draw from these files data pertinent to many areas of medical research. The duplication of expensive research effort could be avoided. Breakthroughs in the diagnosis and treatment of rare diseases could be anticipated if only because this computer system would offer the only possible source for a large body of information on these diseases. With appropriate provision for secrecy and privacy, such a system could substantially add to our well-being.

Consider next a central accounting facility for every person and business in the United States. Currency might become obsolete. A master charge plate, supplemented perhaps by some means of positive identification (such as on-the-spot fingerprints), could serve every purchasing need. Computer accounts could replace currency as a medium of exchange. Earnings from all sources would be credited directly to the account; purchases would be debited. Loans would be arranged, perhaps automatically up to a prescribed limit, to support credit purchases; loan payments could also be made automatically. Of course, the account would also be automatically debited to pay the inevitable taxes. The status of an account could be sent directly to the home, perhaps via a telephone line linked to a typewriter.

Thirdly, let us consider a network of computer-controlled transportation facilities. Perhaps it would be a combination of high-speed express railways between major urban areas and slower local service via monorails or individual railway cars or radio-controlled buses. This service could be supplemented by a combination of throughways for interurban travel, with a computer controlling the entry, exit, and speed of your car, and a network of small buses and moving sidewalks for intraurban travel. This same transportation network would include freight facilities, so that deliveries of purchased goods would be nearly as responsive as the system that ensures payment for the purchase.

This should suffice to indicate why by 1990 even the layman might be expected to consider the electronic digital computer to be one of the prime tools of man.

ANNOTATED SUPPLEMENTARY BIBLIOGRAPHY

The first three references cited below present a good summary of the present and projected impact of the computer on our culture in terms of specific areas of application. The remaining references discuss the computer's impact in broader terms.

1. *Datamation*, pp. 23–24, January, 1966.
2. *Ibid.*, pp. 24–29, December, 1965.
3. Licklider, J. C. R.: "Libraries of the Future," The M.I.T. Press, Cambridge, Mass., 1965.
4. Wiener, N.: "The Human Use of Human Beings; Cybernetics and Society," Houghton Mifflin Company, Boston, 1950. An early warning of the coming of automation by the first cybernetician.
5. Hilton, A. M.: An Ethos for the Age of Cyberculture, *Proc. Spring Joint Computer Conf.*, pp. 139–153, 1964. One woman's view of the cultural impact of computers and of the changes in our society's cultural values that are needed to meet this impact.
6. Fein, L.: Computer-oriented Peace Research, *Proc. Fall Joint Computer Conf.*, pp. 631ff., 1963. For the reader who is not aware of the impact of the computer on this area of our culture.
7. Auerbach, I. L.: The International Impact of Computers, *Commun. ACM*, pp. 466–487, October, 1961. A somewhat dated summary of the computer's impact outside of the United States.
8. "Report of the National Commission on Technology, Automation, and Economic Progress," Feb. 3, 1966. Available in an abridged version from the Government Printing Office in a publication entitled "Technology and the American Economy."

chapter 2

AN HISTORICAL SURVEY OF THE DEVELOPMENT OF THE COMPUTER

2.1 MECHANICAL CALCULATORS

The antecedents of the modern electronic computer can be found in mechanical calculators that are centuries old.   The *abacus* (see Fig. 2.1 and [1]) is probably the oldest and the most important of these calculators; it is still widely used today.   In the hands of a skilled operator, this device rivals modern mechanical desk calculators in the speed of its calculation.

In the mid-seventeenth century, Blaise Pascal, a well-known mathematician and philosopher, used the position of a rotating wheel to indicate the value of a digit in a mechanical calculator he developed.   Carryover was achieved by making special connections between the wheels representing adjacent digits, so that when the right-hand wheel was rotated from position 9 to position 0, the left-hand wheel was advanced one position.   This calculator could only add and subtract, but since

$$4 \times 3 = 4 + 4 + 4$$

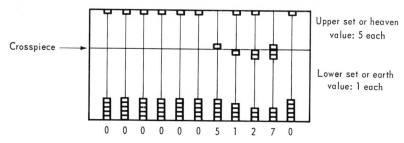

Fig. 2.1 This shows how we would mark the number 51,270 on the abacus. The beads, or counters, represent digits. An upper counter is worth five units, and each lower counter is worth one unit. The value of the digit in each position is determined by summing the values of the counters pressed against the crosspiece.

or, more generally,

$$a \times b = \underbrace{a + a + \cdots + a}_{b \text{ times}}$$

products could be obtained by repeated additions. Near the end of the seventeenth century, Leibniz, who was also a mathematician and philosopher, extended Pascal's ideas to design a desk calculator that could also multiply and divide.

The next important advance in computing was a conceptual one. Near the beginning of the nineteenth century, Charles Babbage, a professor of mathematics at Cambridge University, designed a machine which he called a *difference engine* to help in the construction of mathematical tables. His idea was to reconstruct a mathematical function from its differences.† He built a device that could handle second-degree polynomials, but he ran into some serious technological difficulties when he attempted to construct more complex equipment. The parts could not be made precisely enough to permit them to mesh into an effective machine.

Babbage also conceived of another calculator, an *analytical engine*.

---

† Given a function in the form of a table that lists the functional value corresponding to different, equally spaced values of the argument, one can compute the differences in successive values of the function, which we call *first differences*. The differences in these differences can also be computed. They are called *second differences*. For some smooth mathematical functions, certain differences will follow a prescribed, simple pattern. For example, the second differences of a second-degree polynomial are constant. Babbage proceeded in the opposite way. He started with the simple pattern in the differences and a first entry in the table and, by successive additions, reconstructed the function itself.

This calculator was to have two distinct parts—a store to hold data until they were to act as operands and a mill to process the data. Answers were to be returned to the store for future reference. This is, in principle, the way modern electronic computers function. The analytical engine was never completed.

Until now, we have been discussing mechanical aids that are restricted to the four arithmetic processes. In manipulating data, there is another, more basic process of importance—counting. By *counting*, we mean finding the number of units in a collection, whereas *addition* refers to the combining of two or more numbers into a single number, namely, their sum.

Counting (or enumeration) is a major function of the Bureau of the Census. In the late nineteenth century, Herman Hollerith, an employee of the Census Bureau, realized that punched cards could be used to store digital information by the presence or absence of a series of holes on the card. Once the information is stored in this form, machines could help in the enormous task of enumeration inherent in the taking of a census. Nearly a century before this time, French textile mills were using Jacquard's punched cards to control the weaving patterns of looms. However, this special-purpose application of punched cards was not generalized. Hollerith's scheme was adopted by commercial interests in the decades that followed, and prior to the development of computers, it was widely applied to the processing of large volumes of data in business and statistical applications. Though Hollerith did not foresee the electronic calculator, his punched card is today one of the most important means for entering digital information into a computer.

The punched-card system was not the first of these calculating aids to be used to commercial advantage. A design of the mechanical desk calculator was developed that permitted production on a commercial basis in 1857, but the calculator was not mass-produced until Oldher did so in 1892. Electric power but not control was added to these calculators about three decades later.

At the Bell Telephone Laboratories, in 1937, George Stibitz began building an electromechanical calculator that used open or closed relays, rather than the presence or absence of holes, to record information [2]. The first relay computer, called the *Complex Calculator*, was set up in the Bell Laboratories building in New York City in 1940. Several more elaborate relay computers were developed by the Bell Telephone Laboratories in the next decade.

The ultimate in electromechanical calculators was designed by Howard Aiken at Harvard University in 1937. The machine was constructed by the International Business Machines Corporation (IBM) and presented to Harvard in 1944. Called the *Mark I, Automatic Sequence Controlled Calculator*, it contained 72 adding accumulators.

The Mark I was given its instructions through the use of a combination of punched paper tape, boards which permitted the rewiring of some connections, and various switches and buttons.   The position of a rotating cam replaced the open or closed relay and the presence or absence of a hole on a punched card as the basic unit of digital information.   (Recall that the presence or absence of a hole had, in its turn, replaced the position of a rotating wheel.)   Though the Mark I was truly electromechanical rather than electronic, its use of a battery of accumulators for calculations and of punched paper tape and boards for instructions was carried over in the design of the earliest electronic calculators.

Figure 2.2 contains a chronological summary of the development of mechanical calculators.

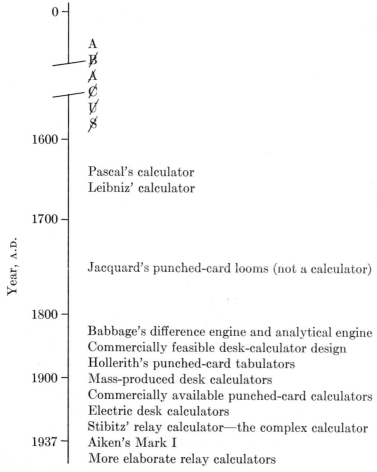

Fig. 2.2   Chronological summary of the development of mechanical calculators.

2.2 THE ELECTRONIC DIGITAL COMPUTER

In 1954, the first installation of an electronic digital computer for business applications was made at the General Electric Appliance Park in Louisville, Kentucky. The Universal Automatic Computer, or *UNIVAC*, installed at this time was manufactured by a company headed by the team of J. Presper Eckert and J. W. Mauchly. These two men, while at the Moore School of Electrical Engineering at the University of Pennsylvania, designed the Electronic Numerical Integrator and Calculator, or *ENIAC*, which was completed in 1945. The ENIAC was installed at the Aberdeen Proving Ground and helped to produce many tables, especially ballistic tables, for the Ordnance Department of the U.S. Army.

The ENIAC used vacuum tubes to record data, in lieu of mechanical relays or holes in cards or positions of wheels. It was programmed by means of boards and switches that established new connections for the sea of cables on the floor and in trays in the computer room. It did not keep both the instructions and the data in its storage facility; only data were stored. However, it was much faster than the Mark I, and the combination of its success and the intensive design effort devoted to similar devices led to a rash of electronic computers in the period 1947 to 1952.

A proposal for a computer to be built for the Institute for Advanced Study in Princeton is worthy of further consideration. This proposal grew out of a study made by a committee headed by the mathematician John Von Neumann. The study was made for the U.S. Army Ordnance Department, which had already had some favorable experience with the ENIAC computer and sought to stimulate further improvements in computers. Entitled "Preliminary Discussion of the Logical Design of an Electronic Computing Instrument," the proposal's recommendations included the use of binary representation, parallel processing, and stored instructions that could themselves be processed.

In *binary representation*, combinations of 0s and 1s represent all numbers in the computer and all calculations are performed with such numbers. A number is ordinarily expressed in the decimal system in terms of powers of 10; that is, a number, read from right to left, indicates how many 1s, 10s, 100s, etc., are in it. For example, 62 contains two 1s and six 10s. In binary representation, powers of 2 are used to indicate the number of 1s, 2s, 4s, etc. This means that only two symbols are necessary, but it also means that the numbers are longer. In binary notation, 111110 is used to represent the decimal number 62.

In *parallel arithmetic processing*, we retain a series of digits in a single group, or word. This word is then processed as a unit, rather than digit by digit. *Serial arithmetic,* as opposed to parallel arithmetic, involves the processing of all numbers digit by digit. It requires less complex equipment than a parallel processor, but it is slower.

The *stored-program concept* permits us to operate on the instructions themselves as if they were data. This means, in effect, that the computer can change its own instructions. This is done in a prescribed way, of course, but it still results in a great deal of versatility. The instruction is itself a number. One part of the instruction is used to designate the operation to be performed. For example, in the IBM 1620 computer, a 21 is used to indicate addition. Other parts of the instruction are used to refer to the operands. The computer has special circuits that analyze this number and cause the codified instruction to be executed.

The history of the computer since 1954 has been one of increasing speed and compactness, reduced purchase and leasing prices, and more versatile devices for communicating with the computer. The use of the transistor, developed at the Bell Telephone Laboratories in 1948, as a computer component reduced the size and cost of computers and also reduced the air-conditioning and maintenance requirements. The changeover to transistors occurred in the period 1956 to 1959.

More recently, improved manufacturing techniques have permitted the miniaturization† of computer components, which not only has made computers more compact and less costly to purchase and operate but also has increased computer speeds.

Computer technology will soon reach the point where the speed of light is a limiting factor in the number of calculations that the computer can perform in a unit of time. Speeds of computer operation are now being measured in *nanoseconds* (billionths of a second), as opposed to *microseconds* (millionths of a second) and *milliseconds* (thousandths of a second). An electric pulse, traveling at the speed of light, will move about 1 foot in a nanosecond, so that the distance the pulse is required to travel will enter into computer-design considerations.

In addition to miniaturization, developments since 1962 include storage devices with enormous capacities, equipment that will accept a few special type fonts printed on paper as an input medium, and equipment that will permit easy communication between the computer and a remote location using a typewriterlike device and a televisionlike display.

Finally, and perhaps most important, the development of elaborate sets of computer programs and special-purpose equipment permits the sharing of a computer facility among several users, each of whom is entering his input and obtaining his results in overlapping time periods.

---

† In one miniaturization process, chip transistors are assembled into a ceramic base with the connective wiring preengraved or printed on the base. This has resulted in the reduction of a circuit that was mounted on a 3×4 inch card to a $\frac{1}{2}$-inch square.

This development will almost certainly result in the more widespread use of computers.

2.3 THE SOFTWARE COMPONENT

A computer system is more than a collection of equipment and its inter-connections; it also includes sets of instructions that permit effective use of this equipment. These sets of instructions are called *software*. Little emphasis in system specification and design was given to software until recently. The situation is changing as computer manufacturers and their customers begin to think of software as a component of the computer system rather than as an appendage to be developed after the equipment is installed.

The history of software as a computer component is short. Even the Mark I, although an electromechanical computer, had a software component that was typical of those developed for almost all the first generation of electronic computers. It consisted of a collection of special prewritten sets of instructions that could be incorporated into a more elaborate series of instructions, thereby avoiding the tedious rewriting of the same sets of instructions. These prewritten sets of instructions are called *subroutines*. In one of the earliest programming manuals [4], the recommended procedure for programming was based on the extensive use of the subroutines available for the EDSAC computer at the University of Manchester in England. Such subroutines are still part of the software component in computers delivered today, but they have become a relatively small part of this component.

The UNIVAC I, the first large-scale electronic computer commercially marketed,† served as the inspiration for the most important software components that were provided with computers in the decade from 1955 to 1965. These were problem-oriented programming languages. Three conceptually important problem-oriented languages were developed, largely under the direction of Dr. Grace Hopper; however, these languages never came into widespread use because of the relatively limited distribution of the UNIVAC I itself and the lack of sufficient effort on the part of the vendor to effectively propagate these tools. These languages were *math-matic* and *flow-matic* [5] and the *A2 compiler* [6].

A great deal more about problem-oriented languages and their antecedents, machine-language programming and assembly systems, will be presented in Chap. 7. Here we need only note that programming computers in their own numerical language is a tedious and difficult task. Assembly systems, which simplified the task somewhat, were developed

† For scientific applications in 1951 and business applications in 1954.

to permit more widespread use of alphabetic characters and symbols in writing programs and, in some cases, to automatically choose storage locations for instructions so as to minimize the running time of the program. However, assembly languages were still very far removed from the language of the problem itself. It was recognized by Dr. Hopper and others that the computer could be used as a translator, or compiler, which accepted as input a series of instructions written in an artificial but more problem-oriented language and which produced as output a machine-language program. Sometimes this had to be done in several steps. For example, in the first step, the input would be the program written in a problem-oriented language and the output would be the same program translated into an assembly language, and in the second step, the input would be the assembly-language program and the output the machine-language program.

The major difficulty in implementing software components during the early history of the computer was that the computer became obsolete before the software component was perfected. The *IBM* 650 *computer*, first available in 1955, was probably the first computer that was around long enough and used widely enough to permit substantial implementation of its software components. *SOAP*, Symbolic Optimizer and Assembly Program, was a widely used optimizing assembly system. The Bell Interpretive System was a less frequently used problem-oriented language.

The *IBM* 704 *computer* served as the inspiration for the development of what is probably the most important and certainly the most widely used problem-oriented language—FORTRAN. In the period 1957 to 1959, this language gained wide acceptance among 704 users [7]. As its name (from FORmula TRANslation) implies, the language is algebraically oriented. Another algebraically oriented language, ALGOL (from ALGorithmically Oriented Language), was developed under the joint sponsorship of the Association for Computing Machinery (ACM) and GAMM, the European professional association of computer specialists. First specifications for this language appeared in 1958 [8]. Its development was intended to result in a broadly accepted, standard algebraic language. However, FORTRAN became the broadly accepted algebraic language in the United States, although ALGOL did become the standard algebraic language in Europe (at least in its later version, known as ALGOL 60). It is also true that many dialects of both FORTRAN and ALGOL were developed in the United States—so that compilers such as FORTRAN II, GOTRAN, BALGOL, ALGO, JOVIAL, and MAD were developed in the period 1958 to 1962.

Thus far we have talked about problem-oriented languages as if there was only one kind of problem—the manipulation of data in scientific applications. A second problem involves the manipulation of large files of data with a minimum of application of formulas. These have been called *business* or *data-processing* applications, though many scientists also have problems of this sort. For example, such scientific applications as numerical taxonomy or the retrieval and use of research data accumulated over a long period of time involve the manipulation of large files of data.

In any case, algebraic languages were not sufficiently problem-oriented for these data-processing applications. In 1959, the Department of Defense organized a committee to develop a problem-oriented language for business applications. The language was to use ordinary English terminology as much as possible and to permit easy manipulation of large files of data. The product of this committee's efforts, COBOL (from COmmon Business-Oriented Language), was first described and made available in 1960 in a version called COBOL 60. This was immediately followed by COBOL 61 [9] and COBOL 61 extended [10] in 1961 and 1962. Despite a United States government ruling that it would not purchase or lease any equipment from a computer manufacturer that did not have a COBOL software component, the implementation of COBOL by computer manufacturers was neither speedy nor complete. For example, the COBOL compiler for the IBM 7090 computer implemented only a fraction of the language specified for COBOL 61 extended. The major reason for the difference in the degree of implementation of FORTRAN and COBOL was probably that the resources of the IBM Corporation were marshalled to help implement FORTRAN.

Other problem-oriented languages were developed in the late fifties and early sixties. These included list-processing, simulation, and general-purpose languages. PL/1 is an example of a general-purpose language.

Users of large, very fast computers soon realized that they required software to:

1. Maintain smooth job flow
2. Call up programs and subroutines, including compilers, as needed, from a library of such programs, which might be stored on a reel of magnetic tape
3. Perform administrative accounting functions, such as keeping track of the amount of computer time used by each job

With the exception of *generalized programming*,† operating systems designed to carry out some or all of these functions were usually developed by individual users for their own installations—until the development of the SHARE Operating System, *SOS* [11]. Like COBOL, SOS was devel-

† Generalized programming was developed for the UNIVAC computer.

oped by a committee of computer users. This time, the computer was the IBM 709 and the users were members of the SHARE organization, an association of users of large IBM computers. The committee prepared specifications for the system, and an internal IBM programming group wrote the system to conform to these specifications. This approach to developing an operating system resulted in some deficiencies; for example, the first version of SOS did not include a capability to compile FOR-TRAN programs. This deficiency was corrected in 1962 by the RAND Corporation.

In the period 1963 to 1966, much effort was devoted to developing software and hardware systems that would permit sharing of the computer facility among many jobs, some of which might be input from remote locations. In some cases, the time-sharing systems were designed to accept input, to form queues of tasks with intricate rules for priority of service, to produce outputs, and in general, to take on many of the tasks of the computer operator and the dispatcher.

One of the first of these systems was developed by the *Systems Development Corporation* in the early sixties [12]. Because it used a one-of-a-kind AN/FSQ-32 computer, manufactured by IBM, it did not get the widespread attention it deserved. It permitted communication with remote computers as well as with remote Teletypewriter terminals and cathode-ray-tube display units. A system intended mainly for the use of undergraduate students was put into operation at Dartmouth Univer-sity in the summer of 1964, using a *GE 225 computer*, supplemented with a *Datanet 30 computer*, to service the remote Teletypewriter terminals. *Project MAC* at the Massachusetts Institute of Technology was developed at about the same time. It has been more widely discussed and is acknowledged by some to be the first working time-sharing system [13].†
It used an IBM 7094 computer and a GE 645 computer in the developmental stages of the project and accepted input from as many as 30 remotely located teletypewriters. The MIT system was designed for use by faculty researchers and graduate students.

In 1965, the IBM Corporation announced the specifications for modular software to be implemented on its System/360 computers [14]. The software consists of distinct programming packages that can be used separately or in combination according to the needs of the user. Some users may need only a simple system, others a more complex one, and still others a system with time-sharing capabilities and extensive job-queueing features. Each user may pick the combination of software components he requires.

† This claim is strongly disputed. In addition to the SDS system and Project MAC, Project Mercury has been considered by some to have instituted the first time-sharing system.

	HARDWARE DEVELOPMENTS		SOFTWARE DEVELOPMENTS	
1945	ENIAC design completed	S		1945
		U		
	ENIAC operation	B		
	Von Neumann's design paper	R		
		O		
		U		
	EDSAC and BINAC	T	Math-matic	
		I	A2 Compiler	
1950	Magnetic-tape input/ output	N	Flow-matic	1950
	UNIVAC commercially marketed	E		
	First computer in business (UNIVAC I)	S		
1955	First computer to gain widespread acceptance (IBM 650)		SOAP (symbolic assembler)	1955
	Magnetic-core storage		FORTRAN	
	Transistorized computers			
1960	Mass-storage systems		ALGOL	1960
			COBOL	
	Thin-film storage			
	Microminiaturization		Time sharing (MAC, SDS, Dartmouth)	
			Modular software components	
1965			PL/1	1965

Fig. 2.3 Chronological summary of the development of electronic computers and their software.

Figure 2.3 contains a chronological survey of the development of the electronic computer and its software components in the two decades between 1945 and 1965.

REFERENCES

1. Yoshino, Y.: "The Japanese Abacus Explained," Dover Publications, Inc., New York, 1964.
2. Stibitz, G. R.: The Relay Computers at Bell Labs, *Datamation*, pp. 35–44, April, 1967, and pp. 45–49, May, 1967.
3. *Datamation*, pp. 24–31, September, 1962, and pp. 36–41, October, 1962.
4. Wilkes, M. V., D. J. Wheeler, and S. Gill: "The Preparation of Programs for an Electronic Digital Computer," Addison-Wesley, Publishing Company, Inc., 1951.
5. Taylor, A. E.: The Flow-matic and Math-matic Automatic Programming Systems, in "Review of Automatic Programming," vol. 1, pp. 196–206, Pergamon Press, New York, 1960.
6. Hopper, G.: The Education of a Computer, *Proc. Natl. Meetings ACM*, pp. 243ff., Pittsburgh, 1952.
7. Backus, J. W., et al.: The Fortran Automatic Coding System, *Proc. Western Joint Computer Conf.*, pp. 188–198, Los Angeles, 1957.
8. Perlis, A. J., and K. Samelson: Preliminary Report—International Algebraic Language, *Commun. ACM*, vol. 1, pp. 8–22, December, 1958.
9. Sammet, Jean E.: Basic Elements of COBOL 61, *Commun. ACM*, vol. 5, pp. 237–253, 1962.
10. Department of Defense: "COBOL-1961 EXTENDED, External Specifications for a Common Business Oriented Language," 1962.
11. Mealy, G. H.: Operating Systems, *RAND Corp. Doc.* P2584, Santa Monica, Calif., 1962.
12. Schwartz, J. V., E. G. Coffman, and C. Weissman: A General Purpose Time-sharing System, *AFIPS Conf. Proc.*, vol. 25, pp. 397–411, 1964.
13. Corbato, F. J., M. Merwin-Daggett, and R. C. Daley: An Experimental Time-sharing System, *Proc. Spring Joint Computer Conf.*, pp. 335–344, 1962.
14. IBM Operating System/360, Introduction, *IBM Systems Ref. Library Form* C28-6534.

ANNOTATED SUPPLEMENTARY BIBLIOGRAPHY

In general, summary references are emphasized in this bibliography. We have also included a reference to the work of Charles Babbage. The titles of these references are self-explanatory, and no further notes are believed necessary.

1. Babbage, R. H.: The Work of Charles Babbage, *Harvard Univ. Symp.*, pp. 13–22, 1947.
2. Chase, G. C.: History of Mechanical Computing Machinery, *Proc. Natl. Meetings ACM*, pp. 1–28, Pittsburgh, 1952.
3. Mesick, B. S.: History of Army Ordnance Electronic Computing Machines, *Office Naval Res. Symp.*, pp. 85–86, 1951.
4. Knuth, D. E.: History of Writing Compilers, *Proc. Natl. Meetings ACM*, paper no. 43, 1962.
5. Rosen, S.: Programming Systems and Languages: A Historical Survey, *Proc. Spring Joint Computer Conf.*, pp. 1–16, 1964.

part 2

FUNDAMENTALS

INTRODUCTION

This portion of the book is intended to provide the groundwork for understanding what computers are like and how processes are implemented on them. Since the discussion is fundamental, it is independent of any one computer or any one technique for describing processes. Two specific languages for describing processes to a computer will be presented in Part 4—FORTRAN IV and PL/1. A specific family of computers, the IBM System/360, will be discussed in Part 5.

Learning about computers begins with an understanding of what computers look like and how information is represented in them. Once this tangible beginning is available, the more abstract subject of the implementation of processes can be attacked. The presentation in Part 2 takes this approach. The representation of information in a computer is discussed first, along with a discussion of how arithmetic processes are executed. The flow of information is discussed next, and then the components of a computer are described. Now, armed with bits, floating points, disks, and light pens, the student is asked to attack the more abstract subjects of algorithms, flow charts, and computer programs. At the conclusion of Part 2, the student should understand how procedures for solving specified problems are developed, recorded, and transmitted to the computer. However, until he masters at least one of the languages for transmitting procedures to a computer described in Part 4 of the book, he will not be able to do all these things himself.

OUTLINE

3. The Representation of Information in a Digital Computer

3 1   Introduction
3.2   The codification of information for a computer
3.3   Positional representation of positive integers
3.4   Conversion from one base to another
3.5   Numbers with nonintegral parts
3.6   Floating-point representation
3.7   Arithmetic processes in a computer

4. A Description of the Components of a Computer

4.1   Introduction
4.2   General flow of information
4.3   Input/output media and devices
4.4   Storage media and devices
4.5   Remote terminals

5. Algorithms

5.1   Definition
5.2   Connection with computer programming
5.3   The sieve of Eratosthenes
5.4   Iteration
5.5   An algorithm for obtaining square roots
5.6   Payrolls
5.7   Testing algorithms
5.8   Errors in implementing algorithms on a digital computer

6. Flow Charts

6.1   Introduction
6.2   The USA standard for flow-chart symbols
6.3   An example of a simple flow chart—the sieve of Eratosthenes
6.4   Detailed and general flow charts
6.5   Flow charts for the payroll problem

7. An Introduction to Computer Programming and a Survey of Programming Languages

7.1   Introduction
7.2   A hypothetical machine language—the 4-address system

chapter 3

THE REPRESENTATION
OF INFORMATION
IN A DIGITAL COMPUTER

3.1 INTRODUCTION

The raw materials with which computers work are sets of digits, which represent the characters being processed by the computer. This chapter contains a discussion of certain conventions used in representing and processing these sets of numbers. The following topics will be covered:

1. The codification of information for a computer
2. The concept of positional notation and the radix, or base, of a number system
3. Procedures for converting from numbers expressed in terms of one base to numbers expressed in terms of another base
4. Floating-point representation of numbers
5. Arithmetic processes as carried out in a computer

3.2 THE CODIFICATION OF INFORMATION FOR A COMPUTER

A computer stores and processes sequences of digits. This means that everything that is to be processed must be reduced to a series of digits.

Codes are used to represent nonnumerical information.   An example of this codification was discussed in Sec. 2.2—the use of two-digit numbers to represent operations.

A variety of codes for representing alphabetic and numeric, or more succinctly, *alphanumeric*, information have been developed.   Different computers represent information in different ways.   The IBM 1620, for example, uses a two-digit decimal number to represent alphanumeric information.   The number 0 is represented by 70, 1 by 71, an A by 41, and a B by 42.   Special characters can also be represented.   Thus, for example, in the 1620, a 23 is used to represent a comma and a 33 an equals sign.   So long as the code is rigidly maintained and so long as the devices, such as the card reader and the printer, that interpret inputs and prepare outputs translate from this code to the appropriate character, the nature of the code itself need not be mastered.

A user should, however, get to know which characters he may employ in any particular application.   For example, in writing instructions for a computer, the set of characters that may be used is determined by the language in which the instructions are to be written.   Characters that are not in the allowed set will not be accepted even though the computer could code and store these characters if they were input in another context.

3.3 POSITIONAL REPRESENTATION OF POSITIVE INTEGERS

The number 437 is understood to mean: four 100s plus three 10s plus seven 1s, or if we reverse the order, $7 \times 10^0 + 3 \times 10^1 + 4 \times 10^2$. Note that multipliers of successive powers of 10 are used to represent the number since, ordinarily, a decimal, or 10-based, system is used.   More generally, if a prescribed positive integer r is used to denote the *base*, or *radix*, of a number system, a positive integer N can be written as follows:†

(F3.1) $N = a_0 r^0 + a_1 r^1 + \cdots + a_m r^m$

where the coefficients a_0, a_1, etc., are to be chosen from the set 0, 1, . . . , $r - 1$.

Conventionally, N is written by listing the coefficients as follows: $a_m a_{m-1} a_{m-2} \cdots a_2 a_1 a_{0_r}$.   In other words, the coefficient of the greatest power of r is written first, then the next greatest, and so on down to the multiplier of r^0, that is, the multiplier of 1.   The base being used is indicated by concluding the number with the base written as a subscript.   If the base is 10, the subscript may be omitted.

† For the reader who is unfamiliar with the notation $\cdots$, it is used to indicate that the pattern established before the three dots will be used to fill in the missing elements in the sequence.   Thus, for example, $a_0 r^0 + a_1 r^1 + \cdots + a_4 r^4$ is a shorthand way of writing $a_0 r^0 + a_1 r^1 + a_2 r^2 + a_3 r^3 + a_4 r^4$.

For example, if we write 11011_2, this is $1 \times 2^4 + 1 \times 2^3 + 0 \times 2^2 + 1 \times 2^1 + 1 \times 2^0 = 27$.

If $r > 10$, new symbols must be added to represent the digits 10, 11, 12, and so on. The convention has been adopted of using the letters of the alphabet, beginning with A to represent 10, B for 11, and so on. Thus in writing numbers to base 16, that is, writing in the *hexadecimal* system, the coefficients would be chosen from among the set 0, 1, 2, 3, 4, 5, 6, 7, 8, 9, A, B, C, D, E, F. For example: $30B_{16} = 3 \times 16^2 + 0 \times 16^1 + 11 \times 16^0 = 779$.

The coefficients in (F3.1) are the digits that a computer processes. Since these digits represent multipliers of different powers of a base, depending on their position in the number, we use the name *positional notation*. Note that there are exactly r distinct choices for digits when using base r; so that if we use base 2, we have only two digits—0 and 1. These are called *binary digits*, which has been shortened to *bits* in ordinary usage.

3.4 CONVERSION FROM ONE BASE TO ANOTHER

Substitution in (F3.1) permits us readily to convert from numbers written in base r_1 to any other base r_2, provided we know how to convert from base 10 to base r. The procedure is: first convert from r_1 to 10 using (F3.1), and then apply the "10-to-r procedure" to convert from base 10 to r_2.

Consider any positive integer N, as represented by (F3.1). If N is divided by r, we have

$$\frac{a_m r^m + a_{m-1} r^{m-1} + \cdots + a_1 r + a_0}{r} = a_m r^{m-1} + \cdots + a_1 + \frac{a_0}{r}$$

that is, an integer dividend, $a_m r^{m-1} + \cdots + a_1$, and a remainder a_0. If the integer dividend is divided by r, we obtain a new integer dividend and a remainder a_1. Since writing N in base r really means finding the coefficients $a_0, a_1, \ldots, a_m$, successive division of N by r will give these coefficients as successive remainders. For example,

$$27_{10} = ?_2 \qquad
\begin{array}{r|l}
2 & 27 \\ \hline
2 & 13 + 1 \\ \hline
2 & 6 + 1 \\ \hline
2 & 3 + 0 \\ \hline
& 1 + 1
\end{array}$$

This means that $a_0 = 1$, $a_1 = 1$, $a_2 = 0$, $a_3 = 1$, and $a_4 = 1$. Or, writing the remainder in the order indicated by the arrow, the result is

$$27_{10} = 11011_2$$

Consider next the problem $30B_{16} = ?_2$. We can proceed by writing $3(16)^2 + 0(16) + 11(1) = 779_{10}$ and then

```
2 | 779
2 | 389 + 1
2 | 194 + 1
2 |  97 + 0
2 |  48 + 1
2 |  24 + 0
2 |  12 + 0
2 |   6 + 0
2 |   3 + 0
        1 + 1
```

to get 1100001011_2. Note also that

$$3_{16} = 0011_2$$
$$0_{16} = 0000_2$$
$$B_{16} = 1011_2$$

So that this result could have been obtained by converting from base 16 to base 2, digit by digit. This procedure will always work when one radix is a power of the other, and it should always be used in this case.

3.5 NUMBERS WITH NONINTEGRAL PARTS

Thus far, only integers have been covered in considering positional notation and conversion from one radix to another. The numbers between 0 and 1 can be considered from the same point of view as the integers discussed above. The number $.134_{10}$ is 1 tenth plus 3 hundredths plus 4 thousandths; that is, it is $1 \times 10^{-1} + 3 \times 10^{-2} + 4 \times 10^{-3}$. In general, any number F between 0 and 1 may be written as

(F3.2) $F = b_1 r^{-1} + b_2 r^{-2} + \cdots + b_n r^{-n} + \cdots$

where the coefficients b_1, b_2, etc., are to be chosen from the set 1, 2, $\cdots$, $r - 1$. The three dots after the term $b_n r^{-n}$ indicate that the representation need not terminate. For example, if $F = \frac{1}{3}$ and $r = 10$, all coefficients are 3 and the representation does not terminate. This means that some nonintegral numbers cannot be represented using any finite number of digits. Every integer, on the other hand, can always be represented with a finite number of digits, regardless of the base used.

All *rational numbers*, numbers that can be expressed as ratios of a pair of integers, either terminate or contain a set of digits that repeats indefinitely. It is conventional to represent nonterminating rational numbers by placing a bar over the set of digits that repeats indefinitely. Thus, $\frac{1}{3} = 0.\bar{3}$, $\frac{7}{12} = 0.58\bar{3}$, $\frac{27}{41} = 0.\overline{65853}$.

Once again, conversion from base r_1 to base r_2 will be made via base 10. To go from r to 10, apply (F3.1). So, for example, $0.101_2 = \frac{1}{2} + \frac{1}{4} + \frac{1}{8} = \frac{5}{8} = 0.625_{10}$. To go from base 10 to base r, apply a series of successive multiplications. Suppose we have $0.b_1b_2b_3 \cdots b_{k_{10}}$ and wish to determine its equivalent to base r.

$$0.b_1b_2b_3 \cdots b_{k_{10}} \times r = \text{integer}_1 + \text{fraction}_1$$
$$F_1 \times r = I_2 + F_2$$
$$F_2 \times r = I_3 + F_3$$
$$\cdots\cdots\cdots\cdots\cdots\cdots\cdots$$

Sooner or later, either $F_m = 0$ or $F_m = F_{m-s}$. In the first case, the representation terminates, and in the second case, there is a nonterminating repeating representation. More specifically, in the first case, the solution is

$$0.b_1b_2b_3 \cdots b_{k_{10}} = 0.I_1I_2 \cdots I_{m_r}$$

and in the second case, the solution is

$$0.b_1b_2b_3 \cdots b_{k_{10}} = 0.I_1I_2 \cdots I_{m-s}\overline{I_{m-s+1} \cdots I_{m_r}}$$

Example $0.25_{10} = ?_2$

$0.25 \times 2 = 0 + 0.5$
$0.5 \times 2 = 1 + 0$, so that the representation terminates, $m = 2$, and
$0.25_{10} = 0.01_2$.

Example $0.3_{10} = ?_{16}$

$0.3 \times 16 = 4 + 0.8$
$0.8 \times 16 = C + 0.8$ or the representation is nonterminating,
$m = 2$, $s = 1$, and $0.3_{10} = 0.4\bar{C}_{16}$.

Example $0.2_{10} = ?_2$

$0.2 \times 2 = 0 + 0.4$
$0.4 \times 2 = 0 + 0.8$
$0.8 \times 2 = 1 + 0.6$
$0.6 \times 2 = 1 + 0.2$
$0.2 \times 2 = 0 + 0.4$, so that the representation is nonterminating,
$m = 5$, $s = 4$, and $0.2_{10} = 0.0\overline{0110}_2$.

Any number can now be converted from base r_1 to base r_2. Given the problem

$$a_m a_{m-1} \cdots a_0.b_1 b_2 \cdots b_{j_{r_1}} = ?_{r_2}$$

1. Write $a_m a_{m-1} \cdots a_0.b_1 b_2 \cdots b_{j_{r_1}} = a_m a_{m-1} \cdots a_{0_{r_1}} + 0.b_1 b_2 \cdots b_{j_{r_1}}$.
2. Apply (F3.1) to get $a_m a_{m-1} \cdots a_{0_{r_1}} = A_{10}$, and $0.b_1 b_2 \cdots b_{j_{r_1}} = B_{10}$.
3. Apply the division procedure to obtain $A_{10} = A'_{r_2}$, and the multiplication procedure to obtain $B_{10} = B'_{r_2}$.
4. The solution is $A'.B'_{r_2}$.

Example $1101.1111_2 = ?_{16}$

1. $1101.1111_2 = 1101_2 + 0.1111_2$
2. $1101_2 = 1(8) + 1(4) + 0(2) + 1(1) = 13_{10}$
   $0.1111_2 = 1(\frac{1}{2}) + 1(\frac{1}{4}) + 1(\frac{1}{8}) + 1(\frac{1}{16}) = {}^{15}\!/_{16} = 0.9375_{10}$
3. $13_{10} = D_{16}$ and $0.9375 \times 16 = F + 0.0$
4. Therefore, the solution is $D.F_{16}$.

Note that the solution could have been obtained directly, since $16 = 2^4$, by grouping the representation to base 2 into sets of four digits each, always proceeding out from the decimal points, and converting each set of four digits to one digit to base 16. Thus $1101.1111_2 = D.F_{16}$ directly, since $1101_2 = D_{16}$ and $1111_2 = F_{16}$.

3.6 FLOATING-POINT REPRESENTATION

Computations with very large or very small numbers are made awkward by the string of concluding or leading zeros carried to fix the decimal point. Scientists avoid this difficulty by writing such numbers in two parts: a *mantissa* that contains only the significant digits and an *exponent* that places the decimal point. If, in addition, the conventions of having no leading zeros in the mantissa and of assuming that the decimal point is to the left of the first digit in the mantissa are adopted, then we shall have arrived at the floating-point representation of numbers for a computer. With these conventions, 1 billion, since it equals 0.1×10^{10}, is uniquely represented by the mantissa .1 and the exponent 10. Or, writing the mantissa first and using the letter E to separate the mantissa from the exponent, 1 billion becomes .1E10. Also, a nanosecond becomes .1E − 8 seconds, a microsecond .1E − 5 seconds, and a millisecond .1E − 2 seconds.

If the decimal point is assumed to be to the left of the first digit in the mantissa and if this first digit is not zero, then

(F3.3) $0.1 \le \text{mantissa} < 1$

The reduction of a floating-point number to this standard form from some other form is called the *normalization* of the number. In general, normalization proceeds by first rewriting the mantissa so that it satisfies (F3.3) and then adjusting the exponent appropriately. For example, 186,000 can be written as 186.E3 in floating-point notation. Since 186. > 1, this number has not been normalized. The normal form is .186E6.

Since zero cannot be represented in this way, it must have a special representation. This representation is specific to each computer. For example, in the IBM 1620, a floating-point zero is represented by a mantissa of zero and an exponent of -99, whereas in the System/360, the mantissa and exponent are both zero.

Floating-point numbers can be written using mantissas and exponents that are themselves written to a base other than 10. Suppose we use M to represent the mantissa and X to represent the exponent, then $M_r E X_r$ would be used to represent M_r times r raised to the power X_r. Note that when using base r, multiplying by r raised to the power X_r is equivalent to moving the *radix point* (we call it a *decimal point* when r is 10) X_r units. For example, $101_2 E 10_2 = 0.101_2$ times 2^{10_2}. Since $10_2 = 2$, we must move the binary point (if $r = 2$, the radix point is called a *binary point*) two units to the right. The result is, therefore, 10.1_2 or 2.5.

When using base r, a number is considered to be normalized only if the mantissa M satisfies

$$r^{-1} \leq \text{mantissa} < r^0 = 1$$

3.7 ARITHMETIC PROCESSES IN A COMPUTER

In carrying out the four basic arithmetic processes—addition, subtraction, multiplication, and division—people make extensive use of tables of sums, differences, and products that they have memorized. Reference to tables seriously slows the progress of a computation; equally so when it is being carried out by an electronic computer. Wired circuits that automatically provide the solution as output, given the operands as input, are faster. (A few older computers—for example, the IBM 1620 Model I—do use tables.) In addition, since the computer represents numbers to base 2, it need only provide for three possible combinations of operands: 0 and 0, 0 and 1, and 1 and 1.† Special circuits have been constructed to provide for the addition of binary numbers based on the fact that $0_2 +$

---

† There is a fourth possibility—1 and 0—but since the results of arithmetic operations are not affected by the order of the operands, for example, $A + B = B + A$, this combination is equivalent to the 0-and-1 combination.

$0_2 = 0_2$, $0_2 + 1_2 = 1_2$, and $1_2 + 1_2 = 10_2$. This addition could also be carried out by referring to a table to determine the sum of these bits.

The way arithmetic processes are carried out in a computer will be illustrated by the discussion of subtraction by means of complements that follows.†

Subtraction can be defined as the addition of two quantities after reversing the sign of one of them. In most computers, subtraction is carried out by adding the complement of the number to be subtracted. The *complement* of a number is obtained by subtracting it from the next highest power of the base (called 10s *complementing* if the base is 10) or from the next highest power of the base less 1 (called 9s *complementing* if the base is 10). If the base is 2, these complements are called 2s *complements* and 1s *complements*, respectively.

For example, the 10s complement of $347 = 1,000 - 347 = 653$, and the 9s complement of $347 = 999 - 347 = 652$; the 2s complement of $101_2 = 1000_2 - 101_2 = 011_2$, and the 1s complement of $101_2 = 111_2 - 101_2 = 010_2$. Note the practice of carrying the same number of digits in the complement as appeared in the original number. Also, since the only possible digits for a binary number are 0 and 1 and since $1 - 1 = 0$ and $1 - 0 = 1$, the 1s complement of a binary number is obtained by merely reversing its digits. Thus the 2s complement of a binary number is most easily obtained by reversing its digits and adding 1 to the result.

Before discussing subtraction, we shall have to modify the definition of complements given in the preceding paragraphs. Instead of subtracting a number from the next highest power of the base, we shall form the complement by subtracting the number from r^d, where d is the number of digits used to represent the number and r is the base. This means that the number of digits, including leading 0s, that are carried in representing a number is critical.

The subtraction of A from B, that is, the addition of B to $-A$, is carried out as follows by using complements:

1. Form the complement of A, call it C, by subtracting A from r^d, where r is the base and d is the number of digits in A, if A has the same number of or more digits than B, or in B if B has more digits.
2. Obtain $B + C$.
3. If $B + C$ has an additional leading 1, the 1 is deleted and the answer is given by the remaining digits with a plus sign.
4. If $B + C$ does not have an additional leading 1, complement the result, again by subtracting it from r^d. The answer is this new result with a minus sign.

† See [1] for a more extensive general discussion of arithmetic processes and [2] for a description of the circuits used in carrying them out.

Example $1011_2 - 1000_2$

1. 2s complement of 1000_2 is 1000_2.
2. $1011_2 + 1000_2 = 10011_2$.
3. Answer is $+0011_2$.

Example $10110_2 - 11011_2$

1. 2s complement of 11011_2 is 00101_2.
2. $10110_2 + 00101_2 = 11011_2$.
3. 2s complement of 11011_2 is 00101_2, and the answer is -00101_2.

Example $110011_2 - 101_2$

1. 2s complement of 000101_2 is 111011_2.
2. $110011_2 + 111011_2 = 1101110_2$.
3. Answer is $+101110_2$.

PROBLEMS

3.1 Convert each of the following numbers to the base 10.
   (a) $FB._{16}$ (b) $0.A8_{16}$ (c) $AC.1D_{16}$ (d) $101._2$ (e) 0.101_2 (f) 10001.0101_2
3.2 Convert each of the following numbers, written in base 10, to the base 2.
   (a) 24. (b) 0.3 (c) 7.7
3.3 Convert each of the following numbers, written in base 10, to the base 16.
   (a) 107. (b) 0.3 (c) 0.606 (d) 1974.414
3.4 Convert each of the following numbers, written in base 16, to the base 2.
   (a) $FB._{16}$ (b) $0.A8_{16}$ (c) $AC.1D_{16}$ (d) 6.4_{16}
3.5 Convert each of the following numbers, written in base 2, to the base 16.
   (a) $101._2$ (b) 0.101_2 (c) 10001.0101_2 (d) 10010001.10011_2
3.6 Normalize the following floating-point numbers. Assume both that the mantissa and the exponents are written to base 10 and that the result should be written to base 10.
   (a) $-104.361\text{E-}2$ (b) $6011.\text{E-}4$ (c) $.00022\text{E-}6$ (d) $136.11\text{E}5$
   (e) $-.0000711\text{E}4$
3.7 Compute each of the following differences by the methods of 10s complements.
   (a) 843_{10} (b) $4,716_{10}$ (c) 617_{10}
       -617_{10} -221_{10} -819_{10}
3.8 Compute each of the following differences by the method of 2s complements.
   (a) 100111_2 (b) 110011_2 (c) 111011_2
       -100001_2 -111101_2 -1001_2

REFERENCES

1. Culbertson, J. T.: "Mathematics and Logic for Digital Devices," chap. 4, D. Van Nostrand Company, Inc., Princeton, N.J., 1962.
2. Bartee, T. C.: "Digital Computer Fundamentals," chap. 6, McGraw-Hill Book Company, New York, 1960.

ANNOTATED SUPPLEMENTARY BIBLIOGRAPHY

Most references on computers or computer programming contain a discussion of the representation of numbers in a computer. Rather than merely listing as many of these as we can recall, we are citing only three supplementary references, each of which has a special feature that makes it worth considering.

1. System/360, Introductory Programming, Book 1, Introduction, *IBM Publ.* R23-2933. A self-teaching manual that is devoted to the representation of numbers and arithmetic operations in a computer, with emphasis on the System/360.
2. Arden, B. W.: "An Introduction to Digital Computing," chap. 7, Addison-Wesley Publishing Company, Inc., Reading, Mass., 1963. A discussion of the representation of numbers in a computer, including a treatment of the problem of scaling.
3. Henrici, P.: "Elements in Numerical Analysis," chap. 15, John Wiley & Sons, New York, 1964. Numerical representation is discussed from an algorithmic viewpoint.

chapter 4

A DESCRIPTION OF
THE COMPONENTS
OF A COMPUTER

4.1 INTRODUCTION

Computers are merely a collection of circuits that are wired together, packaged in pastel-colored boxes, linked to other electronic or mechanical devices that provide input/output or additional storage facilities, and supplemented by sets of instructions that cause the hardware to function in a special way. In this chapter, the functioning of these pastel-colored boxes and their supplements will be discussed from two points of view. First, the flow of information through them will be described, and then a brief description of how some of these devices work will be given. No particular computer will be discussed, and so the presentation can be neither very specific nor very detailed. Section 5 of this book, in which the System/360 is discussed, supplements the presentation in this chapter.

4.2 GENERAL FLOW OF INFORMATION

The flow of information in a computer will be described in two ways: (1) in the form of a diagram depicting this flow in its logical sequence, (2) by tracing the flow through five computer components—input/output, main storage, the processor, the control unit, and auxiliary storage.

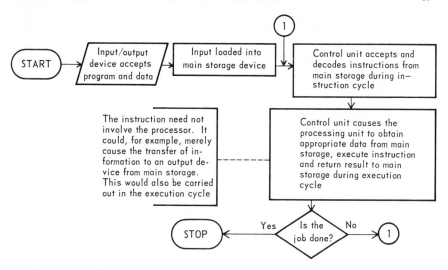

Fig. 4.1 General flow of information in a computer.

Figure 4.1 depicts the logical sequence of the information flow. Note the dichotomous nature of the operation of the computer. *Instruction cycles* alternate with *execution cycles*. In an instruction cycle, a sequence of numbers is obtained from main storage and treated as an instruction. The *control unit* breaks these numbers into their component parts, decodes the number specifying the operation to be performed, and initiates the execution cycle. In the execution cycle, the control unit causes the processor to obtain the operands from main storage, to execute the instruction, and to return the result to main storage for those operations, such as arithmetic processes, that do more than transfer data. The processor need not be involved if the operation involves only the transfer of data. However, such transfers do require the execution of a series of instructions, as does stopping the computer.

This flow sequence illustrates one of the major difficulties a computer user faces. The solution to a problem must be reduced to a sequence of individual, elementary operations. These operations include such things as a single arithmetic operation (e.g., the addition of one pair of numbers), a single transfer of data, or a single modification of the contents of main storage. An enormous number of these individual operations is required to solve a problem. A single error in their construction or ordering could destroy the final result. No wonder there is a need to develop the ability "to construct complex processes out of simple ones"!†

† See [1]. As we shall see in Chap. 7, the situation is not so grim as depicted here. The computer itself is used to permit a user to specify the solution in terms of sets of instructions rather than single instructions and in a language other than a series of numbers.

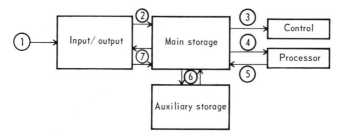

Fig. 4.2 Information flow through the five major computer components.

Figure 4.2 will be used to help us trace the flow of information through the components of a computer. The program and data are loaded into the input/output device (1) and transferred to main storage (2). Instructions are brought into the control unit from main storage (3) during the instruction cycle and are decoded and executed. If the execution involves the processing of data, the operands are brought from main storage to the processor (4); a result is obtained and entered in main storage (5). Exchanges with input/output devices (6) and auxiliary storage devices (7) are made as required.

A special series of instructions, called a *loader routine*, usually is used to initiate the loading of programs in step (2). If such a routine is not available, some other initiating mechanism must be provided to start the instruction sequence.

4.3 INPUT/OUTPUT MEDIA AND DEVICES

The most important input/output media are punched cards, punched paper tape, magnetic tape, disks, the face of cathode-ray tubes, special input forms, and printouts. The devices used to prepare these media and to input/output them are given in Table 4.1.

Figure 4.3 contains a picture of the 80-column *punched card* with the code that is used for recording numeric, alphabetic, and special characters. The card contains 80 columns and 12 rows. Each column is ordinarily used to record a single character. (Several characters may be recorded in a single column by using special input formats.) The top three rows are called the 12, 11, and 0 rows; a hole punched in one of these rows is called an *overpunch*. Note that the code consists in using at most one overpunch combined with one or two punches in rows 1 to 9. These cards are prepared using a keypunch, pictured in Fig. 4.4.

The *keypunch* is a typewriterlike device which permits the entry of one character per column by depressing a single key. The keypunch will then automatically punch the correct combination of holes in the

Table 4.1   Devices associated with input/output media

Medium	*Devices associated with medium*
Punched cards	Prepared by keypunch; input via card reader and output via card punch
Paper tape	Prepared by analog-digital converter or Flexowriter; input via paper-tape reader and output via paper-tape punch
Magnetic tape	Prepared by analog-digital converter or magnetic-tape drive; input/output via drive
Disk	Prepared and input/output via disk drive
Cathode-ray-tube face	Prepared and input/output via terminals incorporating cathode-ray tubes
Special input forms	Prepared manually or on a typewriter; input via magnetic ink or an optical reader (also called an *optical scanner*)
Printouts	Prepared and output via printer or plotter or remote terminals

card.   The code need not be memorized; the key contains the number, letter, or special symbol on its face.   This makes the keypunch as easy to operate as a typewriter.   Professional keypunch operators can prepare about 100 to 150 cards in an hour.

The punched card is the most widely used primary source for computer input, though optical scanners are becoming more and more important.   Because of the widespread use of punched cards, a number of devices have been developed to provide special handling services for them.   These include:

Sorters   The sorter separates a deck of cards in accordance with the entry in a specified column.   This permits the grouping of cards with identical entries.   The cards are grouped in stacks in the sorter.   By removing the cards from the sorter in a prescribed order, the cards can be ordered according to the entry in the column.   In addition, by repeating the process, a deck of cards can be ordered in accordance with the entries in several columns.   Processing speeds are of the order of 500 to 2,000 cards per minute.   A picture of a sorter is presented in Fig. 4.5.

Verifiers   The verifier looks very much like a keypunch but accepts a previously punched card as input.   It indicates an error if the operator strikes a key corresponding to a character other than the one already in that column.   The verifier does not punch any new holes in the card. It permits an independent check of keypunch work, and the speed of operation is about the same as that of a keypunch.

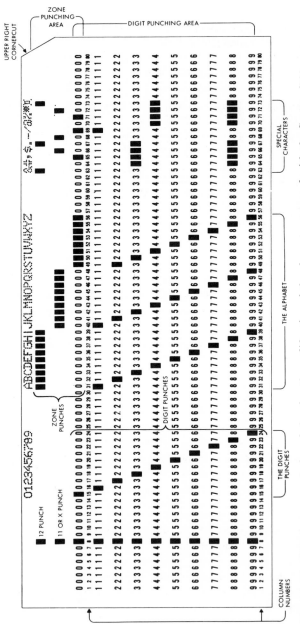

Fig. 4.3 An 80-column punched card showing the codification of the character set used with the System/360.

Fig. 4.4 The IBM 029 keypunch.

Interpreters The interpreter prints, across the top of a card, characters representing the punched entries. (Note that the card in Fig. 4.3 has been interpreted. The keypunch will ordinarily interpret cards as they are punched; however, it may frequently be necessary to interpret cards punched by a computer.) Processing speeds are about 100 to 300 cards per minute.

Collators The collator accepts two decks of cards and merges them into a single deck, depending on the entries in prescribed fields and the manner in which an "instruction board" (also called a *plug board*) is wired. Processing speeds are about 250 to 1,000 cards per minute.

Almost every computer manufacturer offers a *card reader* and *card punch* or a *card reader/punch*, in which both facilities are housed in a single device, as a part of his line of equipment. Card-reader speeds

Fig. 4.5 The IBM 083 card sorter. (*Reprinted by permission from IBM document A24-1034, copyrighted 1961 by the International Business Machines Corporation.*)

vary from about 250 cards to 1,500 cards per minute, while punch speeds vary from 100 to 500 cards per minute.

The punched card has one inherent limitation: a natural break in the information occurs every 80 characters.† Punched paper tapes—as well as magnetic tapes—do not have this limitation. Cathode-ray tubes also have a natural break in the data, which is determined by the maximum number of characters that can be displayed on the face of the tube at any one time. This may vary from as few as 64 to as many as several thousand. Special input forms are limited by the number of characters that can be displayed on a single form. This, too, varies a great deal, but the maximum capacity of a form rarely exceeds several hundred characters.

† It should be pointed out that the absence of a natural break in information is not entirely advantageous. For example, on paper tape and magnetic tape, artificial breaks must be inserted, in such forms as end-of-line characters on paper tape and record marks on magnetic tape.

Paper tape and magnetic tapes are virtually continuous recording devices. A reel of paper tape will usually be about 1,000 feet long and from ⅝ to 1 inch wide. A strip of paper tape is shown in Fig. 4.6. The rows in a reel of tape are called *channels;* the tape depicted has eight channels. (The series of small holes is not a channel; these are sprocket holes for synchronizing and driving the tape.) Paper tape with five channels was widely used in the telegraph industry for many years. Though the computer industry initially conformed—and used a great deal of five-channel tape—the requirements for greater flexibility and provision for checking led to the gradual demise of the five-channel tape in the computer industry.

The significance of each of the eight channels in the tape is indicated in Fig. 4.6. The topmost channel is used to indicate the end-of-line character which is needed to permit the marking of the end of records. The next two rows provide the overpunched facility. The X row is equivalent to the 11 row of the punched card, and the 0 row is equivalent to the 0 row of a punched card.† The equivalent of a punch in the 12 row of the punched card is indicated in the paper tape by a punch in both the X and 0 rows, so that for punched paper tape we have the peculiar equation: $12 = X + 0$. The *check*, or *parity, channel* is used to provide a means for checking on whether a punch is accidentally deleted or added in processing. The check row is punched if and only if the number of punches would otherwise be even. This means that the representation of every character contains an odd number of punches. Note,

† Except that the numerical zero is not indicated by a single punch in the 0 row. Instead, it is indicated by the equivalent of a 10 punch, i.e., a punch in the check, 8, and 2 channels.

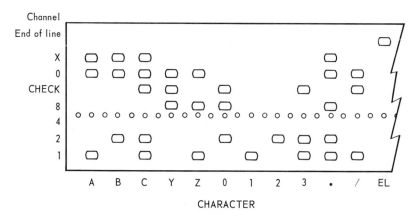

Fig. 4.6 Codification of information on punched paper tape using eight channels.

in Fig. 4.6, that checks are required to represent C, Y, 0, 3, and the slash. The 8, 4, 2, 1 channels are used to represent numerals in the same way that the 1 to 9 rows of the punched card are used. The value of the numeral is indicated by the sum of the values of the channels punched, so that 3 is represented by two punches, 2 + 1, and 7 would be represented by three punches, 4 + 2 + 1.

We shall discuss magnetic tapes and disks in Sec. 4.4 and cathode-ray tubes in Sec. 4.5. This brings us to special input forms and associated devices.

Checks, gasoline-credit slips, and cash-register tapes have been read into computers for several years. Checks first used *magnetic-ink printing*, but more recently, optical techniques have been employed [2]. Account numbers on gasoline-credit slips have been read optically for some time. The *optical scanner* is developing rapidly. A standard for a character set for optical character recognition has been proposed [3], and many computer manufacturers offer an optical scanner of some sort as a part of their line of equipment. The scanner senses differences in the light reflected off the surface of the page being read using one or more optical photodetectors associated with the appropriate optical and mechanical apparatus. The variety of patterns that can be sensed is still quite limited; special type fonts are required. With the development of a standard for the representation of characters, it can be expected that typewriters will be readily available that will reduce the problem of computer input to that of typing. Although this is an important step forward, since ordinary correspondence and manuscripts could be read directly into a computer, the ability to reliably recognize handwritten characters, which is still a subject for research, would provide an even greater breakthrough in the input bottleneck.

The *printer* is certainly the most important computer output device. The ability to produce rapidly large volumes of output that is readily intelligible to people was essential to the extension of the application of computers to nonscientific problems. Today, thousand-line-a-minute printers are commonplace in computer installations, and address labels, checks, employee report forms, elaborate tables—even complete reports—are being prepared by computers using printers.

The three most important printers in use today are character, chain, and cylinder printers. A *character printer* is really a typewriter that is operated by the computer. It operates at speeds of about 15 characters per second. It can be used as either an input or an output device; all other printers are only output devices. Chain printers operate ordinarily at speeds of up to 600 lines per minute, although speeds of up to 1,100 lines a minute can be attained. Cylinder printers operate at speeds exceeding 1,000 lines per minute.

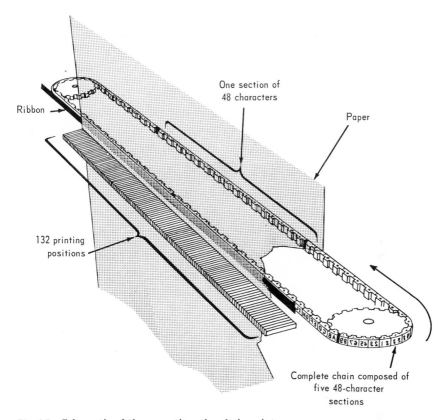

Fig. 4.7 Schematic of the operation of a chain printer.

The *chain printer* uses a continuously moving chain of type slugs that contains several replications of the character set available for printing. Printing is actually done by firing a series of hammers against the paper. The paper is pressed against a ribbon and type slug, and a character is imprinted. (See Fig. 4.7.) The key to the operation of the printer is proper timing in the firing of the hammers, which requires some sophisticated buffering equipment.

The speed of the chain printer is closely related to the character set required. Since the chain is moving at a constant speed, the more sets of the same characters that can be incorporated into a single chain, the faster the operating speed of the printer. Users who require only a limited set of characters—for example, only the 10 numerals and a decimal point—should take advantage of this and order an appropriate chain. Users who require a wide variety of characters either must be satisfied with speeds of about 250 lines per minute or must get a cylinder printer.

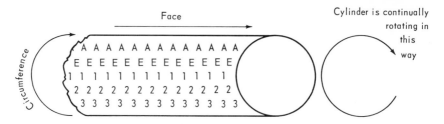

Fig. 4.8 A typical cylinder used in cylinder printers.

The *cylinder printer* uses a continuously rotating cylinder containing around its circumference the set of characters that can be printed. Each character is repeated across the face of the cylinder as many times as there are print positions. (See Fig. 4.8.) Again, the firing of a hammer against the paper, ribbon, and character causes the imprintation. Cylinder printers are also called *line printers* because all the entries of a single character on a line are printed simultaneously. For example, if the sentence "He went to the store." is to be printed on a line, the hammers in the second, fifth, fourteenth, and twentieth print positions would all fire as the row on the cylinder containing the letter e appears opposite them. Again, complex buffering is required to analyze the line to be printed and fire the appropriate hammers at the right time.

Plotters are available that can produce finished graphs and illustrations, including lettered labels and scales, under the control of a computer. They can be quite large, preparing plots as big as a yard square, or compact. A popular model is the Calcomp 565, pictured in Fig. 4.9. It operates by a combination of horizontal movements of the pen across the paper and vertical movements of the paper under the pen. Movements can be made in increments as small as 0.01 inch, so that even though a curve is drawn as a sequence of straight lines, a reasonably good-looking product can be obtained. However, on close inspection, curves do look like step functions.

Because plotters are slow, they should either be adequately buffered—so that the computer is not tied up while the plotter is operating—or be operated by a special device independent of the computer (this is called *off-line* operation). The device might use a reel of magnetic tape or punched paper tape previously generated by the computer or by an analog-digital converter.

Before concluding this discussion of input/output media and devices, we should mention *actuators* and *sensors*. They make possible the widespread use of the computer to control equipment and processes. Signals generated by the computer are transformed by a digital-to-analog converter into appropriate voltages to be input to the actuator. These

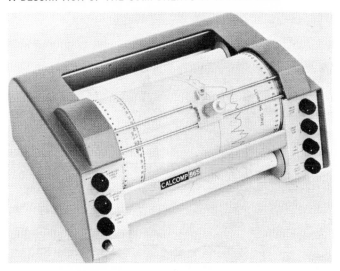

Fig. 4.9 A Calcomp 565 plotter. (*Reprinted with the permission of the California Computer Products Corporation.*)

voltages are translated into a mechanical action of some sort by the actuator. It may close or open a valve, modify the speed of motors or the direction of motion of a shaper table, or modify a tool-bit setting in a lathe. The sensor then monitors the process being controlled, converting its observations into voltages, which are passed through an analog-to-digital converter to be analyzed by the computer in order to determine the next series of process modifications.

4.4 STORAGE MEDIA AND DEVICES

We have already mentioned two important storage media—magnetic tapes and disks. However, these media are not used as the main storage facility of the computer. Most computers use magnetic cores in their main storage.

The electronic computer makes extensive use of *bistable elements.* These are elements that can assume either one of two states and that remain in one of these states until modified from the outside. Vacuum tubes and transistors are either conducting current or not conducting current, punched cards and paper tapes either have a hole or do not have a hole in a given row and column, magnetic tapes and disks either do or do not have a prescribed location magnetized in a prescribed direction, and magnetic-core elements are magnetized in either of two polarities. This bistability in the components of the computer quite naturally leads to binary representation, in which one state is used to represent the digit

Fig. 4.10 A plane of magnetic-core elements. (*Reprinted by permission from document* F22-6517, *copyrighted* 1960 *by the International Business Machines Corporation.*)

0 and the other the digit 1.   In discussing magnetic cores, we shall refer to the two possible polarization states as state 0 and state 1.

Magnetic cores consist of stacks of matrices, or planes, of core elements.   A typical *magnetic-core plane* is shown in Fig. 4.10.   A single *magnetic-core element* in the plane is depicted in Fig. 4.11.   Note that the elements in a plane are connected via a series of wires strung through them.   Each element has four wires passing through it—one oriented along the rows of the matrix, another along the columns, and a third, called the *inhibit wire*, running parallel to the row wire.   The fourth wire, called the *sense wire*, is diagonally oriented and passes through every element in the core plane (as does the inhibit wire).   The other two wires pass only through those elements in the same row or column.   The row and column wires are used to write in the element, and the diagonal wire is used to read from it.   The *inhibit wire* is used in restoring information to the element after reading from it.

Writing is accomplished by sending half the current required to

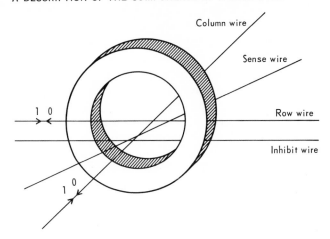

Fig. 4.11   A magnetic-core element.

orient the polarity of the element through the row wire and half the current through the column wire.   This means that only the one element at the intersection of these wires receives the unit of current required to write on the element.   The 0 state is obtained by sending current in one direction; the 1 state by sending current in the other direction.

Reading from the elements is accomplished by attempting to write a zero.   This is called a *destructive read* because it has the effect of erasing core.   If the unit already was in the 0 state, no current is induced in the diagonal wire because the polarity of the element did not change.   If it was in the 1 state, a current is induced in the diagonal wire which is sensed, read, and used to restore the 1 state in the element.   If it were not for this restoration of the 1 state, the process of reading would erase core, which could be disastrous.†   Only one element in a plane is read at any one time, although elements in each of several planes may be read simultaneously.

Magnetic cores are used as the main storage element because of their great speed and reliability.   They have access times in the order of a few microseconds or less.   [*Access time* is the time interval between the instant at which data are called from (or requested to be stored in) a storage device and the instant at which delivery (or storage) is completed.]   However, they are expensive.   Magnetic cores cost about 15 cents per

† Imagine that you are performing an extensive desk calculation which requires you to store intermediate results by noting them on a scratch pad.   Suppose a number was erased as you read it from the scratch pad and not restored.   The calculations would suffer.

bit of storage capacity, whereas drums cost about 0.4 cent, disks 0.05 cent, and magnetic tape about 0.02 cent per bit.†

A *magnetic drum* is a steel cylinder enclosed in a coated copper sleeve. The surface of the copper sleeve is coated with a magnetizable iron or nickel compound. Specific locations—actually, tiny spots—on the surface of the drum are designated as storage locations for a bit. The spot is magnetized in one direction or the other. The drum revolves continually, and each spot can be passed under a read-write head, which can either reorient or sense the direction of the orientation of the spot's magnetization. Unlike core, the process of reading is nondestructive, and restoration is not necessary. The speed of magnetic-drum units is slower than that of core but faster than tapes or disks. Access times for the drums are in the order of 5 to 20 milliseconds. This is more than a thousand times slower than cores. The delay is caused by the need to wait until the desired information is positioned under the read-write head.

Magnetic-tape drives are probably the most widely used auxiliary storage devices. The medium, magnetic tape itself, is a strip of tough flexible plastic material, such as Mylar, coated with a thin layer of iron oxide. The oxide can be magnetized, and spots on the tape are designated as storage locations for a bit. A reel of tape is from 50 to as much as 2,400 feet long, the longer tapes being more commonly used. Characters are represented on the tape using several channels to represent a single character. The *nine-channel tape*, in use with the System/360 family of computers, uses eight channels to record information and one channel for the check, or parity, function.

Figure 4.12 contains a picture of a magnetic-tape drive. The tape is fed from one reel to another, passing over the read-write heads. (They are just below the tape reels in the magnetic drive pictured in Fig. 4.12.) The operation is similar to that of a home tape recorder, except that the tape speeds are much faster—of the order of 6 feet per second—and the density of information on the tape is much greater. Densities as great as 1,600 characters per inch are available. *Tape density* is the number of sets of channels, usually representing characters, per unit of length. This is generally referred to as *bits* per inch, although it should be more properly called *characters* per inch.

Access times for magnetic-tape units are not accepted as a standard

---

† These cost estimates include the cost of interfacing the drums, disks, and tape units with the computer. They are based on the prices quoted by computer manufacturers for supplying this equipment with the computer and the interfacing devices. Prices quoted by specialists in the manufacture of these devices tend to be somewhat less. Also, in the case of drums, larger-capacity, slower devices are available at a cost of about 0.1 cent per bit.

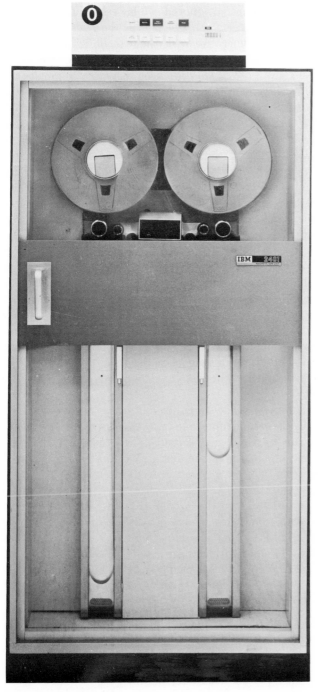

Fig. 4.12   The IBM Model 2401 magnetic-tape drive.

for the speed of the units and are not quoted.   This is because they vary a great deal depending on where on the reel of tape the read-write heads are currently positioned and where we wish them to be.   Criteria such as *tape speed*, in terms of the length of tape moving past the read-write heads in a unit of time, and tape density are used instead.   Though tape can be moved quite quickly, a reel is 2,400 feet long and it can take a relatively long time to position the desired section of the tape over the read-write heads.   A visit to a computer center to watch the operation of a tape drive will convince you that a great deal of time is devoted to spinning tapes.   Access times of the order of minutes can be required in some cases.   In addition, you will probably also note the amount of time required to mount and dismount tapes.

Suppose we cut the tape into 10 or more strips and had 10 or more read-write heads operating, one for each strip.   It is easy to see that this would substantially reduce the need for tape reeling and unreeling. This is the primary reason for the growth of *magnetic-disk storage*.   A disk drive is shown in Fig. 4.13.   The disk drive contains a disk unit or pack (which looks like a stack of phonograph records), a read-write head, and a motor to provide the required motion of its parts.   The disks rotate continuously while the unit is being used.   The read-write heads can either remain stationary, floating over the surface of the disk, or move in and out to the core and the circumference of the disk.   The information is stored in the form of magnetized spots at designated locations, this time on the surface of the disks.   Groups of spots are used to represent characters.

The information on most disks is organized into tracks and cylinders. On some disks, a track is further subdivided into sectors.   A *track* is that portion of one disk surface that can be read or written on by a single read-write head in one revolution of the disk.   A *cylinder* is all the portions of the disk surfaces that can be read or written on by all the read-write heads in a single rotation of the disk.

Access times for disks are of the order of 75 to 200 milliseconds. Disks are available with removable media—that is, a disk pack can be removed from a drive and another one mounted—or with fixed media. Generally, the removable-media drives have a smaller capacity in terms of what is available at any one time; capacities of the order of 10 million characters per drive are common for drives with removable packs, whereas capacities of 50 to 100 million characters per drive are common for fixed media.   However, several drives with removable disks can be linked to a single computer.

We should also note that the storage capacities of magnetic cores currently have an upper limit approaching 2 million characters and that a single reel of high-density, 1,600-character-per-inch tape can hold about

Fig. 4.13   The IBM Model 2311 disk-storage drive.

40 million characters.   Since several tape drives can be linked to a single computer, we see that on-line capacities approaching half a billion characters are available using a tape system.   But even this may not be enough.

Mass-storage devices with even greater capacities are available.   *Magnetic-card devices* are currently available that offer capacities approaching a billion characters.   The cost of the largest devices ranges from $135,000 to $200,000.   The approach used is to store information on strips of magnetic tape attached to a card, which is packaged in a removable cartridge. A cartridge may contain from 128 to 512 cards. A typical card size is $3\frac{1}{4}$ by 14 inches, although somewhat smaller cards and somewhat larger cards are used. The unit reads and writes by first positioning the card at an appropriate head via a series of mechanical operations usually involving movement of the card rather than the head. The strip of magnetic tape stores data in the usual way, and reading and writing are also done as they might be done in a tape drive, once the card is properly positioned.

Before concluding our discussion of storage media and devices, we should mention two promising media that are still being developed— *thin-film memories* and photographic film. Thin film consists of thin spots of magnetic material deposited on an insulated base. The deposit is only one or a few millionths of an inch thick. The magnetizable medium on disks, tapes, and drums is continuous, whereas the medium in thin films is not. A matrix of spots is deposited on a plane of insulator material. A memory would consist of a stack of these planes. Thin-film memories have even shorter access times than core memories, but their fabrication is more difficult and their reliability is not yet established.

Photographic-film storage, because it is multistable rather than bistable, offers much promise. A small, $\frac{1}{64}$-inch square could hold 16 or more distinguishable shades of gray. If color encoding is permitted, then several hundred distinguishable codes might be possible. The ability to store a great deal of information in a small space makes photographic film particularly promising as a mass-storage medium. Because film storage devices can be read photoelectrically, they also have a potential for shorter access times than cores. In this case, however, the sensor is difficult to manufacture, and reliability is also a problem. An even more essential difficulty is that photographic storage is not erasable and could not be used in applications requiring the frequent substitution of new information for old. However, with the increased demand for read-only storages to hold relatively permanent information that is to be protected from erasure, the necessary impetus for promoting the development of film storage devices may be present.

4.5 REMOTE TERMINALS

The growth in the number of time-shared users of computers has caused a parallel growth in the range and capability of the remote terminals available to these users. Initially, the most widely used terminal was a Teletypewriter because it was readily available and could be linked to an established communications network. The time-shared user now has available special-purpose keyboards, cathode-ray tubes and light pens,

Fig. 4.14 Three Teletypewriter terminals. Note the punched paper tape being produced as a by-product of the operation of the rightmost terminal. *(Reprinted by permission from document LINE IOM 664—Issue 1, copyrighted 1964 by the Teletype Corporation.)*

Touch-Tone phones, punched-card and punched-paper-tape readers, and even slide projectors and sound-tape playbacks controlled by the computer. Finally, smaller computers located some distance away can be satellited on larger ones.

As the computer manufacturers develop more and more special terminals, the importance of the *Teletypewriter* as a terminal is rapidly diminishing. It certainly played a prominent role in the first time-sharing systems [4, 5]. The Teletype system and the Data-Phone do not require the installation of new communication lines. Long-established, reliable equipment is available. However, the printing speeds are slow, and Teletype is comparatively noisy. Also, a typewriterlike, character printer is more natural to use if only because it is more familiar to most people. A Teletypewriter, however, has the advantage of providing punched paper tape as a by-product of its operation. A variety of Teletype terminals are pictured in Fig. 4.14.

Little more need be said about *typewriterlike terminals*. They are the equivalents of the character printer that can be found near the console in most computer centers.

Special-purpose keyboard devices have become available to be used for inputs to a computer. Among them are the Bell System *Touch-Tone input device*. This permits the transmission of the equivalent of 10 or more distinct signals, which, with appropriate codification, can permit an inexpensive input of a relatively small set of characters. These devices are being used to process banking transactions. For greater versatility, the IBM 1092 keyboard, pictured in Fig. 4.15, can be used. With the aid of special-purpose overlays, these keyboards can serve to input a wide variety of sets of data. For example, a hospital laboratory could make up a distinct overlay for each type of laboratory report. The overlay would contain information to identify the significance of each key for that report, and the operator would simply transcribe the information from the data sheets directly into the computer via such a terminal.

The face of a *cathode-ray tube* is becoming an important medium at remote terminals. The response to an executive's inquiry, a plot of a mathematical relation, a question for a student to answer as part of a course of instruction, all these are readily displayed on the face of a cathode tube. Earlier difficulties in maintaining a bright, nonflickering picture have been overcome, though the need to add circuitry and storage in order to maintain a good-quality display makes cathode-ray terminals relatively expensive. The cathode-ray tube is similar to a television picture tube in its functioning and characteristics. Numbers are converted to voltages by a digital-to-analog converter. These voltages are then used to control the writing of lines and dots on the face of the tube. The face of a cathode-ray tube can be photographed if a permanent copy

Fig. 4.15 The IBM 1092 programmed input terminal.

Fig. 4.16 The IBM 2260 display station with keyboard input and cathode-ray-tube output.

of the output is desired.   A cathode-ray-tube terminal is pictured in Fig. 4.16.

A light-sensitive cell can be installed in a small pencil-like device, permitting communication with a cathode-ray tube.   These small devices are called *light pens*.   By combining the use of a light pen, to pinpoint the components of a circuit diagram displayed on the face of a tube, with a keyboard input, to request modification in the diagram, an engineer can readily develop new designs. Similarly, by combining the use of a light pen and keyboard, an army officer engaged in a war game can specify troop movements in a convenient way.

Many special remote devices are available. For example, there are terminals that permit the input of punched cards and punched paper tape to be combined with keyboard entries. There are also terminals that permit slide projectors and sound tape recorders to be operated by signals from the computer. This capability, when combined with the usual keyboard input and cathode-ray-tube and/or typewriterlike output, can be especially useful as a student station in teaching applications.

Before concluding our discussion of remote terminals, we should note that the transmission of signals between the terminal and the computer is an important consideration. If existing voice-grade telephone lines are to be used, special linking equipment will be needed and high transmission rates, required for the computer-to-computer communication, are not available. Though voice-grade lines need not be used, transmission costs may become prohibitive when using other lines.

REFERENCES

1. Perlis, A. J., P. Elias, J. C. R. Licklider, and D. C. Marquis: The Computer in the University, in M. Greenberger (ed.), "Computers and the World of the Future," pp. 181–217, The M.I.T. Press, Cambridge, Mass., 1962.
2. Dietrich, W.: Optical Handling of Checks, *Datamation*, pp. 39–42, September, 1964.
3. Proposed American Standard for a Character Set for Optical Character Recognition, *Commun. ACM*, pp. 18–26, January, 1965.
4. Schwartz, J. V., E. G. Coffman, and C. Weissman: A General Purpose Time-sharing System, *Proc. AFIPS Conf.*, vol. 25, pp. 397–411, 1964.
5. Corbato, F. J., et al.: "The Compatible Time-sharing System, A Programmer's Guide," The M.I.T. Press, Cambridge, Mass., 1963.

ANNOTATED SUPPLEMENTARY BIBLIOGRAPHY

A great deal of information is offered by computer manufacturers on the input/output devices available with their lines of equipment. An exhaustive list of references on this subject alone would probably contain hundreds of entries. Specifications for the capacities, access times, processor speeds, and other characteristics of computers are presented from time to time in *Datamation* in the form of a computer-characteristic chart. Some of the more recent issues in which these charts have appeared are listed below. Although the charts were a quarterly feature at one time, they have been published less regularly in recent years.

1. *Datamation*, p. 51, January, 1965.
2. *Ibid.*, p. 76, April, 1965.
3. *Ibid.*, p. 82, July, 1965.
4. *Ibid.*, p. 42, October, 1965.
5. *Ibid.*, p. 55, January, 1966.
6. *Ibid.*, p. 73, July, 1966.
7. *Ibid.*, p. 123, October, 1966.

In addition to the characteristics chart, *Datamation* publishes feature articles describing newly available computers. References to some of the more recent of these articles are given below.

8. The Series 200 from Honeywell, *Datamation*, p. 54, March, 1965.
9. The 1130 from IBM, *ibid.*, p. 51, March, 1965.
10. The 115 from General Electric, *ibid.*, p. 67, April, 1965.
11. Cull, Thomas F.: The Honeywell 8200 Computer, *ibid.*, p. 90, July, 1965.
12. Lynch, John T.: The B8500 from Burroughs, *ibid.*, p. 49, August, 1965.
13. The Sigma 7 from SDS, *ibid.*, p. 53, March, 1966.
14. The Burroughs B2500 and B3500, *ibid.*, p. 75, April, 1966.
15. The Advance 6130 Computer, *ibid.*, p. 61, May, 1966.
16. The Univac 9200 and 9300, *ibid.*, p. 71, July, 1966.
17. The DDP-516 from Honeywell, *ibid.*, p. 30, November, 1966.
18. The SCC 6700, *ibid.*, p. 39, December, 1966.
19. The SDS Sigma 5, *ibid.*, p. 62, January, 1967.

Listed below are a reference on optical character recognition and another on mass storage and two very good general descriptions of the functioning of the elements of the computer. Finally, several references on computers are listed that discuss topics of interest to engineering-oriented readers.

20. Feidelman, L. A., and J. L. Katz: Scanning the Optical Scanners, *Data Process. Mag.*, pp. 34–44, October, 1967. A good summary of the state of the art in optical character recognition. It includes a nice three-page comparison chart. Scanners that read marks other than alphanumeric characters are not discussed.
21. Craver, J. S.: A Review of Electromechanical Mass Storage, *Datamation*, pp. 22–28, July, 1966. An excellent survey article that includes a table of characteristics of more than 130 mass-storage systems.
22. Chapin, N.: "An Introduction to Automatic Computers," pp. 6–150,

D. Van Nostrand Company, Inc., Princeton, N.J., 1963.   This book appears repeatedly in our references and bibliographies.   It is probably the best source for finding the answer to the question "How does a computer work?" by studying the way computer components function and interact.

23. General Information Manual, Introduction to IBM Data Processing Systems, *IBM Publ.* F22-6517.   A nicely illustrated, lucid introduction to computers, with an especially good description of how core storage works.

24. Bartee, T. C.: "Digital Computer Fundamentals," McGraw-Hill Book Company, New York, 1960.   Includes a chapter on logic circuits and another on logic design, as well as a discussion of computer elements from the engineer's point of view.

25. McCormick, E. M.: "Digital Computer Primer," McGraw-Hill Book Company, New York, 1959.   Also touches on questions of logic and design, with an appendix on the mathematics of logic.

26. Culbertson, J. T.: "Mathematics and Logic for Digital Devices," D. Van Nostrand Company, Inc., Princeton, N.J., 1962. This is rather a more mathematically oriented than engineering-oriented book, but logic, nerve nets, and circuit design are given their due.   This book also appears repeatedly in our references and bibliographies.

chapter 5

ALGORITHMS

5.1 DEFINITION

An *algorithm* may be defined as an unambiguous, complete procedure for solving a specified problem in a finite number of steps.† It must include specific steps for both starting and stopping the procedure. Provision for every possible alternative that might be encountered, including provision for erroneous inputs or erroneous results, should also be made to the maximum extent possible. The language in which the algorithm is written and the level of detail required are dictated by the way the algorithm is to be used. In this chapter, we shall be discussing English-language algorithms that would permit a reasonably intelligent person who has no background in the subject matter of the procedure to execute the algorithm. In the next chapter, we shall discuss algorithms in the form of the flow charts that are usually written as an aid to computer

---

† This is not exactly the same as the definition found in dictionaries. For example, "Webster's Seventh New Collegiate Dictionary" [1] defines an algorithm as "a rule of procedure for solving a recurrent mathematical problem (as of finding the greatest common divisor)."

programming. In later chapters, we shall discuss algorithms in the FORTRAN IV and PL/1 programming languages.

5.2 CONNECTION WITH COMPUTER PROGRAMMING

The preparation of an algorithm is an integral part of the general procedure for writing computer programs. This procedure is:

1. Specifically state the problem that is to be solved with the aid of a computer.
2. Formulate an algorithm for its solution.
3. Prepare general and detailed flow charts.
4. Write a computer program.
5. Debug, i.e., test and correct, the computer program.
6. Apply the program to appropriate data and analyze the results.

In some cases, the problem will be small enough or simple enough or the programmer will be proficient enough to permit a telescoping of the procedure. It may even be possible to write the algorithm (step 2) in the form of a computer program directly, so that steps 2 to 4 become just one step. In general, obtaining an algorithm is distinct from writing the program and precedes it.

There is no manual for writing algorithms. Except for a few hints on concluding algorithms, which will be given in Sec. 5.4, and a discussion of the testing of algorithms in Sec. 5.7, the approach will be to present examples of algorithms in the hope that the reader will learn by analogy.

5.3 THE SIEVE OF ERATOSTHENES

Algorithms are not a new subject. In about 250 B.C., Eratosthenes constructed one to answer a question that is still of interest to today's mathematicians. The question is: "What are all the prime numbers between 1 and some specified integer, say N?" (A prime number is a positive integer, other than 1, that is exactly divisible only by itself and 1.) The algorithm, called the *sieve of Eratosthenes*, proceeds as follows:

1. Write down all the integers in numerical order from 2 through N. Call this the *basic list*.
2. Record, in what we shall call the *prime list* (to distinguish it from the basic list), the first uncrossed number in the basic list. Call it M, then cross it off the basic list and every Mth number thereafter.
3. If M is less than $\sqrt{N}$, return to step 2; if M is $\geq \sqrt{N}$, then add all the remaining uncrossed-out numbers to your prime list and stop.

The prime list you have prepared is, in fact, the desired list of primes less than N.

For example, what are all the primes less than 24?   We record

$$2 \quad 3 \quad 4 \quad 5 \quad 6 \quad 7 \quad 8 \quad 9 \quad 10$$
$$11 \quad 12 \quad 13 \quad 14 \quad 15 \quad 16 \quad 17 \quad 18 \quad 19 \quad 20$$
$$21 \quad 22 \quad 23 \quad 24$$

We record 2 and cross off every even number.   Since $2 < \sqrt{24}$, we record 3 and cross off 3, 6, 9, 12, etc.   Since $3 < \sqrt{24}$, we go back to the beginning of the basic list, place 5 on the prime list, and cross off every fifth number.   At this point, our basic and prime lists are

Basic	Prime

$$\text{—2— —3— —4— —5— —6— } 7 \text{ —8— —9— —10—} \quad 2, \quad 3, \quad 5$$
$$11 \text{ —12— } 13 \text{ —14— —15— —16— } 17 \text{ —18— } 19 \text{ —20—}$$
$$\text{—21— —22— } 23 \text{ —24—}$$

Since $5 > \sqrt{24}$, we add 7, 11, 13, 17, 19, and 23 to the prime list and stop.   We conclude that 2, 3, 5, 7, 11, 13, 17, 19, and 23 are the prime numbers less than 24.

A variation of this method was used by Lehmer [2] to produce a list of prime numbers as long ago as 1914.   The list was greatly extended with the aid of the electronic digital computer, and the effort took a new turn.   Large computer facilities competed with each other to find new largest known primes [3], and the sieve was abandoned as a research tool in the study of primes.

5.4 ITERATION

The processes carried out on a computer are often extremely long.   However, it is often the case that the same series of instructions are executed repeatedly with only slight modifications in them or in the data being processed.   The algorithm should be constructed to take advantage of this repetition by returning the procedure to previously written instructions as often as possible.

This was done in the sieve algorithm discussed in the previous section.   The third step provides for returning to step 2, a previously written instruction, if $M < \sqrt{N}$.   Even in the simple numerical example given to illustrate this algorithm, this branching back occurred twice.   More important, by constructing the algorithm in this way, allowance has been made for any number of repetitions of the step 3–step 2 sequence.

In many applications, the repetitive calculations are designed to obtain better and better guided estimates of a desired quantity. Successive estimates of the quantity are obtained by substituting previous estimates in the same procedure. This technique is called *iteration*. Frequently, only the last estimate of the quantity is used to obtain the next estimate. In this case, we would begin with some starting estimate, say E_0. The iterative procedure is then used to obtain the first estimate E_1, using E_0 as an input. E_2 is then obtained using E_1 as input, and so on. The problem is to find a valid procedure, choose an appropriate starting value, and decide on when to stop the iteration. We shall say no more about selecting procedures and starting values. Books on numerical methods, such as [4], should be consulted to find appropriate procedures. They sometimes also contain helpful hints on the choice of a starting value. As regards stopping, in some applications it is possible, given an estimate of the desired quantity, to check on how good this estimate is. For example, if we were estimating the square root of a number, say X, using an iterative scheme, we could square our estimate and compare it with X. In most applications, however, we are forced to rely on a different checking mechanism. It is reasonable to expect that, as we get closer and closer to the true value, successive estimates should differ by smaller and smaller amounts. We could prescribe some small quantity, $\in$, and stop when, ignoring signs, successive estimates differ by less than $\in$. In order to be safe, these checking stop rules are almost always combined with a rule that places an arbitrary, prescribed upper limit on the number of iterations. The iteration is stopped as soon as either this upper limit is reached or the checking criterion is satisfied.

Suppose, for example, we wished to estimate the square root of 1,715. We must first decide on a procedure. A commonly used one is based on Newton's formula, in which the next estimate of the square root of X, say E_n, is obtained from the preceding one, E_{n-1}, and X using

$$(\text{F5.1}) \qquad E_n = \tfrac{1}{2}\left(E_{n-1} + \frac{X}{E_{n-1}}\right)$$

(The mathematical properties of the iterative technique based on the use of this formula are discussed in [4], problem 10 on page 37 and problem 33 on page 315.) Now we need a starting value. It is easy to observe that 40 squared is 1,600 and that 41 squared is $(40 + 1)(40 + 1) = 1,600 + 40 + 40 + 1 = 1,681$. Similarly,

$$(40 + 2)(40 + 2) = 1,600 + 80 + 80 + 4 = 1,764$$

A guess of 41.5 might be reasonable. Finally, we must decide on the error we shall tolerate in terms of the difference between the square of E_n and 1,715. We should also set some upper limit on the number of iterations.   Suppose we insist that the difference between $E_n{}^2$ and 1,715, ignoring signs, be less than 0.0001, and suppose we agree to make no more than 10 iterations.   We find that

i	E_i	$E_i{}^2 - 1{,}715$
0	41.5	7.25
1	41.4126506	0.0076
2	41.4125584	-0.000007

Since 0.000007 is less than 0.0001, we take 41.4125584 as the estimate of the square root.   The beginner should not be misled by the fact that a satisfactory result was obtained so quickly.   The rapid and sharp reduction in the error, as evidenced by the third column in the table, is not typical of iterative procedures.   Newton's formula is especially good, or as the professionals might say, the estimate converges especially rapidly.

We shall discuss an algorithm for estimating the square root of a number in the next section.   It will be based on (F5.1).

5.5 AN ALGORITHM FOR OBTAINING SQUARE ROOTS

Now that we have seen, in rough outline, how one could proceed to estimate the square root of a number, let us try to write a complete, unambiguous procedure—an algorithm—to do this.

We must begin by specifying the number that we are to work with, as follows:

1.   Input X.

The next step is to prescribe a starting value, i.e., a value for E_0. The hunt-and-guess scheme we used in getting the square root of 1,715 might be used in general, but it is very awkward to prescribe.   Instead, we shall use a procedure that is easier to state and that gets us off in the right direction, namely, taking as the starting value half the value of X. So we have:

2. $E_0 = X/2$.

Now we must set up a counter to keep track of which iteration we are currently making.   This must always be done explicitly.   Variables, even if they are subscripts, cannot be introduced into the algorithm without specifying how values are to be assigned to them.   So we have:

3. $n = 1$.

And then:

4. $E_n = \frac{1}{2}(E_{n-1} + X/E_{n-1})$.

Now we must provide for stopping the procedure.   But we have nothing to use for this purpose; we did not input either $\in$, the greatest tolerable absolute difference between $E_n{}^2$ and X, or the maximum number of iterations, say K.   We should modify the first step as follows:

1.   Input X, K, and $\in$.

Now we are ready for the next series of steps.

5.   Is the absolute value of $X - E_n{}^2$, written as $|X - E_n{}^2|$, $< \in$?   If the answer is *yes*, go to 6; if *no*, go to 7.
6.   Output E_n and stop.
7.   Is $n = K$?   If the answer is *yes*, go to 8; if *no*, go to 9.
8.   Output E_n and the message that the maximum number of iterations were executed and stop.
9.   Set $n = n + 1$ and go to 4.

It would appear that this completes the algorithm, but let us now consider the "provision for every possible alternative" discussed in defining the term "algorithm."   Suppose, for example, $X = \frac{1}{2}$.   Well, we know that $\sqrt{X} > \frac{1}{2}$ but that our starting value is actually $< \frac{1}{2}$.   We might modify step 2 as follows:†

2. $E_0 = (X + 1)/2$.

This gives us a value of E_0 that is halfway between 1 and X.   For example, $E_0 = \frac{3}{4}$ if $X = \frac{1}{2}$.   But now what if $X = 0$?   We would get $E_0 = \frac{1}{2}$, and successive applications of Newton's formula would only serve to halve the estimate.   We would be engaged in a lot of wasted effort.   We therefore might find it advisable to check on whether $X = 0$ at the start.   Even more disastrous is a negative value of X.   Such values should also be screened out of the computations.   With these

† Note that this is the value of E_1 that would be obtained if E_0 were taken to be either 1 or X itself.

considerations in mind, we can now rewrite the algorithm as follows:

1. Input X, $\in$, and K.
2. If $X \leq 0$, output X and stop; if $X > 0$, go to step 3.
3. $E_0 = (X + 1)/2$.
4. $n = 1$.
5. $E_n = \frac{1}{2}(E_{n-1} + X/E_{n-1})$.
6. Is $|X - E_n{}^2| < \in$?   If the answer is *yes*, go to step 7; if *no*, go to 8.
7. Output E_n and stop.
8. Is $n = K$?   If the answer is *yes*, go to step 9; if *no*, go to 10.
9. Output E_n and the message that the maximum number of iterations have been executed and stop.
10. Set $n = n + 1$ and return to step 5.

Let us apply the algorithm to a few sets of inputs. We shall take $\in = 0.0001$ and $K = 10$ for each input. We start with $X = 1,715$. We then get $E_0 = 858$ and

n	E_n	$|X - E_n{}^2|$
1	429.991417	More than 158,000
2	216.9899	More than 45,000
3	112.4467	A little less than 10,000
4	63.8492	About 2,362
5	45.3547	About 342
6	41.5839	14.2207
7	41.4129114	0.0292306
8	41.4125584	0.000007

We have arrived at the same estimate, but this time we required eight iterations rather than only three. It would appear that we should improve our procedure for estimating E_0. However, computers perform iterations of this kind quite quickly, and the price we are paying, five additional iterations, is a small one. Even more important, the hunt-and-compute techniques we used to arrive at the better starting value might result in an even longer overall running time for the estimation of the square root if they were implemented on the computer. However, this is not typical of all iteration procedures. In many applications, the choice of a good starting value is critical—we cannot even get an answer if the starting value is poor.

Suppose we next try to estimate $\sqrt{\frac{1}{2}}$; that is, we input $X = \frac{1}{2}$ as well as $K = 10$ and $\in = 0.0001$. This time, $E_0 = 0.75$, and we have

n	E_n	$\lvert X - E_n{}^2 \rvert$
1	0.708333	0.0017356
2	0.70710784	0.000001497

Finally, if $X = -1{,}715$, we would only execute steps 1 and 2 and would output the value of X.

5.6 PAYROLLS

One of the first applications of computers to business problems was the application of UNIVAC I to the generation of the payroll of the General Electric Company.   Because this payroll program included more than 200,000 instructions (according to [5], page 110) and involved some peripheral processing that was interwoven with the payroll processing, a much simpler problem will be discussed for illustrative purposes.†

Some definitions are required before discussing the payroll problem. *Field* denotes a single piece of information, e.g., employee number or gross pay.   *Record* denotes the set of all pieces of information, i.e., fields, pertinent to a single employee.   A *file* is the complete collection of records.   The fields are themselves made up of a series of usually adjacent characters.

Two other terms involve certain data-processing operations.   A *sort* is an ordering of the records in a file in accordance with the entries in a prescribed field.   *Merging* is the process of combining two or more files into a single file while maintaining the order in a prescribed way.

Consider, for example, the collection of all student records at a university.   Each record pertains to a single student and contains such fields as the student's identification number, his home address, and his campus address as well as a series of fields in which his grades are listed. One could sort this student records file according to student number. If this were done, the record corresponding to student number 00002 would follow that for number 00001, and so on.   The file could also be sorted in decreasing order according to quality point index (QPI) or some other quantitative index of the student's average grade.   In this case, after sorting, all students with QPIs greater than 3.5 or those with QPIs less than 2.5 could be easily identified in the file.   A typical merging

---

† We shall, in fact, be dealing with payroll processing itself in a somewhat unrealistic way.   In order to concentrate on algorithmic formulation while at the same time keeping the problem manageable, we have emphasized the computational aspects of the payroll process and have deemphasized the manipulation of information inherent in an accounting operation of this kind.

NUMBER	NAME	REGULAR HOURS	RATE	REGULAR WEEKLY PAY	CUM GROSS PAY	CUM FICA	NUMBER DEDUCT	CUM TAX DEDUCT	WEEKLY HOSP DEDUCT	REGULAR NET PAY
12345	SMITH, JOSEPH E.	40	2.40	96.00	960.00	43.20	0	192.00	4.10	63.38
12347	JOHNSON, PAUL R.	40	2.40	96.00	960.00	43.20	3	144.00	4.10	74.18
12351	FRIEDERICHS, CARL	40	2.80	112.00	1120.00	50.40	3	168.00	4.10	86.06
12353	MASTERSON, JOHN F.	40	2.40	96.00	1050.00	47.25	1	189.00	2.80	71.60
12356	PAULERS, HARRY V.	40	3.10	124.00	620.00	27.90	4	86.80	4.10	96.94
12361	MEYERS, JOAN S.	35	2.00	70.00	700.00	30.50	1	126.00	0.00	54.35
...		...	...	...	...	...	...	...	...	...

Fig. 5.1 Typical master payroll file.

PAYROLL NUMBER	NAME	HOURS WORKED
12347	JOHNSON, PAUL R.	40.00
12351	FRIEDERICHS, CARL	40.00
12353	MASTERSON, JOHN F.	45.00
12356	PAULERS, HARRY V.	40.00
12361	MEYERS, JOAN S.	35.00
...		...

Fig. 5.2 Typical weekly entry file.

operation is to form a new student file at the end of a semester by combining the old file with a file containing the set of grades obtained during that semester.

A payroll file consists of a series of records, one for each employee. The first step in processing the payroll is to sort the file by employee number. This extremely complex program segment is outside our central concern here; it is widely discussed in the computer literature.†

The payroll file stored in the computer will contain the following information in each record: employee number, employee name, regular hours worked, hourly pay rate, regular gross weekly pay, cumulative gross pay to date in the current year, cumulative social security deduction in the current year, withholding tax deduction class, cumulative withholding tax deduction in the current year, hospitalization deductions, and regular net pay. (See Fig. 5.1.)

A series of cards are punched each week, one for each employee, containing the employee's number and name and the number of hours worked during the week. (See Fig. 5.2.) The cards are input to the computer; the program calls up the required information from the payroll file and computes:

1. The actual gross weekly pay. (If no overtime was worked, the actual gross weekly pay will be equal to the regular gross weekly pay; if there has been overtime, the hourly rate will be used to help determine the additional gross pay to be added to the regular gross pay.)
2. Cumulative gross pay to date.
3. Appropriate withholding tax deduction this week.
4. Cumulative withholding tax deduction.
5. Social security tax deduction.
6. Cumulative social security tax deduction.
7. Actual net pay.

Payroll processing begins by matching the number and the name of the first entry in the master file with the number and the name of the first entry in the weekly file. Remember that both the master and the weekly files are sorted in order of increasing payroll number. Normally, a match takes place and the processing goes on to the next step. The abnormal case—no match—is discussed later.

The number of hours actually worked is used to determine the amount of overtime, if any. For example, comparing the entries in the *hours-worked* field in the weekly file, Fig. 5.2, to the entries in the *regular-*

† A whole issue of the *Communications of the Association for Computing Machinery* was devoted to the subject of sorting [6]. A bibliography was included on page 280 of this issue.

hours field in the master file, Fig. 5.1, we see that Mr. Masterson worked 5 hours of overtime.   From this, the program determines gross and net pay for the week.   (It can use the regular figures in the master file for everyone but Mr. Masterson.)   Mr. Masterson's regular hourly rate is $2.40, and since all overtime is paid at a time-and-a-half rate, his overtime rate is $3.60.   This means his gross pay is

$$40(\$2.40) + 5(\$3.60) = \$114.00$$

The deductions to be made are

$4\frac{1}{2}\%$ of gross for social security (FICA) = $ 5.13
18% of gross for withholding income tax =   20.52
Regular deduction for hospitalization   =   2.80

Total deductions = $28.45

Net pay = $85.55

The figure of 18 percent used to compute the withholding tax is determined from the number of deductions claimed by the employee.   We could have put this figure directly in the master file, but we chose to assume that the number of deductions is in the file.   This means that the payroll program must include a table that converts from number of deductions to percentage of gross salary withheld.   For example, the table might be

No. deductions:	0	1	2	3	4	5	6	7	8 or more
% withholding:	20	18	16	15	14	13	12	11	10

The cumulative entries in the master file would now have to be corrected as follows:

Cumulative FICA is now $52.38, that is, $47.25 + $5.13.

Cumulative withheld tax is $209.52, that is, $189 + $20.52.

Cumulative gross earnings are $1,164, that is, $1,050 + $114.

No other changes are made in the master file.   A payroll check for $85.55 is printed, along with an itemized report of his earnings and deductions. The next record in the master and weekly file is then drawn and processed.

Now we shall consider the abnormal case—when the payroll numbers and names in the master and weekly files do not match.   In case of error, a message is printed out so that steps can be taken to correct the files.   There are at least four possible situations:

1.   The payroll number for the master file is less than the number for the weekly file, and the names do not match.

2. The payroll number for the master file is greater than the number for the weekly file, and the names do not match.
3. The payroll numbers are different, but the names are the same.
4. The payroll numbers are the same, but the names do not match.

An appropriate message should be printed out in each case, and the process continued.   If the master-file number is less than the weekly-file number, we print an appropriate message and proceed to draw the next record from the master file.   Similarly, if the weekly-file number is smaller, a message is printed and the next record from the weekly file is drawn.   In either case 3 or case 4, a message is printed and the next record from both files is drawn.

For example, in Figs. 5.1 and 5.2, the first entry in the master file is for employee number 12345, which is less than the first employee number in the weekly file, namely, 12347.   Case 1 applies, and a message is printed.   The record for Paul R. Johnson is drawn from the master file; a match takes place, and his payroll for the week is computed.

The payroll problem defined and discussed above presents a more formidable problem in algorithmic formulation.   We shall construct the algorithm piecemeal, going back and forth between the steps in processing payrolls presented above and the corresponding steps in the algorithm.   This approach is taken in order to more effectively present the reasoning behind the development of the algorithm in the hope that the reader will be able to draw more direct analogies to his own applications.

In any algorithmic procedure, we must assume that we have certain inputs available to the algorithm.   In the sieve, these inputs were N and $\sqrt{N}$.   In the immediate case, we shall assume that two files, the master payroll file and the weekly entry file (see Figs. 5.1 and 5.2), are inputs. We shall also assume that we have a means of sorting these files—just as we assumed that we had a means of inputting and comparing M to the $\sqrt{N}$ in the sieve algorithm.   The algorithm then begins:

1. Input the master payroll file.
2. Sort the master payroll file by employee number.
3. Input the weekly entry file.
4. Sort the weekly entry file by employee number.

We might have assumed that both files were available and sorted by employee number.   In that case, the algorithm would begin at this point.

5. Reposition files at their beginning.
6. Match the number and name of the next entry in the master file to the number and name of the next entry in the weekly file.   (The

phrase "next entry" is used rather than "first entry" in order to be able to return to this step later in the algorithm.)   If both files are exhausted, stop.   If only one file is exhausted, then step 10, below, will apply.

Although, in our earlier discussion of payrolls, it was convenient to assume that a match took place, we cannot do this in constructing an algorithm.   We must provide for all possible outcomes of the match in the algorithm at this time.   The next steps, therefore, are:

7. If both the name and the number match, go to step 21.
8. If the numbers match but the names do not, go to step 11.
9. If the names match but the numbers do not, go to step 13.
10. If neither the names nor the numbers match and if the number in the master file is less than that in the entry file, go to step 15; but if the number in the entry file is less than that in the master file, go to step 18.
11. Output: The employee number and the two names.
12. Go to step 6.
13. Output: The employee name and the two numbers.
14. Go to step 6.
15. Output: The employee name and number and the notation that this employee is in the master file but not in the weekly entry file.
16. Call in the next entry from the master file and match it against the former entry in the weekly file.
17. Go to step 7.
18. Output: The employee name and number and the notation that this employee is in the weekly file but not in the master file.
19. Call in the next entry from the weekly entry file and match it against the former entry in the master file.
20. Go to step 7.

The above steps should take care of all the exceptional matching and provide for both appropriate outputs and continuity.   Now we continue the procedure, treating the usual case—when a match occurs.

21. Compare hours worked (from weekly file) with the regular hours (from master file).   If they are equal, go to step 22.   If the number of regular hours is greater, go to step 23; if the number of hours worked is greater, go to step 24.
22. Set gross pay = regular weekly pay and go to step 25.
23. Set gross pay = regular weekly pay (hours worked/regular hours) and go to step 25.

24. Set gross pay

$$= \text{regular weekly pay} \left(1 + 1.5 \,\frac{\text{hours worked} - \text{regular hours}}{\text{regular hours}}\right).$$

25. Set the cumulative gross pay = previous cumulative gross pay + gross pay.

It is now necessary to compute the income tax and the FICA deductions from gross pay. (It is assumed that the hospitalization deduction is taken directly from the master file.) This is a straightforward task except for the statutory limit of $290.40 placed on FICA deductions in a single year. Because of this limit, we must first compute a potential FICA deduction, check this potential deduction to be sure it does not exceed the limit, and then arrive at the actual FICA deduction. We proceed as follows:

26. Compare cumulative FICA to $290.40. If it is equal, set actual FICA = 0 and go to step 33; if it is not equal, go to step 27.
27. Potential FICA = (0.045) (gross pay).
28. Potential gross FICA = old gross FICA + potential FICA.
29. Compare potential gross FICA to $290.40. If it is less than or equal to it, go to step 30; if it is greater, go to step 32.
30. Actual FICA = potential FICA.
31. New cumulative FICA = previous cumulative FICA + actual FICA. Go to step 33.
32. Actual FICA = potential FICA − (potential gross FICA − $290.40). Go to step 31.
33. Determine withholding tax rate using number of deductions and rate table.
34. Withholding tax = gross pay (withholding tax rate).
35. New cumulative withholding tax = previous cumulative withholding tax + withholding tax.
36. New pay = gross pay − actual FICA − withholding tax − hospitalization deduction.
37. Print a check and an earnings statement. Check forms that include earnings statements can be loaded into the printer and the printer set up so that entries corresponding to the employee name, net pay, gross pay, and deductions are made in the proper position on the check and the form.
38. Reconstruct the master file by making the appropriate entries of new data.
39. Go to step 6.

This completes the basic payroll problem. However, it should be pointed out that algorithms (and ultimately computer programs) must be written to supplement the basic algorithm to permit:

1. Updating the master file or the weekly file. *Updating* a file refers to any modification—such as correcting a field in a record, deleting an entire record, or adding a new record.
2. Initializing the files, especially the master file, at the start of a new payroll year. The major function of this algorithm is to reset cumulative figures to zero. Initializing procedures may also provide for such things as changes in the withholding tax rates or the social security laws.
3. Obtaining special reports from the files such as reports on absenteeism, employee turnover, and summary payroll figures by department.

Note that the basic payroll-processing task is really quite simple, but because of the need to consider all alternatives and the need to break the task into its most elementary parts, it still required 39 steps to state in algorithmic fashion. This is typical of nearly all real-life problems. A. J. Perlis has said (see [1] at the end of Chap. 4), in talking about teaching algorithmic formulation, that "the point is to make the student construct complex processes out of simpler ones."

5.7 TESTING ALGORITHMS

Writing algorithms is a tedious task that offers much opportunity for error. All algorithms should be tested. Ideally, one would like to prove in the mathematical sense that given any input, the result must be correct. It is important in the case of those algorithms using iterative formulas to prove or to find a proof of the fact that the iteration must converge, in the mathematical sense. It may be necessary to consult the literature on numerical analysis to do this; such proofs or references to proofs are frequently found in the source for the formula itself. However, in most cases a proof, in the mathematical sense, of the correctness of the algorithm is not possible—or at least is not readily obtainable. It is then necessary to test the algorithm using specially chosen test inputs.

Since the writing of algorithms is the first step in developing a computer program, the testing of the algorithm could be postponed and, in effect, combined with the checking or debugging of the computer program. However, experience indicates that errors in logic are the most difficult ones to detect in debugging computer programs. For example, Leeds and Weinberg, in a very good discussion of debugging [7], note that "the major errors [of logic or problem interpretation] initially are usually the most difficult to detect." For this reason, it may be easier to invest in a systems analyst's time to check the algorithm for logical errors before any computer instructions are written. This may be preferable to expending a systems analyst's time and computer time in checking both the errors in writing the instructions and the logical errors in the algorithm at the time the program is debugged.

Testing an algorithm for logical errors begins and very nearly ends with the construction of a set of *test inputs*. The set of inputs should be such that, as a whole, they cause every step in the algorithm to be executed. They should also be realistic in both their magnitudes and their signs—covering the range of values that could be expected to appear as input. Finally, several exceptional inputs (values that would only appear in the event of gross input errors) should be included, whether or not it can be anticipated that they would cause new steps in the algorithm to be executed. They may reveal new alternatives for intermediate results that must be accounted for; i.e., they may cause several steps to be added to the algorithm.

Once a set of inputs is established, it is a good practice to give the algorithm and the inputs to a coworker who has never seen either of them before and to ask him to obtain the results. This will both reduce your workload and, more importantly, permit a fresh outlook on the problem. It is surprising how frequently a fresh viewpoint can find dead ends and logical inconsistencies that the person who constructed the algorithm could not see.

Let us try to set up test data for the square-root algorithm. In order to ensure the execution of every step, we include the following sets (the reader should determine which step in the algorithm is executed for the first time by each new set of test input):

Set	X	K	$\in$
1	-1	10	0.001
2	0	10	0.001
3	1	10	0.001
4	10	1,000	0.001
5	10	3	0.000001

For realistic inputs, we include:

Set	X	K	$\in$
6	1047.26	100	0.001
7	0.062172	100	0.00001
8	1.004131	50	0.0001

For grossly erroneous inputs, we add:

Set	X	K	∈
9	10	4.5	0.00001
10	10	−5	0.001
11	10	100	−0.001
12	10	−5	−0.001

Substituting the above inputs in the algorithm would probably cause us to modify the algorithm, so that we first check on whether K is negative or zero and we stop the process if $n \geq K$ (to accommodate a value of $K = 4.5$). We would also probably choose to output X, K, and $\in$ as well as E_n each time an output is made.

5.8 ERRORS IN IMPLEMENTING ALGORITHMS ON A DIGITAL COMPUTER

Algorithms implemented on electronic digital computers may frequently give erroneous results. There are three major reasons for these errors. First, the computer does what it is programmed to do; an erroneous algorithm produces an erroneous result. Second, erroneous input data produce erroneous outputs, or more succinctly, GIGO (garbage in, garbage out). Third, the computer can retain only a finite number of digits in all its calculations. If, for example, the difference of two nearly equal numbers is divided into a third number, the loss of significance in the digits discarded from the first two numbers can be disastrous.

If we use lowercase letters to denote operands and capital letters to denote algorithms, then the procedure X operating on a and b can be denoted by $X(a,b)$. In addition, we use a superscript asterisk to indicate the algorithms and procedures actually used, as opposed to the true algorithms and procedures. The error in applying X to a and b is then given by

$$X(a,b) - X^*(a^*,b^*)$$

This can be rewritten as

$$[X(a,b) - X(a^*,b^*)] + [X(a^*,b^*) - X^*(a^*,b^*)]$$

The first difference is the error resulting from applying the right algorithm to the wrong data and is called the *propagated error*. The second difference results from applying the wrong algorithm to the data actually processed and is called the *generated error*.

There are many sources for propagated errors. Poor data-collection procedures and careless handling of the data in preparing the input can introduce errors. In addition, errors result from the loss of significance in truncating or rounding input data and from using the erroneous result of a previous calculation in the present calculation.†

Generated errors can result from erroneous models for the process under study, clerical errors in preparing the computing program, faulty programming techniques, and poor numerical methodology.

The techniques of statistical design [8,9] should be applied to avoid gathering invalid or incomplete data. Quality-control procedures [10] can be fruitfully applied to the checking of a large volume of input data. For small volumes of data, we recommend a complete check of the final input (usually in the form of a listing of the contents of a deck of punched cards) against the source for the data (e.g., laboratory notebooks, questionnaires, statistical abstracts). Similarly, a complete check of a listing of the program deck should help minimize the number of clerical errors in the program.

Logical errors in programming should be detected in the debugging of the program. There is another class of programming errors, which might be called "sloppy output errors." The organization, labeling, and effective formatting of outputs are essential in order to avoid misinterpretation of valid output.

A sizable area of applied mathematics, numerical analysis, is devoted to the study of the theory of computational algorithms. References [4, 11, and 12] are good introductory books on this subject. This study has produced a set of techniques, or methodologies, that should be reviewed before deciding on a computational algorithm. Reference [13] is an excellent handbook of numerical procedures.

There is no substitute for a penetrating, thorough analysis of the algorithm. It may be that a great deal of experience with a wide range of procedures is required to do an effective job on complex problems. However, a conscientious approach that makes full use of the available references will permit the novice to devise and implement algorithms to solve complex as well as simple problems.

PROBLEMS

5.1 Find all the primes less than 99 using the sieve of Eratosthenes.

5.2 Given M and N, write an algorithm to compare M with the $\sqrt{N}$ that ends if $M > \sqrt{N}$ but goes to another algorithm, say SIEVE, if $M \leq \sqrt{N}$. Do *not* attempt to compute $\sqrt{N}$; it should not be necessary.

5.3 Why does step 3 in the sieve algorithm work? Could you improve on this step—that is, could you rewrite the algorithm by modifying its stop rule so as to obtain a complete list of primes with fewer listings and crossings-out of numbers?

5.4 Suppose we do not assume that the $\sqrt{N}$ is available as input. Rewrite the sieve algorithm so that it could function without this information. Try to do

---

† Some authors apply the term "propagated error" only to this last kind of error. They call the other errors, simply, *input errors*.

this in three ways: (1) by changing the stop rule, (2) by using the result of Prob. 5.2, and (3) by incorporating a computation of $\sqrt{N}$ using Newton's formula.

5.5   Construct a set of test inputs, in the form of several pairs of master and weekly files, for the payroll algorithm. Specify which step in the algorithm would be executed for the first time for each of the inputs. Be sure to include grossly erroneous data—preferably one or two fields in each pair rather than many fields of grossly erroneous data in a single pair.

5.6   Construct an algorithm to solve the following problem: Given a positive integer N, determine the Nth Fibonacci number. The first Fibonacci number is 0, and the second is 1. Each succeeding Fibonacci number is obtained as the sum of the two preceding numbers. Set up a "counter," in the form of a variable that takes on the values 1, 2, 3, . . . , N, to indicate which number was last generated and test the value of the counter against N to determine if the algorithm should be stopped.

5.7   Given three numbers, A, B, and C, write an algorithm which will sort these numbers in decreasing order.

5.8   Write an algorithm to compute $\sum_{i=1}^{N} X_i$, given each X_i and N. Use a counter as in Prob. 5.6. (If you are not familiar with the Σ notation, see Ref. 2 in the Annotated Supplementary Bibliography.)

5.9   Write an algorithm to compute the mean and standard deviation of a series of numbers, X_1, X_2, . . . , X_N, given N and the numbers themselves. The formulas for these statistics are given below. Be sure to include a procedure for computing the required square root.

$$\text{Mean} = \frac{\sum_{i=1}^{N} X_i}{N}$$

$$\text{Standard deviation} = \sqrt{\frac{\sum_{i=1}^{N} X_i^2}{N} - \left(\frac{\sum_{i=1}^{N} X_i}{N}\right)^2}$$

5.10   Construct a set of test inputs for the algorithm written in Prob. 5.9. If your algorithm requires N as input, be sure to include a set of data for which N is given erroneously.

5.11   Write an algorithm to sort a set of N numbers, $X_1 X_2 \cdots X_N$, in decreasing order.

5.12   Construct a set of test inputs for the algorithm written in Prob. 5.11.

5.13   Write an algorithm for computing the point count in a bridge hand (a bridge hand contains 13 cards) using the following point-count scheme:

    (a)   4 points for each ace
    (b)   3 points for each king—but not if the only card in the suit is the king (i.e., not for singleton kings)
    (c)   2 points for each queen and 1 point for each jack—but not if there are two or fewer cards in the suit
    (d)   3 points for each suit in which you have no cards (i.e., 3 points for each void)
    (e)   2 points for each suit in which you have one card (i.e., 2 points for each singleton)
    (f)   1 point for each suit in which you have two cards (i.e., 1 point for each doubleton)

Points for distribution, i.e., points resulting from conditions *d*, *e*, and *f*, are scored independent of the rank or value of the cards held in the suit. For example, a singleton king is worth a total of 2 points (2 for distribution plus none for the king), whereas a singleton ace is worth 6 points (2 for distribution and 4 for the ace).

5.14 Write an algorithm to implement the standard procedure for finding the quotient of two integers. The algorithm should stop if either:

(*a*) The result is exact; i.e., a remainder of zero is obtained

(*b*) You have five digits in the quotient

In the latter case, round the last (the fifth) digit. That is, increase it by 1 if the remainder is greater than half the divisor; otherwise, leave it unchanged.

5.15 Write an algorithm to implement the standard procedure for finding the quotient of two integers, but this time do not stop the algorithm until you know the exact answer. Since the quotient of two integers is a rational number, the result either will be exact (i.e., a remainder of zero will be obtained) or can be expressed using a repeating decimal. Because of this, a procedure for handling repeating decimals will necessarily be a part of the algorithm. Express the repeating portion of the result using the notation of Sec. 3.5.

5.16 Given a pair of integers, *I* and *J*, write an algorithm to find the greatest integer that is a divisor of both *I* and *J*. (*N* is a divisor of *M* if and only if a positive integer *L* exists such that $M = LN$.) It may either encourage you or heighten your frustration to learn that the euclidean school of Greek mathematicians solved this problem thousands of years ago. Their result is known as the *euclidean algorithm*.

5.17 Go to Ref. 4 in the Annotated Supplementary Bibliography and try writing algorithms to solve a few of these problems.

REFERENCES

1. "Webster's Seventh New Collegiate Dictionary," p. 22, G. & C. Merriam Company, Springfield, Mass., 1964.

2. Lehmer, D. N.: A List of Primes from 1 to 10,006,721, *Carnegie Inst. Publ.* 164, 1914.

3. Miller, J. P.: The Search for Large Primes, *Proc. Manchester Univ. Computer Symp.*, 1951.

4. Ralston, A.: "A First Course in Numerical Analysis," McGraw-Hill Book Company, New York, 1965.

5. Hein, L. W.: "An Introduction to Electronic Data Processing for Business," D. Van Nostrand Company, Inc., Princeton, N.J., 1961.

6. *Commun. ACM*, vol. 6, no. 5, May, 1963.

7. Leeds, H. D., and G. M. Weinberg: "Computer Programming Fundamentals," chap. 10, pp. 301–327, McGraw-Hill Book Company, New York, 1961. The quotation is at the top of page 302.

8. Hansen, M. H., W. N. Hurwitz, and W. G. Madow: "Sample Survey Methods and Theory," vols. I and II, John Wiley & Sons, Inc., New York, 1953.

9. Cochran, W. G., and G. M. Cox: "Experimental Designs," 2d ed., John Wiley & Sons, Inc., New York, 1957.

10. Juran, J. M.: "Quality Control Handbook," 2d ed., McGraw-Hill
    Book Company, New York, 1962.
11. Isaacson, E., and H. B. Keller: "Analysis of Numerical Methods,"
    John Wiley & Sons, Inc., New York, 1966.
12. Stanton, R. G.: "Numerical Methods for Science and Engineering,"
    Prentice-Hall, Inc., Englewood Cliffs, N.J., 1961.
13. Ralston, A., and H. S. Wilf (eds.): "Mathematical Methods for
    Digital Computers," John Wiley & Sons, Inc., New York, 1960
    (vol. 1) and 1967 (vol. 2).

ANNOTATED SUPPLEMENTARY BIBLIOGRAPHY

The literature on how to construct algorithms is sparse. Although the
subject is discussed in most introductory computer-programming texts,
it is usually treated too superficially for the discussion to serve as a supplement to this book. A few discussions that are more than superficial
and that can be of help to a person faced with a problem in algorithmic
formulation are referenced below.

1. Chapin, N.: "An Introduction to Automatic Computers," chap. 14,
   D. Van Nostrand Company, Inc., Princeton, N.J., 1963. This discussion is oriented toward the problem of how to go from input to
   output in business applications. Some useful insight is provided,
   but formal algorithms are not really discussed.
2. Culbertson, J. T.: "Mathematics and Logic for Digital Devices,"
   pp. 1–11, D. Van Nostrand Company, Inc., Princeton, N.J., 1962.
   This reference includes a definition of algorithms, one or two examples of algorithms, and a discussion of the Σ notation for sums and
   the π notation for products.
3. Froese, C.: "Introduction to Programming the IBM 1620," chap. 4,
   pp. 13–20, Addison-Wesley Publishing Company, Inc., Reading,
   Mass., 1964. The principal contributions of this reference are a
   definition of recursion and its place in an algorithm and an example
   of a recursive procedure for generating $_nC_r$, that is, for generating the
   ratio of $n!$ to $r!$ times $(n - r)!$.
4. Greenberger, F., and G. Jaffray: "Problems for Computer Solution,"
   John Wiley & Sons, Inc., New York, 1965. The best available set
   of problems for computer solution. Try writing algorithms to solve
   a few of the problems in this book that interest you.
5. Ledley, R. S.: "Fortran IV Programming," chap. 1, pp. 3–26,
   McGraw-Hill Book Company, New York, 1966. A good discussion
   of problem analysis but not of algorithms as such. Reading this
   reference should be postponed until after our discussion of flow
   charting.

chapter 6

FLOW CHARTS

6.1 INTRODUCTION

Flow charts are an especially convenient form for the expression of some algorithms preliminary to computer programming.† In many cases, a systems analyst or programmer will not write out a formal step-by-step algorithm, such as those presented in Chap. 5, but will proceed directly to a flow chart.

Flow charts are widely used because they combine the precision and continuity of an ordinary algorithm with the visual aid inherent in a plot or diagram. In addition, they spotlight dead ends, unaccounted-for alternatives, and special subsections of the algorithms that are particularly susceptible to errors.

The language of flow charts includes some well-known symbols, such as arrows, some very special symbols, which will be described in Sec. 6.2, and ordinary English statements and mathematical formulas. The

† Many professional programmers do not prepare flow charts before writing the computer program. Flow charts are, instead, prepared some time after the program is debugged, for incorporation into the written, detailed description of the program known as the *documentation*.

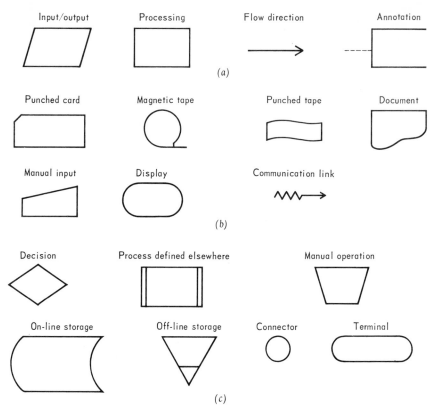

Fig. 6.1 Summary of the most important flow-chart symbols: (*a*) basic symbols, (*b*) specialized input/output symbols, (*c*) special-processing symbols.

arrows are used to indicate the path to be followed from one step to another; the special symbols are the boxes used to enclose the step. The shape of the box categorizes the objective of the step, and the English and mathematical statements prescribe the operation itself.

6.2 THE USA STANDARD FOR FLOW-CHART SYMBOLS

Appendix B contains the United States of America Standards Institute (USA) standard for flow-chart symbols for information processing. Figure 6.1 contains the principal symbols and their meanings. Note that input/output can be indicated either by the slanted quadrilateral or specifically with a distinct symbol for each type of operation.

6.3 AN EXAMPLE OF A SIMPLE FLOW CHART—THE SIEVE OF ERATOSTHENES

Just as with algorithms, one learns how to draw flow charts by example and by doing. In the remainder of this chapter, we shall present two examples of flow charts—one for the sieve and one for the payroll problem—sandwiched in a discussion of the nature and the use of general and detailed flow charts.

A flow chart for the sieve algorithm is given in Fig. 6.2. Note that this time we are including a specific procedure for comparing M with $\sqrt{N}$. The diamond-shaped *decision box* contains the procedure. We use the notation $A:B$ to mean compare A with B, so that this time we are comparing M^2 with N. If $M^2 \leq N$, we continue the procedure of listing and crossing off numbers; while if $M^2 > N$, we proceed to output our results and then to stop. We drew this flow chart somewhat awkwardly in order to be able to include a *connector* (1) in the chart. Ordinarily, one would run the decision diamond to the left rather than to the right of the box which immediately precedes it in order to make a direct connection, without a connector, at (1).

6.4 DETAILED AND GENERAL FLOW CHARTS

Real problems are quite complex, and it is usually too difficult to construct a detailed algorithm for their solution from scratch. Instead, a

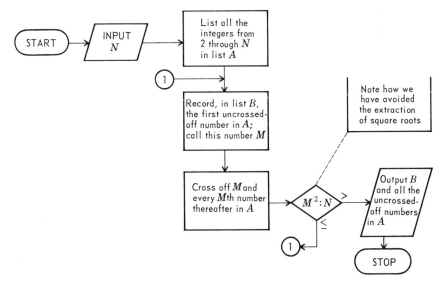

Fig. 6.2 A flow chart for the sieve of Eratosthenes.

general procedure is outlined at the start. This might be called the *overall logic* for the solution of the problem. After reviewing the general procedure for logical correctness and efficiency, a detailed algorithm is built piecemeal, one piece for each major step in the general procedure. A flow chart depicting the general procedure is called a *general flow chart;* those that present the detailed procedure are called *detailed flow charts.*

Another way to distinguish between detailed and general flow charts is to ask: Can I write a computer program directly from the chart? The detailed flow chart should resolve any question that may arise in writing the computer program; the general flow chart will almost invariably leave some questions unanswered.

A third way to distinguish between the charts is to note the kinds of entries that appear in the boxes. Detailed flow charts have a greater number of mathematical formulas and comparisons, whereas general flow charts have a greater number of broad English-language statements or questions. To put this another way, detailed charts assign symbols or values to each variable that is processed and relate the variables via formulas. General flow charts usually deal with variables in generic terms as subjects or objects of English-language statements or questions.

In the next section, we shall discuss both a general and a detailed flow chart for the payroll problem. We shall also pose several important questions that are unanswered by the general flow chart but that are answered by the detailed flow chart.

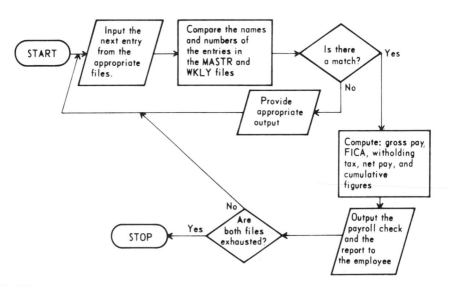

Fig. 6.3   A general flow chart for the payroll problem.

6.5 FLOW CHARTS FOR THE PAYROLL PROBLEM

A general flow chart for the payroll problem is given in Fig. 6.3. For both the general and the detailed flow charts, we shall assume that the master and weekly files have been sorted and are available for our use.

Table 6.1   Definitions of the symbols used in the payroll flow charts

Symbol	Meaning
MNAME	The name of the employee in the record in the master file that is being processed
WNAME	The name of the employee in the record in the weekly file that is being processed
MNO	The number of the employee in the record in the master file that is being processed
WNO	The number of the employee in the record in the weekly file that is being processed
HM	The total number of hours ordinarily worked
HW	The total number of hours actually worked in the preceding week
RWP	The regular weekly pay
GP	The actual gross pay for the preceding week
CGP	The cumulative gross pay for the current year
CFICA	The cumulative social security deductions for the current year
PFICA	The potential social security deduction for the preceding week
AFICA	The actual social security deduction for the preceding week
WTR	The withholding tax rate
D	The number of deductions claimed
WT	The tax to be withheld from the pay for the preceding week
CWT	The cumulative tax withheld in the current year
WHD	The deduction for hospitalization insurance
NP	The net pay for the preceding week
M	A variable that is set to 1 to indicate that the master file has been exhausted
W	A variable that is set to 1 to indicate that the weekly file has been exhausted
NER	The number of special messages generated in processing the payroll
K	A variable that is set to 1 to indicate that MNAME does not match WNAME
MSTR	The name for the master file
WKLY	The name for the weekly file

In comparing the algorithm, as given in Sec. 5.6, with the general flow chart, it is obvious that a great many specific procedures and formulas contained in the algorithm are not given in the general flow chart. Since a knowledge of these procedures is necessary to the programmer, several questions of interest to the programmer that are left unanswered by the general flow chart could be listed immediately.   For example: How are the gross pay, deductions, net pay, and cumulative figures computed?   What is the "appropriate output" to be given in the event of failure to match entries, and which is the "appropriate file" from which to draw the next entry?   These are obvious questions, but there are several others that are left unanswered.   For example: What do we really mean by matching entries?   What are all the possible kinds of output that can be obtained?   How do we go about determining whether or not both files are exhausted?

The detailed flow charts for the payroll problem are given in Figs. 6.4 to 6.6.   The distinction between the two types of charts should become apparent in comparing these figures with Fig. 6.3.   Table 6.1 contains a dictionary of symbols used in the flow charts.

We used several separate charts to present the detailed flow chart because of the dimensional restrictions inherent in presenting the charts

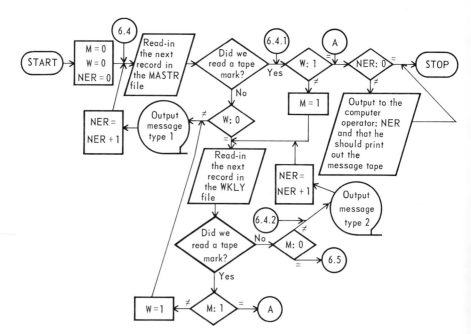

Fig. 6.4 A detailed flow chart for deciding whether to end the processing or to branch to the matching procedure.

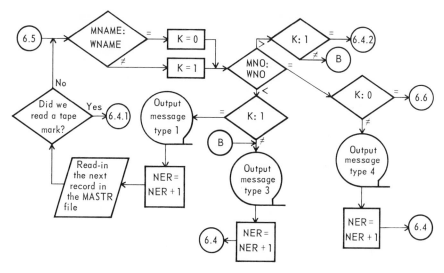

Fig. 6.5 A detailed flow chart for the matching procedure.

on the pages of a book. However, even if we were able to use a large sheet of paper, the charts would be drawn in this way because, in most real problems, one-sheet charts are either impossible (there is no paper in stock big enough) or awkward (the chart becomes too confusing) or avoided for other reasons ("my boss doesn't like it"). In drawing separate charts, it is helpful to tell the user of the charts what the *normal entry* (i.e., most frequently encountered entry) and the *normal exit* are. The normal entry to a flow chart usually appears in the upper left-hand corner.

The first detailed flow chart, Fig. 6.4, describes the procedure for checking on whether the files are exhausted. Note the mechanism used for this purpose. It is assumed that an end-of-file mark is entered on the tape. This is a reasonable assumption since the end of a tape file is marked in a standard way when the file is being written by a computer. The variable M is used to indicate whether the master file has been exhausted, and a W is used for the weekly file. These variables are set equal to 1 when the tape mark is read for the corresponding file. Thus, for example, if W is 1 when the tape mark on the master file is read, both files must have been exhausted. The normal entry is the START, and the normal exit from this chart is connector (6.5). Connector (6.5) is the normal entry to the second detailed flow chart, which provides for the matching of employee names and numbers.

The algorithm is written so that the variable NER will provide a count of the number of times that a match fails to occur of both the

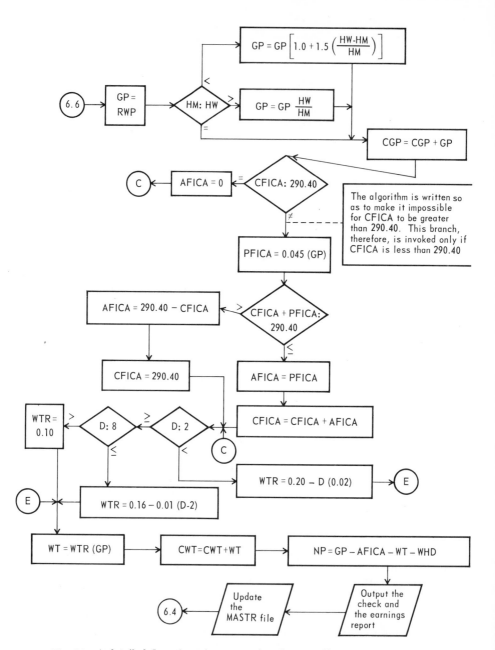

Fig. 6.6 A detailed flow chart for computing the payroll.

Table 6.2   Key to the standard messages used in the payroll flow charts

Message No.	Message	Variables that are output
1	An entry in the master file is not in the weekly file	MNO, MNAME
2	An entry in the weekly file is not in the master file	WNO, WNAME
3	The employee names are the same, but the numbers differ	MNO, WNO, MNAME
4	The employee numbers are the same, but the names differ	MNAME, WNAME, MNO

name and number in the two files.   Each time such a match does not occur, an appropriate message is written on the tape.   If NER is not zero when both files are exhausted, the operator is instructed to print this tape.

Note the use of standard messages.   This facilitates the programming by permitting a single output statement to be used repeatedly. Table 6.2 contains the key to these messages.   The normal exit from the chart in Fig. 6.5 is connector (6.6), which is the normal entry to the last detailed flow chart.

The last detailed flow chart, Fig. 6.6, presents the procedure for calculating the desired payroll figures.   Note the way we reduced the withholding tax table to a kind of mathematical function of the number of dependents.   The normal exit from this chart is via connector (6.4).

PROBLEMS

6.1   Draw a flow chart for finding $\sqrt{N}$ using Newton's formula.   This time, use a combination of all three possibilities (a ceiling on the number of iterations, a bound on the error in the results, and a bound on the difference in successive estimates) to obtain a stop rule.   That is, stop the procedure as soon as one of the three criteria is met.   Be sure to indicate in your output which of the three criteria caused the stop.

6.2   Using some of the test inputs constructed in answering Prob. 5.5, substitute these values in the detailed flow charts for the payroll problem, keeping track of all variables and their current values.

6.3   Prepare a detailed flow chart for finding the Nth Fibonacci number (see Prob. 5.6).

6.4   Prepare a detailed flow chart for sorting three numbers, A, B, and C, in decreasing order (see Prob. 5.7).

6.5   Prepare a detailed flow chart for computing the mean and standard deviation of N numbers, $X_1, X_2, \ldots , X_N$ (see Prob. 5.9).

6.6   Prepare both a general and a detailed flow chart for sorting a set of N numbers in decreasing order (see Prob. 5.11).

6.7 Prepare a general flow chart for solving the bridge point-count problem given in Prob. 5.13.

6.8 Prepared a detailed flow chart for just that portion of the algorithm for finding the quotient of two integers (the algorithm prepared in answer to Prob. 5.15) that tests the remainder to determine whether or not to conclude the division procedure. Assume that the numerator is smaller than the denominator in absolute value and that you have available as input the original numerator, the original denominator, the previous quotients Q_1, Q_2, . . . , Q_{n-1} and remainders R_1, R_2, . . . , R_{n-1}, and the current quotient Q_n and remainder R_n. The output should be either one of two messages: "Stop the division procedure" or "Continue the division procedure." If the message "Stop the procedure" is output, also output the solution using the notation of Sec. 3.5 for recording repeating decimals.

6.9 Prepare a detailed flow chart for the euclidean algorithm (see Prob. 5.16).

6.10 Prepare a detailed flow chart for solving the following problem: Given n and k, compute $\displaystyle\sum_{i=k}^{n} {}_nC_i$, where the symbol ${}_nC_i$ is used to denote

$$\frac{n!}{i!(n-i)!}$$

6.11 Prepare general and detailed flow charts for finding the values of X satisfying $AX^2 + BX + C = 0$. Recall that they are given by

$$X_1 = \frac{-B + \sqrt{B^2 - 4AC}}{2A}$$

and $X_2 = (-B - \sqrt{B^2 - 4AC})/2A$. Be sure to treat the case of multiple roots and imaginary roots appropriately. Assume that you will be asked to solve N such problems. The value of N is input first, followed by N sets of A, B, and C.

6.12 Given n pairs of data points, (X_1, Y_1), $(X_1 + h,\ Y_2)$, $(X_1 + 2h,\ Y_3)$ · · · $[X_1 + (n-1)h,\ Y_n]$, write a detailed flow chart for finding the area under a smooth curve connecting the values of Y using Simpson's rule; i.e., write detailed flow charts that would implement the following general flow chart:

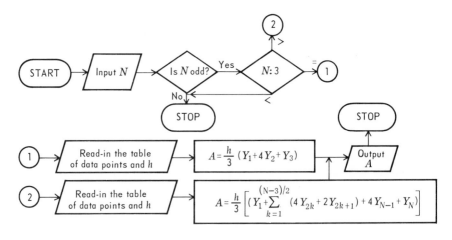

ANNOTATED SUPPLEMENTARY BIBLIOGRAPHY

Most references on computer programming discuss flow charts; in fact, the problem of how to construct an algorithm is frequently absorbed, without too much success, in the discussion of how to construct a flow chart. In addition, not all authors conform to the USA standards in the symbols they use. The following references were chosen because they supplement our discussion even though they may either use different symbols or indirectly attack the problem of how to write algorithms. Before proceeding to these supplementary references, we should note that the USA Standard given in Appendix 2 of this book itself contains appendixes that are not given in our Appendix. They are listed as the first three references below.

1. Appendix A, International Considerations, "USA Standard for Flow Chart Symbols for Information Processing," approved July 9, 1965. Lists those symbols approved by the International Standards Association that are not contained in the USA Standard.
2. Appendix B, Additional Reference Material, *ibid*. References to some background material that influenced the development of the standard.
3. Appendix C, Contributing Organizations, *ibid*. A list of organizations that contributed to the development of the standard.
4. Chapin, N.: "An Introduction to Automatic Computers," pp. 237–254, D. Van Nostrand Company, Inc., Princeton, N.J., 1963. A discussion of flow charts in the context of systems design and analysis. Process charts, work-simplification methods, and related topics are discussed.
5. Davis, Gordon B.: "An Introduction to Electronic Computers," pp. 97–111, McGraw-Hill Book Company, New York, 1966. Includes a carefully defined and illustrated list of each symbol in the USA Standard and a discussion of decision tables and their place in the construction of algorithms and flow charts.
6. Leeds, H. D., and G. M. Weinberg: "Computer Programming Fundamentals," pp. 66–98, McGraw-Hill Book Company, New York, 1961. Probably the most extensive discussion of flow charting currently available.
7. Miller, G. A., E. Galanter, and K. H. Pribra: "Plans and the Structure of Behavior," Holt, Rinehart and Winston, Inc., New York, 1960. The application of information-processing models, including flow charts, to many areas of psychology is discussed in a delightful manner.
8. Schultz, L.: "Digital Processing: A System Orientation," Prentice-

Hall, Inc., Englewood Cliffs, N.J., 1963. The flow chart is discussed in the context of programming ways and means. This leads the author to define and discuss in some detail straight-line vs. looped portions of the chart, iterative programming, looping for address modification, counters, and other concepts that are important to the development of good algorithms and flow charts.

9. Lyachenko, V. F.: The Construction of Flow Charts of Algorithms, *Probl. Peredachi Inform.*, vol. 12, pp. 53–69, 1963. For the reader who understands Russian, the Russian point of view on the construction of flow charts.

chapter 7

AN INTRODUCTION TO COMPUTER PROGRAMMING AND A SURVEY OF PROGRAMMING LANGUAGES

7.1 INTRODUCTION

We now come to the problem of writing complete sets of instructions for a computer, i.e., writing computer programs. The problem is similar to that of conversing with someone who understands no English. You must learn a new language—or at least a part of a new language—in order to satisfy your conversational needs. If your only need is to order meals from waiters, you would soon master the limited vocabulary and grammar required for this purpose. If, however, you wish to live in a foreign country, you need a more complete mastery of the language.

Similarly, if you plan to use the computer infrequently, it may not be necessary to master a programming language at all. Your time might be better spent chatting with the staff of the computer center and contacting people with similar interests in order to find out which programs are already available. If, however, you are a computer-science specialist or will use the computer extensively or in a novel way, then you should master at least one programming language.

It is the purpose of this chapter to present an introduction to computer programming and a smorgasbord of programming languages in the form of a brief description of the most important kinds of languages. Chapter 11 will contain a detailed description of one language, FORTRAN IV, and Chap. 12 of another, PL/1. Many detailed references (see the Annotated Supplementary Bibliography at the conclusion of this chapter) are available for some of the programming languages we shall discuss.

The discussion of lists and list-processing languages in Sec. 7.6 should probably be considered optional reading for all students except computer-science majors, for whom it is mandatory.

7.2 A HYPOTHETICAL MACHINE LANGUAGE—THE 4-ADDRESS SYSTEM

The language actually used by the computer itself is called *machine language*. Because it simplifies the discussion of this subject, a hypothetical rather than a real machine language will be discussed.

The computer communicates in numbers, and the language it understands consists of sequences of digits. These digits must convey all the information the computer requires. The computer carries out its work by executing an instruction that is itself a sequence of digits. These instructions are executed very rapidly—as many as 100,000 or more in a single second—but every task the computer performs must be reduced to sets of sequences of digits; i.e., sets of instructions. In executing an instruction, the computer expects to find in the instruction the answers to certain questions. These may include:

1. What is to be done; i.e., what operation is to be performed?
2. What are the values of the operands?
3. What should be done with the result?

And in order to maintain continuous flow,

4. What should be done next?

The computer is organized in such a way that the answer to the last three questions is given in the form of addresses, i.e., *where to go* for the answer rather than the answer itself. More specifically, the addresses of the operands, rather than the operands themselves, are contained in the instruction. Also, the address at which to store the result and the address of the next instruction may be in the present instruction as answers to questions 3 and 4.

The actual structure of the *instruction word* varies from computer to computer. In order to simplify things, we shall assume that we are dealing with a 4-address computer, that is, a computer with instruction formats providing four addresses. (Problems 7.2 to 7.4, at the end of this chapter, deal with a 2-address system.)   More specifically, we assume that the instruction consists of a 22-digit number setup as follows:

1. The first 2 digits designate the operation to be performed.
2. Digits 3 to 7 contain the address of the first operand, and digits 8 to 12 the address of the second operand.
3. Digits 13 to 17 contain the address at which to store the answer.
4. Digits 18 to 22 contain the address at which to find the next instruction.

Implicit in this approach is the assumption that our addresses consist of five-digit numbers, which means that we have, at most, 100,000 distinct addresses (numbers 00000 to 99999).   All numbers in this chapter will be written to base 10.

Conventionally, the addresses of the operands are called the *alpha address* and *beta address*, the address at which the answer is to be stored is called the *gamma address*, and the address of the next instruction is called the *delta address*.

This means that the instruction word is structured as follows:

Operation	Location of 1st operand	Location of 2d operand	Where to put the answer	Where to find the next instruction
	α address	β address	γ address	δ address
XX	XXXXX	XXXXX	XXXXX	XXXXX

For example, if we used the number 21 to indicate addition, then the instruction 21   12131   14105   13026   17017 would mean: Add the contents of address 12131 to the contents of address 14105, store the answer in location 13026, and go to location 17017 for the next instruction. Similarly, if 14 meant multiply, then 21   12131   14105   13026   17017 followed by 14   13026   12131   13027   16074 would result in our multiplying the answer previously obtained by the contents of location 12131 and storing the answer in location 13027.   The second instruction must be stored in location 17017 for it to be executed immediately after the first.   It is customary to denote the *contents of an address* by placing parentheses around the address, so that (12131) is read: "The contents of location 12131."   If we assume (12131) = x and (14105) = y immediately before the execution of the above two instructions, then (13026) = $x + y$ immediately after the execution of the first instruction and (13027) = $x(x + y)$ at the conclusion of the program.   Note that (17017) = 14   13026   12131   13027   16074 and that the contents of all locations are preserved unless they are written over by the instruction.

Since the program itself is stored as a sequence of digits in main storage, it can appear as an operand and can be modified. The stored-program concept, with the ability to modify programs freely, is a very important one, which greatly enhances the versatility of the computer.†

7.3 THE COMPUTER AS A TRANSLATOR

It should be clear, even to the novice, that machine-language programming is extremely difficult. Operation codes must be memorized, the contents of virtually every address in storage must be noted and modified as changes take place, and every process must be broken down into its most elementary components. It occurred to computer scientists, quite early in the development of computers (see Sec. 2.3 for a history of programming languages), that the computer itself might be used to translate instructions from a more easily mastered programming language to machine language. That is, computer programs could be written that would accept as input instructions which are easier for a person to generate and that would produce as output the corresponding machine-language instructions.

These translating programs are called either *assemblers* or *compilers*. The most elementary translator, an assembler, permits the use of languages, called *assembly languages*, that are just one step removed from machine languages. Assembly languages use mnemonics, such as ADD or MULT for the operation codes, and labels such as X, Y, or PAY for the operands. The computer keeps track of where everything is and will even, upon request, provide a key to the storage locations used for the various operands in the form of a *symbol table*.

Of even greater significance is the inclusion in assemblers of *macroinstructions*. A single macroinstruction can generate many machine-language instructions—the macroinstruction is a kind of program in itself. Once this could be done, it was logical to permit all the instructions to be macroinstructions and in this way to permit programming languages to be even simpler for people to use. The computer program that serves to translate these *higher-level languages*, or *problem-oriented languages*, is called a *compiler*. These higher-level languages will be the subject of the remaining sections of this chapter.

† For an historical note, see Sec. 2.2. Chapter 10 discusses some applications in which this modification takes place, and Prob. 7.4 specifically shows how instruction modification makes a single instruction a great deal more powerful. The modification of the address of an operand in an instruction occurs so frequently that the System/360 has special circuitry and instructions facilitating this function.

7.4 MATHEMATICALLY ORIENTED LANGUAGES—ALGOL AND FORTRAN

Since many of the early computer users were either mathematicians or scientists well versed in mathematics, it was natural for the early higher-level languages to be mathematically oriented.   One of these languages, FORTRAN (standing for FORmula TRANslation), was developed in the late 1950s and became the most widely used programming language of the next decade.   FORTRAN will be discussed in greater detail in Chap. 11.   If Chap. 11 is to be covered, the reader should skip ahead to the discussion of ALGOL.

As its name implies, FORTRAN is ideally suited to the solution of problems containing a series of mathematical formulas.   Instructions such as

$$Y = A/(B*SQRTF(X-Z+2.))$$

are commonplace.   The asterisk stands for multiplication, and the equals sign for "Substitute the value obtained for the expression on the right for the variable given on the left."   SQRTF means "Compute the positive value of the square root of the quantity appearing in the following parentheses."   This means that the above instruction says: "Take the previously computed or input values of X and Z and subtract Z from X. Add 2, and take the positive square root of the result.   Multiply this by the previously computed or input value of B, divide this into A, and call the final result Y."   We could now output Y, if this was the desired result, or use it in still another formula.

A FORTRAN program consists of a sequence of statements.   Each statement is translated into several machine-language instructions (each statement is a kind of macroinstruction).   As with any computer program, the ordering of the statements is a part of the structure of the program.   If a statement is moved to a different place in the program, a new program may result.

In dealing with numbers in FORTRAN programs, a distinction must be made between data that are varying and those that are constant throughout the execution of the program.   Identifiers are used to denote variables, and the number itself is used to denote a constant value.   The identifier, or variable name, really stands for a storage location in the computer in which the changing values of the variable will be kept.   For example, the FORTRAN statement

$$X = X+1$$

serves to replace the current value stored for X with a new value.   This new value is the current value plus the constant 1.

An example of a few lines of code from a FORTRAN program is given below. These instructions provide for the computation of the roots of the quadratic equation $AX^2 + BX + C = 0$. Provision would have to be made for reading in A, B, and C before executing these instructions. Also, valid FORTRAN output statements would have to be written in place of the descriptions given in statements 50 and 60 below, and special concluding statements would have to be added in order to make these instructions into a complete program.

Since an IF statement is used in the example, its format is described. In general, an *IF statement* in FORTRAN is constructed as follows:

IF(arithmetic expression)#1,#2,#3

This statement is executed by computing the value of the arithmetic expression and going to statement #1 if this value is negative, to #2 if it is zero, and to #3 if it is positive. Now the FORTRAN code:

```
     Z=2.*A
     Y=B*B-4.*A*C
     IF(Y)20, 30, 2
  2  ROOT 1=(-B+SQRTF(Y))/Z
     ROOT2=(-B-SQRTF(Y))/Z
     GO  TO  50
 30  ROOT1=-B/Z
     ROOT2=ROOT1
     GO  TO  50
 20  REAL1=-B/Z
     REAL2=REAL1
     XIMAG1=SQRTF(-Y)/Z
     XIMAG2=-1.*(SQRTF(-Y))/Z
     GO  TO  60
```

50 Provision for outputting ROOT1 and ROOT2 must be made, and the program ended after skipping by statement 60.

60 Provision for outputting REAL1, REAL2, XIMAG1, and XIMAG2 must be made and the program ended.

Note that the discriminant, Y, and the denominator, Z, are computed separately at the outset. This is done in order to avoid recomputing these quantities each time they appear in an instruction. Once computed, they are stored in a location labeled Y and Z by the FORTRAN compiler and are then merely called in from storage without being recomputed when they appear in an instruction.

Note also the use of XIMAG1 rather than IMAG1 to denote the imaginary portion of the root. This is done because the first letter in the name of a variable determines whether that variable is to be treated as a floating-point or fixed-point number. The letters I to N are used for fixed-point variables; the other letters for floating-point variables. We wish the root to be treated as a floating-point number, and so its name could not begin with an I.†

Though FORTRAN works well with formulas, it may not handle logical manipulations easily. Its input/output instructions are somewhat awkward, and it cannot process lengthy files of data conveniently.

A more versatile and elegant mathematically oriented language is ALGOL, standing for ALGorithmic Oriented Languages. Though it is better suited to carrying out logical operations, ALGOL still leaves a lot to be desired in its input/output and file manipulations. Despite its superiority in several respects, it never became as popular as FORTRAN, except in Europe and in some American universities.

As we noted in Sec. 2.3, several dialects or variations of ALGOL have been developed. These include MAD, BALGOL, ALGO, and JOVIAL. Variations have been developed for most higher-level computer-programming languages. FORTRAN, being the most widely used language, probably has the greatest number of variations. This presents some problems to the novice who is using a computer with a compiler in one dialect—for example, FORTRAN II—and wants to implement a program written in another dialect, such as FORTRAN IV. Although they are supposedly in the same language, it will not usually be possible to do this without at least some minor modifications of the program. Sometimes the modifications required are so major that it is easier to write the program from scratch in your own dialect. (This is not true of conversions from FORTRAN II to FORTRAN IV.) FORTRAN for the System/360 was also developed in several dialects (E level subset, H level, G level, etc.). In general, FORTRAN programs written for smaller models will run on larger ones, but not vice versa.

One of the first generally accepted dialects of ALGOL, ALGOL 60, will be discussed. The program proceeds by denoting rules for successively assigning values to variables (much as the FORTRAN statement assigns a value to a variable appearing on the left side of the equality). For example, the ALGOL equivalent of FORTRAN's $Z = Z + 1$. is $Z: = Z + 1$. In ALGOL, the programming of a unit or block of instructions, called a *procedure*, within a larger program begins with the word

---

† There are several dialects of FORTRAN. In some of them, it is possible to avoid this nuisance by using a type statement.

BEGIN and ends with the word END.† Declarations in ALGOL that specify the nature of a variable, such as *real, integer,* or *Boolean,* are made within a block and do not hold outside of that block. This permits a programmer to use the same variable in several senses during the course of a program.

A *Boolean variable* takes on only two values—true or false. Boolean variables can be processed in FORTRAN but in an awkward, artificial manner. In ALGOL, however, use of the operators ∧ (logical *and*), ∨ (logical *or*), ≡ (logical equivalence), and] (logical negation) permits the natural processing of Boolean expressions.

The other, more trivial, advantages of ALGOL over FORTRAN are:

1. The use of letters as well as numbers in labeling statements, which permits mnemonic references to statements
2. Branching that can be expressed in the form of an IF-THEN statement

For example, in executing the statement

IF(X>Y)THEN   GO   TO   S21

the program will go to the statement labeled S21 if the value of X most recently obtained is greater than Y; otherwise, it will proceed to the next statement. The IF statement in FORTRAN provides a similar capability, but it is less direct and more awkward to use since its branching depends on the sign of an expression in parentheses. In order to deal with the relation of X to Y, we would have to form X−Y in parentheses.‡

Also, the IF statement in ALGOL permits the use of the term ELSE to provide for alternative, even for conditional alternative, branching. For example,

TEST:T1:IF   X>Y   THEN   S1
ELSE   T2:IF   X>Z   THEN   S2;

In this case, the label for the whole instruction is TEST. The instruction contains two IF statements, labeled T1 and T2. Execution of this instruction will cause the program to branch to S1 if X > Y, to S2 if X ≤ Y and X > Z, and to the next statement if X ≤ Y and X ≤ Z.

Finally, we note the following differences in notation between FORTRAN and ALGOL:

† The last statement in a FORTRAN program must also be the word END; no formal beginning is required. Except for one-line statement functions and some routing of routines via the computed GO TO statement, FORTRAN does not allow separate sections of programs that are to be used repeatedly to be included in the program in which they are to be used; separate programs called FORTRAN *functions* or FORTRAN *subroutines* must be written.
‡ Again, special dialects do permit us to write IF(X.GT.Y)GO   TO   21.

| | Symbol | |
Meaning	FORTRAN	ALGOL
Multiplication	*	X
Greater than	.GT. (FORTRAN IV)	>
Less than	.LT. (FORTRAN IV)	<
Not equal to	.NE. (FORTRAN IV)	≠
Equal to	.EQ. (FORTRAN IV)	=
Substitute value calculated on right for variable appearing on the left	=	:=
Symbol used to enclose subscripts	( )	[ ]

7.5 BUSINESS-ORIENTED LANGUAGES—COBOL

Many computer programs for commercial applications are written in assembly languages rather than higher-level languages in order to reduce the time required to complete processing when using the program (called the *running time* of the program).† This is because a compiler produces stereotyped coding which may be less efficient than the coding a clever programmer can construct using assembly languages. However, the cost of writing programs is an appreciable part of the total cost of using the computer, and higher-level languages are being employed more and more. The most important of these is COBOL, the COmmon Business-Oriented Language.

In a survey of members of the Systems and Procedures Association [1], it was found that a little more than one-fourth of all the analysts polled had used COBOL. It was also found that the analysts believed that the use of COBOL made programming easier and less expensive but that it did not reduce the overall cost of the job. The savings in programming were offset by the increase in costs resulting from the longer running times. However, as computer programs for business become more complex, as information systems rather than routine data processing become more commonplace, and as more and more people are called upon to communicate with computers, higher-level languages will be more widely applied. A poll conducted today would undoubtedly indicate a trend toward higher-level languages.

Programs written in COBOL contain a great many ordinary English-language statements. However, although the user is free to choose his

† In some cases, a compiler to translate from a higher-level language was simply not available and an assembly language had to be used. This is especially true of the smaller IBM 1400-series computers.

own names for files, fields, and variables, a unique code name is specified for operations and other key words.

COBOL permits the processing of files of information, record by record, in a direct manner. It also includes features that make it easier to use the same program on different computers or on differently equipped versions of the same computer. In the remainder of this section, we shall discuss:

1. The three special descriptive divisions of COBOL
2. Some examples of COBOL statements
3. The conditional expression
4. A nice feature, the ENTER verb, that further enhances the versatility of COBOL

The *conditional expression* is singled out for discussion because it provides a convenient vehicle for talking about manipulating variables that take on the value *true* or *false* rather than numerical values. Conditional expressions in COBOL are relatively easy to interpret, which is another advantage of COBOL. Business executives, middle managers, and other personnel in the business community who use the computer but who cannot take the time to master a programming language can translate from COBOL to English. However, an expert is still required to go the other way.

In order to preserve the commonality of the use of COBOL while at the same time providing for the specific needs of the user, COBOL programs have three special divisions. These are the identification, environment, and data divisions. The fourth division of a COBOL program, called the *procedure division,* is really the program itself.

The *identification division* comes first and includes such things as the names of the program and programmer. The *environment division* permits adaptation of a COBOL program to a new computer. It includes such things as the name of the computer in which the program is to be compiled and the one on which it is to be executed, input/output components used on the computer on which the program is to be run, and, perhaps, information on the core-storage capacity of the computer used to compile or execute the program. The *data division* describes the format of the data that will serve as operands in the program. Formats for input/output files, for operands that are generated as intermediate results and therefore do not appear in such files, and for constants are specified in separate sections of this division. Specifications for file elements include the format of the elements and information on the length of the records.

Table 7.1 contains a list of some of the key words and phrases used

Table 7.1   The meaning of some of the key terms used in COBOL

Term	Meaning
COMPUTE	Sets up a series of arithmetic operations. Labels the result with the first word following the word COMPUTE.
TIMES	Used to designate multiplication.
MINUS	Used to designate subtraction.
ADD	Used to set up a series of additions. Labels the answer with the last word used in the series.
SELECT, ASSIGN TO	Assigns files named after the word SELECT to input/output unit named after the phrase ASSIGN TO. This is merely a specification statement; no input/output is executed.
OPEN	Performs the necessary housekeeping tasks to store and process the contents of the file named after the verb OPEN, before actually processing it.
INPUT	Inputs file named after the verb INPUT from the device previously named in the SELECT, ASSIGN TO specification. INPUT is frequently used immediately after OPEN.
READ, RECORD	Reads the records from the file named immediately after the verb READ. Stops when the last record has been processed by noting that an end-of-file indicator has been encountered.
AT END GO TO	Used to specify branching that is to take place at the conclusion of a READ, RECORD operation.

in COBOL and their meanings. An example of the use of each of these terms in an instruction and a discussion of what occurs when these instructions are executed are given below. The instructions listed are unrelated; they do not constitute a portion of a program.

COMPUTE PROFIT FROM VOLUME TIMES(PRICE
MINUS COST).
ADD OVERHEAD,FRINGE-COST,SALARY GIVING TOTAL.
SELECT CUSTOMER ASSIGN TO MTU1.
OPEN INPUT CUSTOMER.
READ CUSTOMER RECORD;AT END GO TO ADDRESSOR.

The first statement causes the computer to obtain PRICE minus COST, to multiply this by VOLUME, and to call the result PROFIT. The second finds the sum of OVERHEAD, FRINGE-COST, and SALARY and calls the result TOTAL. The third specifies that the CUSTOMER file will be found on MTU1, an abbreviation for magnetic-tape unit 1. The fourth opens and inputs the CUSTOMER file, and the fifth causes the records in the CUSTOMER file to be read one by one (and probably processed in accordance with some code that would follow this instruction), branching to the statement labeled ADDRESSOR when the processing of all records in the CUSTOMER file is completed.

COBOL expressions may be either arithmetic or conditional. Arithmetic expressions are similar to those found in FORTRAN; a conditional expression is reduced to a value of either true or false. (Conditional expressions are also permitted in ALGOL and FORTRAN IV. We called them *Boolean expressions* in the discussion of ALGOL.) Compound conditional expressions, uniting several true or false elements, are permitted. For example, we might have

SIZE = SMALL AND PRICE LESS THEN 2.50
OR(COLOR = RED AND PRICE LESS THAN 1.75)

in a compound conditional expression. The following table lists several different combinations of size, color, and price and the corresponding value of this compound conditional.

Size	Color	Price	Value	Size	Color	Price	Value
Large	Green	1.80	False	Small	Green	2.70	False
Large	Red	1.80	False	Small	Green	2.45	True
Large	Red	1.70	True	Small	Red	1.76	True
Medium	Blue	1.70	False	Small	Red	1.74	True
Medium	Red	1.70	True	Small	Blue	1.74	True

The conditional expressions can be put in an IF-THEN statement, so that we might have

IF(SIZE = SMALL AND PRICE LESS THAN 2.50)
OR(COLOR = RED AND PRICE LESS THAN 1.75)IS TRUE
GO TO SPECIAL-DEBUG,OTHERWISE GO TO
INVENTORY-PROCESSING.

Blanks are not permitted in *COBOL names;* however, hyphens may be used to combine several words into a single name.

Although COBOL branching statements require many more characters to write than those in FORTRAN or ALGOL, they are easily interpreted and permit more versatile branching conditions with less chance for error.

The discussion of business-oriented languages will be concluded by discussing a feature in COBOL, the *ENTER verb*, that permits the inclusion of programming in other languages within the COBOL program. When coding in a new language is to begin, the statement ENTER followed by the name of the new language is made. For example, if some symbolic programming for the 1401 computer in the AUTOCODER language is introduced in a COBOL program, write ENTER AUTOCODER before beginning the AUTOCODER programming and ENTER COBOL after completing the AUTOCODER programming and before returning to the COBOL programming.

7.6 LISTS AND LIST-PROCESSING LANGUAGES—IPL

Ordinarily, a computer program is written in order to manipulate numbers. Mathematically oriented languages readily permit extensive computations with these numbers, and business-oriented languages permit both computations and the manipulation of sets of these numbers in a convenient way. In many applications, particularly those in artificial intelligence (see Chap. 10), the computer is processing entities other than numbers; for example, positions on a checkerboard, segments of graphic images, and statements in plane geometry.

These entities are usually structured in a prescribed way. For example, the statements in geometry are grouped and sequenced to form a proof, and the segments of graphic images are also grouped and sequenced, forming graphic entities which, in turn, can be grouped and sequenced to form a picture.† In the latter instance, the picture has a *hierarchical structure* in which whole lists of graphic images are single elements in the list of graphic entities. Consider, as a second example of a *hierarchical list*, a set of hands in a game of bridge. The highest-level list consists of the symbols North, East, South, and West, standing for the frequently used points-of-the-compass designation of bridge hands. Each of these refers to another list containing four elements—spades, hearts, diamonds, and clubs. At the lowest level, each of the suits refers to a list of the cards held in that suit. The elements in this last list are ace, 2, 3, 4, 5, 6, 7, 8, 9, 10, jack, queen, king, void. *Void* is used to indicate that there are no cards in that suit in the hand.

In order for the structure to be preserved as a part of that list, each element listed must contain not only the symbol for the element itself but also connecting links to the next element in the list and, if it is a hierarchical structure, links to another list that contains all the items that go to make up this higher-level element. These connecting links are called *pointers.*‡

† For example, the segments could be small squares of various shades of gray, the graphic entities might be a man or a tree or an x-ray machine or a table, and the picture might be a landscape or an operating room in a hospital.
‡ The use of two pointers in a hierarchical list is not standard. It is done here because it is easier to follow. However, we shall soon see that a widely used list structure—the one used with IPL—contains only a single pointer.

For example, suppose we use 20 characters to denote list elements. The first 10 contain the symbol used to identify the element, the next 5 the address in storage of the next element in this list, and the last 5 the address of the first item on the next lower-level list that contains all the items that are a part of this element. (Thus there would be 10 alphanumeric characters followed by 10 numeric characters. The only feature of the computer that is essential to this approach is that storage addresses are given in five-digit numbers.) Table 7.2 shows what a bridge hand would look like using this 20-character code.

A discussion of the entries in the table may prove helpful in understanding the construction of lists. The symbols used for the elements are the natural choices except for including a letter (N, E, S, or W) in designating the suits to indicate with which hand the particular suit is associated and a letter (S, H, D, or C) to indicate with which suit the particular card is associated. Since the list structure makes the ordering of list elements mandatory, the ordering should be done in a careful manner to simplify the application or to provide additional information. In our example, we ordered hands by bidding sequence, the suits by bidding preference, and the cards by trick-taking value.† The items in the list are scattered around core in a completely unsystematic way. Adjacent items in the list need not be in adjacent addresses—though they could be if it were convenient. They need not even be in the same order in core in which they appear on the list. The structure and linkages are preserved by including the pointer addresses as a part of the item itself. (This is similar, in principle, to the function of the delta address in the instruction word discussed in Sec. 7.2. By using this address, the instruction sequence is maintained regardless of the actual order in which the instructions are stored.) The list in Table 7.2 is entered via address 14172, but it is possible to enter any hand or any suit directly. It is assumed that this feature was needed in the application; otherwise, most of the first 20 items could be deleted. For example, if it was necessary to get to the hands but not the suits, only the first 4 of the 20 items need be retained. More specifically, in the list as it is presently structured, address 12714 permits access to the East hand and address 00477 to the spades in the East hand. Deleting 00477 (as well as 00537, 00567, and 00597), we could link the East hand directly to the cards in the hand via 50001. That is, the contents of 12714 would then be EAST------1910850001. Note that an address consisting of a string of zeros is used

---

† The reader who is not familiar with the game of bridge may find the going rough. It may be helpful to reword this: The hand order is the order in which bids would be made if North were the dealer, the suit order indicates a ranking of the suits that affects bidding, and the card order indicates the value of that card to the player, cards listed first being more valuable.

Table 7.2 A list of bridge hands as stored in a hypothetical computer

ADDRESS	CONTENTS	
14172	NORTH	1271430612
12714	EAST	1910800477
19108	SOUTH	5764300507
57643	WEST	0000013444
30612	SPADESN	3091422114
30914	HEARTSN	3933329006
39333	DIAMONDSN	2741441442
27414	CLUBSN	0000047531
00477	SPADESE	0053750001
00537	HEARTSE	0056751001
00567	DIAMONDSE	0059755001
00597	CLUBSE	0000056001
00507	SPADESS	0150752000
01507	HEARTSS	0153753010
01537	DIAMONDSS	0156754000
01567	CLUBSS	0000057000
13444	SPADESW	0250758000
02507	HEARTSW	0253759000
02537	DIAMONDSW	0256731000
02567	CLUBSW	0000032001
22114	ACES	0301000000
03010	2S	2900600000
29006	JACKH	0404000000
04040	10H	0407000000
04070	3H	4144200000
41442	KINGD	0410000000
04100	QUEEND	0413000000
04130	7D	0416000000
04160	6D	0419000000
04190	4D	0423000000
04230	2D	4753100000
47531	QUEENC	0426000000
04260	2C	5000100000
50001	KINGS	5003100000
50031	10S	5006100000
50061	9S	5009100000
50091	7S	5012100000

ADDRESS	CONTENTS	
50121	6S	5015100000
50151	3S	5100100000
51001	ACEH	5103100000
51031	9H	5106100000
51061	8H	5109100000
51091	2H	5500100000
55001	VOIDD	5600100000
56001	10C	5603100000
56031	8C	5606100000
56061	6C	5200000000
52000	QUEENS	5203000000
52030	8S	5206000000
52060	4S	5301000000
53010	KINGH	5400000000
54000	JACKD	5700000000
57000	ACEC	5703000000
57030	KINGC	5706000000
57060	JACKC	5709000000
57090	9C	5712000000
57120	7C	5715000000
57150	5C	5718000000
57180	4C	5721000000
57210	3C	5800000000
58000	JACKS	5803000000
58030	5S	5900000000
59000	QUEENH	5903000000
59030	7H	5906000000
59060	6H	5909000000
59090	5H	5912000000
59120	4H	3100000000
31000	ACED	3103000000
31030	10D	3106000000
31060	9D	3109000000
31090	8D	3112000000
31120	5D	3115000000
31150	3D	3200100000
32001	VOIDC	0000000000

to indicate termination of a list.   There should be no more than one element in a list, the last one, that has zeros in both of the pointer addresses. (In our example, the last element is not a card, but rather it is the element indicating the void in clubs in the West hand.)   Finally, we note that if it is desirable in the application, the list need not terminate but can turn back on itself.   Such lists are called *threaded lists*.   In our example, the entry at address 32001 would be changed to VOIDC----- 0000014172 to thread the list.   However, it would be wrong to interpret this as meaning that the items in the "void-in-clubs element" are the hands North, East, South, West.   So that threading this list may lead to some difficulties in manipulating it.†

We now turn to *list-processing languages*, that is, computer-programming languages that permit the operands to be lists or elements in a list. Most list-processing languages were developed as a tool for solving problems in artificial intelligence.   Some of these are *IPL* (*Information Processing Language*), developed by Newell, Shaw, and Simon ([2] and also Ref. 24 in the Annotated Supplementary Bibliography); *FLPL* (*Fortran List Processing Language*), developed by Gelertner and his associates [3]; and *LISP* (*List Processor*), developed by McCarthy [4].   The remainder of this section will be devoted to a cursory description of IPL in its fifth version (known as IPL-V).   Reference 24 in the Annotated Supplementary Bibliography is a manual for this language.

In IPL, both the data and the program are lists.   The format for both is prescribed by IPL.   Three fields are used to characterize the elements in a data list, and five fields the elements in a program, i.e., each instruction.   The three entries in the data list are the name of the list, the symbol, and the pointer, or *link*, to the next element in the list.   The instructions have, in addition to these three fields, a *PQ field*, which describes the objectives of the statement, and a *comments* field to permit the programmer and others to interpret the program easily.   In addition, an *H0 field*, also called the *communication cell*, is frequently noted in writing the program to assist the programmer in keeping track of the operands currently available for processing, and an *H5 field*, or *test cell*, is also noted to record special conditions.   The test cell is set to either + or −, with a plus indicating a normal condition and a minus an exceptional condition.   The H0 and H5 fields are not a part of the program.   They are automatically set by the IPL compiler in accordance with the results of the data processing.

An instruction list (i.e., a program) is made up of a series of instruc-

† Changing the contents of 32001 to VOIDC----1417200000 would not help since the entries North, East, South, and West would now be interpreted as cards in the club suit in West's hand.

tions providing for input, list manipulation, and output. The input can be the name of a list or, more frequently, the name of a location in storage that contains the name of the list. (The symbols in an IPL program are really names for the storage locations that contain the entities being referenced.) Proceeding in this way, we can process a list, store the unknown result in a named storage location, and use this result later on without knowing exactly what it was. This is analogous to the use of symbols for numbers in FORTRAN, ALGOL, and COBOL. The Q part of the PQ field is used to distinguish between input which is being named directly and input which is being called from some named location. A zero is used to indicate the former approach, and a 1 to indicate the latter approach.

The processing of lists is simplified by having routines for certain frequently used list manipulations that are on call by name (just as SQRTF called a square-root routine for use in FORTRAN). For example, J66 is the name of a routine that adds a symbol to a list only if it is not already on that list, and J64 is the name of a routine that inserts a symbol in a list in a prescribed location. The library of routines available with IPL is quite extensive. These routines are the key functional statements available to an IPL user. Among the most important capabilities they provide are:

1. Reading the content of symbols of list elements from punched cards
2. Printing out lists, symbols, and special elements called *data terms* (data terms are similar to the constants that would be a part of a FORTRAN or an ALGOL program)
3. Interrupting and restarting a program by reading out its current state on auxiliary storage or cards and then loading it back in at a later time
4. Erasing a data list or routine and making the space occupied by this erased routine available
5. Locating a cell in a list (it need not be there, this will be indicated in the test cell)
6. Inserting or deleting elements in a list
7. Counting the number of items in a list
8. Arithmetic processing of numeric data terms
9. Equality and inequality testing of numeric data terms
10. Identity testing of list elements or nonnumeric data terms
11. Generating a random number (see Sec. 8.5) that is uniformly distributed in a specified range
12. Aiding in debugging, i.e., correcting, the errors in programs
13. Special handling of situations in which errors are detected
14. Manipulating and testing the PQ, SYMB, and LINK fields

Table 7.3   Data list for a bridge hand in IPL

Name	SYMB	Link	Name	SYMB	Link	Name	SYMB	Link
B1	0			E309			S401	
	N101			E307			S411	
	N111			E306			S404	
	N106			E413			S402	
	N105			E410			A110	
	N104			E408			A109	
	N102			E407			A108	
	N213			E406			A103	
	N211			E405			A207	
	N203			S112			A206	
	N313			S107			A205	
	N312			S210			A301	
	N304			S209			A308	
	N302			S208			A305	
	E113			S204			A412	
	E201			S202			A409	
	E212			S311			A403	0
	E310			S303				

We shall now present an example of a very simple IPL data list to illustrate some of the points discussed. Symbols and names in IPL are denoted by a single letter followed by four decimal digits. The data list will be another bridge hand, but this time given as a string of 52 cards. We shall use the letter portion of the symbol to designate the name of the hand (N, E, S, and A)† and the numerical portion to indicate the suit (1, 2, 3, and 4) and value (01 to 13 for ace to king). The data list, which is named B1, is given in Table 7.3.

Note that the entries in the link column are not specified in this case since, unless otherwise specified, each element in a data list is linked to the one that follows it. Note also the use of the symbol 0 to indicate the name entry and the link 0 to indicate the conclusion of the data list. Finally, the entries in the SYMB columns are symbols, not addresses. IPL will assign addresses as a part of its function and record the link address as appropriate.

7.7   MISCELLANEOUS SPECIAL-PURPOSE LANGUAGES

A variety of other computer languages has been developed to satisfy the requirements of special applications. Three of the more important areas

† We cannot use W to designate the West hand because the letter W is reserved to refer to certain system cells in IPL.

of special applications are simulation, symbol manipulation, and language translation. We shall introduce some of the languages developed for these applications in very broad terms in this section.

Simulation has become a very important field of application for computers. (It has become so important that the Communications of the Association for Computing Machinery published a survey article on this subject [5].) *Simulation* may be defined as attaining the essence of an entity without the reality. A definition that is more directly related to the computer has been given in [6]. It is: "Simulation is a numerical technique for conducting experiments on a digital computer, which involves certain types of mathematical and logical models that describe the behavior of a business or economic system (or some component thereof) over extended periods of real time." Except for the restriction to business and economic systems—social, biological, physical, and chemical systems are also simulated—it is a good working definition.

A simulation requires a combination of extensive arithmetic computations and file manipulations. In addition, since most of the files are intended to describe real entities and since the objective of the simulation is to operate on these descriptions of entities, the kinds of manipulations to which the files are subject can be anticipated. For example, in many simulations, at least one of the files pertains to servers. These may be man-machine systems in a manufacturing process, barbers in a barbershop, or claims representatives in a Social Security district office. One of the most important characteristics of servers is their status—that is, whether they are busy or idle. Some simulation languages provide special, direct status-manipulation capabilities.

One common approach to the development of *simulation languages* is to graft macroinstructions, intended to provide special file-manipulation capabilities, on another basic language.† FORTRAN or ALGOL is usually the basic language. For example, *SIMSCRIPT* uses FORTRAN as its basic language, as does *GASP*, while *SOL* uses ALGOL.

Table 7.4 contains a list of six of the more important simulation languages, their developers, the computers on which they have been implemented, and a reference to the entry in the Annotated Supplementary Bibliography pertaining to this language. These six languages are the three mentioned above (SIMSCRIPT, GASP, and SOL) and *GPSS, CLP,* and *CSL*.

Anyone who has done his homework in an algebra course is aware of the tedious activities associated with the reduction of mathematical expressions. Several special-purpose languages have been developed in an effort to enlist the aid of the computer in this task. These languages

† This is true of symbol manipulators and language translators as well.

Table 7.4   Some simulation languages

Name	Developed by	Of	Implemented on	Bibli- ography entry
CLP	Walker, Delfausse, Maxwell, and Conway	Cornell Univ.	CDC 1604	29
CSL	Buxton and Laski	IBM-ESSO-UK	IBM 7090/94	30
GASP	Kiviat and Colker	RAND Corp.	IBM 7040/44 7090/94	32
GPSS II	Efron, Gordon, and Hurowitz	IBM Corp.	IBM 7040/44 7090/94 UNIVAC 1107	33 34
SIMSCRIPT	Markowitz and Hausner	RAND Corp.	IBM 7040/44 7090/94	37
SOL	Knuth and McNeley	Case Inst. of Tech.	UNIVAC 1107	39

treat mathematical symbols as operands and permit the systematic reduction of algebraic expressions.   In treating mathematical symbols as operands, the manipulation of these symbols is an end in itself.   No effort is made in *symbol-manipulation languages* to substitute for these symbols. (Symbol manipulation is also of importance to the computer-science community—a whole issue of the Communications of the Association of Computing Machinery was devoted to the proceedings of the ACM conference on symbolic and algebraic manipulation held in Washington, D.C., in March, 1966 [7].)   Symbol manipulators differentiate, integrate, simplify, edit, and display algebraic expressions.   Inputs are mathematical expressions such as ratios of polynomials, and outputs are also mathematical expressions.   Expressions are not reduced to numerical outputs, although numbers representing constants such as coefficients or exponents of variables may be a part of the input/output.   Polynomial manipulation has probably advanced farther than any other.   Results were reported as early as 1961 on the manipulation of polynomials [8].

Mathematical expressions can be treated as lists, and list-processing techniques and languages have been successfully applied to developing compilers for symbol manipulation.   For example, *COMIT*† was useful in developing *AMBIT*, and *PM* is based on the REFCO III list processor.   Six of the most important symbol-manipulation languages are

† The programmer's manual for COMIT is listed as Ref. 25 in the Annotated Supplementary Bibliography.

Table 7.5 Some symbol-manipulation languages

Name	Developed by	Of	Implemented on	Bibliography entry
ALPAK	Brown, Hyde, and Tague	Bell Telephone Labs.	IBM 7090/94	40
AMBIT	Christensen	Computer Associates, Inc.	Any computer with an ALGOL 60 compiler	41
AUTOMAST	Ball and Berns	Washington Univ.	IBM 7072	42
FORMAC	Bond, Auslander, Grisoff, Kenney, Myszewski, Sammet, Tobey, and Zilles	IBM Corp.	IBM 7090/94	45
Formula ALGOL	Perlis, Iturriaga, and Standish	Carnegie Inst. of Tech.	CDC-G21	46
PM	Collins	IBM Corp.	IBM 7090/94	48

listed in Table 7.5, and included for each language are its developer, the computer on which it has been implemented, and a reference to the entry in the Annotated Supplementary Bibliography pertaining to it. The six are the two mentioned above (AMBIT and PM) and *ALPAK, FORMAC, AUTOMAST*, and *Formula ALGOL*.

The effort devoted to the translation of books and articles, particularly scientific ones, from one natural language to another has increased greatly in recent years. This is particularly true of Russian-English translations. It was recognized that the computer, which has so successfully translated higher-level languages to machine languages, might be useful in translating natural languages, and an applications area known as *machine translation* has developed. However, there is much skepticism regarding the potential of the computer as a translator. See, for example, [9].

Problems in machine translation have several special features that suggest the possible utility of a special-purpose program language. (It seems as if this could be said about almost all applications.) Frequent references to dictionaries are required, systematic restructuring of phrases is useful, and syntactical structures should be readily expressed. A language, SLC, has been developed for machine-translation applications. (See Ref. 48 in the Bibliography.) The sponsoring agency is EUR-

ATOM, a European community of atomic scientists whose interest in translation stems mainly from a desire to read as many pertinent Russian and English scientific articles as possible.

7.8 GENERAL-PURPOSE LANGUAGES—PL/1

FORTRAN, ALGOL, COBOL, LISP, IPL, AUTOCODER, SPS—there are many, too many, programming languages. Some were developed to improve earlier versions of similar languages, others to satisfy a new need. Whatever the reason, it is clear that computer languages have proliferated to the point where one could fill a large bookcase with just the programming manuals for these languages, if they were all available. There is a need for a single, general-purpose language that would satisfy the users of mathematically oriented, business-oriented, list-processing, simulation, and assembly languages. An attempt has been made jointly by SHARE and the IBM Corporation to do this. PL/1, standing for Programming Language 1, is the result. We shall present a detailed description of PL/1 in Chap. 12. If that chapter is to be covered, the remainder of this section can be skipped.

The generality of PL/1 has been demonstrated. It has been used to program both scientific and business applications. Even more indicative of its generality is its use in writing later versions of the PL/1 compiler and in list-processing applications [10].

The approach taken to make PL/1 a general-purpose language was to include an extensive variety of capabilities in its repertoire of instructions. For example, input/output can be handled, in much the same way as it is in FORTRAN, by specifying the layout of each record to be processed. But it can also be handled by doing little more than listing the names of the variables to which numbers are to be assigned in input or whose latest values are to be expressed in the output. For example, by merely writing

PUT LIST(A,B,C);

the latest values of A, B, and C are entered in the output with labels. The following line of output could have been produced using this instruction:

A = 4.2316   B = −6.711   C = 1172.414;

PL/1 will also input/output such things as:

1. Complete files, record by record
2. Structured hierarchical lists (see Sec. 7.6)
3. A stream of characters that is not organized into any kind of structure

In short, almost any kind of input/output required in digital processing can be handled in PL/1.†

The processing of information can also be done in a variety of ways. The arithmetic, formulalike processing of FORTRAN is carried out in much the same way in PL/1. Conditional expressions can be processed, and the IF statement allows the consequential THEN clause and the alternative ELSE clause just as in ALGOL and COBOL. Structures can be easily manipulated. For example, elements in one structure can be substituted for corresponding elements in another structure using a single instruction. These structures must have previously been described in the PL/1 program. The computer cannot "know" which elements correspond; the structures must be defined for it.

Instruction sets can be grouped into blocks, and these blocks can be built into complex program structures with a minimum of restrictions on the ways in which the blocks can be interconnected. (This blocking of PL/1 programs is similar to the use of procedures in ALGOL. See Sec. 7.4, particularly the first footnote on page 100, to contrast this with the situation in FORTRAN.)

Because it has an extensive repertoire of capabilities, the novice should approach PL/1 with trepidation. There is a great deal to be learned. However, PL/1 provides default conditions for any capabilities not explicitly used. This permits the novice to write programs ignoring those capabilities that he does not use. The PL/1 compiler will make all the necessary assignments that the programmer does not make. Although the assignment will nearly always be the one that the programmer would have made (if he knew how to do it), occasionally the default specification will not satisfy a programmer's need. In these cases, he will find that he has errors in his program that he cannot diagnose, and he will have to seek more expert help.

PROBLEMS

7.1 Consider the following series of instructions in our hypothetical 4-address machine language:

```
21  21121  21141  21141  36001
21  21121  21141  21141  36002
14  21121  21141  21141  36003
```

If (21121) = X and (21141) = Y before the execution of the first instruction, then:

(a) What are (21121) and (21141) after the execution of the last instruction?
(b) What are (36002)?
(c) Write an instruction that is to be executed after the last instruction and

† However, some special inputs, such as from an optical scanner, and outputs, such as to a plotter or cathode-ray tube, require additional special hardware and software in order to be serviced when programming in PL/1.

that will store X^2 in location 21142. Follow the previously established
pattern for the delta address. Assume 21 is the code for *add* and 14 the
code for *multiply*.

7.2   The IBM 1620 computer uses a 12-digit, 2-address instruction word. The
first two digits contain the operation code, the next five digits the P address,
and the last five digits the Q address. Listed below is a dictionary for a subset of the machine-language instructions available in the 1620. The form of
the dictionary is to list operation codes and the significance of the P and Q
addresses using the shorthand notation of α and β for the address of operands,
γ for where to store the answer, and δ for the address of the next instruction.
Unless otherwise stated, the address of the next instruction is found automatically by adding 12 to the address of the previous instruction. Each digit
in main storage is individually addressable, but the contents of an address
(except for an instruction) are found by starting at the address specified and
going back to lower-numbered addresses until a flag is found stored along with
the digit. If the digit stored at the specified address has a flag, a minus sign is
attached to the number but the computer proceeds to the next lower digit to find
the end of the contents. This means that there are no one-digit contents.
In the case of instructions, the computer goes to the digit addressed during
the instruction cycle and automatically reads out the next 12 digits as the
instruction, proceeding forward rather than backward and ignoring flags.
Flags are denoted in writing by putting a bar over a digit. Thus, for example,
if we write $(12234) = \overline{1}23\overline{7}$, it means that $\overline{7}$ is stored in address 12234, 3 in
address 12233, 2 in 12232, and $\overline{1}$ in 12231. We still say that the contents of
address 12234 is minus 1,237. Now for the partial dictionary of operation
codes:

Instruction operation		Meaning of five digits	
Meaning	Code	P address	Q address
Add	21	γ, α	β
Subtract	22	γ, α	β
Multiply	23	α	$\beta\dagger$
Transmit the contents of Q to P	26	γ	α
Put a flag at P	32	α	Ignored
Remove flag from P	33	α	Ignored
Go to P only if there is no flag at Q	44	δ, maybe	α
Halt	48	Ignored	Ignored

† Results of a multiplication are automatically stored in location
00099, 00098, and so on back as far as is required. Locations
00080 to 00099 are called the *product area* and are automatically
cleared to zero before the multiplication is executed. If the product
contains more than 20 digits, provision must be made by the programmer to clear locations 00079 and back or an incorrect result
may be obtained.

(a) If $(11234) = \overline{1}234$, $(11236) = \overline{9}6$, $(11241) = \overline{0}0001$, $(11246) = \overline{1}2212$ before the following instruction is executed, what are their contents after it is executed?

INSTRUCTION: 21   11234   11236

(b) Suppose the instruction executed in part *a* is followed by the instruction given below. What are the contents of 11234, 11236, 11241, and 11246 after this second instruction is executed?

INSTRUCTION: 21   11246   11234

7.3 Referring to machine-language programming in the 1620 computer, suppose again that $(11234) = \overline{1}234$, $(11236) = \overline{9}6$, $(11241) = \overline{0}0001$, $(11246) = \overline{1}2212$ before the execution of the first instruction, what are the contents of these locations and the contents of the product area (i.e., of locations 00099 on back) after the execution of the following two instructions:

INSTRUCTIONS: 32   11245   59822
23   11246   11236

7.4 Referring to machine-language programming in the 1620 computer, suppose main storage contains the following digits at the indicated addresses (we are not referring to the formal contents of addresses here but merely to a list of the elements in storage from location 06000 forward to location 06059)

Digit: $3307099\overline{0}200\overline{0}2106030060082\overline{6}07000060114406012070994\overline{8}0000000000$

Address: 06000   06012   06024   06036   06048

Suppose also that the address of the first instruction to be executed in a program is 06000. What can you say about the contents of core after this program is completed?

7.5 Consider each of the following mathematical formulas written in FORTRAN code. Discuss what the computer actually does in substituting in them in the same way as was done for Y =A/(B*SQRTF(X−Z+2.)) in Sec. 7.4.

(a) Z = Z+1.   (b) Z = Z*(B+C)   (c) Y = SQRTF(A*A+(B−C)*D)

7.6 What are the ALGOL statements required to provide the branching indicated in the following FORTRAN IF statements:

(a) IF(X)1,2,3   (b) IF(X*X−Y*Y)3,3,4   (c) IF(Z−(A+B))2,5,5

7.7 Consider the following set of COBOL statements:

IF(PART-NUMBER GREATER THAN 1364 OR COLOR =AMBER)
IS TRUE GO TO EDIT-1,OTHERWISE GO TO TEST-1.
TEST-1.IF(PRICE LESS THAN 1.50 AND GREATER THAN 0.01
AND SUPPLY LESS THAN 20)IS TRUE GO TO INVENTORY,
OTHERWISE GO TO TEST-2.
TEST-2.IF(PRICE LESS THAN 1.50 AND GREATER THAN 0.01
AND SUPPLY GREATER THAN 19)IS TRUE GO TO NEXT-ENTRY,
OTHERWISE GO TO TEST-3.
TEST-3.IF(PRICE GREATER THAN 1.49 AND LESS THAN 9.99
AND SUPPLY LESS THAN 10)IS TRUE GO TO INVENTORY,
OTHERWISE GO TO TEST-4.
TEST-4.IF(PRICE GREATER THAN 1.49 AND LESS THAN 9.99
AND SUPPLY GREATER THAN 9)IS TRUE GO TO NEXT-ENTRY,
OTHERWISE GO TO EDIT-2.

The statement labels appear as the first entry in a statement, and both the labels and the statement are concluded with a period, so that the first statement is unlabeled and the second is labeled TEST-1, etc.

(a) List all the labels of statements that can serve as the next statement to be processed on exiting from this portion of the program.

(b) Draw a detailed flow chart which corresponds to this set of COBOL code.

(c) Indicate which exit would be taken for each of the sets of file entries given below.

Part number	Color	Price	Supply
1716	Blue	1.49	19
1112	Blue	1.50	21
1113	Red	1.49	19
1114	Red	1.50	10
1179	Amber	2.75	10
1363	Yellow	1.48	10
1164	Red	0.00	0

(d) Write the FORTRAN equivalent of statement TEST-1. Use PRICE and SUPPLY for the names of the variables, 101 for the number of the INVENTORY statement, 102 for the number of the TEST-2 statement, and 103 for the number of the TEST-1 statement.

7.8 Reconstruct the bridge hands depicted in the list structures given in Table 7.2 and determine the point count for each of the four hands using the method of Prob. 5.13. If you wrote an algorithm in answer to Prob. 5.13, substitute these hands in that algorithm to further check its validity.

REFERENCES

1. Borenstine, A. J.: Over 1000 Systems Men Evaluate COBOL, *Data Process. Mag.*, pp. 24–30, August, 1966.

2. Newell, A., J. C. Shaw, and H. A. Simon: A Variety of Intelligent Learning in a General Problem Solver, in M. T. Yovits and S. Cameron (eds.), "Self-organizing Systems," Pergamon Press, New York, 1960.

3. Gelertner, H., J. R. Hansen, and C. L. Gerberich: A FORTRAN-compiled List Processing Language, *J. ACM*, vol. 7, pp. 87–101, 1960.

4. McCarthy, J.: Recursive Functions of Symbolic Expressions and Their Computations by Machines, part I, *Commun. ACM*, vol. 3, pp. 184–195, 1960.

5. Teichroew, D., and J. F. Lubin: Computer Simulation—Discussion of the Technique and Comparison of Languages, *Commun. ACM*, vol. 9, pp. 723–741, October, 1966.

6. Naylor, T. H., J. L. Balintfy, D. S. Burdick, and K. Chu: "Computer Simulation Techniques," p. 3, John Wiley & Sons, Inc., New York, 1966.

7. Proceedings of the ACM Symposium on Symbolic and Algebraic Manipulation, Washington, D.C., March 29–31, 1966, *Commun. ACM*, vol. 9, August, 1966.
8. Spielberg, K.: Representation of Power Series in Terms of Polynomials, Rational Approximations and Continued Fractions, *J. ACM*, vol. 4, pp. 613–627, October, 1961.
9. Pierce, J. R., et al.: Language and Machines: Computers in Translation and Linguistics, *NAS Publ.* 1416, Washington, D.C.
10. Lawson, H. W., Jr.: PL/1 List-processing, *Commun. ACM*, vol. 10, pp. 358–367, June, 1967.

ANNOTATED SUPPLEMENTARY BIBLIOGRAPHY

The Annotated Supplementary Bibliography for this chapter is organized somewhat differently than those for the other chapters. Rather than listing references with contents, we have classified our bibliography with respect to the programming language discussed and presented a list of references for each language with a minimum of comment. The phrase "inexpensively bound" is used to indicate a soft cover or other special binding that can be expected to reduce the cost of the book. Many references on computer languages are bound this way.

FORTRAN II

1. Anderson, D.: "Basic Computer Programming," Appleton-Century-Crofts, Inc., New York, 1963. Oriented toward the 1620 computer. Inexpensively bound.
2. Hartkemeier, H. P.: "FORTRAN Programming of Electronic Computers," Charles E. Merrill Books, Inc., Columbus, Ohio, 1966. Inexpensively bound.
3. Organick, E. I.: "A FORTRAN Primer," Addison-Wesley Publishing Company, Inc., Reading, Mass., 1963. Although primarily oriented toward Fortran II, it includes some discussion of Fortran IV. Inexpensively bound.
4. Rule, W. P.: "Introduction to FORTRAN Programming," Prindle, Weber and Schmidt, Boston, 1966. Inexpensively bound.
5. Weiss, E. A.: "Programming the IBM 1620," McGraw-Hill Book Company, New York, 1965. Includes a discussion of assembly-language programming for the 1620 as well as FORTRAN II.

FORTRAN IV

6. Anderson, D.: "Computer Programming," Appleton-Century-Crofts, Inc., New York, 1966. Includes work sheets and is inexpensively bound.
7. Dimitry, D., and T. Mott: "Introduction to FORTRAN IV Pro-

gramming," Holt, Rinehart and Winston, Inc., New York, 1966. Inexpensively bound.

8. Ledley, R. S.: "FORTRAN IV Programming," McGraw-Hill Book Company, New York, 1966. Inexpensively bound.

9. McCracken, D. D.: "A Guide to FORTRAN IV Programming," John Wiley & Sons, Inc., New York, 1965. Inexpensively bound.

10. Pollack, S. V.: "A Guide to FORTRAN IV," Columbia University Press, New York, 1965. Not inexpensively bound, but typewriter-like printing should reduce the cost of this book.

11. Stein, M. L., and W. D. Munro: "A FORTRAN Introduction to Programming and Computers," Academic Press Inc., New York, 1966.

OTHER FORTRAN DIALECTS

12. Stuart, F.: "Introductory Computer Programming," John Wiley & Sons, Inc., 1966. NCE FORTRAN and AFIT FORTRAN are discussed.

FORTRAN WITH NUMERICAL ANALYSIS OR APPLICATIONS

13. Harris, L. D.: "Numerical Methods Using FORTRAN," Charles E. Merrill Books, Inc., Columbus, Ohio, 1964.

14. Kuo, S. S.: "Numerical Methods and Computers," Addison-Wesley Publishing Company, Inc., Reading, Mass., 1965.

15. Pennington, R. H.: "Introductory Computer Methods and Numerical Analysis," The Macmillan Company, New York, 1965.

16. Southworth, R. W., and S. L. DeLeeuw: "Digital Computation and Numerical Methods," McGraw-Hill Book Company, New York, 1965.

17. Schenck, H., Jr.: "FORTRAN Methods in Heat Flow," The Ronald Press Company, New York, 1963.

ALGOL

18. McCracken, D. D.: "A Guide to ALGOL Programming," John Wiley & Sons, Inc., New York, 1962. Inexpensively bound.

19. Baumann, R., M. Feliciano, F. L. Bauer, and K. Samelson: "Introduction to ALGOL," Prentice-Hall, Inc., Englewood Cliffs, N.J., 1964.

COBOL PLUS OTHERS

20. Davis, G. B.: "An Introduction to Electronic Computers," McGraw-Hill Book Company, New York, 1966. Includes two chapters on COBOL and two on FORTRAN, as well as some discussion of FORTRAN II vs. FORTRAN IV. This volume is supplemented by related workbooks that discuss individual computers in detail. A workbook on the System/360 is available.

21. Fisher, F. P., and G. F. Swindle: "Computer Programming Systems," Holt, Rinehart and Winston, Inc., New York, 1964. Includes one chapter each on COBOL, ALGOL, and FORTRAN.
22. Ledley, R. S.: "Programming and Utilizing Digital Computers," McGraw-Hill Book Company, New York, 1962. Includes one chapter on COBOL and one on ALGOL.

MAD WITH NUMERICAL METHODS

23. Arden, B. W.: "An Introduction to Digital Computing," Addison-Wesley Publishing Company, Inc., Reading, Mass., 1963.

LIST-PROCESSING LANGUAGES

24. Newell, A., et al.: "Information Processing Language-V Manual," 2d ed., Prentice-Hall, Inc., Englewood Cliffs, N.J., 1964.
25. "COMIT Programmer's Reference Manual," 2d ed., The M.I.T. Press, Cambridge, Mass., 1961.

COMPUTER PROGRAMMING ORIENTED TOWARD
SPECIFIC COMPUTERS

26. Stein, M. L., and W. O. Munro: "Computer Programming, A Mixed Language Approach," Academic Press Inc., New York, 1964. This book is oriented toward the CDC 1604 computer.
27. Leeson, D., and D. Dimitry: "Basic Programming Concepts and the IBM 1620 Computer," Holt, Rinehart and Winston, Inc., New York, 1962.
28. "Programming the IBM System/360," John Wiley & Sons, Inc., New York, 1966.

SIMULATION LANGUAGES

29. Maxwell, W. L., and R. W. Conway: CLP Preliminary Manual, *Cornell Univ. Dept. Ind. Eng. no.* 3-9850, October, 1963.
30. "Control and Simulation Reference Manual," IBM United Kingdom, Ltd., and Esso Petroleum Company, Ltd., March, 1963.
31. Pugh, A. L.: "DYNAMO User's Manual," The M.I.T. Press, Cambridge, Mass., 1961.
32. Belkin, J., and M. R. Rao: "GASP User's Manual," United States Steel Corporation, Applied Research Lab., Monroeville, Pa., 1965.
33. Reference Manual, General Purpose Systems Simulator II (GPSS II), *IBM Publ.* B20-6346, 1963.
34. Hurowitz, M.: "GPSS II on the UNIVAC 1107, Preliminary User Manual," Univac Division of Sperry Rand Corporation, 1965.
35. "MILITRAN Reference Manual," Systems Research Corporation, Inc., 1964.
36. Bennett, R. P., et al.: "SIMPAC User's Manual, TM-602/000/00,"

Systems Development Corporation, Santa Monica, Calif., April, 1962.

37. Markowitz, H., B. Hausner, and H. Karr: "SIMSCRIPT: A Simulation Programming Language," Prentice-Hall, Inc., Englewood Cliffs, N.J., 1962.

38. Dahl, O. J., and K. Nygaard: "SIMULA: A Language for Programming and Description of Discrete Event System, Introduction and User's Manual," Norwegian Computing Center, Forsknongsveien, Oslo, 1965.

39. Knuth, D. E., and J. L. McNeley: SOL—A Symbolic Language for General Purpose Systems Simulation, *Trans. IEEE*, pp. 401–414, 1964.

SYMBOL-MANIPULATION LANGUAGES

40. Brown, W. S., J. P. Hyde, and B. A. Tague: The ALPAK System for Non-numerical Algebra on a Digital Computer, *Bell Systems Tech. J.*, vol. 42, pp. 2081–2119, 1963; vol. 43, pp. 785–804 and 1547–1562, 1963.

41. Christensen, C.: AMBIT: A Programming Language for Algebraic Symbol Manipulation, *Computer Assoc. Res. Paper* CA-64-4-R, Wakefield, Mass., October, 1964.

42. Ball, W. E., and R. I. Berns: AUTOMAST: Automatic Mathematical Analysis and Symbolic Translation, *Commun. ACM*, vol. 9, pp. 626–633, August, 1966.

43. Guzman, A., and H. V. McIntosh: CONVERT, *ibid.*, pp. 604–615.

44. Symbolic Work in High Speed Computers, *Dartmouth Mathematics Project Rept.* 4, Hanover, N.H., June, 1959.

45. Bond, E., et al.: FORMAC—An Experimental Formula Manipulation Compiler, *Proc. 19th Natl. Conf. ACM*, pp. K2.1-1 to K2.1-11, August, 1964.

46. Perlis, A. J., R. Iturriaga, and T. A. Standish: "A Definition of Formula ALGOL," Carnegie Institute of Technology, March, 1966.

47. Wells, M. B.: MADCAP—A Scientific Compiler for a Displayed Formula Textbook Language, *Commun. ACM*, pp. 31–36, January, 1961.

48. Collins, G. E.: PM—A System for Polynomial Manipulation, *ibid.*, vol. 9, pp. 578–589, August, 1966.

MACHINE TRANSLATION

49. Brown, A.: The SLC Programming Language and System for Machine Translation, Programming Manual, *Euratom Rept.* EUR2418.e, vol. 1, Brussels, May, 1965.

part 3

COMPUTER APPLICATIONS

INTRODUCTION

The next three chapters contain a discussion of computer applications. Ordinarily, the equivalent of only one of these would be covered in a one-semester course. Recommendations for the choice of the applications to be covered, based on the major subject area of the student, can be found in the preface of this book.

The approach taken in Chaps. 8 and 9 is first to provide a description of the application with little or no reference to the computer and then to describe how the computer is used in the application. The algorithms are not given. They are extremely complex and would serve to do little more than decorate the pages of a book intended as a text for a first course. However, references will be made to sources for these algorithms wherever this can be done.

The approach in Chap. 10 is somewhat different. The subjects are discussed in greater depth because this chapter is intended mainly for the computer-science major. Majors in other areas may find it both difficult and uninteresting. A reader who wishes to sample only one application in the area of artificial intelligence should probably read Secs. 10.1 and 10.3.

Applications of computers are discussed in other parts of the book. The processing of payrolls has been described. In fact, algorithms for the solution of this problem were developed and presented. A PL/1 program for implementing these algorithms will be given in Chap. 12. The calculation of square roots has been discussed, and some simple statistical calculations will be described in Chap. 11. The reader who would like to investigate still other applications is referred to the Annotated Supplementary Bibliography at the conclusion of each of the next three chapters.

OUTLINE

chapter **8**

APPLICATIONS
IN THE SCIENCES

8.1 INTRODUCTION

The first applications of computers were to problems in the sciences, and such applications continue to be of great importance. Five applications in the sciences will be discussed in this chapter—one in biology, one in medicine, and three that originate in mathematics but that have been used in the physical and social sciences. The five areas of application are numerical taxonomy, medical diagnosis, the fitting of functions to observed data (with emphasis on the use of spline functions), random-number generation, and linear programming.

The emphasis in the discussion of the last two of these applications is somewhat different from that in the discussion of the other applications. The usual approach is first to provide a broad picture of the application, with little or no mention of the computer, and then to describe how the computer is used. In discussing random numbers, however, the process for generating the numbers is described in some detail. This is because the major area of application in which these numbers are used, simulation, will be discussed in its own right in Chap. 9. The broad picture will be presented there.   Also, the discussion of linear programming is intended to illustrate the mathematical structure of this subject and to define a few of the basic terms used.   Mention is made of some of the problems that have been solved with the aid of this technique, but the intention is to depict linear programming itself rather than those areas in which it has been used.

8.2 NUMERICAL TAXONOMY

Taxonomy, the orderly classification of plants and animals according to their natural relationships, has long occupied biological scientists.   Some taxonomists would call this *classification* and would reserve the word "taxonomy" for the theoretical study of the mechanism of classification itself, including its procedures and rules.   Until recently, most of the work was subjective in nature, indeed so much so that devoted amateurs could make a substantial contribution to the field.   Quite recently, more elaborate, objective techniques have been developed, such as numerical taxonomy, which use mathematical reasoning in their classification procedures.

In general, the taxonomist is concerned with either the classification of a large number of organisms or the assignment of a single organism within a preexisting classification structure.   We shall discuss only the way a numerical taxonomist attacks the former problem.   For a discussion of the latter problem, see [1] or [2].   When faced with the problem of classifying a large number of organisms, the numerical taxonomist will first develop a list of pertinent criteria or characteristics.   (Chapter 5 of [3] contains a good discussion of the considerations that enter into the choice of characteristics.)   Data are then obtained for each characteristic and each organism.   These data may indicate merely the presence or absence of a given characteristic, whether a characteristic is present strongly, mildly, weakly, or not at all, or a numerical measurement such as length or weight.   The problem is to determine, given all the data, how best to group the organisms.

A realistic problem in taxonomy may involve 500 to 1,000 organisms and 100 to 200 characteristics for each organism—about 100,000 pieces of information.   The need for automatic assistance is clearly indicated.

Consider a situation in which we have, say, 500 organisms and 200 characteristics for each organism.   One might first numerically code the data for each characteristic and then summarize the results in a rectangular array, or matrix, in which each organism occupies a single row and each characteristic a single column.   We would then have an array with

500 rows and 200 columns.   A few of its entries might look like this:

	Char. 1	Char. 2	Char. 3	· · ·	Char. 200
Organism 1	1	26.7	3	· · ·	1
Organism 2	0	15.8	3	· · ·	1
· ·				
Organism 500	1	21.2	1	· · ·	0

For characteristics 1 and 200, we have presence or absence; and for characteristic 3, we have four levels of presence or absence.   The code used is:

For char. 1 and 200		For char. 3	
Code	Meaning	Code	Meaning
0	Absent	0	Absent
1	Present	1	Weakly present
		2	Mildly present
		3	Strongly present

Finally, for characteristic 2, we have a measurement—for example, length
in millimeters.

The numerical taxonomist would then compute some sort of measure
of the degree of similarity among the different organisms.   The simplest
of these is the ratio

$$S = \frac{m}{n}$$

where n is the total number of characteristics being compared and m is
the number of characteristics that match.   To employ this measure, the
taxonomist might first reduce all scores to 0 or 1.   He might, for example,
assign a 1 to a score of 3 or 2 and a 0 to a score of 1 or 0 when dealing
with scores in the range 0 to 3.   When dealing with measurements such
as length, he would probably arbitrarily choose a length to act as the cut
between long and short organisms.   In the example we are discussing,
we might decide that a length of 20 millimeters or less is short, and we
might code short with a 0 and long with a 1.   This means that the entries
would become:

	Char. 1	Char. 2	Char. 3	· · ·	Char. 200
Organism 1	1	1	1	· · ·	1
Organism 2	0	0	1	· · ·	1
· ·				
Organism 500	1	1	0	· · ·	0

For this example, $n = 200$, and we could use a computer both to convert the original measurements to 0, 1 scores and to compute S for every pair of organisms. We would then get a different kind of array as an output. This time, both the rows and the columns would refer to organisms and the entries would be similarity scores. For example, if we got the array of S scores given below, organism 1 and organism 2 would have a similarity score of 0.245 and organisms 2 and 500 a score of 0.555.

	Organism 1	Organism 2	· · ·	Organism 500
Organism 1	1.000	0.245	· · ·	0.315
Organism 2	0.245	1.000	· · ·	0.555
· ·
Organism 500	0.315	0.555	· · ·	1.000

The next task is to group those organisms with the largest similarity measures together. One could do this by merely listing all pairs of organisms that, say, had similarity measures greater than 0.80 along with the actual similarity measure. Hopefully, we could arrive at some nonoverlapping classification of some subset of the original 500 organisms in this way. We might then reduce the critical value of the coefficient to 0.70, obtain a further classification, and continue in this way until we decide that we have reached the point where it is best to group the organisms that remain unclassified into a kind of "misfit" classification in itself.

There are many measures of the degree of similarity other than the very simple measure discussed above. Among them are other types of similarity ratios, distance functions, and correlation coefficients. For definitions of these measures and a discussion of them, see pages 128 to 168 of [3]. No matter which measure is used, extensive computation and data manipulation are required and a computer is a necessary tool.

Examples of the application of the techniques discussed in this section to real classification problems can be found in [4 to 6].

8.3 MEDICAL DIAGNOSIS

Although physicians in research have used computers for a number of years, the physician in regular practice has made little or no use of the computer. This situation is slowly changing, and the direct application of the computer to the treatment of patients is increasing. One such application, the fundamental problem of diagnosis, is still being attacked for the most part by research physicians. However, there have been a few applications of the computer to real diagnostic problems [13 to 15].

In addition to quantifying the diagnostic procedure, the computer also uses all the information in an unbiased way. (It is not, for example, biased by recent experience or personal feelings.) The computer can consider more factors, does not make computational errors, and is very fast. It has not yet been widely applied to diagnostic problems because it cannot easily accept narrative histories, physical findings, or laboratory reports. When large volumes of medical records are routinely put into machine-processable form, the techniques of computer-aided diagnosis will probably be more widely applied.

In performing a diagnosis, the physician arrives at a categorization of the patient's state of health from the observations he has made of the patient and his environment. In attacking the problem with the aid of a computer, a specific state is chosen from among a number of mutually exclusive disease states, using information obtained from the patient's medical history, from laboratory tests and physical examinations, and from such things as the relative prevalence of the different disease states in the community at the time that the diagnosis is being made. We shall use the word "symptom" generically to denote all facts regarding the state of the patient. This means that the term will be applied to information obtained from histories, laboratory tests, and examinations. The problem can be restated as follows: "Given the patient's symptoms and information about the local incidence of various diseases, what conclusions can be drawn about the chances that the patient is in each of the various disease states?" Note that the approach used is a probabilistic one. Several probabilistic models have been applied, but the one based on Bayes' theorem is probably the most widely used approach. Any one of the models permits the physician to obtain quantities that indicate the probability that each of the different possible diagnoses is the correct one. (Bayes' theorem is discussed on pages 38 to 40 of [17]. References to other approaches will be given later in this section.)

We shall next discuss a very simple application of Bayes' theorem— intended to provide an example of a diagnostic problem and to help the reader understand how Bayes' theorem is used.

Suppose we are dealing with only two disease states, as follows:

d_1: Asian flu
d_2: not Asian flu

In this situation, we are concerned only with whether Asian flu is present or absent. This is not a realistic example since the category d_2 should be further subdivided into other disease states, but it serves our purpose. Let us suppose we have two patients. One patient, Mr. A, has a set of symptoms, including headache, fever, chills, and general malaise, such that the probability is .95 that if he had the Asian flu he would have these symptoms and only .05 that if he did not have the Asian flu he would have these symptoms. Mr. B, on the other hand, has headache and fever but no chill or general malaise, and the corresponding probabilities in his case are .50 and .50. Let us also assume it is winter and the Asian flu is "going around," so that the probability of Asian flu in the local population is an appreciable .25. Bayes' theorem can now be applied to estimate the probability that Mr. A and Mr. B are in disease state 1. It turns out that these probabilities are .86 and .25, respectively. This would lead us to conclude that Mr. A probably has the flu but that Mr. B probably does not.

Next let us suppose that Mr. A and Mr. B present the same symptoms but that this time the Asian flu is not "going around," so that the probability of Asian flu in the local population is only .001. Applying Bayes' theorem to these data results in our estimating the probability that Mr. A is in state 1 to be .02 and the corresponding probability for Mr. B to be .001. Now we would conclude that neither Mr. A nor Mr. B has the flu.

We see that the local incidence of a disease can strongly affect our diagnosis. Note that Mr. B's symptoms cannot differentiate between d_1 and d_2 (there is a 50-50 chance that either one is appropriate based on his symptoms), so that it is the incidence of the disease in the community that determines the probability of the different disease states in his case.

The preceding example only serves to illustrate the application of Bayes' theorem to medical diagnosis and does not indicate the processing and computational effort needed to apply this approach. Real problems might have 10, 20, 30, or more disease states. The number of different symptom sets that might be observed is enormous.

An algorithm must first be written to reduce the information on symptoms and their relation to disease states to a precise quantity, namely, the probability that a certain symptom would be observed if a given disease state were present. An algorithm must also be written to reduce information on the locale, time of year, and other factors to an estimate of the probability that each of the possible disease states is present in the community at that time. The computation of the diagnostic probabilities, i.e., of the probability of the various disease states in view of the symptoms, follows from Bayes' theorem and is the least demanding computational step.

To be successful, this approach requires a great deal of quantified information that is not readily available. The various probabilities of disease states and of symptom sets corresponding to disease states might be estimated from a national medical-information file, such as the one discussed in Sec. 1.3. Without such a rich source of data, probabilities estimated in this way can do little more than offer some guidance to the diagnostician. The diagnostician must continue to combine such estimates with his own experience and nonquantified observations to arrive at a valid diagnosis.

Several other approaches to diagnosis have been taken. For example, Collen [13] has applied statistical, maximum-likelihood estimates; Overall and Williams [14] have applied the statistical techniques of factor analysis, multiple regression, and discriminant analysis; Ledley and Lusted [16] have combined value theory with the use of Bayes' theorem; and Ledley in [17] discusses the application of conditional expressions and dynamic programming in combination with Bayes' theorem to the problem of medical diagnosis.

8.4 FUNCTION FITTING—SPLINE FUNCTIONS

The problem of how best to describe or summarize data that seem to follow a smooth pattern when plotted has long plagued scientists. In many applications, the scientist is willing to merely draw a smooth curve through the data and to use the resulting graph to represent his function. Frequently, however, it is desirable to specify, in mathematical terms, some sort of functional relation between the plotted variables. This presents two problems: (1) to determine what type of mathematical function is best to use, and (2) given the type of function to be used, to choose from among all functions of this type the one that fits the data best. Scientists sometimes rely on a mathematical model of the process being studied to decide on the appropriate type of function and then use *least-squares techniques* to choose the one best function of this type. The least-squares criterion involves choosing that function that minimizes the sums of the squares of the differences between the observed values and the fitted function. (For a discussion of least squares, see Chap. 6 of [17] or Chap. 9 of [21].) At times, the scientist will use some other criterion for choosing the best function—for example, minimizing the maximum difference between the fitted function and the observed data. This is called *Chebyshev's* (or the *minimax*) *criterion*. (For a discussion of this approach to function fitting, see Chap. 7 of [7].)

The minimax procedure might be appropriate when a scientist is tabulating a relation (such as a planetary orbit) or a mathematical function that is known quite precisely. Minimizing the greatest possible error in the table may be his goal. However, when fitting functions to experimental data, the scientist would probably prefer to use the least-squares criterion. This is because a body of statistical methodology has been developed that is applicable when least squares is used. This theory permits the scientist to make such statements as "Chances are 95 in 100 that the yield of this chemical at a temperature of 84°C will be between 6.14 and 6.32 grams" or "Chances are less than 1 in 20 that we could have obtained these experimental results if the two lines underlying the observed relations were truly identical." In short, a framework exists for the scientist to state the inferences that he draws from his experiments in probabilistic terms.

Frequently, the scientist does not have a mathematical model for his process and wishes to use the data to help him choose the type of function as well as the best function of a prescribed type. Some work has been done by statisticians to assist the scientist in this case [8,9], but the problem still presents some great difficulties. An alternative is for the scientist to return to the "eyeball" fit, but this time attacking the problem in an objective, mathematical way. Fitting by means of spline functions offers just such an approach† since the criteria for fit are related to the smoothness‡ of the result as well as to the deviation of the result from the underlying relation represented by the observed points. In fact, the name "spline function" was chosen because one of these functions approximates the behavior of a mechanical spline, an aid used by draftsmen to draw a smooth curve. This aid consists of a flexible steel or plastic strip to which weights are attached in such a way that the edge of the strip describes a smooth curve that fits the data points.

The spline function is essentially a sequence of polynomials of prescribed degree that are chosen so as to make the overall function as smooth as possible. Of special interest are spline functions that consist of a sequence of third-degree polynomials. (These are just those spline functions that have been shown to approximate the behavior of the draftsman's mechanical spline.) We shall not attempt to describe how such a function is fitted to a set of data. Understanding this description would require mathematical sophistication beyond that considered a prerequisite for this text. Detailed descriptions of how to fit such functions are available in [11] and [12]. We shall, however, note two things about the fitting process, namely, the iterative nature of parts of it and the scope of the process in terms of the number of computations that are required.

The first step in the fitting of spline functions is to estimate the second derivatives of the spline function at the abscissas of the second, third, fourth, and so on, data points up to and including the $(n-1)$st

---

† A number of papers on fitting by spline functions have been published. For a mathematical exposition, see [10]; for detailed information on how to fit spline functions, see [11] or [12].

‡ A spline function is particularly smooth since, given n distinct data points and $k \leq n$, the spline function is chosen so as to minimize the integral of the square of the kth derivative of the function over the range of the abscissas of the data points. In other terms, given data points (X_i, Y_i), for $i = 1, 2, \ldots, n$, such that $X_1 < X_2 < X_3 < \cdots < X_n$ and spline functions $g(x)$ with continuous derivatives through the kth derivative, $k \leq n$, then $\int_{X_1}^{X_n} [g^{(k)}(x)]^2 \, dx$ is minimized.

data point. An iterative technique (see Sec. 5.4) is used. The stop rule is essentially that of prescribing $\in$ and stopping when all the successive estimates of the second derivatives differ by less than $\in$. Initial estimates for the second derivatives at a point are obtained as functions of the data at that point and nearby points.

The computations required are fairly extensive. It has been estimated that to fit an mth-degree spline function to n points requires $(8n + 6m)$ multiplications, $(5n + 2m)$ divisions, and $(8n + 10m + mn)$ additions after the iterations to estimate the second derivatives have been completed. The expected number of iterations is a function of $\in$, of course, and it has also been estimated that $3n(- \log \in)$ multiplications and $5n(- \log \in)$ additions are required to complete the iterations. In summary, if the computations are performed on an electronic computer and if μ, δ, and α are the times required by the computer to perform a single multiplication, division, and addition, respectively, then the total time required for fitting a spline function of degree m to n data points is estimated to be

$$(8n + 6m)\mu + (5n + 2m)\delta + (8n + 10m + mn)\alpha \\ + n(3\mu + 5\alpha)(- \log \in)$$

where $\in$ is the quantity used to determine when to stop the iterative part of the calculations.

For example, for a third-degree spline function with 20 data points and an $\in$ of 10^{-5}, we get 478 multiplications, 106 divisions, and 750 additions. A third-degree spline function was fitted to nine data points in 3.25 seconds using a CDC 1604 computer and in 0.9 second using an IBM 7090 computer.

8.5 RANDOM-NUMBER GENERATION

Random-number generators are widely used in simulations. (See Sec. 7.7 for a definition of simulation and Secs. 9.4 and 9.5 for a discussion of simulation as an area of application.)

When generating any number on a digital computer, we use a completely determined calculation since the computer must be given unique, rigid rules for generating the number. In generating random numbers, the proper random behavior is ensured by designing the calculating procedure so that sets, very large sets, of numbers so generated will pass all the appropriate tests for randomness. This means that we must always check the random-number generator before using it, to be certain that the numbers generated are valid. The term *pseudorandom numbers* has been applied to the sets of random numbers generated by a computer because they are obtained from strictly determined calculations but have the required random properties.†

It is not easy to develop a procedure for generating random numbers. Most procedures are iterative; that is, they generate the next number from the preceding one(s) and repeat the sequence of numbers once they return to their starting point. The number of numbers that the process will generate before restarting the sequence is called the *length*, or the *period*, *of the generator*.

It is obviously desirable, particularly in an application that requires many random numbers, to make this length as great as possible. It is also obviously desirable, in order to conserve storage space in the computer and to save time, to generate the numbers by using a calculating procedure which relies on a few preceding values rather than by reading these numbers from a table previously stored in the computer. How do we do this? We shall discuss three approaches, two that generate numbers *uniformly distributed* between 0 and 1 (that is, every number between 0 and 1 has an equal chance of being selected) and one that generates numbers *normally distributed*‡ with mean 0 and standard deviation 1.

Suppose we start with n numbers, say $X_1, X_2, X_3, \ldots, X_n$, that are themselves randomly distributed between 0 and 1. We might get these numbers, which we call the *seed* for the procedure, from a table [25]. We then generate

$$X'_{n+1} = X_n + X_1$$

and write X_{n+1} = the fractional part of X'_{n+1}. That is, if $X'_{n+1} > 1$, we subtract 1 from it to obtain X_{n+1}; if it is less than 1, we set $X_{n+1} = X'_{n+1}$. We proceed in this way, generating $X'_{n+2} = X_{n+1} + X_2$ and retaining the fractional part.

In general,

$$X'_j = X_{j-1} + X_{j-n}$$
$$X_j = \text{fractional part of } X'_j$$

It has been shown that the length of this generator is k_n times 2^{p-1}, where p is the number of binary digits used in the computer's internal arithmetic and k_n is a constant which is a function of n. Values of k_n

---

† There are schemes for generating random numbers that do not produce pseudorandom numbers. For example, the low-order digits of a microsecond clock have been used to generate random numbers. Such numbers cannot be reproduced.

‡ For a definition and discussion of the normal distribution, see, for example, [21]. The normal distribution has two parameters: a location parameter—the mean—and a dispersion parameter—the standard deviation. It is closely clustered about its mean. For example, two-thirds of the numbers would be expected to be within the interval of mean minus one standard deviation to mean plus one standard deviation.

corresponding to $n = 2, 3, 4, \ldots, 16$ are:†

n	k_n	n	k_n	n	k_n
2	3	7	127	12	3,255
3	7	8	63	13	2,905
4	15	9	73	14	11,811
5	21	10	889	15	32,767
6	83	11	2,047	16	255

If we used $n = 15$ and if our computer retained 24 binary digits in its computations, we would estimate the length of this generator to be $32,767 \times 2^{23}$, or about 2.7×10^{13}, that is, 27 trillion. Statistical tests on the randomness of this procedure [18] have indicated that for $n < 6$ certain nonrandom patterns appear, that for $6 \leq n < 16$ this same nonrandomness is present but can be avoided by actually using every other number that is generated, and that for $n \geq 16$ the numbers so generated pass all the appropriate statistical tests for randomness.

A second procedure uses only the immediately preceding number to generate the next number; in general,

$$X'_j = CX_{j-1}$$

and X_j = fractional part of X'_j.

Now we need two numbers to start: the first number, X_1, and the special multiplying factor, C. Moshman [19] suggests using $C = 7^9, 7^{13}$, or 7^{17} when working with a decimal machine, and Greenberger [20] suggests using $C = 2^{18} + 3$ when working with a binary machine.

Clearly, the appropriateness of the procedure depends on C. The values recommended above have been tested. Any untested value for C would have to be verified by studying the properties of the sequence of numbers that are generated.

In many applications, we do not require random numbers uniformly distributed between 0 and 1 but need instead normally distributed numbers with mean 0 and variance 1. Almost all procedures for generating such numbers first generate uniformly distributed random numbers and then generate normally distributed numbers from these. Box and Muller [22], for example, have suggested generating a pair of random normal numbers, X_1 and X_2, from a pair of uniformly distributed random numbers, U_1 and U_2, by writing

$$X_1 = \sqrt{-2 \ln U_1} \cos (2\pi U_2)$$
$$X_2 = \sqrt{-2 \ln U_1} \sin (2\pi U_2)$$

† This table is reprinted from [26].

In comparing this method with several others in use at the time, Muller [23] concludes that it is best.   However, Marsaglia, MacLaren, and Bray [24] have since developed an even better procedure.   It is too complicated to be described in detail here—the interested reader should consult the basic reference.   We only note here that it uses uniformly distributed random numbers but has available three different procedures to generate the normally distributed number from the uniformly distributed number.   One of these three procedures—a very quick one to implement on a computer—is applied a little less than 95.8 percent of the time; a second one—somewhat slower but still quite fast—is applied a little less than 4.0 percent of the time; the third, very slow procedure is applied a little less than 0.3 percent of the time.   The computer determines which procedure to apply to generate the next number so as to produce a valid set of normally distributed numbers at extremely fast rates.   For example, 10,000 to 15,000 such numbers can be generated in a single second on an IBM 7090 computer.

8.6   LINEAR PROGRAMMING

Linear programming is a computational technique for finding the maximum or minimum of a linear function subject to certain specified linear inequalities.†   A complete understanding of the rigorous mathematical foundations of linear-programming techniques requires some knowledge of convex sets and matrix manipulations.   The actual computational procedure of linear programming is quite simple by comparison, although laborious.

Some examples of problems to which linear programming has been successfully applied are:

Optimum-input problem   Determining the optimum combination of inputs into a manufacturing process which will maximize profits.

Optimum-diet problem   Given that various foodstuffs contain certain vitamins in fixed but different proportions and given the minimum requirements of these vitamins, determining how this requirement can be met in the cheapest way in terms of shipping space or transportation costs.

Bid-evaluation problem   Determining which of a series of bids on a procurement action are minimum.

Resource-allocation problem   Determining the optimum allocation or use of limited resources to achieve some desired objective.

† Many good references on the subject exist; among them we note [27] and [28]. Despite the similarity of their names, linear programming and computer programming are not directly related.   The word "programming" has a different meaning in each case.

An artificial and simple example will illustrate the mathematical structure of the problem and will help in defining some of the commonly used terms.

Two qualified manufacturers, A and B, are available to satisfy a requirement for eight stoppers, five widgets, and seven gizmos. Manufacturer A produces one stopper, one widget, and two gizmos in each unit of his production and charges $2 for each unit. Manufacturer B, on the other hand, produces four stoppers, one widget, and one gizmo in each unit and charges $3 per unit. The problem is to decide how many units to order from A and how many to order from B in order to satisfy the needs at a minimum cost.

These requirements and restrictions are summarized in the following table:

	Stoppers	*Widgets*	*Gizmos*	*Cost* ($)
A's unit	1	1	2	2
B's unit	4	1	1	3
Requirements	8	5	7	Minimum

In mathematical terms: If X_1 denotes the number of units bought from A and X_2 denotes the number from B, then the cost of the purchase, in dollars, is $2X_1 + 3X_2$. This cost function, which is to be minimized, is called the *objective function*. In general, the function that is to be optimized (minimized or maximized) is called the *objective function*.

The needs must be satisfied; i.e., enough units must be ordered from A and B to provide *at least* eight stoppers, five widgets, and seven gizmos, although not necessarily *exactly* this many. It is possible that it would cost more to get exactly this many, and in most cases there is no objection to getting more items for less money. (There may be situations in which this does not apply—for example, in case very limited storage capacities are available.)

Reformulating these needs in terms of the variables, we get

Stoppers	*Widgets*	*Gizmos*
$X_1 + 4X_2 \geq 8$	$X_1 + X_2 \geq 5$	$2X_1 + X_2 \geq 7$

Also, since the manufacturer will not buy from us,

$$X_1 \geq 0 \qquad X_2 \geq 0$$

These restrictions on the choice of X_1 and X_2 are called *constraints*.†

† Strictly speaking, there is another restriction. X_1 and X_2 must be integers, since fractional orders will not be accepted. It happens, quite fortuitously, that the solution that will be obtained does result in integer values for X_1 and X_2. In general, however, if the solution must be integer-valued, we would call this *integer programming*, not linear programming. This subject is discussed in [29].

Note that both the objective function and the functions of the variables in the constraints are linear combinations of the variables; that is, they can be written in the form $A_1X_1 + A_2X_2 + \cdots + A_nX_n$. Thus the name "linear programming." (If we were dealing with quadratic functions of the variables, we would call this *quadratic programming*.)

The problem can now be restated as follows: Choose X_1 and X_2 so as to minimize the objective function $2X_1 + 3X_2$, subject to the constraints

$$X_1 \geq 0 \qquad X_1 + 4X_2 \geq 8 \qquad 2X_1 + X_2 \geq 7$$
$$X_2 \geq 0 \qquad X_1 + X_2 \geq 5$$

A geometric interpretation of the problem is helpful. In Fig. 8.1, we have shaded the region in the X_1,X_2 plane in which the constraints are satisfied. Any value of the variables in this region is called a *feasible solution*. In this case, any point in the shaded region is a feasible solution. The series of three parallel lines, each line corresponding to a fixed cost of our order, i.e., to a fixed constant value assigned to the objective function, indicate that as the cost increases from 0 through 5 and 10, we get closer and closer to the set of feasible solutions. It is clear that we shall intersect the set of feasible solutions first for some cost just a little more than 10. This first intersection will occur at a boundary and, because the boundaries are a sequence of lines, at a corner of the boundary.† In fact, the first intersection occurs at the corner $X_1 = 4$, $X_2 = 1$, which corresponds to a cost of 11, and it is the solution to the problem.

† If the line is parallel to a side of the polygon, the first intersection will involve the whole side, including the two end points which are corners.

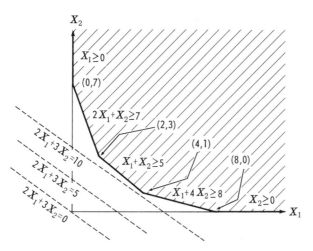

Fig. 8.1 Region of feasible solutions and the objective function.

The behavior of the solution in the above example is typical of what happens when dealing with linear constraints and linear objective functions. It can be shown† that a linear function will always assume its maximum or minimum at a corner of the boundary defining the region of feasible solutions. Of course, it may be that it assumes a minimum there but not a maximum, so that we are not assured that the kind of optimization we seek actually occurs. In this case, a reformulation of the problem may be necessary.

The first numerical procedure for solving linear-programming problems was the simplex method [30], and it is still widely used today.‡

In a practical problem, the number of variables may be in the order of 50 to 100 and the number of constraints may be in the order of 20 to 50. The size of these problems dictates that an electronic digital computer be used in their solution, and many programs have been written for solving problems in linear programming on electronic digital computers. Reference [32] contains an excellent practical discussion, including the underlying methodology, flow charts for an algorithm, and estimates of the running time on an electronic computer. The estimate is

$$3n\{[(9m + 1)(n + 4m + 3) + 3m + 2]\mu + (m + 1)(n + 7m + 6)\alpha\}$$

where n = number of variables

m = number of constraints

μ = unit multiplication/division time of the computer

α = unit addition time of the computer

This means, for example, that for a problem with 50 variables and 20 constraints, it is estimated that about 170,000 multiplications or divisions and 250,000 additions would be required to obtain a solution.

REFERENCES

1. Metcalf, Z. P.: The Construction of Keys, *Systematic Zool.*, vol. 3, pp. 38–45, 1954.
2. Cowan, S. T., and K. J. Steel: A Device for the Identification of Microorganisms, *Lancet*, pp. 1172–1173, 1960.
3. Sokal, R. R., and P. H. A. Sneath: "Principles of Numerical Taxonomy," W. H. Freeman and Company, San Francisco, 1963.
4. Colwell, R. R., and J. Liston: Taxonomic Analysis with the Electronic Computer of Some Xanthomonas and Pseudomonas Species, *J. Bacteriol.*, vol. 82, pp. 913–919, 1961.

† For a proof, see, for example, theorem 19 on page 55 of [28].
‡ A discussion of this method is beyond the scope of this text. Underlying the method is the Gauss-Jordan elimination procedure for solving systems of linear equations. (For a general discussion of elimination procedures, see [8] or [31].) A good elementary discussion of the method can be found on pages 58 to 80 of [28].

5. Rohlf, E. J., and R. R. Sokal: The Description of Taxonomic Relationships by Factor Analysis, *Systematic Zool.*, vol. 11, pp. 1–16, 1962.
6. Sneath, P. H. A., and S. T. Cowan: An Electro-taxonomic Survey of Bacteria, *J. Gen. Microbiol.*, vol. 19, pp. 551–565, 1958.
7. Ralston, A.: "A First Course in Numerical Analysis," McGraw-Hill Book Company, New York, 1965.
8. Hunter, W. G., and G. E. P. Box: The Experimental Study of Physical Mechanisms, *Technometrics*, vol. 7, pp. 23–42, 1965.
9. Cox, D. R.: Tests of Separate Families of Hypotheses, *Proc. 4th Berkeley Symp.*, vol. 1, pp. 105–123.
10. Schoenberg, I. J.: Spline Interpolation and Best Quadrature Formulae, *Bull. Am. Math. Soc.*, vol. 70, pp. 143–148, 1964.
11. Greville, T. N. E.: Numerical Procedures for Interpolation by Spline Functions, *J. Soc. Ind. Appl. Math.*, ser. B, vol. 1, pp. 53–68, 1964.
12. *Ibid.*: Spline Functions, Interpolation and Numerical Quadrature, in A. Ralston and H. S. Wilf (eds.), "Mathematical Methods for Digital Computers," vol. 2, pp. 156–168, John Wiley & Sons, Inc., New York, 1967.
13. Collen, M. F.: Machine Diagnosis for a Multiphasic Screening Program, *Proc. 5th IBM Med. Symp.*, pp. 129–145, 1963.
14. Overall, J. E., and C. M. Williams: A Computer Procedure for the Diagnosis of Thyroid Functioning, in K. Enslein (ed.), "Data Acquisition and Processing in Biology and Medicine," vol. 2, pp. 261–276, Pergamon Press, New York, 1964.
15. Warner, H. R., A. F. Toronto, L. G. Veasy, and R. A. Stephenson: Mathematical Approach to Medical Diagnosis, *J. AMA*, vol. 177, pp. 75–81, 1961.
16. Ledley, R. S., and L. B. Lusted: Reasoning Foundations of Medical Diagnosis, *Science*, vol. 130, pp. 9–21, July 3, 1959.
17. Ledley, R. S.: "Programming and Utilizing Digital Computers," pp. 334–348, McGraw-Hill Book Company, New York, 1962.
18. Green, B. F., Jr., J. E. K. Smith, and L. Klem: Empirical Tests of an Additive Random Number Generator, *J. ACM*, vol. 4, pp. 527–537, 1959.
19. Moshman, J.: The Generation of Pseudorandom Numbers in a Decimal Calculator, *Oak Ridge Natl. Lab. Rept.* ORNL-1532, June, 1953.
20. Greenberger, M.: Random Number Generation, in G. H. Orcutt, M. Greenberger, J. Korbel, and A. M. Rivlin, "Microanalysis of Socio-economic Systems: A Simulation Study," Harper & Row, Publishers, Incorporated, New York, 1961.

21. Cramer, H.: "The Elements of Probability Theory and Its Applications," pp. 108–120, John Wiley & Sons, Inc., New York, 1955.
22. Box, G. E. P., and M. E. Muller: A Note on the Generation of Normal Deviates, *Ann. Math. Statistics*, vol. 28, pp. 610–611, 1958.
23. Muller, M. E.: A Comparison of Methods for Generating Normal Deviates on a Digital Computer, *J. ACM*, vol. 6, pp. 376–383, July, 1959.
24. Marsaglia, G., M. D. MacLaren, and T. A. Bray: A Fast Procedure for Generating Normal Random Variables, *Boeing Sci. Res. Lab. Rept.* 01-82-0219, August, 1962.
25. RAND Corporation, "A Million Random Digits with 100,000 Normal Deviates," The Free Press of Glencoe, New York, 1955.
26. Green, B. F., Jr.: "Digital Computers in Research, An Introduction for Behavioral and Social Scientists," McGraw-Hill Book Company, New York, 1963.
27. Charnes, A., and W. W. Cooper: "Management Models and Industrial Applications of Linear Programming," vols. 1 and 2, John Wiley & Sons, Inc., New York, 1961.
28. Glicksman, A. M.: "An Introduction to Linear Programming and the Theory of Games," John Wiley & Sons, Inc., New York, 1963.
29. Gale, D.: "The Theory of Linear Economic Models," chap. 5, McGraw-Hill Book Company, New York, 1960.
30. Dantzig, G. B.: A Proof of the Equivalence of the Programming Problem and the Game Problem, in T. C. Koopmans (ed.), "Activity Analysis of Production and Allocation," Cowles Commission Monograph no. 13, John Wiley & Sons, Inc., New York, 1951.
31. Ralston, A.: "A First Course in Numerical Analysis," chap. 9, McGraw-Hill Book Company, New York, 1965.
32. Ralston, A., and H. S. Wilf (eds.): "Mathematical Methods for Digital Computers," vol. I, chap. 25, John Wiley & Sons, Inc., New York, 1960.

ANNOTATED SUPPLEMENTARY BIBLIOGRAPHY

A bibliography of computer applications in the sciences would necessarily require hundreds or even thousands of entries. For this reason, a bibliographic reference which is itself a bibliography is listed first. The other references were chosen to present a representative sample of scientific applications in physics, chemistry, astronomy, engineering, the social sciences, and statistics.

1. Youden, W. W.: Computer Literature Bibliography, 1946–1963, *Natl. Bur. Std. Misc. Publ.* 266, March 31, 1965. A comprehensive

bibliography of computer-related articles that could be the first citation in every Annotated Supplementary Bibliography in this book.

2. Freiberger, W. F. (ed.): "Applications of Digital Computers," Ginn and Company, Boston, 1963. Includes a description of applications in artificial intelligence, law, business, fluid mechanics, mathematics, medicine, physics, and statistics. This book should also be considered in connection with both of the next two chapters.

3. Swan, P.: Computational Problems in Theoretical Physics, *Proc. Australian Computer Conf.*, paper B3.2, 1960.

4. Fletcher, R., and C. M. Reeves: An Application of the Monte Carlo Method to the Evaluation of Some Molecular Integrals, *Computer J.*, vol. 6, issue 3, pp. 277–286, 1963.

5. Waldo, W. H., and M. Debacker: Printing Chemical Structures Electro-mechanically, Encoded Compounds Searched Generically with the IBM 702, *Proc. Intern. Conf. Sci. Inform.*, pp. 711–730, 1958.

6. Lipscomb, W. N.: Computing Problems in X-ray Crystallography, *Proc. Harvard Univ. Symp.*, pp. 103–109, 1961.

7. Pearcey, T.: Data Processing in Pure Research with Particular Reference to Radio Astronomy, *Proc. Australian Computer Conf.*, vol. 1, paper 105, 1957.

8. Titener, A. A.: Some Computer Applications to Ship Design Calculations, *Proc. Can. Conf. Computing Data Process.*, pp. 138–157, 1960.

9. Katz, D. L., B. Carnahan, E. I. Organick, and S. O. Navarro: Computers in Engineering Education, 1960–1964, *Proc. Natl. Meetings ACM*, paper 22, 1962.

10. Green, B. F., Jr.: "Digital Computers in Research, An Introduction for Behavioral and Social Scientists," McGraw-Hill Book Company, New York, 1963. Part 3, pages 140 to 274, of this book contains a comprehensive discussion of behavioral-science applications up to 1963. Some of these are really applications in the area of artificial intelligence.

11. Philip, H. W. W.: The Use of Automatic Machines in Social Science, *Proc. Australian Computer Conf.*, paper A7.2, 1960.

12. Meyer, J. R.: Computers in Economics, *Proc. Harvard Univ. Symp.*, pp. 252–261, 1961.

13. Maisel, H.: Best k of $2k-1$ Comparisons, *J. Am. Statistical Assoc.*, vol. 61, no. 314, pp. 329–344, June, 1966. The computer is used as an aid in the planning of statistical tests.

chapter 9

APPLICATIONS IN BUSINESS AND MANAGEMENT

9.1 INTRODUCTION

The electronic digital computer has become an integral part of most large-size business enterprises. Record keeping has been relegated to the computer, and accounts are now stored on magnetic tapes and disks rather than in filing cabinets. Further, the nature of the function of record keeping is changing from routine work to a management information system. This system generates summary reports to management on the status of the different departments, reviews the effects of policy changes, provides measures of productivity, and assists in market research. As it becomes more and more sophisticated, it can assist in analyzing the effects of future policy changes and can provide condensed predictions of the company's market position. Such questions as "What are the probable consequences of a price decrease on the part of my principal competitor?" and "What can I expect to happen if Company B makes a strong pitch for the market in area A?" can be answered with the aid of these systems.

Three specific applications of computers in business and management will be discussed in this chapter: (1) a management and operating

information system for hospitals, (2) the operations of a national wholesale supplier of equipment parts, and (3) the simulation of a Social
Security district office. In addition, the chapter contains a general discussion of simulation, intended to introduce this important area of computer application. Many books have been written that deal almost
entirely with the application of computers in business; among the best of
these are [1 and 2].

9.2 HOSPITAL INFORMATION SYSTEMS

Hospitals, like businesses, are complex, and constant attention to a series
of important details is required. But because a hospital operates around
the clock and because errors may be fatal, the computer may serve a
vital time- and life-saving function in a hospital.

A *hospital information system* will often consist of a whole series of
files and computer programs to process these files. A typical system
might include, among others, the following files:

1. Scheduled-admissions file.
2. Current-patient file.
3. Former-patient file.
4. Hospital-space inventory file.
5. Medical-staff file.
6. Nursing-staff file.
7. Other professional-staff file.
8. Nonprofessional-staff file.
9. Pharmaceuticals file.
10. Laboratories file.
11. A file that contains the names of all the other files. This file is a
    part of a special program that controls the manipulation of all the
    other files.

The computer programs that might be included are:

1. Patient billing program
2. Payroll program
3. Laboratory scheduling and reports program
4. Surgical scheduling and reports program
5. Pharmaceuticals prescription and administration program
6. Admissions program
7. The special controlling program

Before discussing these files and programs further, it is appropriate to consider the equipment setup. At a university hospital, the computer might be a very large one that is shared by the medical school and other schools in the university. The computer might also be a large one located at one hospital and servicing several other hospitals. Finally, it might be a medium-sized computer dedicated to serving only the hospital information system at this one hospital. A typical system will include small-scale computer input/output stations, located away from the computer at nurses' stations, in the admissions office, in the pharmacy, in the dietician's office, and in the laboratories. These stations might contain Teletypewriter terminals or special keyboards or even card readers. (Remote terminals were discussed in Sec. 4.5.) In addition, administrative personnel might have special cathode-ray-tube inquiry terminals permitting them to obtain summary data on various aspects of the hospital functions. Extensive computer output equipment in the computer center itself could generate payroll checks, special reports for research use, space inventories, and similar large-scale outputs.

Two typical problems—patient admissions and the prescription of drugs—may suggest how a hospital information system functions. First, consider a patient appearing in the admissions office for a previously scheduled surgical procedure. The surgeon has already entered into the scheduled-admissions file such things as the nature of the surgery and the time for which it is scheduled, identification of the patient and the physician, and special considerations such as whether or not the patient is a diabetic or has special allergies. On arriving at the hospital, the patient fills out a standard admissions form with identification and billing information, information on previous admissions, medical history, special diet for personal or religious reasons, and so on. This information is immediately entered into the computer network, calling up the scheduled-admissions file and the former-patients file for verification of the information. Any discrepancy would be immediately detected. Next the admissions program calls up the space inventory file, assigns a bed to the patient, updates the space file to account for this new occupancy, and reports the result. Then it initiates a new record in the patient's file and reports the admission to the appropriate nurses' station. Finally, the admissions program calls up the surgical scheduling program to enter information regarding the surgery in the current-patients file and the space inventory file. Reminders will be issued to the medical and nursing staff at appropriate times, and the availability of the surgical facility at the scheduled time for surgery will be ensured.

The second problem concerns a doctor's prescription of a drug for a patient. The doctor prepares the order in the usual way, but the nurse enters the order on a typewriterlike entry board. Before being released, the order is typed back for verification. The "pharmaceuticals prescription and administration" program screens the order to be sure a lethal dose is not being requested and then calls in information from the patient's file to be sure that the order does not grossly violate standard practices. If it does, a message to the nurse temporarily rejects the order and cites the reasons for rejection. The nurse then checks with the physician and, on his orders, overrides the rejection. The pharmaceutical program then makes entries in the pharmaceuticals file, so that the pharmacy is given a prescription, the nurses are reminded to administer the drug according to the prescribed schedule, and a message is sent to the nurses to cease administering the drug at the appropriate time. The nurses, in turn, make an appropriate entry at their station after each administration of the drug, and the patient's file is modified to include information on the drugs administered.

Let us review these two uses of a hospital information system with the aid of Figs. 9.1 and 9.2. Referring first to Fig. 9.1, the physician (1) requests the scheduled admission of a patient for a surgical procedure. The patient appears at the admissions office (2), fills out an admissions

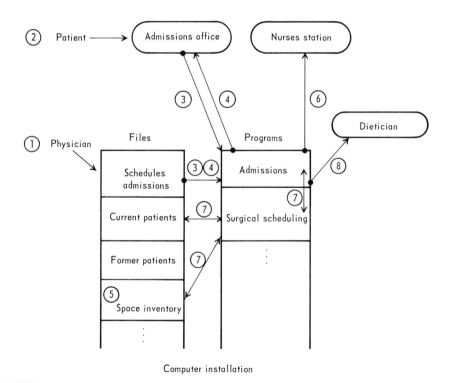

Computer installation

Fig. 9.1 Schematic flow of information in an admission problem.

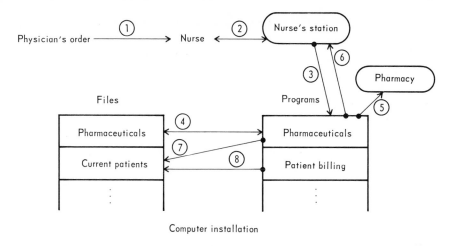

Fig. 9.2 Schematic flow of information in a pharmaceutical problem.

form (3), which is reviewed by the program for exceptions (4). After appropriate corrections are made, the space inventory file (5) is used to assign space to the patient, which is reported to the appropriate nurses' station (6). Surgical scheduling and appropriate space assignments are completed (7), and special messages are generated. For example, the dietician might be sent a message (8) to the effect that this patient must be put on a salt-free diet.

Proceeding to Fig. 9.2, the physician orders the administration of certain drugs to a specified patient (1). The nurse enters this information and verifies it at her keyboard (2) before passing it to the computer (3). The pharmaceuticals program first verifies that the order is neither lethal nor extraordinary (4). It then transmits the prescription to the pharmacy (5), sends messages to the nurses to administer the medicine at the appropriate times (6), and makes entries in the patient's file to reflect administration of the drug (7). Entries are also made in the patient's billing section of the patient's file for the cost of the pharmaceuticals (8).

9.3 NATIONAL PARTS WHOLESALER

Let us next consider a nationwide supplier of equipment parts or similar supplies. Since this application will be discussed hypothetically and is not modeled after an existing system, we shall construct an artificial company with the following characteristics:

1. The company's customers and suppliers are scattered throughout the continental United States.

2. The inventory of the company's merchandise includes thousands of items that vary greatly in price and size.

3. The company uses an elaborate computer-communication system to carry out its operations.

Figure 9.3 presents a schematic summary of the company's operations.

A customer, from his office anywhere in the country, places an order, which is fed directly into the customer-service program (1). The customer-service program then calls in the files it needs to service the order (2), reviews the credit status of the customer, and if it is satisfactory, selects a warehouse to ship the order to the customer. It then calls in the order and shipping program to place the order to ship with the warehouse (3). The order is verified, and the warehouse makes the shipment (4). Information regarding the shipment is sent to the com-

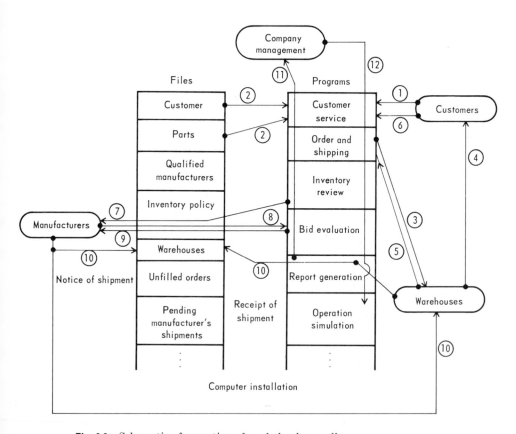

Fig. 9.3 Schematic of operation of a wholesale supplier.

puter (5), and when the order arrives, the customer acknowledges receipt (6).

As an integral part of the operation, the customer files and warehouse files are revised to permit billing and to adjust warehouse inventory. Immediately after the inventory is adjusted, the computer determines whether this shipment depleted the inventory sufficiently to set in motion a reorder mechanism. A field in each record of the parts file will contain the standard reorder quantity, and another field will contain the critical inventory level. Let us assume a critical inventory level was reached. The inventory-review program determines that more supplies are needed and, by using the qualified-manufacturers file and the standard reorder quantity, transmits an invitation to bid to the appropriate manufacturers (7). The bids are then submitted (8) to the bid-evaluation program. This program, perhaps using linear-programming methods, evaluates the bids and chooses the suitable manufacturer or combination of manufacturers. The award is then made (9), and the manufacturer ships the supplies directly to the warehouse (10) and bills the company. Management receives regular and special reports on such things as inventory and customer status and outstanding invitations to bid via terminals that may be located in their offices (11).

Potential policy changes might be transmitted to an operation-simulation program (12), which would substitute these changes in the existing policy and, perhaps using actual operational experience in the past six months or anticipated experience in the next six months, predict the effects of these changes on the company's operations. This prediction would be reported to management, who could then decide which, if any, of these changes it wished to put into effect.

Automation of a business operation is complex and expensive. About half a million dollars would have to be invested in terminal equipment alone if, in the above, we were servicing 100 customers using 10 warehouses. Also, the computer programs might—in total—involve as many as a half million instructions, and though computers are virtually error-free, programmers are not.

9.4 SIMULATION—GENERAL CONSIDERATIONS

Simulation was defined in Sec. 7.7. That definition, slightly revised, is repeated here. Simulation is a numerical technique for conducting experiments on a digital computer involving certain types of mathematical and logical models that describe the behavior of a business, economic, social, biological, physical, or chemical system (or some component thereof) over extended periods of real time.

Much of the efforts of physical and life scientists are devoted to developing mathematical models of natural processes, and some of these models have been subjected to numerical experimentation. Simulation is most widely used, however, in the social and behavioral sciences and in business. This is because the activities in these areas cannot be modeled using strictly determined, unvarying relations. Though some underlying relations may be present, substantial deviations from these relations can be expected to appear in individual results. For example, the orbit of a planet can be predicted quite precisely using an explicit mathematical relation; however, the sales of a firm cannot. Even if management makes no changes in the policies of the firm, fluctuations in the economy, changes in the buying habits of the firm's customers, and many other factors make it impossible to predict sales precisely. This is not to say that a good prediction cannot be made. But it is always just a guess, and a difference between the actual sales and the predicted sales can be expected. It is important to know how great this difference can be. Simulation permits experimental studies of the firm that provide for the natural fluctuation in sales. Estimates of the differences associated with the prediction can be made. Random numbers (discussed in Sec. 8.5) are ordinarily used to introduce the natural fluctuations.

Up to now, we have said nothing about computers and their place in simulation. One can simulate without using any mechanical or electronic aids. Certain simple manual war games or business games are examples of such simulations; more complex games might require mechanical computational assistance. However, once the simulation attempts either to realistically reflect subtle, complex interrelationships or to consider many factors in the model or to deal with a large number of basic units individually, the number of calculations and the extent of record keeping become enormous and an electronic computer is needed.

There are at least five major steps in developing a simulation. These are:

1. Defining the problem
2. Gathering and analyzing the pertinent data
3. Constructing the models
4. Writing and debugging the computer programs
5. Testing and applying the simulation

The definition of the problem should include the preparation of an extensive list of questions that the simulation would be called upon to help answer. Simulations of business enterprises are management tools, and management should be asked: "Suppose you had this tool today, how would you use it?" and "What questions would you try to answer, using this tool, over the next two to three and four or more years?" Responses should be forced, if necessary, and should be as detailed as possible. This step is too often ignored, or inadequately pursued, with disastrous consequences. Management is often disillusioned because the final result is not what they expected and much of the work has to be redone.

Lists of the activities and events to be simulated and a list of the parameters—the variables—to be used in the simulation should result from this definition stage. The list of activities and events might be in the form of a set of diagrams of the process being simulated that includes the connections among the events and activities and some rough estimates of the time between events and the duration of the activities. (An example of one such diagram will be given in the next section in connection with the discussion of the simulation of Social Security district offices.)

The list of parameters is very important. A simulation cannot retain all the features of the process. The analyst always adopts a point of view—sometimes deliberately, sometimes inadvertently. This point of view determines the features to be included, and the list of parameters implements this choice.

All parameters must be listed and defined. The definitions should include specifications for the units to be used. The relationships among the parameters should be given as far as possible, not in terms of specific mathematical functions but rather in terms of which parameters are related to which other parameters.

The second phase of the development of the simulation, gathering and analyzing pertinent data, should not even be designed until after the first phase is completed.† There are at least three sources for pertinent data:

1. Historical records
2. Expert opinion
3. Field studies

Historical records may be useful if the process is changing very slowly or if recent or current records are available. Many historical records are really reports to management. Since the person preparing the record wishes to present the best possible picture, it may be neces-

† However, a pilot data-gathering project might be conducted during the first phase in order to determine what difficulties might be encountered in this kind of enterprise and to acclimate both field and study personnel to data-gathering techniques. This pilot project should be very brief, and it should not be expected that definitive data will be obtained in it.

sary to edit these records carefully before using them. In some cases, the picture may be so distorted that the records are useless.

Expert opinion should not be ignored as a source for data. Subject-matter specialists should be a part of the team developing the simulation. They can frequently provide estimates of the values taken on by some of the parameters and can certainly be helpful in checking historical records and in setting up field studies.

Field studies are the most expensive source for data. They should be undertaken only to fill in the gaps left after the other sources have been exhausted. In order to be most effective at a minimum cost, they must be carefully designed. During the planning of field studies:

1. Representative, approachable field activities should be selected.
2. Specific sites and dates should be decided on.
3. Data-gathering personnel should be selected and trained (these people will actually conduct the field study).
4. Special forms for recording data should be designed and printed, and equipment to be used in the field study should be purchased.

The choice of the units to be studied and the dates of the study should take into account the need to estimate the effects of seasonal factors, account for regional and local idiosyncrasies, and estimate the "observer effect." (Working patterns change when people know that they are being observed. If it is possible to do so, some measurements should be made without these people knowing that they are being observed. If that is not possible or is considered unethical, historical information may prove helpful. An example illustrating how this might be done will be given in the next section.)

If a field study is well designed, the gathering of the data itself should go smoothly. If it is poorly planned, the gathering of the data may encounter some serious obstacles. For example, poorly designed forms may be filled out erroneously, and poorly trained study representatives may confuse the field personnel.

The data gathered in this phase of the study must be thoroughly analyzed. This should include not only the usual reduction of the data to obtain means and standard deviations but also special statistical analyses to do such things as determine the underlying nature of the distributions of the parameters and to fit functions relating the parameters. Frequently, the analysis will reveal gaps in the data that will require some additional data-gathering activities.

The third phase is the construction of models of the process. Actually, the models are being built during the first two phases as well. However, now is the time to be specific and unambiguous. Now is the time to reduce these models to algorithms that can obtain outputs for the process under study given the inputs to this process. Since the models will be implemented in the form of a computer program, the programmer should join the simulation team. From this point forward, the team will include computer programmers and subject-matter specialists as well as operations analysts. The analyst is the mediator between the subject-matter specialist and the computer programmer. He will determine which compromises in the needs of the subject-matter specialist must be made in order to accommodate the restrictions imposed by the programmer.

A set of test data (of the kind discussed in Sec. 5.7) should be constructed concurrently with the development of the algorithms. Computer programming will overlap the development of the models, and the third and fourth phases may be indistinguishable. The last phase, the testing and application of the simulation, should be begun only after the programmer has debugged his programs. The special test set is then run, and after further corrections have been made, other subject-matter specialists and management might be called in for a demonstration of the simulation. If the simulation is a good one, the applications will follow soon thereafter.

The development of computer simulations is often an expensive and time-consuming process. For example, a simulation of land combat (see Ref. 8 in the Annotated Supplementary Bibliography) required for its development about a hundred man-years of effort and 3,000 hours of time on an IBM 7090 computer over a period of $2\frac{1}{2}$ years. The district-office simulation, discussed in the next section, required about twenty-five man-years of effort and several hundred hours of time in all on an IBM 360/65 and GE 245 and 265 computers before its development was completed—about three years after it began.

Several good references on computer simulation techniques are available. Two of them are [5 and 6] in Chap. 7. A third is Chorafas' book [3], which contains a discussion of case histories as well as the mathematical background and some general introductory material. However, statistical methodology and random-number generation are not so well covered in Chorafas' book as in [6] in Chap. 7. Reference 8 in the Annotated Supplementary Bibliography at the conclusion of this chapter contains a description of a simulation of land combat. A description of the simulation of a Social Security district office is given in the next section.

9.5 SIMULATION OF THE OPERATIONS OF A SOCIAL SECURITY DISTRICT OFFICE

The Social Security Administration has several hundred district offices scattered throughout the United States and Puerto Rico. These offices are the principal contact points with the public. Social security account numbers are assigned there, claims are filed, and questions are answered. The efficient and effective operation of these offices is essential to the functioning of the Social Security Administration.

The Bureau of District Office Operations and the Operations Research Staff in the headquarters of the Social Security Administration began a joint study of district-office operations in 1966. A report summarizing the results of the first year's efforts is listed as Ref. [6]. This study was intended to provide a simulation of district-office operations.

District offices come in a variety of sizes and shapes. The largest ones, called *class-A offices*, are located in metropolitan centers. The smallest, called *class-E offices*, are located in rural or small urban areas. Intermediate-size offices—classes B, C, and D, from largest to smallest—can be found in a wide variety of locations. Much of the work of some of the smaller offices is carried out in the field rather than in the office. Contact stations are established in post offices and similar central locations in small communities throughout the area serviced by the district office. These stations are staffed once or twice a week by special district-office employees called *field representatives* or by other employees called *claims representatives*. These field activities were deliberately omitted from the study; the scope of the simulation was limited to the activities in the district office itself. However, studies of the functioning of district offices indicated that the ratio of the number of claims taken in the field to the total number of claims processed may be an important variable in characterizing the activities of the office.

The simulation was developed in accordance with the approach outlined in Sec. 9.4. Management, which in this case includes district-office managers as well as key personnel in the regional† and headquarters offices, were asked how they would use the simulation. Activities of several typical district offices were flow-charted, and lists of activities and parameters were prepared.

A layout of a typical class-C or class-D district office is given in Fig. 9.4, along with a mapping of the path a visitor might follow through the office and a description of the processing of the claim he might submit. There are several categories of employees in the office. These include the manager (M in Fig. 9.4), assistant manager (AM) and administrative clerk (AC), claims representatives (CR), field representa-

---

† Line supervision of district offices is provided by 11 regional offices. The staff in a regional office establish policies for and directly supervise all the district offices in their region. Sitting at the top is the Bureau of District Offices Operations in the headquarters of the Administration, which is responsible for the overall supervision of the district offices.

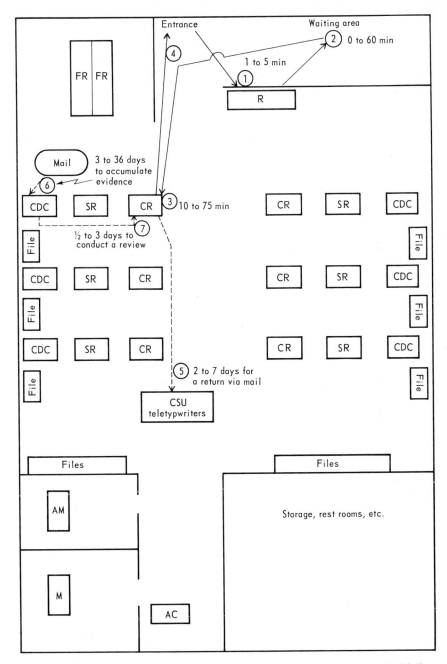

Fig. 9.4 A floor plan of a district office showing the flow of activities. Solid lines indicate the movements of the claimant, and dotted lines the movements of the claim. The scale is approximately 1 in. = 10 ft.

tives (FR), service representatives (SR), claims-development clerical personnel (CDC), receptionists (R), and clearance-service clericals who work in the clearance-service unit (CSU).

The manager and assistant manager share the supervisory and policy-making activities of the office. In addition, they frequently make public appearances in order to more effectively present the social security program. Field representatives also make public appearances from time to time. The administrative clerk helps the manager and assistant manager in carrying out the administrative details associated with their activities. The scope of the simulation did not include these management activities. However, management does help in processing claims from time to time, and these activities were included in the simulation.

Claims representatives and field representatives are responsible for taking and developing a claim, the former in the district office and the latter in the field. However, field representatives also have desks in the district office and occasionally assist the claims representative by conducting interviews or reviewing evidence in the district office. Claims taken in the field are developed in the district office. The service representatives and claims-development clerical personnel also assist the claims representative. Service representatives handle telephone contacts, answer questions about the status of claims or changes and delays in benefits, and evaluate routine evidence. Claims-development clerical personnel gather the evidence, preparing routine requests for additional material, and forward it to the claims representative for evaluation.

The receptionist is the first person contacted by a visitor to the office. In most offices, she will issue account numbers and answer simple questions but will refer a visitor to a claims representative or service representative for interviews regarding the submission of a claim, the development of a previously submitted claim, or delays or changes in benefit checks. The clearance-service unit prepares requests for earnings reports, which are transmitted via Teletype to the headquarters of the Social Security Administration. The earnings records are maintained in magnetic-tape files and are processed by a computer. The district-office Teletypes are connected to headquarters, which records requests for earnings reports directly on magnetic tapes. These tapes are then removed from the recording device and mounted directly on tape drives in the computer center where they are processed.

In many offices, much of the work is carried out over the telephone. These activities were included in the scope of the study. Service representatives are frequently assigned to handling telephone inquiries.

Returning to Fig. 9.4, on entering the office a visitor speaks to the receptionist (1), who determines the purpose of the visit. If the receptionist cannot satisfy the visitor, she determines whom he should see and, if that person is busy, asks the visitor to wait (2). Let us assume that the visitor wishes to submit a claim. He is interviewed by a claims representative (3) and leaves the office (4).

Now we turn our attention to his claim; the visitor has become a claimant. A record of the claimant's earnings is requested via the Teletypewriter at the clearance-service unit (5). The earnings report is mailed to the district office and entered in the folder established for the claim by the corresponding† claims-development clerical employee (6). When sufficient evidence has accumulated, the clerical employee turns the whole file over to the claims representative for evaluation (7). This frequently results in further correspondence among the claimant, the district office, and headquarters. The new incoming mail is entered in the appropriate file (6), and the file is again forwarded to the claims representative for evaluation (7). This process [steps (6) and (7)] may be repeated several times if the claims representative is not satisfied with the evidence that has been submitted.

Note that solid lines have been used to indicate the path of the visitor and dotted lines the path of the claim. The range of times required in visitor stations (1) to (3) has been entered. The range of times required to carry out the processing of the claim associated with steps (5) to (7) has also been entered. For example, it takes from 2 to 7 days to get a response from headquarters to the request for an earnings report [this is noted at step (5)] and from 3 to 36 days to accumulate the evidence associated with a claim.

Historical sources for data were limited to periodic reports to management on district-office operations. These reports either were not sufficiently detailed or were prepared with other objectives in mind and could not be used by themselves as the source for the data required for the simulation. Expert opinion was also of limited use, and it was concluded that a field study would be necessary. Forty-four district offices were studied in the summer and fall of 1967. The 44 offices were 1 in each of the 11 regions in each of the 4 largest classes. Members of the study team were trained in the late spring and summer of 1967. An

---

† Claims representatives, service representatives, and claims-development clerical personnel are often organized into teams. This is the case in the office described in Fig. 9.4. Ordinarily, a single team handles a claim from submission through development and evaluation. It is not passed from one team to another. Account numbers or the first letter of the claimant's surname are used to guide the receptionist in assigning initial interviews to a claims representative's team. Another approach is to maintain separate pools of claims representatives and claims-development clerical employees. The service representatives and claims-development clerical employees do the work as it comes to them regardless of which claims representative took the claim or whether they have worked on this claim before.

instructional booklet was prepared in July, 1967 [4] and revised, after the first series of studies, in August [5]. Extensive analyses of the results of the study were made. Many of these statistical calculations were carried out via a Teletypewriter terminal located in the offices of the Operations Research Staff and linked to a GE 245 computer.

The development of the models was a team effort involving subject-matter specialists from regional and district offices and the Bureau of District Office Operations, mathematicians, operations analysts from the Operations Research Staff, and computer programmers from the Bureau of Data Processing and Accounts in the headquarters of the Administration. The programs were written using the second version of the GPSS language discussed in Sec. 7.7. Most of the computer runs were made on an IBM 360/65 computer in the headquarters of the Administration.

The input to the simulation was mainly a list of values to be assigned to variables. Other inputs included such things as labels and titles for the tables that were to be a part of the output. The values that were input served to characterize the work load in the district office and the way this work load is processed. For example, the total number of visitors per day might be input. This is one way to help characterize the work load. An example of an input that helps characterize the way the work load is processed is a series of numbers that describe the priorities established for answering the telephone. In some offices, claims representatives will interrupt an interview in order to answer the phone; in other offices, they will not. In some offices, the first responsibility of service representatives is to answer the phone; in other offices, some of their other duties have a higher priority. In some offices, a receptionist usually answers the phone and routes the call to another employee if it is not a routine inquiry that she can handle. In other offices, a receptionist almost always answers the phone and makes no attempt to respond to the caller. She routes all calls to other employees. In still other offices, the receptionist answers the phone only if no other employee can answer it. In this case, claims representatives or claims-development clerical employees are responsible for answering the phone. These priorities were coded in terms of a series of 0s and 1s, that is, bits. For example, the third bit in the sequence might specify whether or not the claims representative interrupts an interview in order to answer the phone. If the third bit is a 1, he will interrupt; if it is 0, he will not. The program, that is, the simulation, was able to appropriately interpret this sequence of bits.

The output of the simulation was mainly given in a series of tables that summarized the activities of the district office. For example, a table was obtained that listed each employee and the number of minutes he spent on each of a prescribed set of activities. The set of activities was prescribed as a part of the input.   A second table gave a complete list of the length of time each visitor to the office spent waiting to be interviewed.   There were actually two such tables, one listing the waiting periods before speaking to a receptionist and the other the waiting periods before speaking to a claims representative.   Statistical summaries of these waiting periods were also tabulated.   Another table listed the claims submitted, the time required to complete various stages in the processing of a claim, and statistics summarizing these times.   All told, more than 20 tables were prepared and printed on the computer.

The simulation counted time in the district office in units of a minute. However, a long period of activity in the district office could be simulated in a short time on the computer.   For example, in one early application, a week's activities, about 2,500 minutes of activity, of a district office like that depicted in Fig. 9.4 were simulated in 15 minutes on an IBM 360/65 computer.

The discussion of this simulation will conclude with some comments on the way in which provision was made for correcting for the "observer effect" and other biases in the field studies.   Each district office was actually studied in a one-week, Thursday-to-Wednesday, period.   The district offices make weekly summary reports of their activities that cover this same Thursday-to-Wednesday period.   Reports for the preceding week, the study week, and the succeeding week in the office being studied and for the same three weeks in a similar office in the same region were used.   Systematic differences between offices or between weeks were used to adjust the study results.   That is, data in the summary reports were used to obtain adjustment factors that were applied to the study measurements.   (The variables being measured in the study were not included in the summary report.   Only gross data on the number of cases processed were reported.   Statistics on such things as waiting times and interview times were not reported.)

REFERENCES

1.   Hein, L. W.: "An Introduction to Electronic Data Processing for Business," D. Van Nostrand Company, Inc., Princeton, N.J., 1961.
2.   *Proceedings of the Australian Computer Conferences*, 1957, 1960, 1963. This is a triennial publication.   All proceedings contain at least one discussion of applications of computers to problems in business and management.
3.   Chorafas, D. N.: "Systems and Simulation," Academic Press Inc., New York, 1965.
4.   "District Office Study Representative Instructions," July 3, 1967. Available from the Bureau of District Office Operations, Headquarters Social Security Administration, Baltimore, Maryland.

5. "District Office Data Collection Instruction Booklet," Aug. 4, 1967. Available from the Bureau of District Office Operations, Headquarters Social Security Administration, Baltimore, Maryland.
6. Computer Simulation of the Queuing Characteristics of the Social Security Administration's Claims Process, *Rept.* ORS-2, May 1, 1967. Available from the Operations Research Staff, Social Security Administration, Baltimore, Maryland.

ANNOTATED SUPPLEMENTARY BIBLIOGRAPHY

The electronic digital computer has been applied extensively in business and management. Reference [2] above and bibliographic Refs. 1 and 2 at the conclusion of Chap. 8 are cited first as sources of many descriptions of the use of computers in business and management. In addition, the following are noted:

1. "Electronic Data Processing Symposium, London, October 4–6, 1961," Sir Isaac Pitman & Sons, Ltd., London, 1963. A survey of applications of computers in the United Kingdom in the fields of banking, insurance, government, the petroleum industry, and the aircraft industry. There are also discussions of applications in accounting, payroll generation, inventory control, and market research.
2. A KWIC Index in Operations Research, *IBM Publ.* C20-1673. A survey of articles on operations research that appeared in the period 1961 to 1966 in 15 American and foreign journals. It is quite comprehensive. For example, there are about 100 listings in the area of simulation, 19 relating to hospital applications, and about 100 on inventory problems.
3. Lemays, L. P.: On-line Computer Control of a Chemical Plant, *Proc. Can. Conf. Computing Data Process.*, pp. 258–277, 1962. A discussion of automation at a chemical plant.
4. Scheraga, D. I.: Computer Techniques in Assembly Line Balancing, *Proc. Computer Appl. Symp.*, Armour Research Foundation, pp. 62–75, 1961. A difficult manufacturing scheduling problem solved with the aid of a computer.
5. Hibbard, T. N.: A Simple Sorting Algorithm, *J. ACM*, no. 2, pp. 142–150, 1962.
6. Solomon, N. B.: Icon, A Management Information System, *Proc. Natl. Meetings ACM*, paper 59, 1962.
7. Tiffany, P. C.: The Storage and Retrieval of Physiological and Medical Data in a Modern Hospital, *Proc. Spring Joint Computer Conf.*, pp. 291–306, 1962.
8. Maisel, H., J. Albertini, C. Roberts, and R. Mason: The Centaur War Game, *Proc. U.S. Army Operations Res. Symp.*, Durham, N.C., pp. 107–128, 1963.

chapter 10
ARTIFICIAL
INTELLIGENCE

10.1 INTRODUCTION

Such questions as "Can computers think?" and "Do computers exhibit intelligence?" are indicative of the kinds of reactions people have to automatons that might possibly replace them in some of their activities. People do, of course, have qualities that cannot be duplicated by machine, but we need not duplicate all human qualities in order to perform some tasks previously carried out by people. Only certain well-defined (and usually undesirable) tasks are being given over to automatons. There is no reason for a defensive reaction.

Serious discussions of whether computers can think almost inevitably arrive at problems of artificial intelligence,† or heuristic programming. Computer specialists have attempted to attack some very difficult tasks that defy solution in a straightforward way by providing *heuristics*, i.e., empirically based aids, or by permitting the computer to "learn," i.e., to modify its solution procedure after applying it to a series of specific

† A good detailed reference on artificial intelligence, which includes a description of several more examples and discussions of the relation of artificial intelligence to thought, is [1].

examples. This chapter will first discuss an example of artificial intelligence (theorem proving in plane geometry) that emphasizes heuristics in its solution, then an example (checker playing) that emphasizes learning, and finally an example (pattern recognition) in which both heuristics and learning are used extensively.

Many people do not believe that intelligent behavior by computers has really been achieved. For example, Dreyfus in [15] discusses several attributes of intelligent behavior that he believes the computer has been and will be unable to duplicate.

10.2 THEOREM PROVING IN PLANE GEOMETRY

One of the most impressive and creative activities of man is the mathematician's efforts to discover and to prove general truths about a specified body of knowledge. The truly creative activity, and incidentally the part of the work most satisfying to the mathematician, is the discovery—particularly if it is a surprising one—of a new theorem. The development of a proof can be extremely creative and satisfying in itself but also may be tedious and subject to annoying pitfalls that test the mathematician's perseverance and attention to detail more than his creativity. Some computer specialists recognized the challenge of the combination of tedious attention to detail and creative, intelligent activity that is a part of theorem proving, and *theorem proving by computer* was widely attempted. The most successful work reported thus far is that of Gelertner. He has proved theorems in plane geometry using the computer. In this section, we shall give only a rough sketch of the process. Reference is made to [2] or to pages 134 to 152 of [1] for additional details.

In getting computers to prove theorems, it is natural to first attack an area of mathematics that is both simple and well developed and that has some good heuristics available. Persons proving theorems in plane geometry have long made use of an effective heuristic—a diagram—that could probably be incorporated into a computer's attempts to prove theorems. Furthermore, plane geometry is both simple and well developed, so that it was a natural choice for a first attack on theorem proving.

The broad objective is to have the machine construct proofs of theorems in euclidean plane geometry in much the same way that a high school sophomore does. The specific objective is to obtain a sequence of statements. Each statement must be correct in the language of plane geometry, and the sequence must begin with an axiom or previously proved theorem and conclude with the theorem to be proved. Each succeeding statement either must be inferable from the sequence or some part of the sequence preceding it or must be an axiom or a previously proved theorem.

Considering both the way a sophomore proceeds and the way Newell, Shaw, and Simon [3] proceeded when faced with problems in logical deduction, Gelertner decided to have the computer attack the problem by proceeding backward from the statement of the theorem. Although we are thus assured that the sequence will indeed conclude properly, we cannot be certain that we will generate valid sequences. The next step is to introduce the diagramming heuristic.

Using the techniques of analytic geometry, the information contained in diagrams can be reduced to computationally verifiable statements. Given the coordinates of the vertices of a triangle, for example, the sum of the interior angles can be computed and—allowing properly for rounding—compared to 180°. By using a diagram and terminating the backward-building string when a statement was generated that was not valid in the diagram, Gelertner found that he could already prove a large class of interesting theorems.

The *geometry-theorem-proving machine* is a computer program† too complex to be completely described here. In general, it includes:

1. A subprogram, called a *diagram computer*, that contains a representation of the theorem in terms of collections of coordinates of points and lines. This diagram computer is permitted to draw inferences from the diagram, such as which line segments are opposite which angles and which elements can be called triangles, angles, or line segments.
2. Another subprogram, called a *syntax computer*, that generates sequences of statements.
3. A third subprogram, called a *heuristic computer*, that controls the theorem-proving process, calling in the syntax and diagram computers as needed. The critical step in the functioning of the heuristic computer is its use of *subgoals* in solving the problem.

If we use G_0 to denote the statement to be established by the proof and $G_1{}^j$ to denote the jth statement that is immediately antecedent to G_0, then generalizing we may use G_i (with appropriate superscripts) to denote a statement that is immediately antecedent to some G_{i-1}. We can indicate this linkage graphically, as in Fig. 10.1, where the arrows indicate inferences directly from one statement to another. For example, $G_2{}^2 \Rightarrow G_1{}^1 \Rightarrow G_0$ or $G_2{}^3 \Rightarrow G_1{}^5 \Rightarrow G_0$. (The symbol $\Rightarrow$ is used to denote "implies.")

---

† That is, it is a series of instructions to be executed on an electronic computer. Many investigators in the area of artificial intelligence call their creations *machines* even though they are really only sets of instructions to be executed on a commercially manufactured computer. These "machines" are usually made up of "parts" that are themselves subsets of instructions, i.e., subprograms.

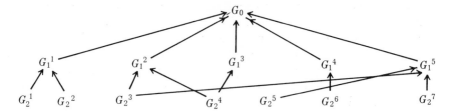

Fig. 10.1   The structure of goals and subgoals.

This graph is developed in the computer early in the procedure and permits subgoals to be chosen.   These are then developed,† and with the aid of the diagrammatic representation of the theorem, a determination is made as to whether these developments are fruitful.   Because of the structure of the graph, as soon as a subgoal can be proved from the axioms, previously established theorems, and premises, there will be a valid proof of the theorem.   This means that a graph could be set up in which the subgoal G_i takes on the position of G_0 in order to find lower-level subgoals.   This is just what is done.   As each lower-level subgoal is rejected, a new one is taken up and tested.   To avoid the redundant checking of subgoals, a special routine is provided to test previously untested subgoals in order to determine whether they are equivalent to previously tested subgoals.

The machine contains other heuristic refinements.   It gives priority in generating subgoals to those things that can be established in a single step—for example, the equality of vertical angles—and to identities such as the equality of all right angles.   Another special heuristic is to consider how far apart a pair of subgoals are, that is, how long a sequence we must use to prove the higher one from the lower one, and to give priority to shorter sequences.

The machine has successfully proved a theorem taken from a high school exam in less than five minutes, the theorem "Diagonals of a parallelogram bisect each other" in about three minutes, and the theorem "Opposite sides of a parallelogram are equal" in less than a minute. (All these times refer to runs made on an IBM 704 computer, which is slow by today's standards.)

10.3   CHECKER PLAYING

Playing games is a human pastime of some significance.   We shall not argue here the extent to which games can be called, in our society, essential (as opposed to frivolous) activity.   In any event, it is clear that

† The procedure used to generate subgoals is complex.   Two of the heuristics used in it are described in the next paragraph.

playing games requires serious intellectual activity, learned skills, and useful heuristics in order to be successful.

The game of chess is recognized by many as an intellectual pastime *par excellence* and so has interested computer specialists for more than a decade. (For example, see [4] and [5]. Pages 39 to 70 of [1] contain a good summary of the development of chess-playing machines.) However, chess playing is sufficiently complicated to have defied the development of a very good chess-playing machine. Checker playing is less complicated but is still intellectually demanding. It has been successfully attacked by A. L. Samuel. (See [6] or pages 71 to 105 of [1].)

Samuel's *checker-playing machine*, like Gelertner's geometry-theorem-proving machine, is really a series of computer programs written for a general-purpose digital computer. The objective of these programs is the same as that of any player—to select a series of moves that will win the game. The approach is to:

1. Look ahead a few moves, producing all possible combinations of checker positions for the opposing players. (A single combination of checker arrangements is called a *board position*.)
2. Score a board position by forming a polynomial which is, in fact, a weighted combination of the various advantages that might result from any given board position. Such factors as piece ratios and positional advantages of various sorts are considered. The machine first will always check to see if victory or defeat is in sight.
3. Select a move. Three heuristics are included in this operation. First, the machine assumes that its opponent will always select the best possible move he can make. Second, the machine starts by evaluating all possible board positions at the end of the series of moves and works backward from these positions. Third, if the machine is losing, it will choose that move that leads to the longest series of moves before defeat is conceded; if it is winning, it will choose that move leading to the shortest series of moves before victory is claimed. This third heuristic is called "giving the program a sense of direction."

Another feature of the checker-playing machine is that it automatically revises all programs on the basis of experience gained in play— for example, it may revise the number of moves to be analyzed and the weights and items used in the scoring polynomial.

Consider Fig. 10.2, in which three moves are depicted—two machine moves and one opponent's move. Looking three moves ahead, the machine first analyzes the values associated with the board positions after the third move. From among these, it picks the positive values

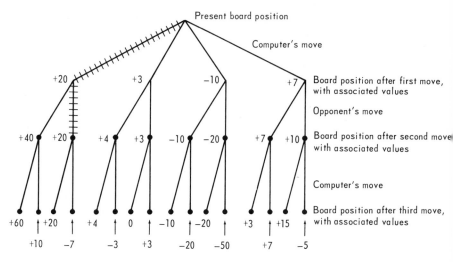

Fig. 10.2 Selection of moves by computer.

and goes back to the second move, which is up to its opponent. Assuming that the opponent will choose the best possible move for him, after the first move is chosen, it selects as the first move the one that will result in achieving the best value after the third move. The hatched path in Fig. 10.2 indicates the selection that would have been made.

The learning capabilities of the checker-playing machine are quite extensive. Two approaches were taken. One, called *rote learning*, involves the accumulation of experience in terms of a reference file of board positions, values of moves, and results. This leads to some intricate cataloging devices to avoid redundancy, to retain only the most valuable results, and to provide ready access to pertinent earlier results. For example, in order to ensure saving only the most valuable results, information is expunged from the catalog if it is not used sufficiently often. Experience with the use of this learning technique indicates that the computer plays a very good opening and ending game but a poor middle game. This computer has been characterized as a better-than-average checker player.

The second learning procedure, called *generalizing*, involves the revision of such things as the number of moves anticipated and the weights and the terms used in the evaluating polynomials. It was found most efficient to implement generalizing by constructing two machine players—called *alpha* and *beta* by Samuel. Alpha frequently changes its weights and terms during the course of a game in an effort to improve them, whereas beta keeps its strategy fixed. If alpha wins a majority of a series of games, beta's fixed strategy is revised to conform with alpha's and a new series is begun.

Regarding generalizing as a learning procedure, Samuel found in the first series of tests that the computer learned quickly but somewhat erratically. For example, it was badly fooled by bad playing on the part of its opponent. This resulted in his adopting the more conservative practice of using a majority of wins by alpha in a series of games rather than a single win to decide on whether or not to revise beta's strategy. Other changes were also made, and the learning pattern became more stable.

Samuel draws the following dramatic conclusion from his work: "As a result of these experiments, one can say with some certainty that it is now possible to devise learning schemes which will greatly outperform an average person and that such learning schemes may eventually be economically feasible as applied to real-life problems."

The program was implemented on an IBM 704 computer, and the sizes of the programs were not very great. For example, the game starting and terminating routine contained 600 instructions, the rote-learning routine 1,500 instructions, and the generalization-learning routine 650 instructions. As for time, it took 2.6 milliseconds to find all available moves from a single board position, 1.5 milliseconds to make a single move and find the resulting board position, 2.4 milliseconds to evaluate a board position using 4 terms, and 7.5 milliseconds to evaluate a board position using 16 terms. Overall, however, the program when running required all the memory capacity (32,000 words) of a 704 for its execution. Running times in the order of half a minute were required on the relatively slow 704 to complete all the computations associated with a single move.

10.4 PATTERN RECOGNITION

The ability to distinguish pertinent information from a wide variety of stimuli is an important characteristic of animal behavior. A great deal of research in psychology has been devoted to perception because of its fundamental place in intelligent behavior. (Reference [7] contains a survey of this research.)

Computer scientists have been interested in perception—perception by computers is called *pattern recognition*—for both practical and academic reasons. The academic motivation results from the fact that perception is an essential feature of intelligent behavior; the practical motivation, from the savings that could be gained if computers could read a variety of printed matter and human handwriting or "hear" voice inputs.

(The preparation of inputs for computers, today usually in the form of punched cards, is an expensive and time-consuming task.)

The richness of applications of pattern recognition makes the treatment of any one case unrepresentative. A rough model will be developed instead, combining common approaches to the problem.

Let us first rule out those approaches to pattern recognition that are not really examples of artificial intelligence. In broad terms, the objective of a pattern-recognizing procedure is to classify inputs. If the classification can be successfully carried out by a straightforward table look-up or by matching with a template, then we can say that we have a *matched filter* for the process and no further work is necessary. In these circumstances, we can recognize and categorize a restricted class of inputs—as, for example, the special type fonts used on bank checks or isolated pure tones on a musical scale. In a somewhat more complex situation, one that is still not representative of pattern recognition as an example of artificial intelligence, we might get inputs that belong to a restricted class but are slightly scrambled or blurred. However, if they are not very scrambled, well-developed mathematical processes are available that can successfully unscramble them and permit a matched filter to uniquely and assuredly classify the inputs. Recognition of Morse code (see pages 238 to 242 of [1]) is an example of this type of problem in pattern recognition.

For the case where learning is an essential feature, the sequence of operations in solving a problem in pattern recognition is summarized in Fig. 10.3. Stimuli are presented and reduced to machine-processable inputs. This usually means that they are quantified by taking measurements of them, which might be done automatically, semiautomatically, or manually. The results of the measurements might be stored in the learning program for future analysis, and the learning program might cause us to modify our measurement process. However, in many applications, the measuring process may not be modified, and this relation with the learning program is then not present. The measurements are passed to a comparing program that resembles the matched filter discussed above except that it cannot arrive at a classification merely by comparing but requires some decision mechanism.

The decision mechanism might be a probabilistic model or a distance function that somehow uses the results of the comparison of the observed measurements with the stored measurements to arrive at a classification. The classification would usually have probabilities associated with it. If we were interpreting a series of handwritten letters, the output might be a U with probability .92, a V with probability .07, and some other character with probability .01. The comparison and discussion procedure is linked with the learning procedure in the same way that the

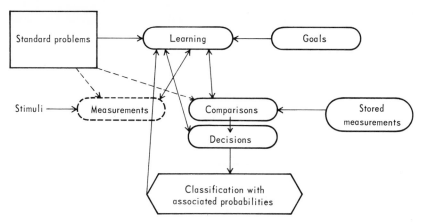

Fig. 10.3 Pattern recognition with learning. Note that an elliptical symbol is used to denote either data or programs that are stored in the computer. The dotted box around measurements indicates that there may be some computer interaction in this process.

measurement procedure is sometimes linked to the learning procedure. This means that the nature of these procedures can be communicated to the learning program and that the program can modify the procedures as a result of previous experience. Note also that the results are returned to the learning program so that it can use these to help evaluate the process.

The learning program permits us to modify our initial rough approximation to a solution by using results obtained with standard, known patterns (indicated by the rectangular box in Fig. 10.3) and comparing these results with the desired results in terms of our goals for an adequate procedure. The procedures are modified, and a series of runs are made to determine which modification is most appropriate. Unknown problems would then be attacked, and the results analyzed in terms of both our goals and the results obtained with the standard problems to see if further modification of the procedures might be necessary.

We shall conclude our discussion of pattern recognition by mentioning a couple of approaches to obtaining measurements and a couple of approaches to the comparison-decision process.

One approach to deciding on which measurements to make is to consider those properties of the stimuli that are invariant within a class but that vary from class to class. Suppose we wish to distinguish among hand-printed alphabetic characters. The letter might be rotated or magnified, but it would still be the same letter; such properties are invariant in this problem. However, if the curvature of the line tracing

the letter were changed, the letter itself might be changed.   Consider
the differences, for example, between a U and a V or an O and a D.
Curvature would be the thing to measure.   Similarly, the number of
straight-line segments and curved-line segments would vary from class
to class but not within a fixed class.   Here, however, since we are dealing with hand printing, a threshold for distinguishing between a straight
and a curved segment must be established.   This threshold might be
resolved by a learning program.   Reference [8] contains some useful
information on the use of invariants in arriving at measurements, with
particular emphasis on the recognition of straight lines.

Another approach to arriving at either measurement criteria or
decision rules is to consider the way the human sensory system processes data.   Much experimentation has been carried out on human perception—particularly on hearing and vision.†   But it is believed that
the use of human sensory systems as a guide to the development of
pattern-recognition devices must await further work on the part of
physiologists, neurologists, and psychologists in characterizing the human
systems in greater depth and detail.‡

Two decision rules that have been used in resolving classification
problems in pattern recognition have already been discussed.   The first
of these is the use of similarity measures, such as the quantity S discussed in connection with the problem of numerical taxonomy in Sec. 8.2.
The second is the use of Bayes' theorem, discussed in connection with
medical diagnosis in Sec. 8.3.   We merely note here, first, that taxonomy
and diagnosis are themselves problems in classifying stimuli and could be
viewed as problems in pattern recognition and, second, that the use of
these decision procedures in problems in pattern recognition would parallel their use in taxonomy and diagnosis.   Different stimuli would merely
be substituted for the organism's characteristics and the patient's symptoms, and different classifications, for the taxonomic classes and the
disease classes.

REFERENCES

1. Feigenbaum, E. A., and J. Feldman (eds.): "Computers and
    Thought," McGraw-Hill Book Company, New York, 1963.

† Broadbent, in [9], presents a survey of what has been done that is pertinent to perception and also offers further references.   At a more detailed level, Vernon [10]
presents a comprehensive survey of the visual process, and Broadbent [11] does the
same thing for hearing.   These results are useful, and Rosenblatt, among others, in
developing the perceptron [12] has obtained some insight from them.
‡ It is interesting to note that a mathematician, using the theory of lie groups and lie
algebras [14] and on the basis of physiological studies of electrical activity in the
brain, has proposed [13] a model for the visual integrative process that may serve as a
guide for and a challenge to these physiologists, neurologists, and psychologists.

2. Gelertner, H.: Realization of a Geometry-theorem Proving Machine, *Proc. Intern. Conf. Inform. Process.*, pp. 273–282, Paris UNESCO House, 1959.

3. Newell, A., J. C. Shaw, and H. A. Simon: Empirical Explorations of the Logic Theory Machine, *Proc. Western Joint Computer Conf.*, pp. 218–239, 1957.

4. Kister, J., P. Stein, S. Ulam, W. Walden, and M. Wells: Experiments in Chess, *J. ACM*, vol. 4, no. 2, pp. 174–177, April, 1957.

5. Bernstein, A., et al.: A Chess-playing Program for the IBM 704 Computer, *Proc. Western Joint Computer Conf.*, pp. 157–159, 1958.

6. Samuel, A. L.: Some Studies in Machine Learning Using the Game of Checkers, *IBM J. Res. Develop.*, vol. 3, pp. 211–229, July, 1959.

7. Beardslee, D. C., and M. Wertheimer (eds.): "Readings in Perception," D. Van Nostrand Company, Inc., Princeton, N.J., 1958.

8. Doyle, W.: Operations Useful for Similarity Invariant Pattern Recognition, *J. ACM*, vol. 9, no. 2, pp. 259–267, April, 1962.

9. Broadbent, D. E.: Information Processing in the Nervous System, *Science*, vol. 150, no. 3695, pp. 457–462, Oct. 22, 1965.

10. Vernon, M. D.: "A Further Study of Visual Perception," Cambridge University Press, New York, 1952.

11. Broadbent, D. E.: "Perception and Communication," Pergamon Press, New York, 1958.

12. Rosenblatt, F.: The Perceptron, A Theory of Statistical Separability in Cognitive Systems, *Cornell Aeron. Lab. Rept.* VG-1196-G-1, Buffalo, N.Y.

13. Hoffman, W. C.: Pattern Recognition and the Method of Isoclines, *Boeing Sci. Res. Lab. Rept.*, 1964.

14. Belinfante, J. G., B. Kolman, and H. A. Smith: An Introduction to Lie Groups and Lie Algebras, with Applications, *Rev. Soc. Ind. Appl. Math.*, vol. 8, no. 1, pp. 11–46, January, 1966.

15. Dreyfus, H. L.: "Alchemy and Artificial Intelligence," RAND Corporation, Santa Monica, Calif., December, 1965. Available through the Clearinghouse for Federal Scientific and Technical Information as Document AD625719.

ANNOTATED SUPPLEMENTARY BIBLIOGRAPHY

The references cited above effectively cover, in a highly selective way, much that is being done in artificial intelligence. Some survey articles on artificial intelligence are listed below, as well as several additional references on this subject that discuss pattern recognition in greater depth and detail.

1. Symposium on Artificial Intelligence, *Proc. Meetings Intern. Federation Inform. Process.*, pp. 478–486, 1962.

2. Symposium on Pattern Recognition, *ibid.*, pp. 467–477.
3. Johnson, D. L., and A. D. C. Holden: Simulation of Human Problem-solving Method, *Simulation*, vol. 3, no. 2, pp. 65–70, August, 1964.
4. Kovaleyskii, V. A.: Present and Future of Pattern-recognition Theory, *Proc. Congress Intern. Federation Inform. Process.*, vol. 1, pp. 37–43, 1965.
5. Marzocco, F. N.: Computer Recognition of Handwritten First Names, *Trans. IEEE*, EC-14, pp. 210–217, April, 1965.
6. Nilsson, N. J.: "Learning Machines: Foundations of Trainable Pattern Classifying Systems," McGraw-Hill Book Company, New York, 1965. A good, but not-for-the-beginner discussion of the theory behind the use of discriminant functions to classify patterns in machines that learn.
7. Sebestyen, G.: "Decision Making Processes in Pattern Recognition," The Macmillan Company, New York, 1962. Some more material on pattern recognition and discriminant functions.
8. Uhr, L. (ed.): "Pattern Recognition: Theory, Experiment, Computer Simulations and Dynamic Models of Form Perception and Discovery," John Wiley & Sons, Inc., New York, 1966. Twenty-two papers that together cover a variety of work in perception quite thoroughly. These include a discussion of the psychology and physiology of perception, experiments in perception, theoretical developments, and computer simulations of complex models.

part 4

THE FORTRAN IV AND
PL/1 PROGRAMMING LANGUAGES

INTRODUCTION

The descriptions of the FORTRAN and PL/1 programming languages, appearing in Part 4, are the main goal of the book. Learning a useful programming language should be the major objective of a first course on computers. There is no effective substitute for the experience that comes from writing real computer programs and attempting to get them to run.

Most students will be required to learn only one language and will read either Chap. 11 or Chap. 12, but not both chapters. The chapters are, therefore, written to be independent of each other. For example, the PL/1 chapter, which comes after the FORTRAN chapter, does not assume a knowledge of FORTRAN.

FORTRAN appears first because it was developed first and because it is somewhat easier to learn than PL/1. However, PL/1 is more powerful and more versatile. The extra effort devoted to learning it will probably be rewarded.

The chapters in this section are the longest ones in the book. Experience indicates that from one-fourth to one-third of a semester is required to cover one of these chapters. Problems should be assigned before the chapter is completed. For example, in Chap. 11, Prob. 11.1 should be assigned after Sec. 11.2, Probs. 11.2, 11.3, and 11.5 after Sec. 11.14, Probs. 11.4, 11.6, and 11.7 after Sec. 11.20, and Probs. 11.8 and 11.9 after Sec. 11.21. Selections should be made from among Probs. 11.10 to 11.16 for laboratory exercises if a computer is available. If a computer is not available, the program written in answer to these problems should be carefully reviewed for errors; the students might exchange programs in class and attempt to find each other's errors under the guidance of the instructor.

The FORTRAN and PL/1 programming languages contain many special features that cannot be covered in a first course on computers. Wherever possible, mention will be made of these features in the text and references will be given to IBM manuals for a definition and further discussion of them. IBM manuals are updated frequently. This means that the text must necessarily refer to outdated, earlier versions of manuals. However, the manuals usually retain the same overall structure, and page references to an earlier version can frequently be helpful in finding the corresponding discussion in a newer version of the same manual.

OUTLINE

11. The FORTRAN Language

chapter 11

THE FORTRAN LANGUAGE

11.1 INTRODUCTION

Early users of the electronic digital computer were mainly scientifically oriented. Substitutions in elaborate formulas were frequently required, and it might be expected that the first popular compiler would make the programming of formulas easy. FORTRAN, developed in the late 1950s by the IBM Corporation, does that. However, strings of characters are not so easily accommodated, and input/output is awkward. Even formula manipulation can get to be annoying because of the restrictions in some versions of the language on mixing floating-point and fixed-point arithmetic, the use of parentheses, the size of arrays, etc. However, FORTRAN was certainly there "fustest with the mostest," and its prominent place is a testimony to its advantages as a programming language and to the influence of the IBM Corporation.

FORTRAN comes in a variety of dialects and versions within dialects. FORTRAN II was developed for smaller computers, such as the IBM 1620, and FORTRAN IV for larger ones, such as the IBM 7090. The dialect of FORTRAN implemented in the System/360 is FORTRAN IV. However, it comes in several versions, each associated with the letter code used to indicate core size in the System/360.† The FORTRAN language described in this chapter is the G-level version of FORTRAN IV for the System/360. Table 11.1 contrasts the G-level and H-level versions of FORTRAN for the System/360. The E-level version does not implement all the features of FORTRAN IV. Features that are in both the G- and H-level versions but not in the E-level version are listed in Appendix E of the manual for the E-level subset of FORTRAN IV [1].

FORTRAN is being discussed in this book in order to accommodate the physical scientist who might prefer FORTRAN to PL/1. For this reason, the scope of the discussion is limited to those features that are useful in scientific calculations. Other features—for example, those associated with character and file manipulations—will not be discussed. However, there are many good references on FORTRAN IV. The reader interested in learning more about the language should return to the Annotated Supplementary Bibliography at the end of Chap. 7 in order to select a suitable reference.

† This letter code for FORTRAN is as follows: E for cores of 32,000 bytes, G for 131,000 bytes, and H for 262,000 or more bytes. IBM will not supply FORTRAN compilers for System/360 computers with fewer than 32,000 bytes of core.

Table 11.1   Differences between the G-level and H-level versions of FORTRAN for the System/360

	Implementation in	
Feature	G level	H level
Direct-access I/O statements	Allowed	Not allowed
DEBUG statement	Allowed	Not allowed
Automatic typing of generic functions, depending on the argument	Not done	Done
Nonsubscripted array variables	Not allowed	Allowed; assumes implicit subscript of 1, outputs a warning diagnostic
Complex constant of form (real, integer)	Allowed; converts integer to real	Not allowed
Logical expressions combined using relational operators	Not allowed	Allowed
Mixed BCD and EBCDIC	Allowed when BCD is specified, but a dollar sign ($) is flagged as an error	Allowed when BCD is specified

11.2 A FORTRAN PROGRAM

A FORTRAN program is introduced at this point to expose the reader to its general appearance and to discuss some general considerations in writing these programs. The program in Figs. 11.1 and 11.2 is designed to find the roots of a quadratic polynomial.† Note that it is presented on a FORTRAN coding form. These forms are useful because the writing of FORTRAN programs is rather stereotyped with respect to the punched card. Individual statements appear on different cards. The statement is actually entered in columns 7 to 72 of the card. Columns 1 to 5 are reserved for the statement number, a number that serves as a cross-reference to the statement. Column 6 is used to indicate *continuation cards*. Column 6 is ordinarily left blank; however, if more than one card is required to record a single statement, then something other than a zero must be punched in column 6 in all cards after the first one. A good practice is to punch successively greater digits in column 6, beginning with a 1 on the first continuation card. No more than 19 continuation cards, i.e., a total of 20 cards, can be used to record a FORTRAN statement. Column 1 also serves a rather special purpose. A C entered in this column causes the FORTRAN compiler to ignore the remainder of the card. Thus one or more *comments cards* are easily inserted in FORTRAN programs by just beginning the card with a C in column 1. Finally, columns 73 to 80 in the card are always ignored. The programmer can use these in any way he sees fit. He might enter his name in these columns, or he might use them to sequentially number the cards.

The last statement in a FORTRAN program must be an *END statement*. It serves to tell the compiler that no more FORTRAN code will follow. It is *nonexecutable;* that is, it does not result in a series of corresponding machine-language statements. The *STOP statement* is executable. It results in a series of machine-language instructions that will return control of the computer to the operating system when the program is completed.

Operating systems were discussed in Sec. 2.3. They are computer programs that provide for the smooth flow of jobs through the machine, that call up compilers and other frequently used programs when they are needed, and that maintain records on the utilization of the computer. Special instructions to the operating system are given in *control cards*.

---

† Cross-references to Chap. 12 will be avoided in the text of this chapter because it is intended that Chaps. 11 and 12 be studied independently. However, those who are interested in contrasting the languages will find that the chapters are developed in a similar way. For example, a PL/1 program to solve this same problem can be found in Sec. 12.2.

IBM

FORTRAN Coding Form

PROGRAM	QUADRATIC ROOTS		PUNCHING INSTRUCTIONS	GRAPHIC		PAGE 1 OF 2
PROGRAMMER H. MAISEL	DATE JUNE 15, 1967			PUNCH		CARD ELECTRO NUMBER

```
C     A PROGRAM TO COMPUTE THE ROOTS OF A QUADRATIC POLYNOMIAL
      WRITE(6,10)
   10 FORMAT(1H1)
      DOUBLE PRECISION A,B,C,D,ROOT1,ROOT2,REAL,XIMAG
      READ(5,2,END=5) A,B,C
    2 FORMAT(3F10.4)
      IF(A*A+B+C+C) 1,1,8
      IF(A) 9,20,9
      D=B*B-4.*A*C
      IF(D) 3,4,4
C     THE ROOTS ARE REAL
    4 ROOT1=(-B+DSQRT(D))/(2.*A)
      ROOT2=(-B-DSQRT(D))/(2.*A)
      WRITE(6,6) A,B,C,ROOT1,ROOT2
    6 FORMAT(1H0,44HTHE ROOTS OF THE QUADRATIC WITH COEFFICIENTS/1H ,2HA
     1=,F16.7,10X,2HB=,F16.7,10X,2HC=,F16.7/1H ,T30,'ARE'/1H ,6HROOT1=,F
     2=,F16.7,20X,6HROOT2=,F18.8,8)
      GO TO 1
C     THE ROOTS ARE COMPLEX
    3 REAL=(-B)/(2.*A)
      XIMAG=(DSQRT(-D))/(2.*A)
      WRITE(6,7) A,B,C,REAL,XIMAG
    7 FORMAT(1H0,44HTHE ROOTS OF THE QUADRATIC WITH COEFFICIENTS/1H
     1=,F16.7,10X,2HB=,F16.7,10X,2HC=,F16.7/1H ,66HARE COMPLEX CONJUGATE
```

Fig. 11.1   The first 24 statements in the quadratic-roots program.

IBM FORTRAN Coding Form X28-7327-5 Printed in U.S.A.

PROGRAM QUADRATIC ROOTS
PROGRAMMER H. MAISEL DATE JUNE 15, 1967
PUNCHING INSTRUCTIONS GRAPHIC PUNCH PAGE OF CARD ELECTRO NUMBER*

STATEMENT NUMBER | CONT. | FORTRAN STATEMENT | IDENTIFICATION SEQUENCE

```
     2S WITH THE FOLLOWING REAL AND IMAGINARY PARTS/1H ,10HREAL PART=,F1       25
     38.8,20X,15HIMAGINARY PART=,F18.8)                                        26
      GO TO 1                                                                  27
   20 WRITE(6,15)                                                              28
   15 FORMAT(1H0,'A IS ZERO')                                                  29
      GO TO 1                                                                  30
    5 STOP                                                                     31
      END                                                                      32
```

*A standard card form, IBM electro 888157, is available for punching statements from this form

Fig. 11.2 The remaining statements in the quadratic-roots program.

In some computer installations, these cards are prepared by the programmer and their preparation has become a necessary adjunct to programming. In other installations, the programmer need not worry about control cards. Nothing more will be said about their preparation here; the staff of the computer installation should be consulted.

11.3 THE CHARACTER SET

A FORTRAN program is an algorithm. It consists of a sequence of statements, or instructions. A statement corresponds to a box in a flow chart or to a step in an English-language algorithm. The sequence determines the order in which the statements are to be executed.

The main objective of this chapter is to permit the reader to state an algorithm in the FORTRAN language. The approach taken will be to present a repertoire of statements, the rules for their formulation, and the significance of their application. However, we must begin at the beginning. We shall first specify the set of characters that can be used in the words that appear in FORTRAN statements.

There are three kinds of characters: alphabetic, numeric, and special. The alphabetic characters include all 26 letters and the dollar sign ($). Only capital letters are permitted; there are no lowercase letters in FORTRAN. The dollar sign has been arbitrarily added to the usual set of 26 alphabetic characters. The numeric set contains no surprises. There are 10 numeric characters, the digits 0 to 9. The special characters permitted in FORTRAN include characters representing arithmetic processes: the plus sign ($+$), the minus sign ($-$), a slash for division ($/$), and an asterisk (*) for multiplication. Also available are left and right parentheses ( ), an equals sign ($=$), a period (.), a comma (,), an apostrophe ('), and an ampersand (&). Finally, we must not forget the blank space, an important special character. In summary, the 49-character set is:

Alphabetic characters:	A B C D E F G H I J K
	L M N O P Q R S T U V
	W X Y Z $
Numeric characters:	0 1 2 3 4 5 6 7 8 9
Special characters:	$+$ $-$ / * ( ) = . , ' &
	blank space

11.4 SYNTAX NOTATION

Syntax has been defined in [2] as "the way in which words are put together to form phrases, clauses, or sentences." In computer programs, the basic language element is the statement, and the syntax for computer-programming languages is concerned with the rules for combining words and other symbols to form a statement. In general, the syntax for programming languages is more rigid than that for natural languages. This makes it easier to provide direct, syntactical definitions of the different types of statements permitted in programming languages.

In order to avoid ambiguity, we shall adopt some special conventions for presenting the syntax of FORTRAN statements. These conventions are not a part of the FORTRAN language. They apply only to syntax expressions in this chapter and not to the FORTRAN statements themselves. In this section, we are defining a language for talking about FORTRAN; we are not talking about FORTRAN itself. For example, lowercase letters will be used in syntax expressions for words that are notation variables; lowercase letters are not even in the FORTRAN character set.

Notation variables are used in syntax expressions to denote parts of a statement that can be changed from statement to statement. They are written using lowercase letters but may also contain decimal digits and hyphens. However, they must begin with a letter.

Capital letters are used to denote *notation constants*. These are fixed and must appear exactly as they are given in the syntactical definition.

In addition, we shall adopt the convention of italicizing the character that would ordinarily appear in column 7 of the input card.† Consider the following example of a syntactical definition:

statement-number *G*O TO statement-number

The word "statement-number," which is used twice and is in lowercase, denotes a notation variable. Statement numbers would be substituted for these variables in implementations of the statement. The words "GO TO," on the other hand, are notation constants and would appear beginning in column 7.

Examples of program statements corresponding to this syntactical definition follow:

10   GO TO 36

GO TO 114

Note that the second of the statements is not itself numbered. This indicates that the first number is optional. Optional items will be denoted

† More precisely, this character is the first one in the text of the statement. It may appear anywhere in columns 7 to 72, preceded by blanks beginning in column 7, since blanks in FORTRAN are ignored.

by enclosing them in brackets. The above syntactical specification now becomes

[statement-number] *GO TO* statement-number

A brace is used in the syntactical definition to enclose several choices for items that can be used in a given statement. The brace is not a notation constant. The alternatives can either be stacked vertically or listed horizontally separated by a vertical stroke (the vertical stroke in this context is not a notation constant). For example, either {integer-variable|integer-constant} or $\left\{\begin{array}{l}\text{integer-variable}\\\text{integer-constant}\end{array}\right\}$ can be used to indicate that either an integer variable or an integer constant can appear in the FORTRAN statement at this point.

Special punctuation marks—especially commas and parentheses, which are used extensively in FORTRAN programs—are notation constants. For example, in the specification:

[statement-number]{READ|WRITE}(data-reference[,format-

reference])[variable-list]

the comma and the parentheses are notation constants but the brackets, braces, and vertical strokes are not. Examples of FORTRAN statements corresponding to this specification can be found in lines 2, 14, and 22 of Fig. 11.1 and line 28 of Fig. 11.2.

11.5 CONSTANTS IN FORTRAN STATEMENTS

Within the scope of the applications of the language we plan to discuss, the operands in FORTRAN statements will be either constants, variables, or data aggregates called *arrays*. *FORTRAN constants* are denoted by merely entering their value in FORTRAN statements. *Integer constants* are written without decimal points. *Real constants* can be specified by either writing the number with a decimal point or writing the number using floating-point representation. In the latter case, the mantissa must have a decimal point and the exponent must contain one or two digits. A decimal point is not allowed in the exponent. The letter E is used to separate the mantissa from the exponent if the number is to be stored in the short form (using four bytes),† and the letter D is used if the number is to be stored in the long form (using

---

† A *byte* is a unit of storage capacity in the System/360. It is analogous to the words found in other computers. A byte contains nine bits; one of these is ordinarily a parity bit, and the other eight are used to record information. More will be said about the byte in Chap. 13.

eight bytes).   Commas should not appear anywhere.   The following are valid representations of 7,900:

   7900.

   7.9E3

   7.9E03

   7.9D03   (8 bytes used in storage)

   790000.E − 02

The following are invalid representations of real numbers:

   7,900.

   7900

   7900.E

Complex constants are represented by writing a pair of real constants in parentheses, separated by a comma.   The first constant represents the real part, and the second the imaginary part of the number.   The following are valid representations of $-6.4 + 8.71I$:

   $(-6.4, 8.71)$

   $(-6400.E − 3, 871.E − 2)$

   $(-.64D1, .871D1)$

The last number uses eight bytes to store each part.   The following are invalid representations of complex numbers:

   $(-.64D1, .871E1)$ (because both parts must have same length)

   $(64, 8.7)$

   $(64., 8.7E)$

Literal constants are enclosed in single quotation marks, that is, in apostrophes, and represent a string of characters.   An example of a literal constant can be found on line 16 of Fig. 11.1.   The constant is the word "ARE."

   Other constants are permitted in FORTRAN programs; however, they will not be discussed here.   They are discussed on pages 9 to 13 of [5].

11.6 FORTRAN VARIABLES

FORTRAN variables really are names for storage locations that contain a value associated with that variable.   Though they may be thought of as algebraic variables in constructing formulas, this will sometimes prove to be confusing. For example, the following FORTRAN statement is algebraically nonsensical: $N = N + 1$. However, it is a legitimate FORTRAN statement that permits us to replace the value currently stored for N with a value that is a unit greater. Note that a variable is assigned a new value by having it appear to the left of an equals sign in a FORTRAN statement. It may also be assigned a value in an input statement. Every variable that appears in a FORTRAN statement must have been assigned a value either in that statement or in a preceding statement.

A variable is denoted by any combination of alphabetic and numeric characters, with the following restrictions:

1. The first character must be alphabetic.
2. There can be no more than six characters in a single variable name.
3. No special characters can appear in a variable name.

FORTRAN variables may take on integer, real, complex, or logical values. A given variable name can be used to denote any one type of variable. Logical variables take on the values *true* or *false*, real variables are assigned floating-point values, and complex variables are assigned pairs of floating-point values—one for the real and the other for the imaginary part. Integer variables take on only integer values. This may lead to some peculiar arithmetic. For example, the quotient of two integers is not generally an integer. However, in FORTRAN, the quotient of two integers is an integer. The integer result is obtained by merely dropping the fractional remainder. This means that, in integer arithmetic, 10 divided by 3 is 3, as is 11 divided by 3.

Unless otherwise specified, variables beginning with the letters I to N are integer and all other variables are real. The programmer may override these arbitrary assignments using the IMPLICIT or type statement. (These statements will be discussed in Sec. 11.15.)

The standard amount of space reserved for FORTRAN variables in the System/360 is four bytes for integer, real, and logical variables and eight bytes for complex variables. Optional lengths are available. For example, we have already mentioned the long form for storing real numbers that uses eight bytes. Other optional lengths are implemented using the IMPLICIT or type statement and will be discussed in Sec. 11.15.

11.7 ARRAYS AND THE DIMENSION STATEMENT

An *array* consists of a collection of homogeneous items that can be thought of as arranged in some geometric pattern. Thus we can speak of an array of one dimension, two dimensions, three dimensions, and so on. A two-dimensional array is a rectangular arrangement—a *matrix*—of items. Two-dimensional arrays, or matrices, are frequently encountered in applications, and special attention will be devoted to them in the discussion that follows.

The manipulation of matrices is frequently encountered in statistical calculations and is also of importance in a variety of other applications. This is largely because linear systems can be succinctly represented in matrix notation and the solution of such systems can frequently be reduced to the inversion of a matrix. Consider the following simple example, consisting of a series of n equations in n unknowns. We can write the system as follows:

$$a_{11}x_1 + a_{12}x_2 + \cdots + a_{1n}x_n = y_1$$
$$a_{21}x_1 + a_{22}x_2 + \cdots + a_{2n}x_n = y_2$$
$$\cdot \cdot \cdot \cdot \cdot \cdot \cdot \cdot \cdot \cdot \cdot \cdot \cdot \cdot \cdot \cdot \cdot \cdot \cdot \cdot \cdot$$
$$a_{n1}x_1 + a_{n2}x_2 + \cdots + a_{nn}x_n = y_n$$

In matrix notation, we write simply: $Ax = y$. It is understood that A is an $n \times n$ matrix and that x and y are one-dimensional arrays. The solution of the problem, that is, finding a set X's that simultaneously satisfy the n equations, is (as one would conclude from the matrix equation) $X = A^{-1}y$. Since matrix multiplication is a straightforward computational problem, finding the solution is reduced to finding the inverse of A. This is not a straightforward problem, and a great deal of analytical effort and computer time has been devoted to its solution. (See, for example, Chaps. 9 and 10 of [3] and Part II of [4].)

Any name that could be used for a variable name can be used for an array name. Individual elements in an array are denoted by the use of the array name and *subscripts* that pinpoint the element's location. Subscripts are enclosed in parentheses and are separated by commas. Thus, for example, A(3,4) refers to the element in the third row and fourth column of A. There may be a maximum of seven subscripts associated with a single array name; that is, an array may have a maximum of seven dimensions. The subscripts can themselves be arithmetic expressions (see Sec. 11.9), but they must not take on nonpositive values or values that exceed the specified maximum for that particular subscript. Logical or complex-valued subscripts are not permitted.

Maximum values for each subscript in an array are presented in a *DIMENSION statement* or in a type statement. These statements are not executable. The syntax of the DIMENSION statement is given below. The type statement will be discussed in Sec. 11.15.

$DIMENSION$ array-name(integer-constant[,integer-constant] . . .
[,integer-constant])[,array-name(integer-constant[,integer-constant]
. . . [,integer-constant])] . . . [,array-name(integer-constant
[,integer-constant] . . . [,integer-constant])]

The integer constant must be positive; it indicates the maximum
value that may be attained by the corresponding dimension. The sets
of three dots are not punctuation-notation constants. They are used,
as in mathematical notation, to indicate that the pattern established by
the elements appearing in the sequence before and after the dots is to be
used to fill in a variable number of elements in place of the dots. In this
case, the dots are used to indicate that several sets of integer constants,
separated by commas, may appear in the set of subscripts associated
with a single array. Also, the third set of dots is used to indicate that
any number of arrays may be dimensioned in a single statement. Consider, for example, the statement:

DIMENSION A(10,6),B(100),INTEG(3,4,3,4)

This statement specifies, among other things, that A can have no more
than 10 rows, that the array INTEG has four dimensions, that A and B
are made up of real numbers, and that INTEG is made up of integer
numbers.

The order of the *storage of elements in an array* is prescribed by the
FORTRAN compiler. They are stored so that the value of the first subscript increases most rapidly and the value of the last subscript increases
least rapidly. Thus, for example, a one-dimensional array is stored as
a list. The first element is stored first, the second in the next higher
storage location, and so on. Multidimensional arrays are stored column-
wise. The first element stored is the element in the first row, first column, and the next is the element in the second row, first column. Thus
all elements in the first column are stored before any element in the second column is stored. This process is continued until the last column is
stored.

11.8 THE OPERATIONS

We shall discuss the arithmetic and logical operations available in
FORTRAN in this section. Table 11.2 contains definitions of these
FORTRAN operations and examples of their use. The operands are
variables, including array elements, or constants in each case. Operations on arrays as a whole are not permitted. The operands in logical
operations are either binary or decimal variables. The result is always
binary—true (1) or false (0).

Table 11.2 FORTRAN operations

Symbol	Definition	Example	Value of operands	Result
		ARITHMETIC		
**	Exponentiation	A**B	A = 2., B = 3.	8.
*	Multiplication	A*B	A = 2., B = 3.	6.
/	Division	B/A	A = 2., B = 3.	1.5
+	Addition	A+B	A = 2., B = 3.	5.
−	Subtraction	A−6.	A = 2.	−4.
		LOGICAL		
.GT.	Greater than	A.GT.B	A = 2., B = 3.	F
.GE.	Greater than or equal to	A.GE.B	A = 2., B = 2.	T
.LT.	Less than	A.LT.B	A = 2., B = 3.	T
.LE.	Less than or equal to	A.LE.B	A = 2., B = 3.	T
.EQ.	Equal to	A.EQ.B	A = 2., B = 3.	F
.NE.	Not equal to	A.NE.8	A = 2.	T
.NOT.	Not	.NOT.A	A = 1	F
.AND.	And	A.AND.B	A = 1, B = 0	F
.OR.	Or	A.OR.B	A = 1, B = 0	T

Arithmetic operations are executed in the following order: exponentiation first, multiplication and division second, addition and subtraction third. Operations at the same level are executed from left to right. Expressions in parentheses are always evaluated first. For example, if A = 2., B = 3., and C = 4., then

$$A**B+C = 12. \quad \text{but} \quad A+B**C = 83.$$

$$A/C*B = 1.5 \quad \text{as does} \quad B*A/C$$

$$A/C+B = 3.5 \quad \text{as does} \quad B+A/C \quad \text{but} \quad A/(C+B) = .\overline{285714}$$

Two successive arithmetic operations are not permitted. If, for example, A is to be multiplied by −B, it must be written as A*(−B) rather than A*−B.

Some logical operations are used mainly to check on whether certain inequalities hold. These *comparison operations* are the first six logical operations in Table 11.2. They may have expressions as operands so that, for example, if A = 2., B = 3., and C = 4., then

$$(A**B+C).GT.(A+B**C) \quad \text{gives the result false (0)}$$

$$(A/C*B).EQ.(B*A/C) \quad \text{gives the result true (1)}$$

$$(A/(C+B)).LE.(A/C*B) \quad \text{gives the result true (1)}$$

Logical operations may be quite elaborate. For example, if A = 2., B = 3., and C = 4., then

$$((A**B+C).GT.(A+B**C)).OR.((A/C*B).EQ.(B*A/C))$$

gives the result 1 because the OR operation is true (gives result 1) if either of the operands is true (has value 1). However,

$$((A**B+C).GT.(A+B**C)).AND.((A/C*B).EQ.(B*A/C))$$

gives the result 0 since both operands must have value 1 in order for the AND operator to give the result 1. In the absence of parentheses, the order of execution of logical expressions is to evaluate the arithmetic parts first and then to carry out the logical operations. Among the logical operations, the comparison operations are executed first. These six operations are of equal priority and so would be executed from left to right in the order in which they appear. .NOT. is executed next, followed by .AND.. The operation .OR. has the lowest priority and is executed last. Thus, for example, the numbers under the operands in the following expression indicate the order in which they are to be executed:

A.GT.B.AND.C.GT.D.OR.A**N − X.LE.B/C*D+F
  6   9   7   10   1   4   8   2 3 5

11.9 EXPRESSIONS AND THE ASSIGNMENT STATEMENT

Any valid combination of operands and operations constitutes a *FORTRAN expression*. If all the operations are arithmetic, then the expression is called an *arithmetic expression*.

Values may be assigned to variables by means of the assignment statement, which has the following form:

[statement-number]variable = expression

The variable on the left may be subscripted, and the expression on the right may be any valid FORTRAN expression. The expression is evaluated, and the result is substituted for the value, if any, currently stored for the variable on the left. Lines 9, 12, 13, 20, and 21 of Fig. 11.1 contain examples of FORTRAN assignment statements. In each case, the expression on the right is an arithmetic expression. But this need not be the case. If, for example, A = 2., B = 3., and C = 4., then the assignment statement

$$L = ((A**B+C).GT.(A+B**C)).AND.((A/C*B).EQ.(B+A/C))$$

assigns the logical value 0 to L. Of course, L must have been declared to be a logical variable.   (The declaration of variables will be discussed in Sec. 11.15.)

Note that statements 12, 13, and 21 in Fig. 11.1 contain the factor DSQRT(D) or DSQRT($-$D).   The FORTRAN compiler contains in it a series of *FORTRAN library programs*, each of which can be used by merely writing its name followed by an argument or arguments in parentheses.   DSQRT is the name of the library program that computes the square roots of the argument using long-form representations of real numbers.   CSQRT computes square roots using complex arithmetic, and SQRT computes square roots using short-form representations.   There are many other library programs, including the trigonometric functions, the absolute-value function, logarithmic and exponential functions, hyperbolic functions, and the normal-error function.   A description of a few of the most important of these library programs is given in Appendix C of this book.   A complete list is given on pages 109 and 110, Appendix C of [5], version 4.

11.10   INPUT/OUTPUT—GENERAL CONSIDERATIONS

Input/output (I/O) must provide for communication with a wide variety of units—magnetic-tape devices, disk-storage devices, card readers and punches, printers, plotters, etc.   The instructions must also be people-oriented.   They must permit the computer to accept inputs and produce outputs that are easily prepared and interpreted.   These requirements almost inevitably cause the I/O instructions in a programming language to appear cumbersome and unnecessarily complex.

I/O statements process data sets.   A *data set* is a collection of data items that is external to the program during its execution.   Input and output can now be defined as follows: *input* transfers one or more data items from the data set to the program, whereas *output* transfers one or more data items from the program to the data set.

There are several I/O statements available in the FORTRAN language.   We shall discuss only two of them: the READ statement and the WRITE statement.   In addition, we shall discuss the FORMAT and NAMELIST specifications associated with FORTRAN I/O.   The END FILE, REWIND, BACKSPACE, DEFINE FILE, and FIND statements will not be discussed.   Also, the use of the READ and WRITE statements in connection with direct-access I/O will not be covered.   These statements are discussed in [5] on pages 69 to 76 of version 4.

An I/O statement and the corresponding FORMAT statement should provide four basic pieces of information.   These are:

1. Whether the operation is an input or an output. The word "READ" is used for inputs, and "WRITE" for outputs.
2. The computer component from which inputs are to be read or on which outputs are to be recorded. This is called the *data-set reference* and is indicated by the first of two numbers in parentheses after the word "READ" or "WRITE." The second number is a reference to the FORMAT statement associated with the I/O statement.
3. The list of variables in the program to which numbers are being assigned or from which numbers are being outputted. This list appears at the end of the I/O statement.
4. A sequence of specifications for the format in which the data will appear on input or in which the data are to appear on output. These specifications are given in the FORMAT statement. Each variable in the list is associated with a corresponding specification in the FORMAT statement, proceeding from left to right.

The next four sections, Secs. 11.11 to 11.14, will be devoted to a detailed description of how this is done. A fifth section on I/O, Sec. 11.16, contains a discussion of the NAMELIST statement. This statement can be used to input or output a list of variables in a standard way. Detailed specifications for formats are not required, and a corresponding FORMAT statement is not used. The NAMELIST statement is not generally available in other versions of FORTRAN IV.

11.11 THE READ STATEMENT

Input is carried out by means of a READ statement and its associated FORMAT specification. The *READ statement* contains the following basic information:

1. Where the information that is to be read in can be found, i.e., the data set reference
2. The statement number of the FORMAT specification associated with this READ statement
3. The names of the variables to which numbers are being assigned using this statement

The syntax for presenting this information is

*R*EAD(data-set-reference, statement-number)list-of-variables

Standard data-set references have been established for the System/360. For example, 5 is normally used to indicate that the card reader is the input device and 6 is normally used to assign the printer as the output device. Thus, almost every READ statement will begin

READ(5,

Control cards can change these standard references and can establish references for data sets on magnetic tapes, disks, and other devices. Additional information on setting up and processing data sets can be found on pages 8 and 9, 17 to 23, and 38 to 50 of the programmer's guide [6].

The statement-number reference is the link to the corresponding FORMAT statement.† The computer must be told what it can expect to see in the input set. Rather than clutter up the READ statement with the specifications for the input set, the programmer includes the specifications in a separate FORMAT statement. The statement number connects the two statements.

The list contains a series of variable or array names, separated by commas. It controls the assignment of items in the data set to variables. Assignments are made in the order in which the variables appear on the list. The list controls termination of input; that is, items are read from the set and assigned to elements in the list until the list is exhausted. If the data set is exhausted, the execution of the program will be terminated unless an END option is used.

There are additional special features available with the READ statement that enhance its usefulness. The END option is just one of these features. Others are the ERR option and the NAMELIST approach to input mentioned at the end of the preceding section. With these options and also with the option of numbering the READ statement itself, the syntax for the READ statement becomes

[statement-number]READ(data-set-reference[,{statement-number-1 |namelist-name}][,END = statement-number-2][,ERR = statement-number-3])[list-of-variables]

Now we are using "statement-number-1" to refer to the statement number of the corresponding FORMAT statement. It is optional, as is the list of variables now, because neither the FORMAT specification nor the list of variables appears in a READ statement that employs the NAMELIST option. The *END option* permits the programmer to branch to another statement in the program if the data set is exhausted

† A name of a FORMAT array may also be given. This option will not be discussed. It permits the programmer to specify the format of his input (or output since it can be done with the WRITE statement as well) at the time the program is executed. This option is called an *object time FORMAT statement* and is discussed on page 47 of version 4 of the manual [5].

but the variables list is not. The program branches to statement-number-2. The *ERR portion*, if it is used, specifies that the program should branch to statement-number-3 if an input error is encountered. In the absence of an ERR option, the execution of the program is terminated when an input error is encountered.

Note that the READ statement on line 5 of Fig. 11.1 contains an END option: END = 5. Since statement 5 is the STOP statement, the program will cease execution—but in a normal way, without any error messages—when all the input data set is exhausted. This approach is frequently taken when an undetermined number of sets of input data are to be processed.

An example of a READ statement using the NAMELIST option will be given in Sec. 11.16. In addition, consider the following examples:

READ(5,25)X,Y,Z

READ(5,25,END = 20,ERR = 16)X,Y,Z

Both statements will cause values to be assigned to X, Y, and Z from the first, second, and third numbers in the data set in accordance with the specifications detailed in statement 25. The first statement will cause the program to be terminated if either the data set is exhausted or an input error is encountered. For the second statement, the program will branch to statement 20 if the data set is exhausted and to statement 16 if an input error is encountered.

11.12 THE WRITE STATEMENT

The syntax of the *WRITE statement* is

[statement-number]WRITE(data-set-reference[,{statement-number-1|namelist-name}])[list]

The various portions of the WRITE statement have meanings similar to those of the corresponding portions of the READ statement. In this case, the data set reference will usually be 6, in order to obtain printed output. Note that END and ERR options are not permitted.

Just as for the READ, the list contains a series of variable names separated by commas. The values stored for the elements in the list are entered as items in the data set in the order of the elements listed.

Both the READ and the WRITE statements permit the indexing and incrementing of arrays that are listed. For example, it is permissible to say

READ(5,10)(A(I),I = 1,7,2),X

WRITE(6,10)(B(K),K = 1,L),Y

Note the parentheses around the indexed and incremented portion to indicate that it is all a single list element. In the first case, the list as given is equivalent to A(1),A(3),A(5),A(7),X. In the second case, it is equivalent to B(1),B(2), . . . , B(L),Y, where L is assumed to have been assigned an integer value before this point. We shall return to the specification of such lists in Sec. 11.18.

If an array appears as a list element, all the elements in the array are assigned values (READ) or written out (WRITE). The DIMENSION statement serves to specify the number of elements that are involved.

Examples of WRITE statements can be found on lines 2, 14, and 22 of Fig. 11.1 and line 28 of Fig. 11.2. An example of a WRITE statement using the NAMELIST option will be given in Sec. 11.16.

11.13 FORMAT STATEMENTS—GENERAL CONSIDERATIONS

A FORMAT statement is used to indicate the way data sets are to be interpreted, in input, or constructed, in output. This is done by prescribing the interpretation or construction of each element in the variable list by a corresponding entry in the FORMAT statement. Certain FORMAT codes must be used for entering the prescription; they will be discussed in the next section. A FORMAT statement may be placed anywhere in the program.

The form of the *FORMAT statement* is

statement-number *F*ORMAT(specification[,specification] . . . [,specification])

The specifications may be any of the FORMAT codes or a slash. If a slash is used, the comma separating specifications may be omitted. Parentheses may be used to group specifications, and multiple entries of the same specifications may be indicated by premultiplying that specification with the appropriate constant. Commas may also be omitted where parentheses appear.

In the absence of slashes, the parentheses in a FORMAT statement are used to enclose a single record. A FORTRAN record may be thought of as a single card on input or a single line of printing on output. If other I/O media are used, the record must be appropriately defined. This is covered in the reference on setting up and processing data sets, on pages 8 and 9, 17 to 23, and 38 to 50 of version 0 of the programmer's guide [6]. A slash is used to mark the end of a record. For example, the following FORMAT statement refers to three records:

67 FORMAT(F10.4/I4/F20.8)

Multiple slashes will cause records to be skipped and can be used to insert blank lines in printouts or to skip cards in input.

Recall that the variables list, rather than the FORMAT statement, controls the processing. That is, so long as there are variables in the list, an attempt will be made to continue input or output. If the specifications in the FORMAT statement are exhausted, the next variable is assigned to the first specification. However, if there are parentheses in the FORMAT specifications, the rule is more complicated. The procedure is then as follows:

1. Ignore the left parenthesis immediately after the word "FORMAT."
2. Proceed from right to left.
3. Stop at the first left parenthesis not entirely enclosed in another pair of parentheses (remember that the first left parenthesis is ignored and so is not enclosing anything).
4. Assign the next variable to the first specification to the right of this parenthesis.

Consider the following examples:

43 FORMAT(---(---(---)--)---)

44 FORMAT(---(---)----(----)----)

The assignment of specifications proceeds as indicated by the arrows.

FORMATS for printer outputs must include a special *carriage-control specification* at the beginning of each new record. The carriage control is indicated by entering a literal character. This can be done using either quotes or the H FORMAT code. More specifically, using a "b" to indicate a blank character:

If the first entry for a printed record is		Then the carriage will make the following advance before printing
Either	Or	
1Hb	'b'	One line
1H0	'0'	Two lines
1H1	'1'	First line of next page
1H+	'+'	No advance

Ordinarily, carriage-control characters will not appear in FORMAT statements associated with nonprinted output. Since the carriage-control character is a literal entry, it would be entered in the output record of nonprinted outputs if it were erroneously included in the FORMAT statement.

The first line of printed output for a FORTRAN program will be entered under control of the operating system. It may appear at the start of a new page or embedded in a series of messages related to the set of control cards used. In order to set off the printed output on a new page, it may be desirable to begin the program with a pair of statements similar to those appearing on lines 2 and 3 of Fig. 11.1.

11.14 FORMAT CODES

We shall discuss only the G, I, F, H, X, T, and literal codes. See the discussion of FORMAT codes on pages 50 to 67 of version 4 of the manual [5] for information on the D, E, L, C, A, and P codes.

The *G FORMAT* code is a general one that can be used to transfer integer, real, complex, or logical data. Its general form is

[factor]G field-length[.significant-digits]

The factor is a positive-integer constant used to denote a number of repetitions of the code. So that, for example, we may write 4G8.3 in lieu of G8.3, G8.3, G8.3, G8.3. The field length indicates the total number of positions in a record (e.g., columns in a card, positions in a printed line) spanned by this code reference. The significant-digits portion specifies the number of significant digits to be included in the output or retained in the input. This portion is optional only for I/O of integer or logical data.

From this point on, we shall use the letter a to refer to the factor, the letter w to refer to the field length, and the letter s to refer to the number of significant digits. We shall also use the letter d to refer to the number of digits to the right of the decimal point.

Consider, for example, the following sequence of I/O statements:

        READ(5,1)A,B,C
    1   FORMAT(3G10.5)
        WRITE(6,2)B,C,A
    2   FORMAT(1Hb,G15.6,G12.6//1Hb,G15.6)

The FORMAT associated with the READ statement indicates that we shall read A from the first 10 columns of the first data-input card, B from columns 11 to 20 of this same card, and C from columns 21 to 30. If the card had the following entries stored in it:

    Columns 1–10:   .25631E02b
    Columns 11–20: b−6.14E08b
    Columns 21–30: 171.114132

then the value stored for A would be .25631E02, that for B would be −.61400E09, and that for C would be .17111E03. Note that, because of the choice of the names for these variables and in the absence of any IMPLICIT or type statement to the contrary, the variables are all real-valued, short-form numbers.

Since the WRITE statement is executed immediately after the READ statement, the values assigned to these numbers have not been changed. From statement 2, we see that the printout will look as follows:

Line 1: bb−0.614000Eb09b171.110bbbb
Line 2: All blank
Line 3: bbbb25.6310bbbb

Note that B is printed in E FORMAT. This is because its absolute value is outside the range 0.1 to 10**s. Superfluous leading zeros after the decimal or concluding zeros before the decimal would have been required if B was printed in the same way that A and C are printed. (B is actually greater than 10**s in absolute value and would have required superfluous concluding zeros.) Note also that both A and C contain four concluding blanks in their fields. This is because four positions must always be allotted for the possibility of an exponent, and if there is none, four blanks appear at the end of the field. Except for this, the number is right-adjusted in the field.

Suppose, instead of A, B, and C, we were reading in K, L, and M and writing L, M, and K using the same FORMATS. Suppose also the input card contained

Columns 1–10:   bb4621bbbb
Columns 11–20: bbbbbb3161
Columns 21–30: 1234567bbb

Then the value 4621 would be stored for K, 3161 for L, and 12345 for M. (Incidentally, if we had omitted the optional s specification, 1234567 would have been stored as the value for M.)

The printout is

Line 1: bbbbbbbbbbb3161bbbbbbbb12345
Line 2: blank
Line 3: bbbbbbbbbbbb4621

Complex numbers are treated as an ordered pair of real numbers both in input and in output. For example, if D is a complex number, then the statement READ(5,1)D would use the first specification in the corresponding FORMAT statement to read in the real part of D and the second to read in the imaginary part. This means that if we had the same input card as was used to read in A, B, and C and the same FORMAT, the value assigned to D would be .25631E02−.61400E09I.

Logical constants take on the values *true* or *false*, denoted by a T and an F or a .TRUE. and a .FALSE., respectively, in the data set.

For example, if Q is a logical constant with the value *true*, then the statements

WRITE(6,3)Q

3   FORMAT(1Hb,G3)

would result in the following printout:

Line 1:   bbT

The *I FORMAT code* is used to transfer integer data.   It has the form

[a]Iw

Blank spaces to the right of the first significant digit in the field are read as zeros on input.   The leftmost print positions are filled with blanks on output.   If the number of digits to be printed is greater than w, asterisks are printed in the whole field.   If, however, the number of digits is equal to w but the number is negative, its positive value is printed.   Thus, for example, using the I4 specification:

If the internal value is	The printed result is	If the following appears in the input field	The stored result is
−7132	7132	−11b	−110
64241	****	bb12	12
0	bbb0	bbbb	0
−323	−323	−b11	−11
−6	bb−6	1212	1212

The *X FORMAT code* is used to indicate the insertion of blanks in the output or the skipping of positions in the input record.   Its syntax is wX.   In all FORMAT codes, w must be less than 256.   The X code is not associated with a variable in the list.   Examples of the use of the X code can be found on lines 16, 17, and 24 of Fig. 11.1 and on line 26 of Fig. 11.2.

The *T FORMAT code* is used to specify a position in a record where the transfer of data is to begin.   Its syntax is Tw.   The T code is not associated with a variable in the list.   An example of its use appears on line 16 of Fig. 11.1.   It would cause the first character to be output in the twenty-ninth print position of the line.

The *F FORMAT specification* is used to transfer real data.   It has the form

[a]Fw.d

Provision must be made for a sign and a decimal point on output. If there are more than d digits to the right of the decimal in the internal value, the last digit that is retained is rounded before the value is printed. So that, for example, if the stored value for A is 6.317, then

WRITE(6,20)A

20   FORMAT(1Hb,F5.2)

would result in the value 6.32 being printed on the next line of the output. The integer portion of the number is treated as the integer number was, using the I code. If there are too few positions to print the integer portion, then asterisks will be printed. Also, if there is no room for the minus sign of a negative number, the positive value will be printed. The following table illustrates these rules.

If the internal value is	Then the following is printed using an F6.2 specification
114.11	114.11
−321.16	321.16
−16.272	−16.27
3217.14	******
−13.1	−13.10
.377	bb0.38

If a decimal is punched in the input field, the d specification is ignored. So that, for example, if .31721 appeared in the input field and the specification F6.2 was used, .31721 would be stored. In the absence of a decimal point, the d specification is used to place the decimal. If 317222 appeared in the input and the specification F6.2 was used, then 3172.22 would be stored.

The *H FORMAT code* is used to present literal information. We shall discuss only the output of literal information. Literal input is discussed on pages 64 and 65 of version 4 of the manual [5]. The H code is frequently used to label outputs. See, for example, lines 15, 16, 23, and 24 of Fig. 11.1 and lines 25 and 26 of Fig. 11.2. The syntax is

wH message

The message, which must be w characters long, counting blanks, is inserted in the output at this point. The H code is not associated with a variable in the list. The output for the quadratic-roots problem, corresponding to the use of the H code in Fig. 11.1, is given in Fig. 11.3.

Literal data in a FORMAT statement can also be denoted by writing the string of characters enclosed in single quotation marks, i.e., by enclosing the statement in apostrophes. A quotation mark itself within a

```
THE ROOTS OF THE QUADRATIC WITH COEFFICIENTS
A=        0.2430000           B=         2.4730000           C=        0.2170000
                              ARE
ROOT1=       -0.0906619                      ROOT2=       -2.53818212

THE ROOTS OF THE QUADRATIC WITH COEFFICIENTS
A=        1.0000000           B=         2.0000000           C=        1.0000000
                              ARE
ROOT1=       -1.0000000                      ROOT2=       -1.0000000

THE ROOTS OF THE QUADRATIC WITH COEFFICIENTS
A=        1.0000000           B=         2.0000000           C=        5.0000000
ARE COMPLEX CONJUGATES WITH THE FOLLOWING REAL AND IMAGINARY PARTS
REAL PART=       -1.0000000                  IMAGINARY PART=       2.0000000

A IS ZERO
```

Fig. 11.3 Printout obtained in a run of the quadratic-roots program.

literal string is indicated by the use of two apostrophes. For example, "I CAN'T READ" is entered as literal data in a FORTRAN statement by writing

'I CAN''T READ'

The use of literal data in FORMATS for output is similar to that of the H code. In fact, literal data are frequently used in order to avoid counting the number of characters in the message associated with an H specification. An example of the use of literal data appears on line 16 of Fig. 11.1 and on line 29 of Fig. 11.2. The use on line 16 serves to insert the word "ARE" in the output. Since it is preceded by the specifications /1Hb,T30, the word "ARE" actually appears beginning in print position 29 of a new line. The use of literal data on line 29 of Fig. 11.2 serves to cause the message "A IS ZERO" to be printed.

11.15 THE IMPLICIT, TYPE, AND DOUBLE PRECISION STATEMENTS

As we pointed out earlier, FORTRAN variables may be integer, real, complex, or logical. Logical variables take either of two values, *true* or *false;* the other variables take on the kinds of values indicated by their names. Unless otherwise specified, variables beginning with the letters I to N are integer and all other variables are real. However, the programmer may override this specification by means of the IMPLICIT statement. The *IMPLICIT statement* must be the first statement in the program, and there can be only one in each program. It has the form

IMPLICIT type[*length](character-specification)[,type[*length] (character-specification)] · · · [,type[*length] (character-specification)]

The type can be any one of the following: INTEGER, REAL, COMPLEX, or LOGICAL. The character specification can be in the form of either a list of first letters of names or a range of first letters of names to be assigned to that type. For example, the IMPLICIT statement below maintains the usual specifications for variable names beginning with the letters A to Q. However, variable names beginning with R to X have been reserved for complex variables, and those beginning with Y or Z have been reserved for logical variables.

IMPLICIT INTEGER(I–N),REAL(A–H,O–Q),

COMPLEX(R–X),LOGICAL(Y,Z)

The optional "*length" specification in the syntax for the IMPLICIT statement refers to the number of bytes to be reserved for storing the value of this variable. If no length is specified, the standard length is allotted. The *standard lengths for FORTRAN variables* are four bytes for integer, real, and logical and eight bytes for complex. The *optional lengths for FORTRAN variables* are 2 for integer, 8 for real, 16 for complex, and 1 for logical. The programmer thus has a choice of two lengths in each case. We have been calling this the *short-form* and *long-form* representations in talking about real variables. If we use this terminology for all types of variables, then we can say that the long form is standard for representing integer and logical data and the short form is standard for representing real and complex numbers.

Another way to specify the type or length of FORTRAN variables is by means of the *type statement*. The form of this statement is

type[*length]variable-name[(array-specification)][/initialization/]
[,[*length]variable-name[(array-specification)][/initialization/]] · · ·
[,[*length]variable-name[(array-specification)][/initialization/]]

This statement serves to declare the type of a variable or an array by its name rather than by its initial character. In addition, it permits specification of the length of the variable, the bounds for subscript values, and the initialization of variables. The type is declared first. Again the choice is from among INTEGER, REAL, COMPLEX, and LOGICAL. The optional length is specified exactly as for the IMPLICIT statement. The name of the variable follows, and then the array specification, if any. The array specification may also be given in a DIMENSION statement if the programmer prefers that approach. Bounds for each subscript, separated by commas, are entered in the parentheses. Initial assignment of values to variables may be made by placing each value between a pair of slashes. Any number of variables may be included in a single type statement.

Examples of two type statements are as follows:

INTEGER ARRAY(6,10,2),X/20/,I/5/,*2J/0/

REAL ITEM(4,6),TOT/0./,*8Y,*8BIG/4.2D+06/

The first statement declares ARRAY, X, I, and J to be integer-valued. Except for J, they will all use four bytes of storage. J uses two bytes. ARRAY is three-dimensional, with bounds of 6, 10, and 2 for the subscripts. X is initialized at 20, I at 5, and J at 0. The second statement declares ITEM, TOT, Y, and BIG to be real. ITEM is a two-dimensional matrix with bounds of 4 and 6 for its subscripts. TOT is initialized at zero, and both TOT and the elements of ITEM use four bytes of storage. Y and BIG use eight bytes of storage, and BIG is initialized at 4,200,000. (Note the use of the D in initializing BIG.)

A special *DOUBLE PRECISION statement* permits a programmer to specify that a list of variables and/or the elements of whole arrays are real and of eight bytes length. In addition, bounds for subscripts can be specified, just as they were in the DIMENSION and type statements. Line 4 of Fig. 11.1 contains an example of a DOUBLE PRECISION statement. A second example is given below. This example declares the elements of MATRIX to be real and of length eight; it also specifies that MATRIX is a 6 × 4 array.

DOUBLE PRECISION MATRIX(6,4)

The syntax of a DOUBLE PRECISION statement is

DOUBLE PRECISION variable-name[(array-specification)] [,variable-name[(array-specification)]] · · · [,variable-name[(array-specification)]]

11.16 THE NAMELIST STATEMENT

The list of variables and arrays that appears in a READ or WRITE statement may be given in a separate *NAMELIST statement*. This is done as follows:

1. Add to the program a NAMELIST statement that includes a name for and a definition of the list. The NAMELIST statement must appear before the corresponding READ or WRITE statement.
2. Insert the name of the list in the READ or WRITE statement in lieu of the number of a FORMAT statement.
3. Omit the list of variables from the READ or WRITE statement.

The syntax of the NAMELIST statement is

*N*AMELIST/list-name/list[/list-name/list] · · · [/list-name/list]

Note that several lists may be named in a single NAMELIST statement. The list contains a sequence of variable or array names separated by commas, just as in the lists in a READ or WRITE statement. The list-name cannot appear as an argument in any other FORTRAN statement.

Since a FORMAT specification is not given, the *I/O of a named list* must proceed in a standard way. On input, the first character in the record in the data set is ignored. The second character must be an ampersand (&), followed immediately by the list-name. A blank follows, and then a series of assignments of constants to variables and/or arrays is given. These assignments are of the form

variable-name = constant   or   array-name = set-of-constants

The assignments are separated by commas, as are individual constants in the set used for assigning values to an array. The number of constants in an assignment of values to an array name must equal the number of elements in the array. The constants may be integer, literal, complex, or logical. Also, if k identical constants are to be stored in successive elements in an array, the form "k* constant" may be used to make all k assignments in one step.

The input is concluded with an ampersand and the word "END."

Output using a WRITE statement and an associated NAMELIST statement generates records that look like inputs to a READ statement using the same NAMELIST. This means that we get an ampersand as the second character, followed by the name of the list, a blank, and a series of assignments of the form "variable = constant" or "array name = set of constants."

Consider, for example, the following program:

DIMENSION ARRAY(3,3)

NAMELIST/LIST1/A,B,C,ARRAY/LIST2/A,ARRAY

READ(5,LIST1)

WRITE(6,LIST2)

STOP

END

Suppose the following was input:

Cols.	Contents
2	&
3–7	LIST1
8	b
9–15	A = 2.17,
16–27	B = 1.045E − 02,
28–36	C = 6.1712,
37–65	ARRAY = 1.0,3*0.0,1.0,3*0.0,1.0
66–69	&END

The values 2.17, .01045, and 6.1712 would be stored for A, B, and C, respectively. Also, a 3 × 3 unit matrix would be stored in ARRAY. The printout obtained in running this program was:

Line 1: &LIST2

Line 2: A = bb2.1699991bbbb,ARRAY = bb1.0000000bbbb,
b0.0bbbbbbbbbbb,b0.0bbbbbbbbbbb,
b0.0bbbbbbbbbbb,bb1.0000000bbbb,b0.0bbbbbbbbbbb,

Line 3: b0.0bbbbbbbbbbb,b0.0bbbbbbbbbbb,bb1.0000000bbbb

Line 4: &END

The list of results begins on a separate line, and the ampersand and END are also printed on a separate line. A neatly blocked output is obtained with a clear indication of the beginning and end of the results. Note that real values are printed as if they were in format G15.8, except that a zero is printed simply as 0.0. Finally, we note that the value of A was changed from 2.17 to 2.1699991 because the number is stored hexadecimally and the conversion from decimal to hexadecimal and back to decimal caused this change in A.

11.17 CONTROL STATEMENTS

A FORTRAN program is ordinarily executed by proceeding to the next statement after executing the present one. Sometimes it is desirable to branch to some other location in the program after executing a statement. *Control statements* permit such branching to be carried out.

The simplest control statement is the *GO TO statement*. It has the following form:

[statement-number-1] *GO* TO statement-number-2

This statement will cause statement-number-2 to be executed next. Examples of GO TO statements can be found on line 18 of Fig. 11.1 and lines 27 and 30 of Fig. 11.2.

A more versatile branching tool is available in the form of a *computed GO TO statement*. Now the form is

[statement-number] *GO* TO(statement-number-1[,statement-number-2] · · · [,statement-number-n]),integer-variable

The integer variable must not be subscripted. The value of the integer variable is determined. Say it is i. The program then branches to statement-number-i. For example, if N = 3, then

GO TO(43,16,17,21,1005),N

would cause the program to branch to statement 17.   If the integer variable takes on a value outside the allowable range, the program executes the next statement.   (For example, a value of N of 0 or 6 would have been outside the allowable range in the above example.)

The most powerful FORTRAN control statement is the *IF statement*.   It comes in two varieties, the arithmetic IF statement and the logical IF statement.   The *arithmetic IF statement* has the form

[statement-number] *I*F(arithmetic-expression)statement-number-1, statement-number-2,statement-number-3

Note that only arithmetic expressions are permitted.   In fact, the expression must not be complex-valued.   The effect of the statement is to branch to statement-number-1 if the expression is negative, to 2 if the expression is zero, and to 3 if the expression is positive.   For example, if $A = 2.$, $B = 3.$, and $C = 4.$, then the statement

IF$(A - B + C)$10,15,20

will cause the program to branch to statement 20.   But if $A = 2.$, $B = 10.$, and $C = 4.$, the program will branch to statement 10.

The *logical IF statement* has the form

[statement-number] *I*F(logical-expression)statement

The statement portion can be any valid FORTRAN statement except a specification, a DO statement, or another logical IF statement.   In most cases, it will be either a GO TO or an assignment statement.   The statement portion will be executed only if the value of the logical expression is true (that is, 1).   If the value is false, the next FORTRAN statement will be executed.

Consider, for example,

    IF(A.LE.B)GO TO 26
    GO TO 27
26 IF(C.LT.D)C = D
27 . . . .

The effect of the first logical IF statement would be to skip the GO TO 27 statement if A is less than or equal to B.   This means that the program would proceed immediately to set $C = D$ if C is less than D. If A is greater than B, the second logical IF will not be executed and the value of C is unchanged.   Also, if C is greater than D, the value of C is unchanged.   For example, if $A = 2.$, $B = 21.$, $C = .4$, and $D = 1.073$, then the program would branch to statement 26 and the value of C would be changed to 1.073. If, on the other hand, $A = 21.$, $B = 2.$, $C = .4$, and $D = 1.073$ or if $A = 2.$, $B = 21.$, $C = 1.073$, and $D = .4$, then C is not changed.

To illustrate how the IF statement might be used in a program, suppose, given values of the argument x, we wished to output corresponding values of the following function:

$$f(x) = \begin{cases} 1 \text{ if } x \geq 1 \\ x \text{ if } 0 \leq x \leq 1 \\ 0 \text{ if } x \leq 0 \end{cases}$$

The following program will do this:

```
      WRITE(6,20)
  20  FORMAT(1H1,'ARGUMENT',20X,'FUNCTION F')
   8  READ(5,1,END=10)X
   1  FORMAT(F20.10)
      IF(X)2,2,3
   2  F=0
      GO TO 6
   3  IF(X-1.)4,4,5
   4  F=X
      GO TO 6
   5  F=1.
   6  WRITE(6,7)X,F
   7  FORMAT(1Hb,F16.6,10X,F16.6)
      GO TO 8
  10  STOP
      END
```

Note the use of the WRITE statement and corresponding 20 FORMAT statement to both start the output on a new page and prepare a header for the table of outputs. Note also the spacing used in the 7 FORMAT statement to ensure alignment of the header and output.

11.18 THE DO STATEMENT

Suppose we are given a one-dimensional array A, containing N real elements, and wish to compute the sum of the elements in the array. We could proceed in any of the following ways:

```
   SUM=0.0
   I=1
 2 SUM=SUM+A(I)
   IF(I-N)1,3,3
 1 I=I+1
   GO TO 2
 3 WRITE(6,4)SUM
 4 FORMAT(5H1SUM=,F16.6)
   STOP
   END
```

```
   SUM=0.0
   I=1
 2 IF(I.GT.N)GO TO 3
   SUM=SUM+A(I)
   I=I+1
   GO TO 2
 3 WRITE(6,4)SUM
 4 FORMAT(5H1SUM=,F16.6)
   STOP
   END
```

```
   SUM=0.0
   I=1
 2 SUM=SUM+A(I)
   I=I+1
   IF(I.LE.N)GO TO 2
   WRITE(6,4)
 4 FORMAT(5H1SUM=,F16.6)
   STOP
   END
```

It is assumed, of course, that values were assigned to the elements of A and N earlier in the program. Note that the carriage-control character in the three FORMAT statements is combined with the initial literal output.

The above can be done more succinctly using the DO statement. The DO statement has the form

[statement-number] *DO* statement-number-1 integer-variable = initial-value,test-value[,increment]

"Statement-number-1" is called the *range of the DO* and is the statement number of the last statement to be repeatedly executed. The integer variable is called the *DO variable*. It cannot be subscripted and serves as a counter in executing the DO. ("I" served as the counter in the above example.) It may or may not appear as a variable in the FORTRAN statements within the range of the DO. However, upon completion of the DO, it is undefined and cannot be used until it is redefined. The *initial value, test value*, and *increment* must each be either an integer constant or a nonsubscripted integer variable. They must also always be positive. The increment is optional, and it is set equal to 1 if it is not given.

The DO statement acts as follows: The DO variable is set equal to the initial value, and the statements in the range of the DO are executed. The DO variable is incremented, and the statements in the DO are again executed. The statements are executed for the last time when the DO variable takes on the greatest value less than or equal to the test value.

Using the DO statement, the section of a program used to compute the sum of the elements in the array A becomes

```
      SUM = 0.0
      DO 2 I = 1,N
    2 SUM = SUM + A(I)
      WRITE(6,4)SUM
    4 FORMAT(5H1SUM = ,F16.6)
      STOP
      END
```

Note that the variable SUM takes on the values 0, A(1), A(1) + A(2), and so on during the execution of the program. SUM must be assigned an initial value, 0.0 in this case, because it would otherwise appear on the right of an assignment statement (statement 2) before it is assigned a value. That is, when I = 1, statement 2 serves to assign a new value to

SUM which is equal to the old value plus A(1). But there would be no old value if the value of 0.0 had not been previously assigned to SUM.

It was noted that the DO variable need not appear in the statements in the range of the DO loop. It then serves merely as a counter. Suppose, for example, we wished to duplicate the output of a program N times. We could include in the program the following section:

```
    . . . . . . . . . . .
    DO  10  I = 1,N
    WRITE(6,4)-----
4   FORMAT(1H1,---)
10  CONTINUE
    . . . . . . . . . . .
```

The last statement in the range of a DO must be executable.† If it is not, then a dummy statement called a *CONTINUE statement* should be added to serve to conclude the DO. The CONTINUE statement has the form

[statement-number] *CONTINUE*

Although it may appear that the statement number is mandatory because the statement serves as the last statement in the range of a DO, it is indeed optional. The programmer may insert unnumbered CONTINUE statements at other places in his program if he chooses to.

There are other do's and don't's with respect to DO loops. They can be summarized as follows:

1. Do not branch into a DO from outside its range.
2. Branching out of a DO before it is completed is permitted.
3. Do not change the values of the initial value, the test value, and the increment, within the range of the DO.

Returning to the input and output of arrays, first discussed in Sec. 11.12, it should now be evident that the notation of the DO statement was used in that section. The subscript in the array is the DO variable, and the initial value, test value, and increment are used to indicate which elements are to be input or output. Thus, for example,

READ(5,20)(X(I),I = 1,5,2)

would result in values being input for X(1), X(3), and X(5). In dealing

---

† Also, it must not be a GO TO, PAUSE, STOP, RETURN, or arithmetic IF statement, or another DO statement.

with matrices, we must account for two subscripts, and we could write

READ(5,20)((X(I,J),I = 1,5,2),J = 1,7,3)

if we wished to assign values to X(1,1), X(3,1), X(5,1), X(1,4), X(3,4), X(5,4), X(1,7), X(3,7), and X(5,7) in that order.   Note that, since the subscript I is in the innermost parentheses, it is changing most rapidly. That is, we are reading in values column by column.   If we wished to assign values to these same elements of X(I,J) row by row, we would write

READ(5,20)((X(I,J),J = 1,7,3),I = 1,5,2)

Now the elements are assigned values in the order X(1,1), X(1,4), X(1,7), X(3,1), X(3,4), X(3,7), X(5,1), X(5,4), and X(5,7).   Just as for ordinary DO statements, if the increment is 1, it need not be given.

Note that the word "DO" does not actually appear in the READ or WRITE statement.   As a result, the phrase *implied DO* has been used to refer to the use of the DO notation in input/output.

Finally, if all the values in an array are to be input or output, only the name of the array need appear in the list of variables; the implied DO notation need not be used.   The DIMENSION statement serves to determine the test value, and the initial value and increment are assumed to be 1.   The elements are assigned values or written out column by column for a matrix.   More generally, the first subscript changes most rapidly, the next changes next most rapidly, and so on.   Thus, for example, the statements

DIMENSION X(2,2,2)

READ(5,20)X

would result in values being assigned to the elements of X in the following order: X(1,1,1), X(2,1,1), X(1,2,1), X(2,2,1), X(1,1,2), X(2,1,2), X(1,2,2), X(2,2,2).

11.19 A FORTRAN PROGRAM FOR OBTAINING THE ROOTS OF A QUADRATIC

The time has come to apply our knowledge of FORTRAN to the writing of a complete program.   A program to obtain the roots of a quadratic polynomial will be developed in this section, and one to find the mean and standard deviation of a set of data in the next.

The roots of $AX^2 + BX + C$ can be obtained from the formulas

$$\text{ROOT1} = \frac{-B + \sqrt{B^2 - 4AC}}{2A} \quad \text{and} \quad \text{ROOT2} = \frac{-B - \sqrt{B^2 - 4AC}}{2A}$$

The inputs are the coefficients A, B, and C, and the outputs are the two roots.   We should be able to process several sets of input in a single run. The output should be neatly formatted and labeled.

A critical consideration in computing the roots is whether $B^2 - 4AC$, the discriminant, is positive, negative, or zero.   If it is negative, the roots will be complex.   In this case, we have a choice of either using complex arithmetic or dealing with the real and imaginary parts separately as real numbers.   The former would require us to declare the roots, and certain

Program statements	Comments
WRITE(6,10)	We're off and running at the top of a new page.
10 FORMAT(1H1)	
DOUBLE PRECISION A,B,C,D,ROOT1,ROOT2, REAL,XIMAG	Why be half-safe?
1 READ(5,2,END = 5)A,B,C	The coefficients, punched in columns 1–10, 11–20, and 21–30 are read in.
2 FORMAT(3F10.4)	
IF(A*A + B*B + C*C)1,1,8	Really, if they are all zero, let's give up.
8 If(A)9,20,9	If A = 0, the polynomial is not a quadratic.
9 D = B*B − 4.*A*C	The discriminant is computed.
IF(D)3,4,4	The critical consideration.
4 ROOT1 = (− B + DSQRT(D))/(2.*A)	The real roots are obtained, using
ROOT2 = (− B − DSQRT(D))/(2.*A)	the double precision square root.
WRITE(6,6)A,B,C,ROOT1,ROOT2	
6 FORMAT(1H0,44HTHE ROOTS OF THE QUADRATIC WITH COEFFICIENTS/1Hb, 2HA = ,F16.7,10X,2HB = ,F16.7,10X,2HC = , F16.7/1Hb,T30,'ARE'/1Hb,6HROOT1 = , F18.8, 20X,6HROOT2 = ,F18.8)	The messy details required to obtain the printout given in Fig. 11.3 if the roots are real.
GO TO 1	Go back for another set of data.
3 REAL = (− B)/(2.*A)	The real and imaginary portions of
XIMAG = (DSQRT(− D))/(2.*A)	the complex roots are obtained.
WRITE(6,7)A,B,C,REAL,XIMAG	
7 FORMAT(1H0,44HTHE ROOTS OF THE QUADRATIC WITH COEFFICIENTS/1Hb, 2HA = ,F16.7,10X,2HB = ,F16.7,10X,2HC = , F16.7/1Hb,66HARE COMPLEX CONJUGATES WITH THE FOLLOWING REAL AND IMAGINARY PARTS/1Hb,10HREAL PART = ,F18.8,20X, 15HIMAGINARY PART = ,F18.8)	The messy details required to obtain the output given in Fig. 11.3 if the roots are complex.
GO TO 1	Go back for another set of data.
20 WRITE(6,15)	The output if A = 0.
15 FORMAT(1H0,'A IS ZERO')	
GO TO 1	Go back for another set of data.
5 STOP	We'll get to here if there are no more data.
END	That's all, folks!

Fig. 11.4 An annotated FORTRAN program to compute the roots of a quadratic polynomial.

variables used to obtain the roots, to be complex. The latter would require us to be very careful about formatting the output. We decided to use the latter approach in order to illustrate how printed output may be labeled.

An annotated FORTRAN program to compute the roots of a quadratic is given in Fig. 11.4. The listing and the accompanying comments should be studied in order to better understand how to convert the formulas and the I/O and other considerations into a program. Certain details, such as continuation marks, which would appear in column 6, and comments cards, have been omitted. The complete program, without annotated remarks, can be found in Figs. 11.1 and 11.2. The printout obtained in one of the runs of this program is given in Fig. 11.3.

11.20 A FORTRAN PROGRAM TO COMPUTE MEANS AND STANDARD DEVIATIONS

We shall now develop a FORTRAN program to compute the mean and standard deviation of each of several sets of input data. We shall assume that each set begins with a card on which is punched the number of observations in the set, also called the *sample size*. This will be denoted by N in the program. This is followed by the observations, eight to a card, 10 columns to an observation. We shall also assume that the observations are real, with a decimal point punched somewhere in the field.

Given a set of N observations, $X_1, X_2, X_3, \ldots, X_N$, the mean XBAR and the unbiased estimate of the population standard deviation,[†] SIGHAT, are given by

$$\text{XBAR} = \frac{\sum\limits_{i=1}^{N} X_i}{N}$$

$$\text{SIGHAT} = \sqrt{\frac{N\left(\sum\limits_{i=1}^{N} X_i^2\right) - \left(\sum\limits_{i=1}^{N} X_i\right)^2}{N(N-1)}}$$

We shall compute the sum and the sum of squares of the observations by adding the value of X_j and X_j^2 to $\sum\limits_{I=1}^{j-1} X_I$ and $\sum\limits_{I=1}^{j-1} X_I^2$, until $J = N$. The next principal consideration is to conserve storage space in writing the program. If we read in all the observations, or even a single set of

[†] Refer to [7], page 78, for a definition of the population standard deviation, to page 171 for a definition of the sample standard deviation, to page 192 for a definition of bias, and to page 182 for a derivation of the unbiased estimate of the population standard deviation.

observations, we shall soon find that core storage will be exhausted. Suppose, instead, we read in the observations eight at a time, i.e., record by record. We could then process these eight and use the same storage space (i.e., the same variable names in the FORTRAN program) for the next eight. This is what was done in our program. We must, of course, also keep a separate counter that will tell us when we have read in all the data in a single set. The approach taken in the program is to define a new integer variable, M, equal to N plus 7 divided by 8. M is the number of records to be read in if there are N observations. [In carrying out integer arithmetic, the fractional part of a result is truncated. For example, $(19+7)/8$ is 3.] The disadvantage of this approach is that blanks or zeros must appear in the last data card in each set after the Nth observation. Other characters appearing in these positions will be read in as data and can either cause an error that will interrupt execution or give an erroneous result.

Figure 11.5 contains an annotated FORTRAN program to compute means and standard deviations. The output from a run of this program

Program statements	Comments
WRITE(6,10)	
10 FORMAT(1H1,'SAMPLE SIZE',20X,	The table of outputs, beginning at the
'MEAN',20X,'SIGMA HAT')	top of a new page, now has a heading.
DIMENSION X(8)	
DOUBLE PRECISION X, SUMX,SUMX2,XBAR,	We'll need this because ΣX^2 gets big and
SIGHAT	$N\Sigma X^2 - (\Sigma X)^2$ can go awry.
5 READ(5,2,END = 20)N	The sample size is input; if there are no
	more data, then we go to statement 20.
2 FORMAT(I4)	
SUMX = 0.	We must set the storage locations that
SUMX2 = 0.	will hold ΣX and ΣX^2 to zero.
M = (N+7)/8	N observations give M records.
DO 7 J = 1,M	Each of the M records will be processed
	in the same way.
READ(5,3)(X(I),I = 1,8)	The Ith record is read.
3 FORMAT(8F10.4)	
DO 7 I = 1,8	ΣX and ΣX^2 are calculated.
SUMX = SUMX + X(I)	
7 SUMX2 = SUMX2 + X(I)*X(I)	
XBAR = SUMX/N	
SIGHAT = DSQRT((N*SUMX2 - SUMX*SUMX)	Now we have one set of results.
/((N - 1)*N))	
WRITE(6,6)N,XBAR.SIGHAT	The results are entered in the table.
6 FORMAT(1Hb,I8,20X,F16.6,10X,F16.6)	
GO TO 5	Go back for another set of data.
20 STOP	
END	That's all there is, there isn't any more.

Fig. 11.5 An annotated FORTRAN program to compute means and standard deviations.

is given below:

Line 1:	SAMPLE SIZE	MEAN	SIGMA HAT
Line 2:	112	20.924107	5.811688
Line 3:	17	1.889465	7.225034

11.21 SUBPROGRAMS—STATEMENT FUNCTIONS, FUNCTION SUBPROGRAMS, AND SUBROUTINE SUBPROGRAMS

If a series of instructions is to be executed several times with different arguments and at different points in a FORTRAN program, it may be desirable to use a *subprogram*. The series of instructions is written once, using dummy variables. This subprogram is then called in at the different points where it is needed with the appropriate variables substituted for the dummy variables.

There are three kinds of subprograms available in FORTRAN IV. These are statement functions, FUNCTION subprograms, and SUBROUTINE subprograms. The choice of a subprogram depends on the number of instructions required in it and the number of outputs it is to provide. Table 11.3 contains a summary of the characteristics of each of the three subprograms that are available.

Subprograms may be named in the same way that variables are named. Since a statement function and a FUNCTION subprogram

Table 11.3 Characteristics of FORTRAN subprograms

Type	Length	Outputs	Called by	Requires in subprogram
Statement function	One statement	One value	Use of function name, with actual arguments, in an arithmetic expression	Name(dummy-arguments) = expression
FUNCTION subprogram	Several statements	One value	Use of function name, with actual arguments, in an arithmetic expression	FUNCTION name(dummy-arguments) . . . . RETURN END
SUBROUTINE subprogram	Several statements	Any reasonable number of values	CALL name(actual-arguments)	SUBROUTINE name(dummy-arguments) . . . . RETURN END

return a single value, it is this value that is really stored in the location corresponding to the name of the program.   Any of the techniques used to declare special properties for variables can be used to declare special properties for the statement function or the FUNCTION subprogram. That is, the name of either of these two kinds of subprograms can appear in a type statement.   Also, the use of an IMPLICIT statement to revise the convention for assigning properties to variables is applicable to the names of these subprograms.   Finally, FUNCTION subprograms can be declared of special type in the FUNCTION statement itself.   This will be discussed later in the section.

A *statement function* is defined in a single statement that has the form

$$name(\text{dummy-arguments}) = \text{arithmetic-expression}$$

The *dummy arguments* are nonsubscripted variables separated by commas. These variables should appear in the arithmetic expression on the right. The expression must not contain any subscripted variables.   The definition of an arithmetic function must precede the first executable statement in the program.   Suppose, for example, we wished to repeatedly compute the sum of five arguments, using this sum in different ways during the execution of the program.   We could write

$$S5(A,B,C,D,E) = A + B + C + D + E$$

If we wished to later compute

$$(SUM + X + Y + Z + F)/(TOT + RHO + SIGMA + SIG2 + VAR)$$

and call the result RATIO, we could write

$$RATIO = S5(SUM,X,Y,Z,F)/S5(TOT,RHO,SIGMA,SIG2,VAR)$$

A *FUNCTION subprogram* is defined in several statements that result in a single output.   It is compiled separate from the main program and so must conclude with an END statement.   In addition, it must include RETURN statements, which serve the same purpose as the STOP statement in the main program.   The *RETURN statement* causes control to be transferred to the main program in much the same way that control is passed to the operating system by the STOP statement.

The first statement in a FUNCTION subprogram has the form

$$FUNCTION \; name(\text{dummy-arguments})$$

The arguments will ordinarily appear on the right side of assignment statements in the subprogram.   The name will ordinarily appear on the left side of assignment statements in the subprogram.   These statements serve to assign a value to the named function in terms of the dummy variables.

Consider, for example,

> FUNCTION YTWO(X)
>
> IF(X)40,40,30
>
> 40   YTWO = 5.*X+1.0
>
> RETURN
>
> 30   YTWO = .2*X+2.0
>
> RETURN
>
> END

This FUNCTION subprogram defines the following function of X:

$$YTWO(X) = \begin{cases} 5X+1.0, X \leq 0 \\ .2X+2.0, X > 0 \end{cases}$$

If we wished to compute $(YTWO(6))^2$ in the main program and call it SQUARE, we need only write

> SQUARE = (YTWO(6))*(YTWO(6))

Since FUNCTION subprograms and subroutines are compiled separate from the main program, it is permissible to use the same name for different variables in these subprograms and the main program. Of course, since the named subprogram itself appears in both, this is not true of the name of the subprogram.

Now that we have seen what FORTRAN functions look like, the declaration of FORTRAN functions using the *FUNCTION statement* will be discussed. A more general syntactical definition of the FUNCTION statement is

> [type]FUNCTION name[*length](dummy-arguments)

For example,

> REAL FUNCTION YTWO*8(X)
>
> INTEGER FUNCTION TOTAL(I,J,K)

In the first case, the real value YTWO, returned from the subprogram, is expressed using the long form. In the second case, TOTAL is declared to be an integer function name.

Subroutines tend to be more elaborate than functions. Also, since they may return several results, the set of dummy variables associated with them includes output as well as input variables. A special *CALL statement* is required before using the values that are returned from the subroutine. It has the form

> CALL name(actual-arguments)

The actual arguments are variables appearing in the main program that
are to be substituted for the dummy input and output variables in the
subroutine. The first statement in the subroutine is the *SUBROUTINE
statement*, which has the form

SUBROUTINE name(dummy-arguments)

Except for the inclusion of output variables in the set of dummy arguments, this statement is much like the FUNCTION statement without
type or length specifications. Most programmers list input variables
first and outputs last, but this is not a syntactical requirement.

Consider, for example, the following subroutine:

```
      SUBROUTINE LARGE(ARR,I,BIG,J)
      DIMENSION ARR(10,10)
      BIG = ABS(ARR(I,1))
      J = 1
      DO 70 K = 2,10
      IF(ABS(ARR(I,K)) − BIG)70,70,71
   71 BIG = ABS(ARR(I,K))
      J = K
   70 CONTINUE
      RETURN
      END
```

After some analysis, it should be clear that this subroutine finds the
element in the Ith row of the array, ARR, that is largest in absolute
value. It assigns the dummy variable BIG to the absolute value of this
element and the dummy variable J to the column in which BIG appeared.
We might use this subroutine as follows:

```
      DIMENSION COVAR(10,10)
      . . . . . . . . . . . . . . . . . .
      CALL LARGE(COVAR,J,DIV,ICOL)
      DO 10 I = 1,ICOL
   10 COVAR(J,I) = COVAR(J,I)/DIV
      . . . . . . . . . . . . . . . . . .
```

This serves to replace the elements in the Jth row of COVAR, up to
and including the element with the biggest absolute value in the row,
by the original element divided by this biggest absolute value. Note
that two variables, I and J, are used to denote different things in the

subroutine and the main program. For example, J is the column in which BIG appears in the subroutine and J is also the row in COVAR that we are changing in the main program.

Normally, control is passed to the statement immediately after the CALL statement in the calling program after a subroutine is executed. However, it is possible to branch to another statement in the calling program by using a nonstandard RETURN. The RETURN statement in a SUBROUTINE subprogram has the form

> RETURN[{integer-variable|integer-constant}]

If the optional integer variable or constant is present, then a *nonstandard RETURN* is implemented. It functions in much the same way as a computed GO TO. The SUBROUTINE statement would have asterisks in lieu of some of its dummy variables. The corresponding actual variables in the CALL statement would contain statement numbers, designated by an ampersand followed by the number. If the integer constant is 1 or if the variable takes on the value 1, the first listed statement number is executed on return. If it is 2, the second one is executed, and so on. Suppose, for example, we had:

Calling program	*Subroutine*
CALL SPEC(A,B,C,&25,&31,&7)	SUBROUTINE SPEC(X,Y,Z,*,*,*)
7 · · · · · · · · · · · · · · · · · · ·	
· · · · · · · · · · · · · · · · · · ·	· ·
	IF(X*X+R)10,20,30
31 · · · · · · · · · · · · · · · · · · ·	10 RETURN 1
· · · · · · · · · · · · · · · · · · ·	20 RETURN 2
	30 RETURN 3
	END
25 · · · · · · · · · · · · · · · · ·	
· · · · · · · · · · · · · · · · ·	

If $X*X+R<0$, return will be made to statement 25; if $X*X+R=0$, return will be to statement 31; and if $X*X+R>0$, return will be made to statement 7. If the integer variable or constant is out of the allowable range (less than 1 or greater than 3 in this example), return is made to the first executable statement after the CALL statement.

It is also possible to enter a SUBROUTINE or FUNCTION subprogram at some point other than the first executable statement after the FUNCTION or SUBROUTINE statement. This is done by adding *ENTRY statements* to the subprogram. The syntax is

> ENTRY name(dummy-arguments)

The name must be distinct from the name used for the subprogram or for any other entry points. If the subprogram is a subroutine, the appearance of this name in a CALL statement will result in the execution of the subroutine beginning with the first executable statement after the ENTRY statement. If the subprogram is a function, the appearance of this name in an arithmetic expression will result in the execution of the function beginning with the first executable statement after the ENTRY statement.

There are some do's and don't's with respect to FUNCTION subprograms and subroutines. They include:

1. IMPLICIT statements may appear in FUNCTION subprograms and SUBROUTINE subprograms, but they must be placed immediately after the FUNCTION or SUBROUTINE statement.
2. SUBROUTINE statements and FUNCTION statements may not appear anywhere other than as the first statement in these subprograms.
3. Subprograms may call other subprograms.
4. The dummy arguments must agree in type and length with the actual variables. Arrays that appear as dummy arguments must have the same dimensions as arrays in the main program. However, it is permissible to assign maximum values to the subscripts in arrays in subprograms using integer variables. These integer variables must be subprogram arguments. This makes the dimensions of dummy arrays adjustable, a feature that is called *adjustable dimensions*. This feature is discussed, with examples, on pages 81 and 82 of version 4 of the manual [5].

11.22 DEBUGGING A FORTRAN PROGRAM

The FORTRAN compiler and language have several features that can assist a programmer in debugging a FORTRAN program. However, since debugging a program is really another kind of algorithm testing, Sec. 5.7 should be reviewed before reading about these special features. It is most important to prepare an adequate set of test data in accordance with the recommendations in that section.

We shall discuss three major aids to debugging available in FORTRAN. These are:

1. The diagnostic messages produced by the FORTRAN compiler
2. The sectioning of a program into subprograms
3. The use of NAMELIST-oriented output

In addition, a special DEBUG facility has been incorporated into the FORTRAN IV G compiler. However, limited experience with it indicates that it is not suitable for use by a novice. It is described in Appendix F of the manual [5].

The FORTRAN compiler provides diagnostic messages in the output to indicate to the programmer the kind of error that may be present. *FORTRAN error and warning messages* are printed on the source listing, which should always be obtained as a part of the output during debugging. The errors are flagged by a dollar sign, which is printed immediately under the character believed to be in error. No more than four errors are flagged in a single line of code. A coded error message is also printed on the next line. For example, in running the quadratic-roots program, the following appeared in the program listing:

    1   READ(5,2,END = K)A,B,C
                          $

        01)   IEYO131ISYNTAX

The dollar sign under the K indicates that the compiler believes this character is erroneous. The message, number 01 because it is the first one for this program, then provides another description of the trouble. A dictionary of diagnostic messages can be found in Appendix D of the guide [6]. IEY0131I is used to denote a SYNTAX error, indicating that this portion of the statement does not conform to the required syntax. Syntax requires a statement number, not a variable, to appear at this point in a READ statement.

FORTRAN status messages indicate that compilation was terminated in some nonnormal fashion. These messages appear at the very end of the printout. They are defined in the dictionary in Appendix D of [6]. In writing the quadratic-roots program, the statement on line 18 of Fig. 11.1 was erroneously punched as GO TO 5. Since the first set of coefficients yielded real roots, this branch of the program was executed first. As a result, only one set of outputs was obtained even though several sets of coefficients were input. The diagnostic message was

    IHC230I SOURCE ERROR AT ISN 0012
    EXECUTION FAILED AT SUBROUTINE MAIN

The abbreviation *ISN* is used for internal statement number. The erroneous GO TO 5 statement was numbered 0012 in the program listing. The clue was quite effective.

The bugs that remain after the syntactical errors have been corrected are the hardest ones to detect. This is particularly true of long, complex programs. One way to simplify the debugging is to break the program into smaller parts. For example, if a long program can be separated into logically distinct sections, it may be advantageous to write the program by using several subroutines. Test data can be inserted, and the input and output of each subroutine can be checked separately. The major disadvantage is that it is somewhat awkward and wasteful of computer time, since each subroutine is compiled separately.

NAMELIST statements and corresponding WRITE statements can be added to a program during debugging in order to obtain intermediate results that would not ordinarily be output. The use of a NAMELIST approach is recommended because:

1. The statements can be easily removed after the program is debugged.
2. The printout is always conveniently labeled.
3. The set of variables to be output can be varied by modifying the NAMELIST statement.

Consider, for example, the following NAMELIST statement, which could be added during the debugging phase at the beginning of the program to compute means and standard deviations:

NAMELIST/DEBUG1/M/DEBUG2/SUMX,SUMX2

Then, the statement

WRITE(6,DEBUG1)

could be inserted after the statement $M = (N+7)/8$. Also, the statement

WRITE(6,DEBUG2)

could be inserted after statement 7 if only the last values of ΣX and ΣX^2 were desired. If intermediate values of these sums were desired, this same statement could be inserted immediately before the statement $SUMX = SUMX + X(I)$. (This would result in all sums, including the initial value but excepting the last one, being printed out for each set of input data. If all sums except the initial value, but including the last one, were desired, something else could have been done. See Prob. 11.4.)

Excerpts from the printout obtained from the means and standard-deviation program when the NAMELIST and WRITE statements were added to the program are given in Fig. 11.6. The second WRITE statement was inserted immediately before $SUMX = SUMX + X(I)$ in the program. Note the repetition of the same values of SUMX and SUMX2 in the last excerpt. This results from the blank fields that fill out the last data card. SUMX and SUMX2 are recomputed, adding zero to each of these values, once for each set of 10 blank columns at the end of the last card. Also note that the mean and standard deviation are embedded in the set of partial sums. This awkward structuring of the

```
SAMPLE SIZE                        MEAN                   SIGMA HAT
&DEBUG1
M=        14
&END
&DEBUG2
SUMX=  0.0                     ,SUMX2=  0.0
&END
&DEBUG2
SUMX=  22.0000000000000       ,SUMX2=  494.0000000000000


&END
&DEBUG2
SUMX=  1386.499999999919      ,SUMX2=  32277.74999999999
&END
&DEBUG2
SUMX=  1411.499999999999      ,SUMX2=  32902.74999999998
&END
&DEBUG2
SUMX=  1444.500000000000      ,SUMX2=  33991.74999999999


&DEBUG2
SUMX=  2321.499999999998      ,SUMX2=  52300.74999999998
&END
          112                      20.924107                  5.811688
&DEBUG1
M=          3
&END
&DEBUG2
SUMX=  0.0                     ,SUMX2=  0.0
&END
&DEBUG2
SUMX=  4.632109999999996      ,SUMX2=  21.45644305209997


&DEBUG2
SUMX=  32.12090999999997      ,SUMX2=  895.9092600320981
&END
&DEBUG2
SUMX=  32.12090999999997      ,SUMX2=  895.9092600320981
&END
&DEBUG2
SUMX=  32.12090999999997      ,SUMX2=  895.9092600320981
&END
           17                       1.889465                  7.225034
```

Fig. 11.6   Excerpts from the printout obtained in a run during the debugging of the program to compute means and standard deviations.

output occurs only in the debugging phase.   After the special NAME-LIST and WRITE statements are removed, a conveniently formatted output will be obtained.

11.23   THE PRECISION OF FORTRAN COMPUTATIONS

The number of digits carried in FORTRAN computations is dictated by the number of bytes used in representing the variable, i.e., by the length specification.   Real numbers ordinarily are stored in their short form, using four bytes.   This results in approximately seven decimal digits being represented.   The long form may be specified.   Eight bytes are used, and about 16 decimal digits are represented.   Complex numbers are pairs of real numbers and so require either 8 bytes in their short form or 16 bytes in their long form.   Integer numbers ordinarily are stored in their long form using four bytes.   They may optionally be stored in two bytes.   Logical values ordinarily are stored in four bytes, but they may be stored in one byte.

The major decision to be made by the programmer is usually whether the long-form representation of real numbers is desirable.   A safe approach is to use the long form if storage requirements permit it. (For example, note the "Why be half-safe?" comment in Fig. 11.4.) However, in some applications, the long form is absolutely necessary, and some means must be found to implement it even if, at first, storage requirements prohibit its use.   This is the case in the means and standard-deviation program.   The computation of the standard deviation involves the difference $N\Sigma X^2 - (\Sigma X)^2$.   The quantities $N\Sigma X^2$ and $(\Sigma X)^2$ are usually of the same order of magnitude and may be quite large.   Significant digits can be lost if the long form is not used.   To compensate for the additional storage requirements, we wrote the program so as to retain only eight observations in storage at any one time.

What of the number of digits used and retained in carrying out operations on operands of different types and different lengths?   In general, if a real variable in long form appears in the computations, the calculations are carried out in long form.   The type and length of the variable on the left of the assignment statement determine how much of the result is ultimately retained.   However, a number with 7 significant digits that is stretched to contain 16 digits is still accurate to only 7 digits. If 16 digits of precision are required, it might be best to use a DOUBLE PRECISION statement in order to be sure that all the intermediate operands, as well as the final ones, are represented using the long form.

More specifically, since any arithmetic expression is the result of a series of pairwise operations, it is sufficient to define the type and mode of the result of every pairwise combination of operations.   This is done in Table 11.4.   The abbreviations I for integer, R for real, and C for

Table 11.4   The type and length of the results of arithmetic operations

If the first operand is	*The result is as tabulated if the second operand is*					
	I2	*I4*	*R4*	*R8*	*C8*	*C16*
I2	I2	I4	R4	R8	C8	C16
I4	I4	I4	R4	R8	C8	C16
R4	R4	R4	R4	R8	C8	C16
R8	R8	R8	R8	R8	C16	C16
C8	C8	C8	C8	C16	C8	C16
C16	C16	C16	C16	C16	C16	C16

complex are used. Some study of the table leads to the following conclusions:

1. Operations with operands of the same type and length give results of that type and length.
2. The type and length of the operands can be ordered as follows: complex 16, complex 8, real 8, real 4, integer 4, integer 2. Operations with operands of different type and length yield results with the type and length of the higher-ordered operand. There is one exception—if real-8 and complex-8 operands are combined, the result is complex 16. The reason should be obvious; the long form of the real portion must be retained.

Suppose, for example, that X and Y are real and of length 4 and that N and M are integer and of length 2. Any expression involving all these operands must yield a result that is real and of length 4. Thus $(X+Y)/(N*M)$, $X+Y+N+M$, and $(X*N)/(Y-M)$ would all yield a real result of length 4. Note, however, that the denominator in the first expression is integer and of length 2.

PROBLEMS

11.1 Which of the following are invalid names for FORTRAN variables? Assume that parentheses are always used to enclose subscripts and that the type of each variable is determined in the standard way. Give reasons for your choice.

VVV   INTEGER 1   1SUM   A4719   N(6*M,4*J)   INTEG1
A(−7,21)   X*   LENGTH   X/21   POST   PLUS

11.2 What values will be assigned to the variables X, Y, and Z using the input statements

    READ(5,1)X,Y,Z
  1 FORMAT(G10.2/F20.4,26X,F14.4)

if the following appears on the input cards:

Card	Cols.	Contents	Card	Cols.	Contents
1	1–9	−bbb43891	2	1–10	6423.17191
	10–80	Blank		11–50	Blank
				51–60	1234567891

11.3 Rewrite the program to compute quadratic roots using quotes, rather than the H specification, to designate literal data.
11.4 Modify the program to compute means and standard deviations, given in Fig. 11.5, as follows: Using the NAMELIST approach, output all values of SUMX and SUMX2 except the initial value, for each set of input data.
11.5 Describe the output that will be obtained from the program written in answer to Prob. 11.4 if the input is as follows:

Card	Cols.	Entries	Card	Cols.	Entries	Card	Cols.	Entries
1	1–4	bb10	2	1–10	bb6.1bbbbb	2	61–70	bbbb2.1bbb
	5–80	Blank		11–20	b−3.2bbbbb		71–80	bbbbbb3.bb
				21–30	bbbbbbbb.6	3	1–10	Blank
				31–40	bb−4.5bbbb		11–14	−4.2
				41–50	bb0.1bbbbb		15–80	Blank
				51–60	000.3bbbbb			

11.6 Write a FORTRAN program to compute and output the correlation coefficient of X and Y, the mean of X, the unbiased estimate of the standard deviation of X, the mean of Y, and the unbiased estimate of the standard deviation of Y. Assume that the number of pairs of observations of X and Y, denoted by N, will be input in columns 1 to 4 of the first input card. Assume that X will be punched, with a decimal point, in columns 1 to 10 of each succeeding card and that the corresponding value of Y, with a decimal point, will be punched in columns 11 to 20 of the same card. The correlation coefficient is given by

$$r = \frac{N\Sigma X_i Y_i - \Sigma X_i \Sigma Y_i}{\sqrt{[N\Sigma X_i^2 - (\Sigma X_i)^2][N\Sigma Y_i^2 - (\Sigma Y_i)^2]}}$$

where all sums, Σ, are from $i = 1$ to N. Label all output and try to minimize the storage space required.

11.7 Modify the program written in answer to Prob. 11.6 so that any number of sets of input data can be processed in a single run. Output the result in tabular form. Include the sample size in the output.

11.8 Write a FORTRAN subroutine that will return the product of a complex number and its conjugate, given the complex number as input. Assume that all variables are real and of length 8; that is, treat the complex number as two distinct real numbers.

11.9 Write a FORTRAN program to reduce a ratio of complex numbers $(a + bi)/(c + di)$ to the form $e + fi$, where e and f may involve ratios of real numbers. Call the subroutine written in answer to Prob. 11.8 in this program.

Problems 11.10 to 11.16 are given by means of the table below. In each case, a FORTRAN program should be written to implement the algorithm and/or flow chart previously developed in working problems in Chaps. 5 and 6. A brief title for the problem is also given in the table.

	Write a FORTRAN program to implement	
Problem	The algorithm developed in solving the given problem in Chap. 5	Corresponding to the flow chart developed in solving the given problem in Chap. 6
11.10	5.6—Fibonacci numbers	6.3
11.11	5.7—Sort three numbers	6.4
11.12	5.11—Sort N numbers	6.6
11.13	5.13—Bridge problem	6.7
11.14	5.16—Euclidean algorithm	6.9
11.15	—	6.10—$_nC_i$
11.16	—	6.12—Simpson's rule

REFERENCES

1. IBM Operating System/360 FORTRAN IV (E Level Subset), *IBM Systems Ref. Library Form* C28-6513.
2. "Webster's Seventh New Collegiate Dictionary," p. 894, G. & C. Merriam Company, Springfield, Mass., 1961.
3. Ralston, A.: "A First Course in Numerical Analysis," McGraw-Hill Book Company, New York, 1965.
4. Ralston, A., and H. S. Wilf (eds.): "Mathematical Methods for Digital Computers," John Wiley & Sons, Inc., New York, 1960 (vol. 1), 1967 (vol. 2).
5. IBM System/360 FORTRAN IV Language, *IBM Systems Ref. Library Form* C28-6515.
6. IBM System/360 Operating System FORTRAN IV (G) Programmer's Guide, *IBM Systems Ref. Library Form* C28-6639.
7. Cramer, H.: "The Elements of Probability Theory and Some of Its Applications," John Wiley & Sons, Inc., New York, 1958.

ANNOTATED SUPPLEMENTARY BIBLIOGRAPHY

Six references on FORTRAN IV can be found in the Annotated Supplementary Bibliography at the end of Chap. 7. In addition, anyone who expects to do a great deal of programming in FORTRAN for the System/360 should get the manual ([5] above) and the programmer's guide [6]. The manual is reasonably well written.

chapter 12

THE PL/1 PROGRAMMING LANGUAGE

12.1 INTRODUCTION

A PL/1 program consists of a series of basic programming elements called *statements*. These statements are really commands to the computer, and ordinarily they are carried out in the order in which they are given. However, some of the statements can serve to command the computer to proceed to a statement other than the next one. PL/1 is a compiler-type language, and so these statements must be translated into machine-language instructions before the program is executed.

A general-purpose language, PL/1, provides a wide range of capabilities that are rarely all used in a single application. This presents problems to the designer of the language, to the person describing it, and to the user of the language. The designer must so construct the language that any unused capabilities can be safely ignored by the programmer. The describer must choose from among all the capabilities, describing some in detail, others superficially, and some not at all. The user must be aware of the particular implementation of PL/1 with which he is dealing; different computer manufacturers can be expected to vary the specification for the language they are implementing, and different computer centers may modify the language as delivered by the manu-facturer. The implementation described here is the PL/1 F-level language for IBM System/360 computers.

The approach taken in this introductory book is to describe those aspects of PL/1 in detail that are essential to the novice and the other aspects superficially, with syntactical structures and references to the appropriate manuals wherever possible. In this way, it is hoped that the novice will be able to write some relatively simple PL/1 programs after reading the chapter and also will use the chapter as an index for further information on the more advanced features of the language.

The designers of PL/1 solved their problem by providing default conditions for any capabilities not specified by the user. The PL/1 compiler assigns its own selected characteristics to constants and variables if the programmer does not. This permits a novice to write programs with little concern for the very special characteristics that PL/1 variables may have. However, on those rare occasions when the default specification does not satisfy his needs, the novice may become involved with errors he cannot diagnose.

PL/1 statements contain various parts of speech, which are, in turn, made up of a series of characters. The PL/1 language has been designed to permit the processing of many different kinds of information. Because of this, the set of characters, some of the parts of speech that can be used, and the kinds of information that can be processed must be described before the basic elements, the statements, can be discussed. Sections 12.3 to 12.11 contain these descriptions. In Sec. 12.12, at last, a PL/1 statement—the DECLARE statement—will be introduced. From that point on, the discussion will concentrate on how to write PL/1 statements.

12.2 A PL/1 PROGRAM

At this point, a PL/1 program for finding the roots of the quadratic $Y = Ax^2 + Bx + C$ is presented with the intention of exposing the reader to the general appearance of PL/1 programs and to some general considerations in writing these programs. The program follows.

```
QUAD_ROOTS: PROCEDURE OPTIONS(MAIN); PUT LIST
('ROOTS OF A*X*X+B*X+C=0')PAGE; NULL:; GET DATA
(A,B,C); IF(A*A+B*B+C*C)=0 THEN GO TO REND; IF
A=0 THEN GO TO ONEROOT, PUT DATA(A,B,C)SKIP(2);
Z=A+A; X=B*B-4.0*A*C; IF X<0 THEN DO; CALL
COMPLX; GO TO END_QUAD; END; X=SQRT(X);
ROOT_1=(-B+X)/Z; ROOT_2=(-B-X)/Z; PUT DATA
(ROOT_1,ROOT_2)SKIP(1); GO TO END_QUAD; COMPLX:
```

PROCEDURE; DECLARE(ROOT_1,ROOT_2,Y)COMPLEX FLOAT; Y=X; ROOT_2=SQRT(Y); ROOT_1 = (−B + ROOT_2)/Z; ROOT_2=(−B−ROOT_2)/Z; PUT DATA (ROOT_1,ROOT_2)SKIP(1); END COMPLX; ONEROOT: PUT LIST('ERROR IN INPUT,A=0')SKIP(2); END_QUAD: GO TO NULL; REND:END QUAD_ROOTS;

The semicolon is used to conclude a statement in PL/1. Note that separate statements did not appear on separate lines and no special effort was made to group the statements or to insert comments in order to improve the readability of the program. Comments should be used freely to improve the readability of the program. Comments are inserted in PL/1 programs by writing

/* comment */

Semicolons need not be inserted after comments. The programs should also be set out in a convenient way. There is no great advantage in using the minimum number of lines to record a PL/1 program. Thus we may rewrite the above program, improving its readability but not changing the way it will be executed, by writing it as follows:

/* A PROGRAM TO COMPUTE THE ROOTS OF A QUADRATIC POLYNOMIAL */ QUAD_ROOTS: PROCEDURE OPTIONS(MAIN);

PUT LIST('ROOTS OF A*X*X+B*X+C=0')PAGE;

NULL:; GET DATA(A,B,C,);

IF(A*A+B*B+C*C)=0 THEN GO TO REND;

IF A=0 THEN GO TO ONEROOT;

PUT DATA(A,B,C)SKIP(2);

Z=A+A; X=B*B−4.0*A*C;

IF X<0 THEN DO;

CALL COMPLX; GO TO END_QUAD; END;

/* THE ROOTS ARE REAL */

X=SQRT(X);

ROOT_1=(−B+X)/Z; ROOT_2=(−B−X)/Z;

PUT DATA(ROOT_1,ROOT_2)SKIP(1);

GO TO END_QUAD;

/* THE ROOTS ARE COMPLEX */

COMPLX: PROCEDURE;

```
    DECLARE(ROOT_1,ROOT_2,Y)COMPLEX FLOAT;
    Y = X;  ROOT_2 = SQRT(Y);  ROOT_1 = (-B+ROOT_2)/Z;
    ROOT_2 = (-B-ROOT_2)/Z;
    PUT DATA(ROOT_1,ROOT_2)SKIP(1);  END COMPLX;
/* THE POLYNOMIAL IS NOT QUADRATIC */
    ONEROOT:
    PUT LIST('ERROR IN INPUT,A = 0')SKIP(2);
/* REPEAT THE OPERATION IF THERE ARE MORE
DATA TO PROCESS */
    END_QUAD: GO TO NULL;
/* ALL GOOD THINGS MUST END */
    REND: END QUAD_ROOTS;
```

Ordinarily, a PL/1 program begins with a labeled PROCEDURE OPTIONS (MAIN) statement. The conclusion of the program is indicated by an END statement, which usually contains a reference to the label used in the PROCEDURE OPTIONS (MAIN) statement. In the above example, the label of the PROCEDURE OPTIONS (MAIN) statement is QUAD_ROOTS, and so the program is concluded with an END QUAD_ROOTS statement.

The program is usually prepared for input by punching the series of statements and comments on cards, one line per card, using a keypunch. In most instances the deck of cards is then submitted to a computer center, where it is processed by a professional computer operator. The results are then returned to the programmer. Ordinarily, the program will be punched beginning in column 2 and proceeding no further than column 72. These are the standard limits for entering PL/1 programs on punched cards. These limits are called the *source margin*.

Source-margin changes and some other important specifications are implemented via *control cards*. At some computer centers, the preparation of control cards has become a necessary adjunct to the preparation of computer programs. At other centers, the control cards are prepared by the staff of the center. These control cards serve to transmit special instructions to the operating system. Operating systems were discussed in Sec. 2.3. These systems are computer programs that provide for the smooth flow of jobs through the machine, call up compilers and other frequently used programs when they are needed, and maintain records on the utilization of the computer. Nothing more will be said about the preparation of control cards here; the staff of the computer center should be consulted.

12.3 THE CHARACTER SET

PL/1 programs can be written using either one of two character sets, the 60-character set or the 48-character set.   Ordinarily, the 60-character set is used.   The 48-character set is available for those programmers who do not have access to a keypunch that can punch all the characters in the 60-character set.   Once a set is chosen for a particular program, that set must be used for writing the entire program.   Both character sets contain only capital letters—lowercase letters are not available.   In a control card, the programmer indicates to the PL/1 compiler which character set has been chosen.

The *60-character set* is composed of alphabetic characters, digits, and special characters.   There are 29 *alphabetic characters*, which include the 26 letters A to Z and three additional characters.   These three are the currency symbol ($), the number sign (#), and the commercial *at* sign (@). There are 10 digits, the digits 0 to 9, and 21 *special characters*.   One of these special characters is a blank space; the other 20 are given in Table 12.1.

The break is used to provide a spacing in a group of characters to improve readability.   This is very useful to the programmer as it allows

Table 12.1   The special characters in the 60-character PL/1 set

Name	Symbol
Equals, assignment	=
Plus	+
Minus	−
Asterisk, multiply	*
Slash, divide	/
Left parenthesis	(
Right parenthesis	)
Comma	,
Decimal point, binary point, period	.
Quotation mark, apostrophe	'
Percent	%
Semicolon	;
Colon	:
Not	¬
And	&
Or		
Greater than	>
Less than	<
Break character	—
Question mark	?

him to write a variable name which is naturally two words without actually employing a space. (A blank space is not permitted in a name.) The following examples illustrate the use of this break character:

X_AXIS

JOB_NO

MASTER_FILE

Some additional symbols may be created by writing two consecutive special characters. The multiple-character symbols are as follows:

Symbol	Meaning	Symbol	Meaning
**	Exponentiation	]<	Not less than
]>	Not greater than	‖	Concatenation
>=	Greater than or equal to	/*	Left-hand border for comment
]=	Not equal to	*/	Right-hand border for comment
<=	Less than or equal to	—>	Special pointer qualification used only with list processing

In the *48-character set*, four symbols from the 60-character set are eliminated altogether and eight others are replaced by multiple-character symbols. The four symbols which are not available with the 48-character set are the break character (—), number sign (#), commercial *at* sign (@), and question mark (?). The symbols which are denoted by a combination of characters are given in Table 12.2. The first eight of these replace characters in the 60-character set. The combinations of letter symbols, such as in CAT or LE or NE, cannot be used for any other purpose. For example, when using the 48-character set, it is not permissible to name a variable CAT.

Throughout the remainder of this book, the 60-character set will be used.

12.4 SYNTAX NOTATION

Syntax has been defined in [1] as "the way in which words are put together to form phrases, clauses or sentences." In most higher-level programming languages, the basic language element is the statement, and the syntax for computer-programming languages is concerned with the rules for combining words and other symbols to form a statement. In general, the syntax for programming languages is more rigid than that for natural languages. This makes it easier to provide direct, syntactical

Table 12.2   Designation of symbols in the 48-character set using multiple characters

	60-*character symbol*	48-*character symbol combination*
Colon	:	..
Semicolon	;	,.
Percent	%	//
Greater than	>	GT
Less than	<	LT
Not	⌐	NOT
Or	|	OR
And	&	AND
Less than or equal to	< =	LE
Concatenation	||	CAT
Exponentiation	**	**
Not less than	⌐<	NL
Not greater than	⌐>	NG
Not equal to	⌐=	NE
Special pointer	—>	PT
Greater than or equal to	> =	GE
Left comment enclosure	/*	/*
Right comment enclosure	*/	*/

definitions of the different types of statements permitted in programming languages.

In order to express a syntactical definition in a compact, unambiguous way, it is desirable to establish certain conventions for syntactical notation.   The conventions to be used to syntactically define PL/1 statements are described in this section of the chapter.   (The system used in the manual [2] is followed throughout in order to facilitate the use of the manual as a further reference.)   These conventions apply only to the syntactical definitions and not to the PL/1 statements themselves.   In this section we are defining a language that will be used to talk about PL/1, we are not discussing PL/1 itself.   For example, lowercase letters are used in syntactical definitions; they are not even available for use in PL/1.

Lowercase letters will be used for words that are *notation variables*. Notation variables may also contain decimal digits and hyphens; however, they must begin with a letter.   Notation variables are used to denote parts of a statement that can be changed from statement to statement.

Capital letters are used to denote *notation constants*.   This means that terms appearing in capitals in syntax definitions also appear, in just the same way, in the corresponding PL/1 statement.

Consider the following example of a syntactical definition:

label:PROCEDURE;

The word "label," in lowercase, denotes a notation variable. It will be replaced in the PL/1 statement by some word that will serve to label this statement for reference at other points in the program. The word "PROCEDURE," a notation constant, must appear in the PL/1 statement exactly as it is given here.

Special characters, usually punctuation marks, are also notation constants and must appear exactly as in the syntactical definition, so that the colon and semicolon must appear exactly as they do in the example.

Examples of program statements corresponding to this syntactical definition are

COMPLX:PROCEDURE;

ROOT:PROCEDURE;

FIRSTA:PROCEDURE;

A1:PROCEDURE;

A brace is used in the syntactical definition to enclose several choices for items; one of these is to be selected for use in the statement. The brace is not a notation constant; it does not appear in a PL/1 statement. The alternatives can be either stacked vertically or listed horizontally separated by a vertical stroke (the vertical stroke in this context is not a notation constant). For example, either $\begin{Bmatrix} BIT \\ CHARACTER \end{Bmatrix}$ or {BIT|CHARACTER} can be used to indicate that the notation constant BIT or the notation constant CHARACTER can appear in the PL/1 statement at this point. Neither the brace nor the vertical stroke would appear in the PL/1 statement.

A bracket is used to enclose optional items and is itself not a notation constant. Consider, for example, the following syntactical definition:

identifier{BIT|CHARACTER}(length)[VARYING]

The only punctuation notation constants are the parentheses. This syntax indicates that the statement begins with an identifier; the word "BIT" or "CHARACTER" is next followed by the length, enclosed in parentheses. The word "VARYING" may or may not appear, depending on the intentions of the programmer. Examples of PL/1 statements corresponding to this specification are

VARLAB CHARACTER(10)

TSTDIG BIT(8)VARYING

The meaning of these statements will become clear later; the reader should only understand the nature of the syntax notation and the sense in which the above examples are substitutions in the corresponding syntactical definition.

There may be some ambiguity in the use of characters in syntactical definitions that can also appear in PL/1 statements. For example, the vertical stroke is a legitimate special character with a different meaning in PL/1 statements than it has in syntactical definitions. Where ambiguity may result, the item in the PL/1 language is underlined. For example, consider a situation in which the PL/1 programmer has a choice between the symbol for *and* (&) and the symbol for *or* (|). This is indicated syntactically by

$\{\& | \underline{|}\}$

An exception to the use of lowercase letters to denote notation variables occurs with the symbols "min" and "max." They are used to permit specification in the syntactical definition of the minimum and maximum possible values of a constant or variable or some set of constants or variables. They do not denote parts of a statement that can be changed from statement to statement. For example,

min 3 max 31{digit|letter}

is used to indicate that a combination of at least 3 but no more than 31 digits and letters may follow. The corresponding PL/1 statement will contain only the storing of from 3 to 31 characters.

12.5 STATEMENT LABELS

A *statement label* is a word, attached as a prefix to a statement, that permits other statements in the program to refer to the labeled statement. In general, the syntax for a statement is

[statement label:] · · · [statement label:]statement body;

Note the brackets, indicating that the label is, in general, optional. However, for certain statements, a label is required, for example,

label:PROCEDURE;

The three horizontal dots are used, as in mathematical notation, to indicate that the pattern established by the elements appearing in the sequence before and after the dots is to be used to fill in a variable number of elements in place of the dots. They are not punctuation notation constants. In this case, they merely indicate that any number of labels may be associated with a single statement. Multiple labels are treated as alternative identifiers, so that the statement

ADD1:ADDONE:X = X + 1;

could be referred to as either ADD1 or ADDONE.

Since every statement may have one or more labels, the specification for labeling a statement will be omitted from the syntax of PL/1 statements. However, this will only be done if the omitted specification would have appeared first and would have been

[statement label:] · · · [statement label:]

Thus, for example, the syntax for a PROCEDURE statement will include a reference to the statement label in order to indicate that at least one label must be used.

12.6 IDENTIFIERS

An *identifier* is a set of not more than 31 consecutive alphabetic, digital, and/or break characters which is used as a name for an entity in the program or as a means of helping to specify the purpose of a statement or the characteristics of a variable. The first character must be alphabetic. A statement label is an example of an identifier used to name statements. In addition to naming statements, identifiers are used to name data items, input/output files, and data aggregates.

Some examples of identifiers are:

COMPLX

X_AXIS

#643

PLOT#9

ACCOUNT_649_HERCULES_CORP

Z

ANTIDISESTABLISHMENTARIANISM

The novice may find it advantageous to restrict his identifiers to a length of only 7 characters, rather than 31. This is because one type of identifier, external names, is truncated to seven characters by the PL/1 compiler. The first four characters are combined with the last three characters of the name. (External names will be defined and discussed in Sec. 12.31.)

12.7 KEYWORDS

The PL/1 compiler recognizes the function of a statement or the significance of parts of a statement by employing unique identifiers called *keywords*. Keywords are not reserved; that is, they may appear elsewhere in the program and may be used for other purposes. For example, it is permissible to name a variable PUT or GET or BY even though these are all keywords.

An exhaustive list of the 221 keywords in PL/1 can be found in alphabetical order in Appendix D. This appendix also contains, for each keyword listed:

1. The abbreviation for the keyword where such an abbreviation is permitted
2. The kind, or type, of keyword that it is
3. A page reference to the manual [2] where the keyword is discussed
4. An example of its use

There are eight types of keywords. We shall define only three of these types here; the other five types are defined and discussed later in the chapter. (These other five are conditions, discussed in Sec. 12.30; data attributes, Sec. 12.9; file attributes, Secs. 12.15 and 12.27; formats, Sec. 12.26; and options, Sec. 12.27.) Note that only seven of these eight are recognized in the type assignments given in Appendix D. Separating keywords are not identified in the appendix.

There are five keywords used to separate parts of a statement. They are called, appropriately enough, *separating keywords*. These are

BY   THEN   WHILE

ELSE   TO

Keywords used to convey the purpose of a statement are called *statement identifiers*. A few of the more important statement identifiers are

BEGIN	DO	GET	READ
CALL	END	IF	RETURN
DECLARE	ENTRY	PROCEDURE	STOP
DISPLAY	FORMAT	PUT	

Built-in function names are keywords used to call up previously written algorithms that are available to a programmer using the PL/1 language. This permits the programmer to obtain square roots, trigonometric functions, absolute values, and a variety of other functions by merely employing the appropriate keyword and specifying the arguments for the function. The built-in function keywords can be easily recognized in the table in Appendix D since they are almost always of the form

keyword(argument[,argument] · · · [,argument])

Also, the page reference for these words can be found in the first column (1) in the "Type of Keyword" section. A more elaborate listing and definitions of the built-in functions useful in arithmetic computations can be found in Appendix E. A list and description of all the built-in functions in PL/1 can be found in Appendix 1 of the manual [2].

12.8 THE REPRESENTATION OF CONSTANTS

PL/1 is a general-purpose programming language and so must provide for not only the arithmetic manipulation of a variety of numbers but also the processing of information. The information is ultimately codified as a series of bits in the computer, but the PL/1 language must permit the programmer to think of it in terms of the representation he would use. This means that since the data in PL/1 programs may sometimes include collections of alphabetic or even special characters as well as numbers (collections of digits), virtually any combination of characters in the character set should be admissible as data.

In addition, a distinction must be made between data sets that can be varying and those that are constant. In the case of numbers, this is done by using identifiers to denote variables and using the number itself to denote its constant value. So that in the statement

ADD1:X = X + 1;

X is a variable and the 1 at the extreme right is a constant. Note that the 1 at the left is merely part of the statement label. In general, the DECLARE statement (see Sec. 12.12) is used to specify the characteristics of variables. The representation of constants in PL/1 statements will be discussed in this section. The characteristics, or attributes, of variables will be discussed in the next section.

Collections of characters are called *character strings* in PL/1. A character string is a connected sequence of any of the characters in the admissible character set, including the blank space. Single quotation marks are used to enclose references to character strings in PL/1 statements. When the quotation mark itself appears in a character string, it is represented by a pair of quotation marks. Thus, for example,

'CAN''T FIND A LABEL'

PL/1 also permits the processing of *bit strings*, which are connected sequences of the characters 0 and 1, that is, character strings that contain only 0s and 1s. References to bit strings in a PL/1 statement must also be enclosed in quotation marks, and to distinguish them from character strings, they must be concluded with the letter B. Examples are

'010'B

'1'B

'1011000011101110000'B

But '010' is a character string because it is not concluded with a B.

Numeric data, or *arithmetic data*, as it is called in PL/1, comes in five varieties. Decimal and fixed, decimal and floating, binary and fixed, binary and floating, and sterling and fixed. The *fixed-point sterling* representation permits the handling of British sterling currency in the PL/1 language. Data are written as: pounds.shillings.pence L. The letter L indicates that sterling currency is being represented, for example,

3.2.4L

12.4.6L

No further use or discussion of this data type will appear in this book.

Both fixed- and floating-point numbers can be written to either base 2 (binary) or base 10 (decimal). Binary representations are distinguished from decimal representations in the same way that bit strings are distinguished from character strings. The binary number contains a concluding B. Otherwise, the rules for writing the numbers are the same. Signs precede the digits; a decimal or binary point is optional. If it is not given, it is assumed to be immediately to the right of the low-order digit. Examples of binary fixed and decimal fixed numbers follow. The reader should verify that these numbers are equivalent.

Binary fixed	Decimal fixed
101B	5
1101B	13
110.1B	6.5
−1010B	−10
−101.1B	−5.5

Floating-point numbers consist of a mantissa and an exponent separated by the letter E. In writing decimal floating numbers, both the mantissa and the exponent are written to base 10; whereas for binary floating numbers, the mantissa is written to base 2 but the exponent is written to base 10. However, the exponent is a power of 2; that is, it moves the binary point the indicated number of places. Negative signs may be used for either the mantissa or the exponent; decimal or binary points can appear only in the mantissa.   The letter B is also used to conclude binary floating numbers.   Examples are:

Binary floating	Decimal floating
1.01E2B	5E0
$-1011E-3B$	$-1375E-3$
1101E$-$1B	65E$-$1
1101E4B	2.08E2

Each of the four nonsterling types of arithmetic data can be used to represent complex numbers.   The imaginary parts are written by concluding the representation with the letter I.   Thus,

$$5E0 + 65E - 1I$$

$$5 + 6.5I$$

$$101B + 110.1BI$$

are all valid representations of the same complex number.

12.9 VARIABLES AND THEIR ATTRIBUTES

A *variable* is a quantity that can assume any one of a set of values.   A *scalar variable* is a variable that denotes a single data item (as opposed to a variable that refers to an aggregate of data items).   The specifications for the characteristics of variables are called *attributes*.   Attributes are assigned to variables in a DECLARE statement (see Sec. 12.12).

Arithmetic-type variables refer to numbers rather than strings.   They are given attributes with respect to base, scale, and mode.   The *base* can be decimal or binary, the *scale* fixed or floating, and the *mode* real or complex.

In PL/1, every attribute of a variable has been given a *default* interpretation.   If no alternative is selected by the programmer, the compiler will automatically assume one of the choices.   This choice, which the compiler will make in lieu of specifications from the programmer, is called the *default condition* or *option*.

If the attributes of an arithmetic-type variable are not declared, then the default conditions are assigned as follows: If the first letter of the name is any of the letters I, J, K, L, M, or N, the default conditions are fixed, binary, and real.   If the first letter is any other than those mentioned, the defaults are floating, decimal, and real.

If some, but not all, of the attributes of a variable are declared, then the remaining attributes are assigned as floating, decimal, and real.   For example, the following statement declares the scale of TENSION as fixed:

DECLARE TENSION FIXED;

Since only the scale attribute is declared, the default conditions for base and mode apply. The three attributes of TENSION are then fixed, decimal, and real.

Another attribute must also be given for arithmetic data or it is assigned by default. This is the *precision attribute*, which specifies the number of significant digits (either binary or decimal) that are to be carried in the computations. The default and maximum precisions for F-level PL/1 are:

	Default precision	*Maximum precision*
Fixed decimal	5	15
Fixed binary	15	31
Floating decimal	6	16
Floating binary	21	53

Complex data are made up of two real data items, one for the real part and one for the imaginary part of the complex number. The precision of complex data then is the same as for the corresponding real variables.

String variables are used to denote string data. String variables must be assigned the attribute character or bit.

Examples of the assignment of attributes to arithmetic and string variables will be given in Sec. 12.12. A string variable may be described as having either fixed length or variable length. If it is of fixed length, its length should be specified. If it is of variable length, its maximum length should be specified.

12.10 DATA AGGREGATES

It is possible in PL/1 programs to assign a single name to a collection of data items. In addition, names can be assigned to subsets and individual items in the collection. Collective naming does not alter the data; its purpose is to give the programmer a convenient means for manipulating whole sets. There are two kinds of collections which can be treated as a whole in PL/1, arrays and structures.

An *array* consists of a collection of homogeneous items that can be thought of as arranged in some geometric pattern. Thus we can speak of an array of one dimension, two dimensions, three dimensions, and so on. A two-dimensional array is a rectangular arrangement—a *matrix*—of items. Two-dimensional arrays, or matrices, are frequently encountered in applications, and special attention will be devoted to them in the discussion that follows.

Two examples of rectangular arrays, i.e., matrices, are given below. In one example, the homogeneous items are fixed-point decimal numbers; in the other example, they are character strings.

Suppose we had the following three equations in three unknowns:

$$6x_1 + 22x_2 - 13x_3 = 4$$
$$-3x_1 + 16x_2 - x_3 = 7$$
$$x_1 + 2x_2 - 101x_3 = 26$$

The coefficients of x_1, x_2, and x_3 can be arranged in an array in which the rows are the different equations and the columns the different variables. Thus there would be three rows, since there are three equations, and three columns, since there are three variables. The array would be

```
 6   22   -13
-3   16   -1
 1    2   -101
```

Consider as a second example a manufacturing plant that has three different assembly lines. Suppose that there are five stations in each line and that one employee works at each station. We can succinctly describe the assignment of employees to stations in the form of an array in which each row represents an assembly line and each column the corresponding stations in the different lines. The matrix might be

GOLDEN	HARRINGTON	O'ROURKE	THOMAS	WASHINGTON
SMITH	BOSTON	KLEIN	DETTALI	FERGUSON
HARRIS	O'NEILL	SIEGEL	FEURST	DAYTON

From this matrix we see, for example, that Golden, Smith, and Harris service the same stations in the different lines and that O'Rourke works at the third station of the first line.

Individual elements in an array are identified by using the array name followed by a series of subscripts. There is one subscript for each dimension, and the subscripts are enclosed in parentheses and separated by commas. In a one-dimensional array, a single subscript is used to indicate the position of the element in the array. Two subscripts are used in a matrix. The first designates the row, and the second the column.

If, for example, we name the array of coefficients COEF, then the coefficient of x_1 in the third equation would be called COEF(3,1). In fact, COEF(3,1) = 1. Similarly, we see that if we call the array of assignments of employees to assembly-line stations WORK, then the statement that O'Rourke works at the third station of the first line can be more succinctly expressed by saying: WORK(1,3) is O'Rourke.

It may be useful to label the rows or columns of a matrix in an unusual way. For example, suppose the WORK matrix really referred to stations 7 to 11 in the assembly lines. It might be nice to be able to use these numbers, rather than the numbers 1 to 5, in the subscript referring to the elements in the matrix. This can be done in PL/1. Now we could say that WORK(1,9) is O'Rourke. This tells us that O'Rourke works at station 9 in the first line.

Also, it is sometimes desirable to allow a subscript to vary. For example, suppose we wished to study the makeup of the first assembly line. We could use WORK(1,J) to denote the Jth station in the first line. We could then manipulate the value assigned to J in order to move from one station in the first line to another station in this same line.

Structures consist of a hierarchical collection of not necessarily homogeneous items. Since they are hierarchical, they are graded into different levels. The *major-structure name* refers to all the items in the whole structure and is the first level. Certain subsets of the first level (i.e., of the whole structure) are then named, and these constitute the second level. Subsets of these subsets would constitute the third level,

Table 12.3 Structure of the master and weekly payroll files

Hierarchical level and file element	PL/1 identifier
1 Master file	MASTER
2 Employee number	MNO
2 Employee name	NAME_M
3 First name	FIRSTM
3 Middle initial	INITLM
3 Last name	LASTM
2 Regular hours worked	HM
2 Hourly pay rate	RATE
2 Regular gross weekly pay	RWP
2 Cumulative gross pay to date in the current year	CGP
2 Cumulative social security withheld in the current year	CFICA
2 Withholding tax deductions class	D
2 Cumulative withholding tax deduction in the current year	CWT
2 Hospitalization deduction	WHD
2 Regular net pay	RNP
1 Weekly file	WEEKLY
2 Employee number	WNO
2 Employee name	NAME_W
3 First name	FIRSTW
3 Middle initial	INITLW
3 Last name	LASTW
2 Number of hours worked during the week	HW

and so on. In general, .the $(N + 1)$st level consists of subsets of collections in the Nth level. Items which are not themselves major structures but which contain subsets are called *minor structures*. Items which contain no subsets are called *data elements*.

Consider, for example, the master and weekly payroll files first discussed in Sec. 5.6. The structures associated with the records in these files are outlined in Table 12.3. These structures are data aggregates in the PL/1 program that are useful in processing the information in the files. (The files are in the data external to the program; i.e., they are on magnetic tapes or disks.) The numbers used in Table 12.3 indicate the level of the structure associated with the given element, and the series of capital letters at the far right is the identifier associated with this element in the PL/1 program.

For example, the identifier NAME_M refers to the employee's full name in the master-file structure, whereas the identifier LASTM refers to his last name in the same structure. The identifier MASTER provides access to the master structure as a whole and is a major-structure name as is WEEKLY. NAME_M and NAME_W are minor-structure names; all other items are data elements.

12.11 PROGRAM STRUCTURE—STATEMENTS AND GROUPS

A PL/1 program is an algorithm. It is a series of commands, or *statements*, to a computer that are to be executed in the order in which they are given. There is also a collection of statements, called a *group*, that is not really a unit in the structure of the program. However, because it is convenient to do so, groups will also be defined in this section.

Statements may be either of two types, simple or compound. The *simple statement* has the following general form:

[[statement-identifier]statement-body];

The optional identifier, if it is present, determines the purpose of the statement. A statement without an identifier but with a statement body is called an *assignment statement*. As the name implies, an assignment statement is used to assign a new value to a variable. (This statement will be discussed in some detail in Sec. 12.18.) Note that both the identifier and the statement body are optional. This means that a statement could consist of only a semicolon; this is called a *null statement*. An example of each of the three types of simple statements follows:

GO TO END_QUAD;   (simple statement with identifier GO TO)

ROOT_1 = (−B+ROOT_2)/Z;   (assignment statement, assigning a new value to ROOT_1)

;   (null statement)

Each statement could, of course, have one or more labels attached.

A *compound statement* is one which specifies more than one action and which will contain two or more keywords. There are only two types of compound statements, the IF statement and the ON statement. Examples of these are

IF A=0 THEN GO TO ONEROOT;   (keywords are IF, THEN, and GO TO)

ON ZERODIVIDE GO TO FIX_NUMBER;   (keywords are ON and GO TO)

The function and form of both statements will be discussed in detail in later sections. The commands inherent in these statements are just those that might be guessed from their English-language interpretation. For example, in executing the first statement, the current value assigned to A is checked. If it is zero, the program will execute the statement labeled ONEROOT next. If A is not zero, the next statement in sequence will be executed.

"Group" is really a convenient name for certain sets of PL/1 statements. This name is useful in presenting the syntax of some PL/1 statements. For example, some of the clauses of an IF statement can be selected from among any of the sets of statements that constitute a group.

A group is either a single statement, other than those listed below, or a special collection of statements called a *DO group*. The following types of statements may not, by themselves, constitute a group:

PROCEDURE   DECLARE   DO   FORMAT

BEGIN   ENTRY   END

The form of a DO group is

DO statement;

program-element 1;

program-element 2;

. . . .

program-element k;

END[label];

The DO statement is called the *heading statement* of the DO group. Each program element may be one or more statements. The end of the group is indicated by the END statement. An example of a DO group is

START: DO I = 1 TO N;

X(I) = Y + Z(I);

END START;

The functions of the DO statement as well as the usefulness of the DO group will be discussed in detail in Sec. 12.20.

12.12 THE DECLARE STATEMENT

The *DECLARE statement* is a nonexecutable statement. It does not specify any action but is used to describe the attributes of identifiers.

The general format of the DECLARE statement is

DECLARE[level]name[attributes] · · · [,level]name[attributes]];

Since this is one of the first syntax specifications, we shall translate it for the reader. The first word, "DECLARE," is in capital letters and is therefore a notation constant. This means that this statement must begin with the word "DECLARE." The word "level," and all other words, are in lowercase and so are notation variables. The word "level" will not appear in the statement, but some level (which, it turns out, is a positive integer) may be specified. Since "level" is in brackets, the specification of a level is optional. Next, the name of a variable is given whose attributes are being assigned, followed by a list of the attributes. The attributes are optional since the statement can be used only to declare the level of a variable. Several sets of attributes may appear in a single statement. This is indicated by the three dots and the optional additional set of the notation variables: level, name, and attributes.

If the variable being declared is arithmetic, then attributes can be specified with respect to base, scale, and mode. That is, the attributes portion of the DECLARE statement is

[{DECIMAL|BINARY}]
[{FLOAT|FIXED}][{REAL|COMPLEX}]

These specifications are optional; the default attributes discussed and designated in Sec. 12.9 will apply in the absence of a complete set of attributes.

If the variable named is a string variable, then the attributes portion of the DECLARE statement is

{{CHARACTER|BIT}(length)[VARYING]|PICTURE 'character-picture-specification'}

CHARACTER and BIT are used to distinguish character-string variables from bit-string variables. If the string is to be fixed in length, then this length is enclosed in parentheses and the option VARYING is not included. If the string is to be variable in length, then the length given in parentheses is the maximum length and the attribute VARYING must appear.

The length may be given by means of an arithmetic formula. These formulas are called *expressions* in PL/1. The length in this case will be the value of the expression truncated to an integer. If the value is less than zero, the length is zero.

The general form shows that the PICTURE attribute may be used to describe string data in lieu of a CHARACTER or BIT specification. This attribute will be discussed in Sec. 12.26.

Some examples of string attributes used in a DECLARE statement follow.

DECLARE SMALL BIT(15),
LARGE CHARACTER(LNGTH+10),
MESSAGE CHARACTER(16)VARYING;

The name "SMALL" is described here as a fixed-length bit string of length 15. "LARGE" is a fixed-length character string whose length is equal to the value of the variable LNGTH plus 10 converted to an integer. "MESSAGE" is a variable-length character string whose maximum length will be 16 characters.

One statement can declare the attributes of any number of names. However, the attributes must be separated by commas, and they must follow the names to which they refer. The level is a positive decimal integer constant that serves to assign a structure-level number. If a level is not specified, then a 1 is assumed. Except for certain attributes of FILE names, all the attributes that are to be assigned to a variable must be given together in one statement. The same variable name should not appear more than once in a single DECLARE statement, nor should it appear in more than one DECLARE statement.

An example of a DECLARE statement is

DECLARE ERROR CHARACTER(15),NUMBR FLOAT;

Here, the name "ERROR" is described to be a character string of fixed length 15. "NUMBR" is a floating point and, by default, decimal and real arithmetic variable.

If it is desired to give the same attributes to more than one name, then these attributes may be factored by enclosing the name declarations in parentheses.   Consider the following DECLARE statement:

DECLARE NUMBR FLOAT,JOB FLOAT;

It could be factored as follows:

DECLARE(NUMBR,JOB)FLOAT;

Additional attributes can be included with the names inside the parentheses.   For example,

DECLARE(NUMBR REAL,JOB COMPLEX)FLOAT;

describes NUMBR and JOB to be floating-point variables.   However, NUMBR is real-valued, while JOB is complex.

The general format for describing the *precision attribute* for a variable in a DECLARE statement is as follows:

(number of digits[,scale factor])

This precision attribute must immediately follow a scale, base, or mode attribute.   The "number of digits" is a positive decimal integer constant specifying the number of binary or decimal digits to be retained.   For example,

DECLARE VARIABLE FLOAT(12);

describes VARIABLE as a floating-point decimal real variable with a precision of 12 digits.

The *scale factor* may be given only with fixed-point data.   It is a decimal integer constant which may be negative or positive, and it is used to define the decimal point or binary point, whichever applies. The scale factor, if it is positive, indicates the number of digits to the right of the point.   If the scale factor, say $-s$, is negative, then the result is obtained by adding s concluding zeros to the number.

Consider:

DECLARE N FIXED(5,2),T FIXED(5,-2);

Both N and T are fixed, decimal, and real and have five significant digits. However, two of these five digits are to the right of the decimal point in N, whereas the true value of T is obtained by adding two concluding zeros to the five digits that are stored.   Suppose, for example, 12345 is the stored value of N; then the true value of N is 123.45.   If, on the other hand, 12345 were the stored value of T, the true value of T would be 1234500.

The next five sections of this chapter are devoted to a further discussion of the declaration of variables. Statement labels and their declarations are discussed in the next section, followed by a discussion of the use of the DECLARE statement to initialize variables and a discussion of the declaration of aggregates. Some guidelines for choosing attributes are then given, and finally, the declaration of the variables in the quadratic-roots and payroll problems is discussed.

12.13 STATEMENT-LABEL VARIABLE

A *statement-label variable* is a variable which has a statement as its value. The LABEL attribute is used in the DECLARE statement to specify that the variable named is a statement-label variable. In addition, this same DECLARE statement can also specify the values which the variable may take on during the execution of the program. If a list of values is specified for a label variable, then that variable may have only the members of the list as values. The general format for the DECLARE statement with a LABEL attribute is

DECLARE name LABEL[(statement-label-constant · · · [,statement-label-constant])];

For example, in

DECLARE VARINAME LABEL(BEGIN,START,BGN);

the identifier VARINAME is described as being a LABEL variable which may be assigned any one of the values BEGIN, START, or BGN.

The usefulness of this type of variable is shown in the following example:

DECLARE LABL_VAR LABEL;

· · · · · · · · · · · · · · · · · · ·

LABL_VAR = STAT_D;

· · · · · · · · · · · · · · · · · · ·

GO TO LABL_VAR;

STATMT:Statement body

STAT_D:Statement body

Here, the identifiers STATMT and STAT_D are label constants, while LABL_VAR is a LABEL variable. The statement

LABL_VAR = STAT_D

assigns to LABL_VAR the label constant STAT_D. Then, where the GO TO LABL_VAR statement is executed, control will be transferred to the statement labeled STAT_D.

A LABEL variable declared with no list of values may have any statement-label constant as its value.

12.14 INITIAL ATTRIBUTE

Variables can be assigned initial values by using the *INITIAL attribute* in the DECLARE statement. The general format is

INITIAL(item · · · [item])

For example,

DECLARE SUM FIXED(6,2)INITIAL(21)

sets up a fixed-point decimal real variable named SUM whose initial value is 0021.00.

The items listed can be string or label constants as well as arithmetic. A character-string variable then could be initialized. For example,

DECLARE NAMES CHARACTER(5)INITIAL('FRANK');

initializes the character string NAMES, which is five characters long, with the elements FRANK.

If the attributes of several variables in a DECLARE statement are factored, then these variables must be initialized to the same value (if they are initialized at all). For example,

DECLARE(X1,X2,X3)FIXED(7)INITIAL(1);

specifies that the three variables X1, X2, and X3 are each fixed, decimal, and real, with a length of seven digits, and that they are all initialized to 1.

If all the variables are not to be initialized to the same value or if only some of the factored variables are to be initialized, then the INITIAL attribute must appear with the variable to be initialized. For example, if we wish to initialize X1 to 1 and X3 to -6, the DECLARE statement would be

DECLARE(X1 INITIAL(1),X2,X3 INITIAL(-6))FIXED(7);

12.15 THE DECLARATION OF ARRAYS AND STRUCTURES

Since the data elements in an array are assumed to be homogeneous, the attributes of these elements should be identical. This means that only one set of attributes should be given in the *declaration of arrays*. In addition to this set of attributes, the bounds for each of the subscripts of the array should be declared. The specification for the bounds precedes the attributes. The format for the portion of a DECLARE statement used to declare an array is

Name of array(bound[,bound] $\cdots$ [,bound])
[attribute] $\cdots$ [attribute]

The bound is given by

{[lower bound:]upper bound|*}

An asterisk may be used in place of a numerical value. If an asterisk is not used, an upper bound must be given and a lower bound may be given for each subscript. The bounds given will ordinarily be decimal integers. However, they may be formulas. The formula is evaluated, and the result is truncated to an integer in order to obtain the bound. The asterisk indicates that bounds will be assigned elsewhere. It is sometimes advantageous to allow the bounds for the dimensions of an array to be assigned, using certain specific mechanisms, during the course of the execution of the program.

For example, using

DECLARE A(5,5)FIXED;

A will have five rows and five columns and will consist of fixed and, by default, decimal real scalar variables. But using

DECLARE A(*,*)FIXED;

A will have an, as yet, unspecified number of rows and columns. It will still consist of fixed, decimal, and real scalar variables.

Consider next:

DECLARE BOX(−6:4,12)BINARY;

The rows of BOX will be numbered −6, −5, . . . , 4, and the columns 1, 2, . . . , 12. The elements of BOX are floating, binary, and real.

If we write

DECLARE JOSH(X*X+Y:100,X*X+Y*Y);

the rows of JOSH will be numbered $X^2 + Y$, $X^2 + Y + 1$, . . . , 100, and the columns 1, 2, . . . , $X^2 + Y^2$. The elements of JOSH are fixed, binary, and real.

Recall the array WORK, first discussed in Sec. 12.10, that is used to specify the assignment of employees to assembly-line stations. Its elements are character strings, and the subscripts vary from 1 to 3 and from 7 to 11. The longest character strings in the array are 10 characters in length. There are two elements that are this long, HARRING-

TON and WASHINGTON. They are denoted by WORK(1,8) and WORK(1,11), respectively. If we wished to use this array in a PL/1 program, we could declare it as follows:

DECLARE WORK(3,7:11)CHARACTER(10);

If, however, this array is to contain not only the present assignment of employees but all future assignments, it will be changed from time to time, and the length of the character strings should be sufficient to accommodate these future employees. In this case, we might declare WORK as follows:

DECLARE WORK(3,7:11)CHARACTER(15);

Note that we did not choose to declare the character strings to be VARY-ING. This is because varying-length character strings must be closely monitored by the PL/1 compiler. This wastes a great deal of computer time, and beginners should almost never use them. They are permitted in PL/1 programs only because they can be very handy in some advanced, very special applications.

Structures are declared by listing the elements along with the associated level numbers and the attributes, if necessary, of the data elements. The elements of structures are not assumed to be homogeneous, and different elements may have different attributes. An example of a DECLARE statement for a structure will be given in Sec. 12.17.

This concludes our description of the DECLARE statement. A number of special features that have not and will not be discussed here may be of interest to the more sophisticated user. Chapter 4, pages 38 to 67, of version 3 of the manual [2] contains a description of these features.

12.16 CHOOSING ATTRIBUTES

At this point, the reader is probably anxious to learn how to choose the attributes to be assigned to the variables in his program. There are no strict rules—only rough guidelines.

One simple approach, which may be adequate for the beginner, is to:

1. Use no DECLARE statements.
2. Begin the names of all variables, except those appearing in subscripts, with one of the letters A to H or O to Z.
3. Begin the names of all variables appearing in subscripts with one of the letters I to N.

This serves to assign all attributes by default. All variables, except those in subscripts, will be floating, decimal, and real, with a precision of six decimal digits. Variables in subscripts will be fixed, binary, and real, with a precision of 15 bits.

Though these default specifications may be adequate in most beginning applications, sooner or later the programmer must deal with complex numbers or character strings or must worry about how many digits he really has to carry in the computations. A few additional guidelines are offered next.

Variables, other than subscripts, that are going to appear in extensive computations will almost always be floating point, decimal, and real, with a precision of either 6 digits (the default precision) or 16 digits (the maximum precision). Though 7, 8, 9, and so on up to 15, digits can be specified, it is probably best to go all the way if more than 6 digits are required. This is because the computer will use 16 digits in the computations it executes and truncate the results if you specify a precision that is between 7 and 15 digits. If storage space is available, you might just as well retain all the digits.

Integer variables, especially subscripts, should be fixed, binary, and real. They are fixed in order to save time and storage space and binary in order to save processing time. There are occasions, however, when variables which take on only integer values give noninteger results. For example, if $I = 9$ and $J = 4$, then I divided by J is not an integer. If the result is also declared to be an integer, then the answer will be 2, not 2.25. If fixed-point variables are used in computations, the formulas must be reviewed in order to be certain that the truncations that are made do not vitiate the results. Also, the default precision of 15 bits is equivalent to only four or five decimal digits. Again, the formulas should be reviewed in order to be certain that more digits are not required.

Variables that are assigned such values as names, identification numbers, and text will probably be declared to be character strings of fixed length. The VARYING attribute should be used sparingly, particularly by beginners.

Character strings need not be converted into numbers in order to be compared. For example, the character strings A and B that appear in the statement

IF A = B GO TO MATCH;

will be compared as character strings. The equals sign in this case means that the character string A must be identical to the character string B. If the strings are identical, the next statement executed will be the one labeled MATCH; if they are not identical, the next statement in sequence will be executed. There is no need to reduce the strings to numbers in order to do this. The PL/1 compiler will automatically generate the machine-language instructions required to compare the character strings.

12.17 EXAMPLES OF THE USE OF THE DECLARE STATEMENT

We shall now apply our knowledge of the DECLARE statement to
writing the DECLARE statements for the quadratic-roots and payroll
problems.   In the quadratic-roots problem, we shall want the coefficients
A, B, and C to be real floating-point numbers.   The roots, denoted by
ROOT_1 and ROOT_2, should be complex numbers only if $(B^2 - 4AC)$
< 0.   This means that we need not declare A, B, and C.   (The default
conditions are just what we want.   This illustrates why these default
conditions were chosen; they are natural in many applications.)   It also
means that we have to declare ROOT_1 and ROOT_2 only in the separate procedure for computing the complex roots.   This is necessary
because we are using the same names for the roots even though they
have different attributes.   All in all, the quadratic-roots program requires
only one DECLARE statement, which should be a part of the procedure
block for computing complex roots.   It is

DECLARE(ROOT_1,ROOT_2,Y)COMPLEX FLOAT;

The variable Y is required to handle the quantity $\sqrt{B^2 - 4AC}$
conveniently.

In the payroll problem, the considerations involved in writing the
DECLARE statements are more complicated and lengthy.   A systematic approach is required.   Each variable to be used in the program
should be listed.   This assumes that some means for obtaining such a
list is available.   A detailed flow chart could be used for this purpose.
The attributes associated with each variable are then listed with the
variable.   This is done in Table 12.4.   The appropriate DECLARE
statements are then constructed from the table.

Some of the attributes in Table 12.4 are easily determined; others
were determined only after some analysis of the problem.   For example,
the first name of an employee is clearly a character string, but what
should be its maximum length and should it be varying?   It was decided
that it would be easier to process the employee files if the character string
were fixed.   This will result in concluding blanks being inserted in names
that are shorter than 14 letters.   It was also decided that truncating
first names that are longer than 14 letters can do no harm.   In applications where storage is at a premium, it may be desirable to truncate
first names at 10 or even 7 letters.   This presents some problems in
printing checks, but it may be adequate to print merely the initials of
the first and middle names on the check.   The precision specification
also required some analysis.   In most cases, it was merely a matter
of deciding on the maximum value assumed by the variable.   For
example, weekly earnings are limited to $999.99.   Table 12.5 contains the

Table 12.4 The attributes of the variables in the payroll problem

Variable	Name	Attributes
Employee number in master file	MNO	Fixed, decimal, and real, with precision 6
First name in master file	FISTM	Character string, fixed length 14
Middle initial in master file	INITLM	Character string, fixed length 1
Last name in master file	LASTM	Character string, fixed length 14
Employee number in weekly file	WNO	Fixed, decimal, and real, with precision 6
First name in weekly file	FIRSTW	Character string, fixed length 14
Middle initial in weekly file	INITLW	Character string, fixed length 1
Last name in weekly file	LASTW	Character string, fixed length 14
Regular hours worked	HM	2 digits
Hours actually worked that week	HW	2 digits
Hourly pay rate	RATE	4 digits, 2 to right of decimal
Regular weekly pay	RWP	5 digits, 2 to right
Cumulative gross pay	CGP	7 digits, 2 to right
Cumulative social security withheld	CFICA	5 digits, 2 to right
Number of deductions	D	2 digits
Cumulative tax withheld	CWT	7 digits, 2 to right
Weekly hospitalization deduction	WHD	4 digits, 2 to right
Regular net pay	RNP	6 digits, 2 to right
Probable social security to be withheld	PFICA	5 digits, 2 to right
Actual social security to be withheld	AFICA	5 digits, 2 to right
Income tax to be withheld	WT	6 digits, 2 to right
Net pay	NP	6 digits, 2 to right
Actual gross pay for week	GP	6 digits, 2 to right
Withholding tax rate	WTR	2 digits, both to right

† All these variables are fixed, decimal, and real; only the precision is tabulated.

Table 12.5   The DECLARE statements in the payroll problem

```
DECLARE 1  MASTER,
     2  MNO FIXED,
     2  NAME_M,
        3  FIRSTM CHAR(14),
        3  INITLM CHAR(1),
        3  LASTM CHAR(14),
     2  HM  FIXED(2),
     2  RATE  FIXED(4,2),
     2  RWP  FIXED(5,2),
     2  CGP  FIXED(7,2),
     2  CFICA  FIXED(5,2),
     2  D  FIXED(2),
     2  CWT  FIXED(7,2),
     2  WHD  FIXED(4,2),
     2  RNP  FIXED(6,2);
DECLARE 1  WEEKLY,
     2  WNO  FIXED,
     2  NAME_W,
        3  FIRSTW  CHAR(14),
        3  INITLW  CHAR(1),
        3  LASTW  CHAR(14),
     2  HW  FIXED(2);
DECLARE(PFICA,AFICA)FIXED(5,2),(WT,NP,GP)FIXED(6,2),WTR  FIXED(2,2);
```

DECLARE statements required in the PL/1 payroll problem. The neatly structured layout of the first two statements is convenient but not necessary.

12.18   EXPRESSIONS, ASSIGNMENT STATEMENTS, AND OPERATIONS

An *expression* is a valid combination of identifiers and operations. In most cases, an expression represents an arithmetic formula or serves to manipulate character or bit strings.

Expressions can be of three types: scalar, array, and structure. A *scalar expression* manipulates (computationally or otherwise) scalar variables. That is, the operands in a scalar expression are variables that refer to a single number and/or constants, and the value assigned to the expression is a single number.

An *array expression* contains arrays or arrays and scalars as its operands and produces an array as a result. Similarly, *structure expressions* have structures or structures and scalars as their arguments and produce structures as results.

Expressions are frequently found in an *assignment statement*. The *scalar assignment statement* serves to assign the value obtained in resolving a scalar expression to one or more scalar variables. Its syntax is

scalar-variable[,scalar variable] · · ·
[,scalar variable] = scalar expression;

Each of the variables on the left will be assigned the value of the scalar expression on the right. Note the use of the equals sign to indicate the assignment of the value on the right to the variable(s) on the left. The following is a valid assignment statement:

J = J + 1;

It causes the current value of J to be incremented by 1.

Before beginning the discussion of operators, it is necessary to distinguish between prefix and infix operators. A *prefix operator* accompanies a single operand and is placed immediately before it. An *infix operator* is used with two operands and is placed between them. The + and − symbols represent both prefix and infix operators. The choice is made according to the context of the expression. Prefix + or − assigns a sign to the operand, whereas infix + and − refer to addition and subtraction, respectively.

Table 12.6 contains a list of PL/1 scalar operators, their relative priorities, and their meanings. The priority is used to resolve ambigui-

Table 12.6 PL/1 scalar operators

	Operator			Example of	
Priority	Symbol	Name	Type of operator	Operation	Result is
1	⌐	Not	Prefix-bit string	⌐A(A = 110101)	001010
1	**	Exponentiation	Arithmetic	A**B(A = 2,B = 3)	8
1	+	Prefix +	Arithmetic	+A(A = 2)	+2
1	−	Prefix −	Arithmetic	−A(A = 2)	−2
2	*	Multiplication	Arithmetic	A*B(A = 2,B = 3)	6
2	/	Division	Arithmetic	A/B(A = 6,B = 3)	2
3	+	Addition	Arithmetic	A + B(A = 2,B = 3)	5
3	−	Subtraction	Arithmetic	A − B(A = 2,B = 3)	−1
4	> =	Greater than or equal to	Comparison†	A > = B(A = 2,B = 3)	0
4	>	Greater than	Comparison	A > B(A = 2,B = 3)	0
4	⌐>	Not greater than	Comparison	A⌐ > B(A = 2,B = 3)	1
4	⌐=	Not equal to	Comparison	A⌐ = B(A = 2,B = 3)	1
4	=	Equal to	Comparison	A = B(A = 2,B = 3)	0
4	<	Less than	Comparison	A < B(A = 2,B = 3)	1
4	⌐<	Not less than	Comparison	A⌐ < B(A = 2,B = 3)	0
4	< =	Less than or equal to	Comparison	A < = B(A = 2,B = 3)	1
5	&	And ‡	Bit comparison	A&B(A = 1100,B = 1010)	1000
6	|	Or ‡	Bit comparison	A|B(A = 1100,B = 1010)	1110
7	||	Concatenation	String	A||B(A = 'NOTON'B = 'GIVE') A||B = 'NOTONGIVE'	

Result is 1 if comparison is true and 0 if false

† Comparison operators may be applied to character and bit strings as well as arithmetic variables and expressions. Characters have been given a unique order for this purpose; for example, the blank is lowest, A < B < C, etc. (See [5], page 82 of version 1.) The comparison is made character by character, and the result is a bit string.

‡ Each of these comparisons is made bit by bit. A|B is 0 if and only if both the bit in A and the bit in B are 0, whereas A&B is 1 if and only if both the bit in A and the bit in B are 1.

ties in the order of execution of operations. For example, $A = B + C/D$; would yield $A = 5$ if $B = 2$, $C = 6$, and $D = 2$, since the division is executed first (it has a higher priority). For $A = B*C/D$;, we would get $A = 6$ since the multiplication, appearing to the left of the division, has the same priority as the division and the left-to-right ordering determines the order of execution. Parentheses may be used, in which case the contents of the innermost parentheses are evaluated first. Thus $A = (B + C)/D$ gives $A = 4$.

The type of operator indicates the kind of operation that is taking place. The prefix *not* operates on a bit string and changes all the 1s to 0s and all the 0s to 1s. Except for exponentiation, no more need be said about arithmetic operators. An operator for exponentiation is necessary because all the characters in a PL/1 statement must lie on the same line. There is no provision for raising some characters a little above the level of the line. Exponents must be set off in some other way. (Similarly, subscripts had to be set off in a complicated way because dropping some characters below the level of the line is not permitted.) The approach taken is to represent A^B by using A**B. So that, for example, $[2.6(X + Y)]^{(3+Z)}$ is written as $(2.6*(X + Y))**(3 + Z)$.

Comparison operators, as the first footnote in Table 12.6 states, are infix operators that can have either arithmetic or string expressions as operands. The beginner will probably use these operators with string operands in only one context, that is, in checking on whether two names are identical or in putting them in alphabetical order. Either of these things can be done by merely comparing the names. This works because the strings are stored with the first character in the leftmost position and the comparisons are made from left to right. For example, suppose we had

DECLARE(A,B)CHARACTER(10);A = 'HERB';B = 'DON';

The first statement serves to declare both the variables A and B to be fixed character strings of length 10. The next two statements assign the string HERB to A and DON to B. Using a b to indicate a blank character, the stored strings would be

A:HERBbbbbbb

B:DONbbbbbbb

Suppose next we write

X = (A < B)|(A = B);

In fact, DON precedes HERB, so that $A < B$ is false, i.e., has the value 0. Similarly, $A = B$ has the value 0, and since neither operand is 1, X has the

value 0.   Since X did not appear in a DECLARE statement, it is assigned
the attributes real, decimal, and floating by default.   The bit string 0 is
converted to the floating-point number 0 and stored for X.   If we had
rewritten the DECLARE statement as follows:

DECLARE(A,B)CHARACTER(10),X BIT(1);

no conversion would have taken place.

There is one other complication in dealing with comparisons of character strings that should be discussed.   Punctuation symbols in names,
e.g., the apostrophe in O'Rourke, will mix up the alphabetical ordering.
If alphabetical ordering is a part of the program, it might be best to delete
the apostrophe, e.g., to treat O'Rourke as Orourke.   Punctuation marks
in names do not interfere with tests to determine if two names are
identical.

The operations *and* and *or* are infix operators with bit strings as
operands.   The bit strings are compared bit by bit from left to right.
These operations are equivalent to the logically defined *and* and *or* if a
1 bit is used to represent *true* and a 0 bit to represent *false*.   Since this
is exactly what is done in obtaining the result of comparison operations,
the operator *and* or *or* is frequently applied to the results of comparison
operations.   Examples of this can be found on the last two lines of
Table 12.7.

A few examples of assignment statements containing scalar expressions are given in Table 12.7.   The reader should evaluate them and
compare his answer with those given in the table.

Array operators include prefix $+$ and prefix $-$, multiplication by a
scalar, and the addition, subtraction, and multiplication of arrays.   In

Table 12.7   Examples of PL/1 assignment statements

Statement	Value of variables before execution of statement	Result
ROOT_2 = (− B − ROOT_2)/Z;	B = 3,ROOT_2 = 5,Z = 2	ROOT_2 = − 4
FULLN = FIRSTN‖MIDINTL‖LASTN;	FIRSTN = 'JOHN', MIDINTL = 'A',LASTN = 'DOE'	FULLN = 'JOHNADOE'
ROOT_2 = − B − ROOT_2/Z;	B = 3,ROOT_2 = 5,Z = 2	ROOT_2 = − 5.5
X = A|B|C;	A = 1,B = 0,C = 0	X = 1
X = A&B&C;	A = 1,B = 0,C = 0	X = 0
X = ((A >B)&(C >D))|(E >F);	A = 1.47,B = 2000,C = 0, D = − 5,E = 0,F = 0.5	X = 0
X = ((A >B)&(C >D))|(E >5);	A = 1.47,B = 1.46,C = 0,D = − 5, E = 0,F = 0.5	X = 1

general, if we use $A = [a_{ij}]$ and $B = [b_{ij}]$ to denote two arrays, where i goes from 1 to n and j from 1 to m (i.e., both arrays have n rows and m columns), then

$-A$ results in $[a_{ij}]$ becoming $[-a_{ij}]$ for all i and j.
$3*A$ results in $[a_{ij}]$ becoming $[3*a_{ij}]$ for all i and j.
$A+B$ results in an array $[a_{ij}+b_{ij}]$ for all i and j.
$A-B$ results in an array $[a_{ij}-b_{ij}]$ for all i and j.
$A*B$ results in an array $[a_{ij}*b_{ij}]$ for all i and j.   (*Note:* This is not the usual definition of matrix multiplication.)

For example, if

$$A = \begin{bmatrix} 2 & 6 \\ 3 & 1 \\ 4 & 7 \end{bmatrix} \quad \text{and} \quad B = \begin{bmatrix} 1 & -1 \\ 2 & 0 \\ 3 & 4 \end{bmatrix}$$

then

$$-B = \begin{bmatrix} -1 & 1 \\ -2 & 0 \\ -3 & -4 \end{bmatrix} \quad \text{and} \quad 3*B = \begin{bmatrix} 3 & -3 \\ 6 & 0 \\ 9 & 12 \end{bmatrix}$$

$$A+B = \begin{bmatrix} 3 & 5 \\ 5 & 1 \\ 7 & 11 \end{bmatrix} \quad A-B = \begin{bmatrix} 1 & 7 \\ 1 & 1 \\ 1 & 3 \end{bmatrix}$$

$$A*B = \begin{bmatrix} 2 & -6 \\ 6 & 0 \\ 12 & 28 \end{bmatrix}$$

The results of structure operators and expressions are similar to those for arrays. That is, the operation is applied to corresponding data elements in each of the structures and a new structure is formed. For example, if we have the following two files with the indicated declarations:†

```
DCL 1  MASTER,              and   DCL 1  WEEKLY,
    2  MNO FIXED,                     2  WNO FIXED,
    2  NAME_M,                        2  NAME_W,
       3  FIRSTM CHAR(14),               3  FIRSTW CHAR(14),
       3  INITLM CHAR(1),                3  INITLW CHAR(1),
       3  LASTM CHAR(14);                3  LASTW CHAR(14);
    2  HM FIXED(2);                    2  HW FIXED(2);
```

† Many of the PL/1 keywords can be abbreviated. DCL is the allowed abbreviation for DECLARE. A complete list of allowable abbreviations is given in Appendix D.

Then the assignment MASTER = WEEKLY, results in the execution of the following set of assignments:

MNO = WNO

FIRSTM = FIRSTW

INITLM = INITLW

LASTM = LASTW

HM = HW

That is, data elements in the MASTER structure are replaced by corresponding elements in the weekly structure. In order to determine corresponding elements, it is necessary that the structures be identical. (Though the level numbers after the first need not be identical. For example, NAME_W and HW could be assigned level 3 and FIRSTW, INITLN, and LASTW level 5 without affecting the result. Level assignments need only follow the rule that sublevels must have a greater level number.)

Substitutions can be made between structures that are not identically ordered by using the assignment BY NAME instruction. Its syntax is

structure name[,structure name] . . . [structure name] = structure expression, BY NAME;

In this case, after the expression is evaluated, structure elements in all the right-hand structures are assigned to the left-hand elements. Further information can be found on page 108 of the manual [2].

The roots of a quadratic $AX^2 + BX + C$ are obtained from the formulas

$$\text{ROOT\_1} = \frac{-B + \sqrt{B^2 - 4AC}}{2A}$$

and

$$\text{ROOT\_2} = \frac{-B - \sqrt{B^2 - 4AC}}{2A}$$

If $B^2 - 4AC \geq 0$, these formulas can be written in PL/1 as follows:

ROOT_1 = (−B+SQRT(B*B−4.*A*C))/(2*A);

ROOT_2 = (−B−SQRT(B*B−4.*A*C))/(2*A);

(*Attributes of constants* are assigned in accordance with their appearance. A 2 and a 4 would ordinarily be treated as a FIXED DECIMAL REAL number because of their appearance. However, since the above computations would be carried out in floating-point arithmetic, the 2 and 4 would be converted to FLOAT DECIMAL REAL for purposes of these computations. They would continue to be stored in their implicitly declared FIXED format.)

Since $B^2 - 4AC$ must be evaluated before computing the roots and since $2A$ appears twice, it is natural to break up the above computations as follows:

X = B*B − 4*A*C;

Z = A+A;   (Adding is faster than multiplying.)

X = SQRT(X);   (This is done after testing X < 0; we then do not need $B^2 - 4AC$ and so need not waste storage space on it.)

ROOT_1 = (−B+X)/Z;

ROOT_2 = (−B−X)/Z;

If the roots are complex, we would proceed as follows (after declaring ROOT_1, ROOT_2, and Y to be complex-valued):

X = B*B − 4*A*C;

Z = A+A:

Y = X;   (This changes X to a complex number called Y; its imaginary part is zero.)

ROOT_2 = SQRT(Y);   (This results in an imaginary value for ROOT_2; the argument of SQRT must be complex if a complex result is to be obtained.)

ROOT_1 = (−B+ROOT_2)/Z;

ROOT_2 = (−B−ROOT_2)/Z;   (Now we discard the value of $\sqrt{B^2 - 4AC}$ since it is no longer needed.)

The assignment statements in the payroll problem are chiefly concerned with the computation of the payroll itself. Some of these are

GP = RWP;

If HM = HW, then we obtain immediately

CGP = CGP+GP;

If $HM > HW$, then

$$GP = GP*(HW/HM), \quad \text{and} \quad CGP = CGP + GP;$$

Otherwise,

$$GP = GP*(1 + 1.5*((HW - HM)/HM)); \quad \text{and} \quad CGP = CGP - GP;$$

The computation of the FICA is dependent to an even greater extent on comparisons, and discussion of the computation and the associated assignment statements will be postponed until after the IF statement is discussed.

12.19 BASIC CONTROL STATEMENTS

When a PL/1 program is being executed, the normal program flow is sequential. The statements that will be discussed in this section, the GO TO and IF statements, allow this sequential execution of statements to be modified.

The *GO TO statement* causes control to be transferred to a specified statement. Its general form is

GO TO {label-constant|scalar-label-variable};

If a label constant is specified, control will be transferred to the statement having that label. If a label variable is specified, control will be passed to the statement which has as a label the value of the label variable specified. Specifying the label variable may then allow the same statement to pass control to different statements, depending upon the value the variable takes on during a given execution of the program.

While the GO TO statement always causes control to be transferred to some other labeled statement, the *IF statement* causes the flow of the program to depend on the value of an expression. The general format is

IF scalar-expression THEN unit-1[ELSE unit-2]

The *units* referred to are either groups or begin blocks. (Groups were defined in Sec. 12.11; begin blocks will be discussed in Sec. 12.31.) The terminating semicolon of the unit is used to effect the termination of the statement. Since a group or begin block may each have its own label, each unit may have its own label.

The statement functions as follows: The scalar expression is evaluated according to the rules previously described. The result is then converted to a bit string if it is not already in that form. If any bit in the resulting string is a 1, then unit 1 is executed and control is passed

to the statement following the IF statement. If the expression has a
value whose bits are all zero, then unit 2 is executed if the *ELSE clause*
has been specified.   If the ELSE has not been specified and the bits are all
zero, control is transferred to the next statement following the IF statement.   Consider the following examples:

IF A = B THEN I = I+1;

In this example, if A is equal to B, then I is incremented by 1; otherwise,
I retains the same value.

IF A = B THEN I = 1;ELSE I = 2;

Here, if A = B, I is set to 1; otherwise, I is set to 2.
    A GO TO statement could also serve as either unit 1 or unit 2, or
both.   In that case, control might not necessarily be passed to the statement following the IF statement.   The following is an example of this.

IF X < (Y+Z) THEN GO TO QUIT;

ELSE GO TO NAPLES;

In this case, the next statement executed is either QUIT or NAPLES.
    The next example shows how a DO group could be used as the THEN
clause.   This provides the ability to have more than one statement in a
unit.

IF X < (R*5+5) THEN DO; X = X+Y;

R = .5*R;

END;

ELSE X = X−Y;

In this case, if X is less than R*5+5, then X will be incremented by
Y and R will be divided by 2 before going on to the next statement following the IF statement.   If the expression is false, that is, $X \geq R*5+5$, then
X will be incremented by −Y and control will be passed to the next
statement.
    Both unit 1 and unit 2 may themselves be IF statements.   These are
called *nested* IF statements.   Each ELSE clause in a nested IF statement
is associated with the innermost unmatched IF.   It may then be necessary in some cases for a *null ELSE* (i.e., an ELSE clause which is a null
statement) to be added.   The following example illustrates this.

IF C = 9 THEN

IF V < 10 THEN GO TO L1;

ELSE;

ELSE GO TO L2;

Here the null ELSE is used because the ELSE GO TO L2 clause should be associated with the IF $C=9$ portion of the statement. Without the null ELSE, ELSE GO TO L2 would be associated with the IF $V<10$ portion.

12.20 THE DO GROUP

The basic structure of a DO group was described in Sec. 12.11. The DO statement indicates the start of the group, and an END statement specifies the end. One of the useful functions of this program structure was shown in connection with the IF statement. The DO group was used there to permit a whole set of statements to serve as an alternative in an IF statement. The DO group has several other forms which make it a very powerful tool for specifying and controlling the repeated, or iterative, execution of a set of statements.

One form of the DO heading statement is

DO WHILE(scalar-expression);

The scalar expression enclosed in parentheses is treated similarly to the expression in an IF statement in that the value is ultimately converted to a bit string, so that it has a value *true* ('1'B) or *false* ('0'B). If the expression is true, then all the instructions following the DO and before the END are executed. Control is then returned to the DO statement, and the expression is reevaluated. This continues until the expression is false, at which time control is passed to the first statement following the END statement. For example:

$E=1; X=N/2$

DO WHILE$(E>1.0E-9)$;

$Y=(X*X+N)/(X+X)$;

$E=(X-Y)**2$;

$X=Y$;

END;

Each iteration through the DO loop calculates a new value for X. The iteration stops when the square of the difference between the new and old values is less than or equal to 10^{-9}.

Another format for the DO header statement is

DO scalar-variable = specification[,specification] $\cdots$ [,specification];

Each of the specifications shown in the DO has the following general form:

expression-1[TO expression-2[BY expression-3]][WHILE (expression-4)]

The TO and BY options shown may also be reversed; i.e., the BY could appear before the TO or by itself without the TO.

With this type of header, expressions 1, 2, and 3 are first calculated and their values retained. The designated scalar variable is assigned the value obtained from expression-1, and the DO group is executed so long as the value of expression-1 $\leq$ expression-2 and the WHILE, if present, is satisfied. The variable is then incremented by expression-3, and the DO group is executed provided expression-1 $\leq$ expression-2 and the WHILE, if present, is satisfied. This process is continued until the provision is not met, at which time the second specification, if present, controls execution of the DO in the same way the first did. If there are no additional specifications, control is passed to the first statement after the END.

A flow chart for the action of this type of DO is given in Figure 12.1. Consider, for example,

DO INDX = 1 TO 10 BY 1;

statement 1

statement 2

. . . .

statement n

END;

The sequence of events is as follows:

1. The variable INDX is set to the value 1.
2. The value of INDX is checked against the number 10. If INDX > 10, then control is transferred to the first statement following the END statement. If INDX $\leq$ 10, statements 1 through n are executed.
3. The value of INDX is incremented by 1, and we return to step 2.

The syntax shows that the BY expression is optional. If it is omitted, the value of expression 3 is taken to be 1. The DO statement shown in the example above could then have been written as

DO INDX = 1 TO 10;

The TO expression is also optional. In the following example, both the TO and BY options are omitted.

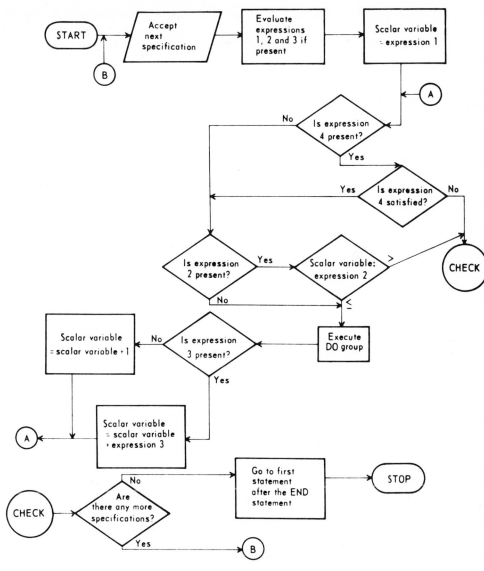

Fig. 12.1 Flow chart for the execution of DO groups with specifications.

DO KEY = Z*R+S;

. . . .

END;

Here, the statements within the DO group are executed just once, with
the variable KEY having the value of the expression Z*R+S.   Since a

series of specifications may be included, separated by commas, a series of statements could be executed a number of times, with the variable taking on a different value each time. The next example illustrates this.

DO KEY = Z*R+S,A,X,X+Z;

. . . .

END;

Here, the statements within the DO group will be executed four times. The first time KEY will have the value Z*R+S, the second time KEY will have the value A, the third time X, and the fourth time X+Z.

The next example shows a means of stopping the execution of the statements in a DO group using the WHILE option and at the same time ensuring that there will be some maximum number of iterations.

E = 1; X = N/2;

DO I = 1 TO 15 WHILE(E > 1.0E − 9);

Y = (X*X+N)/(X+X);

E = (X − Y)**2;

X = Y;

END;

As before, control will pass out of the DO group to the first statement following it whenever the value of E becomes less than or equal to 10^{-9}. If this does not happen before the value of I exceeds 15 (i.e., before the statements have been executed 15 times), control will be terminated even though the value of E is still greater than 10^{-9}. This permits us to establish both a maximum number of iterations and a minimum difference between successive iterations as criteria for terminating a procedure.

Notice that in the previous example, the DO statement had only one specification and that the specification included the WHILE option. If the DO statement had been written with two specifications, as follows, a quite different process results.

DO I = 1 TO 15,16 BY 1 WHILE(E > 1.0E − 9);

In this case, the statements would have first been executed 15 times. Following that, the statements would continue to be executed until E became less than or equal to 10^{-9}. Since I starts at 16 in executing the WHILE and is incremented by 1, the variable I does provide a count of the number of iterations.

DO groups may be nested to any depth. That is, DO groups may be contained in other DO groups. Also, control may be transferred to a statement within a DO group from outside the DO group but only if iteration is not specified in the DO.

12.21 INPUT/OUTPUT IN PL/1—GENERAL CONSIDERATIONS

Input/output (I/O) instructions must provide for communication with a wide variety of units—magnetic-tape drives, disk-storage drives, card readers and punches, printers, plotters, etc. The instructions must also be people-oriented. They must permit the computer to accept inputs, and produce outputs, that are easily prepared and interpreted. These requirements almost inevitably cause the I/O instructions in a programming language to appear cumbersome and unnecessarily complex.

Input/output in PL/1 is probably more complex than I/O in other languages. In designing special-purpose programming languages, assumptions can be made that simplify the language at the expense of its versatility. This cannot be done for a general-purpose language such as PL/1. As a result, PL/1:

1. Contains an enormous repertoire of I/O statements and specifications
2. Permits specification of I/O units during either the compilation or the execution of the program
3. Provides default conditions that implicitly establish specifications for identifiers

The major dichotomy in the sizable repertoire of PL/1 I/O instructions is between record-oriented and stream-oriented I/O. *Stream I/O* views the information being processed as a character string. *Record I/O* views the information being processed as a series of records whose structure is specified as a part of the instruction. Since stream-oriented I/O is easier to master and permits the novice to accommodate virtually all of his requirements, it will be emphasized in the discussion that follows. Record-oriented I/O is discussed in detail on pages 62, 63, 97 to 101, 112, 120, 126, 129 to 131, and 161 to 163 of version 3 of the manual [2]. The novice should begin with the discussion on pages 97 to 101.

The choice of an I/O unit may be specified at the time a program is executed by using a special control card called a *DD card* (data-definition card). Control cards for PL/1 programs are discussed in the manual on the job-control language [3]. The DD card is discussed on pages 21 to 25 in version 1 of [3]. In the absence of a designated device, standard devices for I/O are established. Most installations establish the card reader as the standard input device and the printer as the standard output device.

I/O statements process data sets. A *data set* is a collection of data items that is external to the program during its execution. Any of the data types discussed in Sec. 12.8 can serve as elements in a data set. Input and output can now be defined as follows: *input* transfers one or more data items from the data set to the program, whereas *output* transfers one or more data items from the program to the data set.

The next eight sections of this chapter will be devoted to a discussion of the statements used in I/O in PL/1. The simpler approach to I/O, the stream-oriented approach, will be discussed first and more completely than the record-oriented approach. All three kinds of stream-oriented I/O—DATA-directed, LIST-directed, and EDIT-directed—will be covered. The choice among these three kinds will be dictated by the volume of input or output, the format of the input, and the desired format for the output. If the input is labeled with the name of a variable or if there is a small volume of output that can be easily interpreted if it is labeled only with the name of a variable, then DATA-directed I/O will be useful. If the input is unlabeled but has spaces or commas between data items or if the output need not be labeled, then LIST-directed I/O will be useful. Finally, if extensive editing of the input or editing and labeling of the output are required, EDIT-directed I/O should be used. EDIT-directed I/O is the most difficult of these three approaches to master.

Record-oriented I/O is useful in processing data that is organized as a series of records in files. This is the case in the payroll problem, and the discussion of record-oriented I/O will emphasize the facilities needed to handle this problem. The discussion is sketchy, and references to the manual will frequently be given in order to permit the reader to follow up on topics that are of interest to him.

12.22 STREAM-ORIENTED I/O—THE GET AND PUT STATEMENTS

There are three types of stream-oriented I/O: DATA-directed, LIST-directed, and EDIT-directed. All three types use a GET statement for input and a PUT statement for output. The formats for these statements are

GET[FILE(filename)]data-specification[COPY];

PUT[FILE(filename)]data-specification;

The optional FILE portion of the statement serves to designate an input or output unit on which the data set is to be found as well as the particular data set on this unit. In the absence of a FILE designation, the established standard input file unit (usually the card reader) and the established output file unit (usually the printer) are assumed.

The novice will ordinarily not designate a file in his GET or PUT statement and will rarely use the COPY option. This means that the data specification is all that the beginner should master. It is the requirements for the data specification that distinguish among DATA-, LIST-, and EDIT-directed I/O.

Before proceeding to a discussion of the simplest of the directed I/O —DATA-directed I/O—we shall briefly discuss the COPY option.

The *COPY option* causes the entire input stream to be copied on the print file without alteration. Every data item will be copied, not just those items that are to be incorporated into the program.

12.23 DATA LISTS

Both LIST-directed and DATA-directed transmission require that a data list be included in the I/O statements. Since the format of the lists and the nature of the list elements are the same, specifications for data lists for both LIST-directed and DATA-directed I/O will be given in this section.

The general format for a data list is

(element[,element] . . . [,element])

The following can serve as an element in an input statement: a scalar variable with or without subscripts, an array name, a structure name, or a repetitive specification. For outputs, the permissible elements are a scalar expression, an array expression, a structure expression, and a repetitive specification. Note that input elements may be subscripted.

Two examples of input data lists follow:

(R,S,T)

(((A(I,J)DO I = 1 TO X)DO J = Y BY R TO Z),X,Y,Z)

The second list will cause elements of the array A to be read in the following order:

$A(1,Y)$, $A(2,Y)$, . . . ,$A(X,Y)$, $A(1,Y+R)$, . . . ,$A(X,Y+R)$, . . . , $A(1,T)$, . . . ,$A(X,T)$, where T is the greatest number of the form $Y+kR, k = 1, 2, . . .$, that is, $\leq Z$.

Two examples of data lists for outputs are

(R,S,T)

(R*S+T),(B(K)DO K = 1 TO 9),'X = ',Z*Z)

Note the appearance of the character string 'X =' in the list. This is a valid expression consisting of the character-string constant 'X ='. The two characters X and = will be placed in the output stream immediately after the array B(K).

Unless otherwise specified, elements of an array are transmitted in row order. This means, for example, that an array, say A(I,J), with two rows and three columns would be transmitted in the order $A(1,1)$, $A(1,2)$, $A(1,3)$, $A(2,1)$, $A(2,2)$, and $A(2,3)$.

12.24 DATA-DIRECTED I/O

The syntax for a DATA-directed input statement is

GET DATA [FILE (filename)] [({scalar-variable | array | structure},
. . . ,{scalar-variable|array|structure}][COPY];

and the syntax for a DATA-directed output statement is

PUT DATA[FILE(filename)]({scalar-variable|array|structure|array
element|structure element}, . . . ,{scalar variable|array|structure|array
element|structure element});

The contents of the parentheses following the FILE(filename) portion of the GET and PUT statements are data lists. The alternatives for the elements in these lists have been spelled out in detail as a reminder to the reader. We might have written merely

GET DATA[FILE(filename)][(data list)][COPY];

PUT DATA[FILE(filename)](data list);

The items in data-oriented I/O data sets are self-identifying; i.e., they are labeled. This is done by writing "scalar variable = constant" in the input or output stream. Consider, for example, the statement

GET DATA(A, B, CHEESE,DIAL_1);

The input stream that is to be read using this statement could be

DIAL_1 = 43.1   A = 20,B = 'INSIDE'   CHEESE = −41.1;

The GET DATA statement would assign the value 20 to A, 'INSIDE' to the character string B, −41.1 to CHEESE, and 43.1 to DIAL_1. Note that the order of the variables in the list need not match the order in the input stream and that successive variable assignments in the input may be separated either by a comma or by one or more spaces. The semicolon is used to define the end of the data stream. The next stream-oriented input statement would begin to read the character string at the first character after the semicolon. For example, suppose the following appeared on three successive cards:

Card	Contents
1	DIAL_1 = 43.1
2	CHEESE = −41.1;A = 20
3	C = 17.7432,D = 41.4 B = 'INSIDE';

If we used the same GET DATA statement, values would be assigned only to DIAL_1 and CHEESE because the semicolon after -41.1 marks the end of the first set of data. A feature in the PL/1 compiler would alert the user to this incomplete matching. A *NAME condition* is established whenever an item in a data list does not appear in the input stream or an item in the input stream does not appear in the data list (providing a data list is used). The programmer can deal with this condition in his own way by using the ON CONDITION statement (see Sec. 12.30). In the absence of specific instructions from the programmer, the operating system will treat the NAME condition in a standard way. Unmatched names are ignored, and a message is printed in this standard approach to indicate that the NAME condition occurred. (For additional details, see page 162 of version 3 of [2].) If problems in input are expected, the COPY option may prove helpful since its use will cause the whole input stream to be included in the output.

In the absence of an input list, the GET DATA statement inputs all the values appearing in the input stream. (The values must be labeled in the input stream.) For example, the statement

GET DATA

would assign the value 20.7 to B, -64.4 to C, and 11.1 to A if the following appeared in the input stream:

$B = 20.7, C = -64.4 \qquad A = 11.1; STYLE = 'FREEFORM';$

The statements

GET DATA;GET DATA;

would make these same assignments and also assign 'FREEFORM' to the character-string variable STYLE.

In data-oriented output, each item is separated by blank characters and a semicolon is written after the last item in the list. A new line is begun whenever the next item is too long to fit in the remaining space in the present line. An output item is split between two lines only when it is more than one line long.

Input or output of data aggregates can be effected using the GET DATA and PUT DATA statements. Though an array listed in a GET statement cannot be subscripted, the identifiers of the items in the data stream can be subscripted. For example, if A was declared as follows:

DECLARE A(5)FIXED(6,2);

then the statement

GET DATA(A);

can accept data items such as

$$A(1) = 3.47, A(3) = -11.11$$

from the input stream. As long as at least one element of a listed aggregate appears in the stream, the NAME condition will not be raised. Therefore, it will not be raised in this case even though A(2), A(4), and A(5) do not appear in the stream.

Since scalar variables in the PUT statement can be subscripted, individual elements in an array can be output. In addition, a *repetitive specification* can be used. It employs the verb DO in the data list. For example,

PUT DATA(A(K) DO K = 1 TO 5);

would cause A(1), A(2), A(3), A(4), and A(5) to be output. It is equivalent to

DO K = 1 TO 5;

PUT DATA(A(K));

END;

Since A has only five elements, each of the above is equivalent to

PUT DATA(A);

Therefore, in the absence of a subscript, the whole array is output. Similarly, if only the major name for a structure is given in the output list, the whole structure is output. If we wished to output only A(1), A(3), and A(5), we could write

PUT DATA(A(K) DO K = 1 TO 5 BY 2);

If the element in a data list is a structure name, it must be sufficiently qualified to avoid ambiguity. For example, consider the structure declared as follows:

DECLARE 1 MASTER, 2 LAST, 2 FIRST, 1 WEEKLY, 2 LAST, 2 FIRST;

If the statement

PUT DATA(LAST);

is used, it is not clear whether we are referring to MASTER.LAST or WEEKLY.LAST. The statement must be given as

PUT DATA(MASTER.LAST);

or

PUT DATA(WEEKLY.LAST);

12.25 LIST-DIRECTED I/O

The syntax for LIST-directed input is

GET LIST[FILE(filename)](data list)[COPY];

and the syntax for LIST-directed output is

PUT LIST[FILE(filename](data list);

LIST-directed input proceeds by associating elements in the data
list with elements in the data stream in the order in which they appear
in the list and the stream.   Elements in the data stream may be separated
either by a comma or by one or more blank spaces—as were elements in
the DATA-directed input stream.   Transmission stops when all the
elements in the data list have been matched.   A semicolon should not
appear in the data stream.

Elements in the data list can be skipped by having two successive
commas in the data stream.   For example, suppose the statement

GET LIST(A,B,C,D);

was used to read the following data stream:

−16.1, ,43.4, '101'B

The result would be to assign the value −16.1 to the variable A, to leave
the value of variable B unchanged, and to assign 43.4 to C and '101'B
to the bit-string variable D.   It is assumed that D has been declared
to be a bit-string variable.   If it has not, something other than '101'B
would be assigned to D.   This is because input data are always converted,
if necessary, to conform to the attributes declared for the corresponding
variable in the data list.   The rules for this conversion can be found on
pages 88 and 89 of version 3 of the manual [2].

In LIST-directed output, the value of a scalar variable is converted
to a character representation according to the attributes of the variable
and a set of rules that take into consideration the total number of digits,
the number of digits to the right of the decimal point, etc.   These rules
can be found beginning on page 89 of version 3 of the manual [2].

Printed output is structured according to prescribed rules that cause
each item to begin at particular positions in each line.   If there is no
room for an item in the space remaining in the line, it is put on the next
line.   This causes the printed output to have the appearance of a rectangular array; the rows are the lines, and the columns begin at the
particular positions in the line established for entering output items.
Output to some device other than a printer is in the form of a data stream
whose items are separated by blank characters.   Quotation marks are

not printed around character or bit strings when using LIST-directed output to a print; DATA-directed output would print quotation marks.

12.26 EDIT-DIRECTED I/O

The advantages of taking the list approach to I/O is that the input or output stream consists only of data (as opposed to both data and identifiers) with appropriate separation characters. This is called *free-form I/O*. The separation characters are either blanks or commas for the input stream and blanks for the output stream. However, the list approach does not readily permit editing of the input or output stream. This makes it difficult to select a subset of the input stream for processing or to organize and label the output to improve its legibility. EDIT-directed I/O facilitates these operations.

EDIT-directed I/O allows the programmer to be selective in input and legible in his outputs by requiring him to describe the format of the input or output in a format list. The syntax of the EDIT input statement is

GET EDIT[FILE(filename)]data-list format-list[data-list format-list] . . . [data-list format-list][COPY];

and the syntax of the output statements is

PUT EDIT[FILE(filename)]data-list format-list[data-list format-list] . . . [data-list format-list];

Writing EDIT-directed I/O statements requires mastering the repertoire of format items that may appear in the format list. The items are of two types: *control-format items* and *data-format items*. Control items specify such things as spacing within a line, skipping lines, going to the next page. Data items are used to describe the appearance of each of the items in the data list. In executing EDIT I/O statements, items in the data list are associated, in order, with data items in the format list. As was the case with LIST-directed I/O, transmission is terminated when the last item in the data list is matched. Control items appearing after the last-matched data items are not processed.

Format items in the format list are separated by commas. A series of items enclosed in parentheses may be preceded by an iteration factor. This factor may itself be an expression enclosed in parentheses. If it is a constant, it must be a decimal integer. If it is an expression, it is truncated to its integer value. If this value is positive, it is used as the iteration factor, and if it is negative or zero, the whole format item that it precedes will be ignored.

There are a great variety of format items available in PL/1. We shall discuss only those items that can be expected to be useful to the novice. These are the items for control formats, fixed- and floating-point formats, bit and character formats, and picture formats. A list of all items and where they can be found in version 3 of the manual [2] follows:

Format item	Page	Format item	Page	Format item	Page
Bit-string	95	Control	96	Picture	95
Character-string	95	Fixed-point	94	Remote	96
Complex	95	Floating-point	94		

The format for *character-string-format items* has the general form A(w). The letter w represents the total number of characters in the data. The w can be omitted only on output. If it is omitted, the number of characters transmitted would be the current length of the string. Also, if the length w is less than the length of the character string being output, truncation is performed on the right. If w is greater than this length, the string in the output is filled out on the right with blanks. In input, the character string is truncated on the right if it is longer than w characters in the stored form.

The following three output statements would give the identical result:

EXAMPLE ONE

in the output stream:

    PUT EDIT('EXAMPLE ONE')(A(11));

    PUT EDIT('EXAMPLE ONE')(A);

    PUT EDIT('EXAMPLE ONETWO')(A(11));

Note that quotes do not appear in the output stream in EDIT-directed output. Similarly, a character string transmitted using EDIT-directed input is not enclosed in quotes in the input stream.

The general format of *bit-string-format items* is B(w). The rules are very similar to those for character-string-format items. The w may be omitted on output but not on input. On input, the data field of length w can contain the character representations of the bit string anywhere within that field. A *CONVERSION condition* is raised if the field contains either all blanks or characters other than 0s and 1s. The character representation of the bit string on output is left-adjusted in the field. The following statements would produce the characters 1011 in the output stream:

    PUT EDIT('1011'B)(B);

PUT EDIT('1011'B)(B(4));

PUT EDIT('101111'B)(B(4));

Fixed-point data-format items can appear in any one of the following three general formats:

option 1: F(w)

option 2: F(w,d)

option 3: F(w,d,p)

A d is used to represent the number of positions to the right of the decimal point, and a p to represent a scale factor.

The fixed-point-format item specifies the appearance of the character representation of a fixed-point number in the data stream. The number to be input may be located anywhere within the field of length w. If the d is specified, as in the second option, and if the number in the field does not have a decimal point, the decimal point is assumed to be immediately before the last d digits. Trailing blanks are ignored. If the d is specified and a decimal point appears in the number, the d specification is ignored. Option 1 is treated, on input, just like F(w,0).

The precision of the number as it is retained in the program is determined by the attributes of the variable to which the number is assigned. Consider the following set of statements:

DECLARE X FIXED(6,2);

GET EDIT(X)(F(10,2));

Here X has been declared as a fixed-decimal variable of length 6, with two digits to the right of the decimal point. From the format specification, we see that the data item in the input stream is to be found in the next 10 successive characters. The following table shows the digits that would actually be assigned to X for various forms of data items appearing in the input field. A b is used to indicate a blank character in the stream.

Characters in the input	*Internal representation of X*
bb379.62bb	037962
379.620bbb	037962
bbbbb37962	037962
bbb379620b	037962
bbb37.962b	003796

The third option for fixed-point-format items provides a means of changing the value of the data item before it is stored. The scale factor, p, multiplies the data item by 10 raised to the power p. For example, the format F(10,2,1) applied to the data item 379.62 appearing in the input stream would store the number 3796.2.

On output, the external decimal number is always right-adjusted in the field of w characters. Here, option 1 will transmit only the integer portion of the number, and no decimal point will appear. Option 2 will transmit both an integer and a fractional part. A decimal point is always inserted before the last d digits. However, if d is zero, a decimal point will not appear. Option 3 works as for input except that the internal value is multiplied by the p power of 10 before being transmitted to the data set. The value stored in memory is unchanged. If a data item is negative, the character representation will include a minus sign as one of the characters. The possible need for two additional characters, one for the minus sign and a second for the decimal point, in options 2 and 3 should be considered in determining w. The following table shows the character string in the data set when using various format items corresponding to a number having an internal value of 379.62.

Format	External representation
F(8,2)	bb379.62
F(8,1)	bbb379.6
F(8,0)	bbbbb379
F(8)	bbbbb379
F(8,3,−2)	bbb3.796

The attributes of variables need not agree with the format prescribed for the data item. The proper conversion is made to conform to the format on output and to the attribute on input.

If data items or values are too large in magnitude to be represented conveniently in fixed point, the *floating-point-format item* may be used. It has the following general format: E(w,d[,s]). The w and d represent, as before, the total field length and number of digits after the decimal point. The s represents the number of significant digits to appear; it is used only for output. The form of a floating-point number in the data set for input is

[±]fixed-point-number[{[E]±|E[±]}exponent]

The fixed-point number is the mantissa. The syntax indicates that the mantissa can be separated from the exponent by a sign alone, by an E alone, or by both a sign and an E. All of the following are valid representations of 3.1415 in the input:

3.1415
31415E−4
31415−4
.31415+1
.31415E1

If no decimal point is included in the fixed-point number on input, then one is assumed to be before the last d digits. If a decimal point appears, it overrides the d specification, just as for the fixed-point format.

On output, the representation of the data items is as follows:

[−]integer-part.fractional-part E{+|−}exponent

The integer part will contain s − d digits, and the fractional part d digits. If the s does not appear in the format item, then it is taken to have the value d + 1. Also, if d is specified to be zero, then no decimal point is written. The following table shows the output stream corresponding to the value 17152 when using the listed floating-point-format items.

Format item	External representation
E(13,4)	bbb1.7152E+04
E(13,3)	bbbb1.715E+04
E(13,0)	bbbbbbbb1E+04
E(13,4,5)	bbb1.7152E+04
E(13,4,6)	bb17.1520E+03
E(13,4,7)	b171.5200E+02

It is often desired to skip over a number of consecutive characters in an input stream or to put blank items in an output stream in order to separate data items. This can be done with a control-format item called a *spacing-format item*. The general form is X(w).

On input, this item specifies that the next w characters in the input stream are to be ignored. Although the skipped characters may be blank, it is not required that they be blank. Anything that appears is ignored. On output, w blank characters are inserted into the output stream. In either input or output, w may be zero. If it is, then no characters are skipped or added to the stream. If w is less than zero, it is treated as though it were zero.

The other control-format items are all *printing-format items*. They apply only to printed outputs. They are the PAGE, SKIP, LINE, and COLUMN format items.

The syntax for these specifications is

[PAGE][SKIP[(expression)]][LINE(expression)]

Two or more of these specifications can be given as separate format items in the same format list.   Commas must appear between the items. The PAGE specification causes the printer to go to the top of the next page before proceeding to carry out the output associated with the next format item.   In carrying out the LINE specification:

1. The expression is evaluated.
2. The result is truncated to an integer, say i.
3. Printing is begun on the ith line.

For example, the format item

LINE(23)

would cause the next line to be printed on the twenty-third line of the current page.   If we were already printing below the twenty-third line, the printer would skip to the first line of the next page.   If we were already printing below the twenty-third line or anywhere else on the page and the specification

PAGE,LINE(23)

were used, the next line would be printed on the twenty-third line of the next page.   The SKIP item causes the expression to be evaluated, if it is present, and then truncated to an integer, say j, and printing to begin after $j - 1$ blank lines are inserted in the output, i.e., after the printer skips to the jth line after the last one printed.   If the expression is not given, the printer skips to the next line, i.e., acts as if $j = 1$.   If j is less than zero, the next line is printed over the last one.

The remaining control-format item has the general form COL-UMN(w).   This causes blank characters to be inserted into the stream so that the next character will be the wth character of the current line. If at least w characters have already been written on the line, then enough blanks will be inserted so that the next character will be the wth character of the next line.   The following example shows how some of these format items work:

PUT EDIT(X,Y,Z)(F(10,2),SKIP(3),F(10,2),COLUMN(50), F(10,2));

The value of X will be printed in the first 10 characters of line 1.   SKIP(3) and F(10,2) will cause the value of Y to be printed as the first 10 characters of line 4.   The COLUMN(50) and F(10,2) format items will cause the next 40 characters of line 4 to be blank and the value of Z to be printed in characters 51 to 60 of that line.

It frequently happens that many GET or PUT statements in the same program have identical format lists. A *remote-format item* is provided to permit the programmer to use the same format list in different places in the program. The general format is R(statement-label-designator).

The *statement-label designator* is a statement-label constant or variable whose value is the label of a FORMAT statement. This FORMAT statement then specifies the format list to be used in place of the remote-format item. The general form of the FORMAT statement is

label:[label:] . . . [label:]FORMAT format-list;

For example, the following statements would give the same results as in the previous example:

PUT EDIT(X,Y,Z)(R(USE_REM));

USE_REM:FORMAT(F(10,2),SKIP(3),F(10,2),X(40),F(10,2));

The following set of statements would also give the same results:

PUT EDIT(X,Y,Z)(F(10,2),R(USE2));

USE2:FORMAT(SKIP(3),F(10,2),X(40),F(10,2));

The *picture-format specification*, as its name implies, permits the programmer to present a digit-by-digit or character-by-character picture of a data item. Both numeric and character-string fields can be formatted using this specification. The programmer encloses a string of characters in quotes in the format list. Each character in the input or output is represented by a generic character in the specification. This format item has the syntax

P'specification'

A few of the most important of the generic representations that can be used in the specification follow.

The letter A is used to denote a generic letter.

The digit 9 is used to denote a generic decimal digit.

The digit 1 is used to denote a generic binary digit.

The letter X is used to denote a generic character.

The letter V is used to indicate where the decimal point would appear, but a decimal point is not included in the output.

The mark . is used to indicate where the decimal point is to be placed.

The letter Z is used to indicate that if a leading zero appears here, then suppress it.

The mark * is used to indicate that if a leading zero appears here, replace it with an asterisk.

The mark , is used to indicate the placing of a comma at this point, except if it is preceded entirely by suppressed zeros.

The mark $ is used to indicate the placing of a dollar sign at this point.

The picture format is used extensively in outputting fields that represent cash values. For example, the entry of the cash field in a check might be given the picture specification

P'$***9.99'

This would permit the check to have a maximum value of $9,999.99. If the check were to be in the amount of $3.56, then the output would be $***3.56. For 56 cents, the output would be $***0.56. Note that if the specification

P'$ZZZ9.99'

had been used, the entries in the check would have been $bbb3.56 and $bbb0.56. (Again, the b is used to indicate the blank character.) The recipient of the check could then enter additional digits in the blank spaces that would increase the value of the check.

12.27 PRINTING OPTIONS

The layout of printed EDIT-directed output was made easier by the use of PAGE, LINE, SKIP, and COLUMN control-format items. Since the easy formatting of output is also desirable when using the LIST- and DATA-directed approaches, it would be nice if these capabilities were available as options in the PUT statement. Three of them are. The COLUMN item is not available.

The syntax for the PUT statement now is

PUT[FILE(filename)][data-specification][PAGE][SKIP[(expression)]][LINE(expression)];

These options should be used only in connection with printed output. Recall that the use of:

1. The PAGE option causes the printer to go to the top of the next page before printing the output.

2. The LINE option results in an expression being evaluated and then truncated to an integer, say i, and printing to begin on the ith line.
3. The SKIP option causes the expression, if it is present, to be evaluated and then truncated to an integer, say j, and printing to begin on the jth line following the last one printed. If an expression is not used, printing begins on the next line; that is, j is taken to be 1.

These options are executed before transmission of the data begins. However, several PUT statements can be combined to obtain neatly formatted outputs. For example

PUT DATA(X,Y,Z)PAGE;PUT SKIP(2);PUT DATA(U,V);

will cause the last values assigned to X, Y, and Z to be printed at the top of a new page, with labels, and the values of U and V to be printed, with labels, after inserting a blank line in the output. A typical output would be

line 1: X = 2.347   Y = 6.163   Z = −104.21;
line 2: Blank
line 3: U = 1046.21   V = −.04726;

12.28 FILES—THE OPEN AND CLOSE STATEMENTS

In many applications, data sets are organized into files. Though they are collections of records, files can be processed using either stream-oriented or record-oriented I/O. However, in most instances, record-oriented I/O will be used because it is more convenient. In either case, a file can be assigned attributes in a DECLARE statement or, for certain attributes, in an OPEN statement.

Before a file can be processed in a PL/1 program, it must be opened. This can be done either explicitly, using the OPEN statement, or implicitly by referring to the file in some other statement. The OPEN statement permits additional attributes to be declared. These same attributes may later be rescinded using a CLOSE statement. This ability to "turn on" and "turn off" the attributes of a file is very useful. For example, it permits the programmer to intermittently prohibit writing on a file in a data set by giving the file the *INPUT attribute* in an OPEN statement and then rescinding it in a CLOSE statement. The INPUT attribute permits the file to be passed from a data set to the program but not from the program to the data set. This makes it impossible to write on this file when it appears in the data set. Similarly, it is possible to intermittently prohibit reading a file from a data set by giving it the *OUTPUT attribute*, since the output attribute allows the file to go from the program to the data set but not from the data set to the program. Also, it is possible to permit the file to be processed by reading in a record, modifying the record, and writing it in place of itself in the data set. This is done by associating the *UPDATE attribute* with the file. The syntax of an *OPEN statement* is

OPEN options-group[,options-group] · · · [,options-group];

Each options group specifies one file and the options associated with that file. Since a single OPEN statement may contain several options groups, more than one file can be opened with a single statement. A partial format for the *options group* is given below. Many options associated with record-oriented files have been omitted. A more complete description of the options can be found on pages 123, 124, 61 to 63, and 84 and 85 of version 3 of the manual [2].

FILE(filename)[{INPUT|OUTPUT|UPDATE}][{STREAM|REC-ORD}][PRINT][LINESIZE(expression)][PAGESIZE(expression)]

The options may appear in any order after the FILE(filename) portion of the statement. *STREAM files* are treated as a continuous string of characters and are processed using stream-oriented I/O statements. *RECORD files* are considered to be collections of records whose attributes will be specified elsewhere. They are processed using record-oriented I/O statements. Use of the *PRINT attribute* ensures that proper control of the printer carriage can be implemented. It may be specified only with a STREAM file. The *LINESIZE option* and *PAGESIZE option* apply only to files that have the PRINT attribute. The expression in parentheses is truncated to an integer, which is then used to specify the number of characters on a line (LINESIZE) and the number of lines on a page (PAGESIZE).

Alternative attributes of files are those which must be present either explicitly or implicitly. The {INPUT|OUTPUT|UPDATE} and {STREAM|RECORD} attribute choices are alternative. The specifications assigned implicitly by default are INPUT and STREAM, respectively. *Additive attributes* are those that may be optionally included at the discretion of the programmer and so are not implicitly assigned by default if not present. PRINT is an example of an additive attribute. Some examples of OPEN statements are

OPEN FILE(MASTR)RECORD UPDATE,FILE(WKLY)REC-ORD INPUT;

OPEN FILE(WRITE)OUTPUT PRINT PAGESIZE(22);

Note that the attribute STREAM is assigned to WRITE by default.

The DECLARE statement could also be used to assign attributes. In this case, they cannot be turned on and turned off. The attributes for MASTR, WKLY, and WRITE specified above in the OPEN statements could have been specified in a DECLARE statement as follows:

DECLARE MASTR FILE RECORD UPDATE,WKLY FILE RECORD INPUT, WRITE FILE OUTPUT PRINT;

In this context, FILE is an attribute. PAGESIZE and LINESIZE cannot be specified in a DECLARE statement. They are printing options, not attributes.

Closing a file can also be either explicit or implicit. A file is implicitly closed at the termination of a program. It is explicitly closed, and the attributes specified in the corresponding OPEN statement are rescinded, by using a CLOSE statement. The CLOSE statement also serves to reposition the file to its logical beginning. This means that a CLOSE statement could be used (in fact, must be used) to *rewind tapes in PL/1*. The syntax of the CLOSE STATEMENT is

CLOSE FILE(filename)[,FILE(filename)] . . . [,FILE(filename)];

An example of a CLOSE statement is

CLOSE FILE(MASTR),FILE(WKLY),FILE(WRITE);

12.29 RECORD-ORIENTED I/O

Record-oriented I/O permits the input or output of whole records uniformly and rapidly. In most cases, a single transmission will result in a complete record being read from or written into a structure or an array. Conversions are not made. The format in output will be identical to the internal representation of the elements in the record. The internal format on input will be identical to the format in the data set. There are many complicated and useful options available with record-oriented transmission. The discussion that follows is intended merely to introduce this subject.

A READ statement is used for record input, and a WRITE statement for record output. The formats of these statements are

READ FILE(filename)INTO(variable);

WRITE FILE(filename)FROM(variable);

Note that the file must be named. There are no standard system files in record-oriented I/O. The variables must not be subscripted. Variables referring to structures must be at level 1. Consider the following example from the payroll problem:

INWK:READ FILE(WKLY)INTO(WEEKLY);

This statement, labeled INWK, will read the next record in the file named WKLY into the structure WEEKLY. This approach to the reading in of the weekly file presupposes that the file WKLY was previously written using a WRITE statement in order to be sure that entries in the file are in the proper format.

Record I/O is used in the payroll problem because it simplifies the programming and speeds the execution of the program. Programming is easier because whole records can be inputted and outputted using a single statement and because special instructions are available for updating files. Execution is faster because data conversions are not made.

The ordinary READ statement is all that is required to read in records that are to be updated. Modification of the record is completed using the appropriate PL/1 statements, and the record is returned to its old place in the file using the *REWRITE statement*. This statement has the following format:

REWRITE FILE(filename)FROM(variable);

Consider the following example of this process from the payroll problem:

REWRITE FILE(MASTR)FROM(MASTER);

The effect of this instruction is to write the current contents of the MASTER structure in place of the last record that was read in from the MASTR file.

The *DISPLAY statement* is used to print out messages to the computer operator. Its syntax is

DISPLAY(scalar-expression);

In executing this statement, the scalar expression is evaluated and converted to a character string, where necessary. Consider the following examples from the payroll problem:

DISPLAY(NER||'ERRORS HAVE OCCURRED');

DISPLAY('LIST ERROR TAPE');

As a result of these two successive statements, two lines of messages to the operator are displayed. On the first line, the value of NER, which is the cumulative number of errors that have been found in executing the program, is printed along with the label ERRORS HAVE OCCURRED. On the second line, the message LIST ERROR TAPE is printed. A typical result would look like this:

6 ERRORS HAVE OCCURRED

LIST ERROR TAPE

The DISPLAY statement may also be combined with a *REPLY statement* (see page 113 of version 3 of [2]).

If a REPLY statement is used, execution of the program is suspended pending some interaction with the operator. In the absence of a REPLY, execution continues uninterrupted.

12.30 ON CONDITIONS AND ON STATEMENTS

In executing a PL/1 program, anomalous conditions can arise that usually cause the execution to be interrupted. Some of these conditions reflect machine problems; others, programming errors. It is possible that correct and appropriate, but unusual, results may lead to such a condition. This will happen only rarely, but it should be anticipated by the programmer. These anomalous situations in execution are said to be *ON conditions*.

Sometimes, when an ON condition occurs, a message is printed and execution is continued. At other times, a message is printed and execution is terminated. At still other times, nothing is done unless the programmer takes some action. The program is not even interrupted at these times. The ON conditions for which this is the case are the SUBSCRIPTRANGE and SIZE conditions. For these conditions, and only for these conditions, the standard response is not invoked unless the programmer asks for it. He does this by means of an ON-condition SYSTEM statement.

A complete list of all the ON conditions and the standard system responses to them is given in Appendix 3 of the manual [2], beginning on page 162 of version 3. A list of a few of the more important ON conditions and descriptions of when they can be expected to occur is given in Table 12.8.

A programmer can override the standard response by using an *ON statement*. Its syntax is

ON   condition{on-unit|SYSTEM;}

The "on-unit" can be either an unlabeled single statement or an unlabeled BEGIN block. (BEGIN blocks will be discussed in the next section.) It specifies the action to be taken. The use of the *SYSTEM specification* will cause the standard response to be used. It is generally used to rescind special responses provided by the programmer, but it also serves to interrupt programs that would not otherwise be interrupted if either a SUBSCRIPTRANGE or a SIZE condition occurs.

A new ON statement automatically overrides all preceding ON statements referring to the same ON conditions. Consider the program outlined in Fig. 12.2. (The braces are used to refer to sections of the

called in at the different points where it is required using a single statement, and the appropriate set of actual variables to be used at this point is substituted for the dummy variables. This avoids the tedious rewriting of virtually the same set of instructions.

Also, a section of a program might be blocked off from the remainder of the program in order to handle a special situation conveniently. For example, in computing the roots of a quadratic, say $Ax^2 + Bx + C$, the roots are complex if and only if $B^2 - 4AC$ is negative. Since variables that take on complex values can be handled directly if they are declared to be complex, it might be convenient to block out that portion of the program that computes complex roots. The variables could be declared to be complex in this blocked-out portion of the program and real in the rest of the program. This changing of attributes from block to block is allowed in PL/1. The quadratic-roots program, first presented in Sec. 12.2, does, in fact, contain a separate procedure, called COMPLX, to compute and output complex roots.

Another reason for collecting a series of statements into a block is that the syntax of the PL/1 language sometimes requires it. For example, the THEN and ELSE clauses of the IF-THEN statement can be either a group or a BEGIN block. This means that if the programmer would like the clause to contain a collection of several statements, other than a DO group, he must use a BEGIN block. This syntactical requirement is one of the major reasons for the use of BEGIN blocks.

There are two types of blocks, BEGIN blocks and PROCEDURE blocks.

The general form of the *BEGIN block* is as follows:

```
BEGIN;
program-element 1;
program-element 2;
. . . . . . . . . . .
program-element k;
END [label];
```

The general form of the *PROCEDURE block* is only very slightly different. It is as follows:

```
label: [label:] · · · [label:] PROCEDURE statement;
                  program-element 1;
                  program-element 2;
                  . . . . . . . . . . .
                  program-element k;
                  END [label];
```

Both blocks have a heading statement which identifies the block type, and both must end with an END statement. Note that in the PROCEDURE block, since at least one label must be given for the heading statement (the PROCEDURE statement), the syntax does include the label portion of the statement. A BEGIN block does not require a label, although one or more may appear. A PL/1 program must have at least one PROCEDURE block but need not have any BEGIN blocks.

In order to begin execution of any procedure, except the first, the procedure must be called. This is done with a *CALL statement* of the following form:

CALL entry-name;

The entry name represents the entry point of the procedure and is usually the label of the PROCEDURE statement. Execution of the statement

CALL NEWPROG,

would transfer control to the procedure named NEWPROG.

As was noted in Sec. 12.2, the first procedure of a program must have the OPTIONS(MAIN) attribute specified in the PROCEDURE statement. This means that at this point, the syntax of the PROCEDURE statement is

entry-name[entry-name:] · · · [entry-name:]PROCEDURE [OPTIONS(MAIN)];

An example showing a program containing two procedures follows.

OUTSIDE:PROCEDURE OPTIONS(MAIN);
        program-element 1
        program-element 2
        CALL INSIDE;
        program-element 3
        program-element 4

INSIDE:PROCEDURE
        program-element 5
        program-element 6
        END INSIDE;
        program-element 7
        END OUTSIDE

Here, the PROCEDURE OUTSIDE, having the attribute OPTIONS(MAIN), is the first procedure executed after loading. Control then proceeds sequentially from program element 1 to program element 2 and then to the CALL statement. The CALL statement invokes the

procedure INSIDE. After program elements 5 and 6 are executed, the END INSIDE statement transfers control back to the next statement following the CALL statement. The program then continues through program elements 3 and 4. The next statement in line is the PROCEDURE, and since this can only be invoked by a CALL, control is passed to the next statement after the PROCEDURE INSIDE, program element 7. The program ends with the statement END OUTSIDE, which is the END statement corresponding to the MAIN procedure. In summary, the program elements are executed in the following order: 1, 2, 5, 6, 3, 4, 7.

Examples of PROCEDURE blocks will be given in the next section. Another example of a PROCEDURE can be found in the program to compute the roots of a quadratic first presented in Sec. 12.2 and discussed in greater detail in the section after the next one, i.e., in Sec. 12.33. The PROCEDURE, called COMPLX, is used to compute and output complex roots of the quadratic.

A BEGIN block is activated by normal program flow. It is not invoked with a CALL statement. Every BEGIN block must be included in some other block and therefore must be included in some PROCEDURE. Thus we could have

```
OUTSIDE:PROCEDURE OPTIONS(MAIN);
          program-element 1;
          program-element 2;
          INSIDE:BEGIN;
          program-element 3;
          END INSIDE;
          program-element 4;
          END OUTSIDE;
```

In this case, the BEGIN block named INSIDE is executed in line, and the order of execution of the program elements is 1, 2, 3, 4.

BEGIN blocks are not so widely used as PROCEDURE blocks. They are frequently used in order to permit the programmer to temporarily change the attributes of some of his variables. This is possible because the attributes of an identifier are applicable in that block, say A, to which the DECLARE statement is internal and in all other blocks, say B, C, D, E, etc., which are contained in A, unless the identifier is redefined in one of the blocks B, C, D, E, etc. This last sentence is, of course, incomprehensible at this point. The remainder of this section will be devoted to a discussion of what is internal and external to a block and to the scope of the declaration of attributes for identifiers. The sentence will be repeated near the end of the section, and by that time, its meaning should have become clear.

A procedure which is not included in any other block is called an *external procedure*. The entry names of an external procedure are called *external names*. A block which is included in another block is called an *internal block*. Blocks can be nested to any depth; that is, any block, A, can include another block, B, so long as B is contained entirely within A. All the text of a block, except the entry name, is said to be *contained in* that block. That part of the text of block A which is not contained in any other block contained in A is *internal to* block A. The following example should help to clarify this definition.

```
A:PROCEDURE;
    program-element 1
    program-element 2
B:PROCEDURE;
    program-element 3
    program-element 4
C:PROCEDURE;
    program-element 5
    program-element 6
    END C;
    program-element 7
    END B;
    program-element 8
    END A;
```

There are three procedures in the example. Procedure A is external; procedures B and C are internal. Program elements 1, 2, and 8 are internal to A; elements 3, 4, and 7 are internal to B; and elements 5 and 6 are internal to C. Entry name A is an external name; entry name B is internal to procedure A, and entry name C is internal to procedure B.

The END statement may itself have several labels and may conclude with a label. If it does not conclude with a label, it is assumed to conclude that unended group or block whose heading statement precedes and is nearest to the END statement. For example:

```
A:PROCEDURE;
B:DO;
    . . . . . . . . . .
    END;
    END;
```

The first END concludes the DO group B, and the second END concludes PROCEDURE A. If an END statement with a concluding label terminates a group or block, it also terminates all unended groups or

blocks contained within it. The above example could be written as follows:

```
A:PROCEDURE;
B:DO;
      . . . . . . . . . .
END  A;
```

The END A statement automatically ends B as well.

The END statement of a procedure serves both to delineate the text of the procedure and to return control to the statement in the program following the CALL statement that invoked the procedure. Control can also be returned by means of the RETURN statement, which is written simply as

```
RETURN;
```

Control may also be passed to a statement outside the procedure by using the GO TO statement within the procedure (see Sec. 12.19).

PL/1 programs may be quite lengthy and contain many procedures. It sometimes may happen that a programmer will accidentally use the same name for two distinct variables in different procedures or that a programmer may wish to use the same name for two distinct variables. In either event, a special feature of the PL/1 language permits this to be done. Attributes declared for a given identifier are applicable in that block, say A, to which the DECLARE statement is internal and in all other blocks, say B, C, D, E, etc., which are contained in A, unless the identifier is redefined in one of the blocks B, C, D, E, etc. (It may not be redefined in block A.) Each redefinition establishes a new distinct identifier with the same name. This rule is said to establish the *scope of identifiers*. For example:

```
A:PROCEDURE;
  DECLARE(X,Y)FLOAT;
  . . . . . . . . . . . . . . . .
B:BEGIN;
  . . . . . . . . . . . . . . . . .
  DECLARE  Y  FLOAT;
  . . . . . . . . . . . . . .
END  B;
END  A;
```

The floating-point variable Y in BEGIN block B is not the same variable as the floating-point variable Y in PROCEDURE A. Since X is not declared in B, X in B is identical to X in A.

```
A:PROCEDURE;
   DECLARE Y FLOAT;
   . . . . . . . . . . . . .

B:PROCEDURE;
   DECLARE X FIXED;
   . . . . . . . . . . . . .

   END B;
   X = Y*Y;
   . . . . . .

   END A;
```

The statement X = Y*Y is internal to A since it appears after the END B statement. It serves to implicitly declare X in A. (The default specifications apply.) The explicit declaration of X in B, by means of the DECLARE X FIXED statement, automatically results in the X in B being different from the X in A. If X were not explicitly declared in B but were used in B, then the X's in B and A would be the same.

12.32 BUILT-IN FUNCTIONS AND PROGRAMMER-DEFINED FUNCTIONS AND SUBPROGRAMS

A number of special functions are provided with the PL/1 compiler that permit a programmer to obtain frequently derived values without writing special routines for this purpose. These built-in functions were first discussed in Sec. 12.7 and are described in Appendix E. They include such standard mathematical functions as the trigonometric functions, the exponential and logarithmic functions, the hyperbolic functions, the square root, and the absolute-value function. The arguments can be scalar expressions. In addition, special array functions are provided. For example, the function SUM(X) will compute the sum of all the elements in the array X.

The programmer can provide his own function to compute frequently derived values if none of the built-in functions satisfies his needs. This is done by writing a procedure for this purpose and adding it to the program. When a function reference appears in an expression, a function procedure is invoked. This is true for both programmer-supplied and built-in functions. The procedure is then executed, and the result is passed back to the statement invoking the procedure, where it is substituted for the function reference. Though some built-in functions may return more than one value, programmer-supplied functions must return only a single value. However, the value returned can be derived from several values.

The returning of values from function procedures to the statement

invoking the procedure is implemented by means of a RETURN statement in the procedure. The format of this statement is

RETURN(expression);

The expression in parentheses is evaluated, and this result is returned. Consider the following example:

```
A:PROCEDURE OPTIONS(MAIN);
  DCL(X,Y,Z)FIXED(4);
  · · · · · · · · · · · · · ·
  R=S*ADD3+T*T;
  · · · · · · · · · · · ·
  Q=V+(ADD3+R)/T;
  · · · · · · · · · · · · ·
  L=ADD3/M;
  · · · · · · · ·
  ADD3:PROCEDURE;
        RETURN(X+Y+Z);
        END ADD3;
  END A;
```

The sum (X+Y+Z) is computed each of the three times ADD3 is used, and the result is substituted for ADD3 in the expression. Note that though X, Y, and Z are fixed-point variables, the value substituted for ADD3 is in floating point because of the name of the function (ADD3).

Suppose we had to form a sum of three variables many times in a program, but suppose they were a different three variables each time. We would then use a procedure name with arguments to indicate which variables were to be summed. For example, in the procedure below, R, Y, and Z are summed in obtaining a new value for R, while R, X, and T are summed in getting Q, and R, Q, and V are summed in getting L.

```
A:PROCEDURE OPTIONS(MAIN);
  DCL(L,M,Q,R,S,T,V,X,Y,Z)FLOAT;
  · · · · · · · · · · · · · · · · · · · · · · ·
  R=S*ADD3(R,Y,Z)+T*T;
  · · · · · · · · · · · · · · · ·
  Q=V+(ADD3(R,X,T)+R)/T;
  · · · · · · · · · · · · · · · · · · ·
  L=ADD3(R,Q,V)/M;
  · · · · · · · · · · · · · ·
  ADD3:PROCEDURE(A,B,C);
        DCL(A,B,C)FLOAT;
        RETURN(A+B+C);
        END ADD3;
  END A;
```

It is possible to specify attributes for the value of the expression being returned, that is, for (A+B+C) in the above example, in the PRO-CEDURE statement that heads the special procedure. In the absence of such a specification, the name of the procedure is used to assign attributes to the value being returned by default. In this case, since the name begins with an A, these attributes are FLOAT, DECIMAL, and REAL.

We can now see that the general syntax for a *PROCEDURE statement for a programmer-supplied function* is

    entry-name:[entry name:] · · · [entry name:]PROCEDURE
    [(parameter[,parameter] · · · [,parameter])][data attributes];

For each parameter listed, there must be a matching argument in the invocation of the procedure. A *parameter* may be any scalar, array, or structure name that is unsubscripted and unqualified. An *argument* may be any of these or an expression. Every parameter listed is declared, implicitly or explicitly, within the procedure. A parameter is, therefore, a separate and distinct variable. In order to avoid additional conversions and to conserve storage space, parameters should have the same attributes as the corresponding arguments. However, they can be given distinct attributes. This requires a special declaration in the invoking procedure using the ENTRY attribute. Additional details can be found on page 52 of version 3 of the manual [2].

It may be convenient to enter a procedure at some point other than the PROCEDURE statement. This is done by means of an *ENTRY statement* having the following general form:

    entry-name:[entry name:] · · · [entry name:]ENTRY[(parameter
    [,parameter] · · · [,parameter])][data attributes];

The statement format is identical to that for the PROCEDURE statement given above except that the word ENTRY replaced the word PROCEDURE.

Suppose, for example, we wished to repeatedly evaluate either a linear or a quadratic function. That is, we wished to evaluate either $A + BX + CX^2$ or $A + BX$. The following procedure would provide the desired result:

    POLY2:PROCEDURE(A,B,C,Y)FLOAT BINARY;
        DCL(A,B,C,Y,S)FLOAT;
        S = C*Y;GO TO TWO;

    POLY1:ENTRY(A,B,Y)FLOAT BINARY;
        S = 0;

      TWO:RETURN((S+B)*Y+A);

      END POLY2;

If we now had the expression POLY1(FOX,G1,Z) in our program, it would be replaced by FOX+G1*Z in executing the procedure. If we had POLY2(H,J,R,X) in our program, it would be replaced by H+J*X+R*X*X.

If several values are to be returned, then a function will not do; a subroutine is required. Subroutines are invoked by using a special statement—a CALL statement. Merely writing the entry name is not enough. Also, the RETURN statement in the subroutine must not have an expression associated with it, and the PROCEDURE and ENTRY statements cannot specify data attributes. The reason for these last two restrictions is that several derived values with possibly different attributes are to be returned.

Suppose, for example, we wish to form an array whose rows consist of a single element. This element is to be the sum of the elements in the corresponding row of a given array. Let us call the given array A and the array of row sums B. If A has 10 rows and 10 columns, then the following subroutine will permit us to obtain B:

```
ROWSUM:PROCEDURE(A,B),
        DCL(A(10,10),B(10))FIXED;
        L1:DO K=1 TO 10;S=A(K,1);
        L2:DO I=2 TO 10;S=S+A(K,I);END L2;
        B(K)=S;END L1;
        RETURN;
        END ROWSUM;
```

This subroutine could be invoked using the statement

CALL ROWSUM(X,Y);

where X and Y have been declared to be (X(10,10),Y(10))FIXED. Whenever an argument is an array name, the number of dimensions and its bounds must agree with those declared for the corresponding parameters in the invoked procedure. Also, if an argument is a string, its length must be the same as that of the corresponding parameter.

If the bounds or the lengths are not known when the procedure is written, an asterisk may be used instead of the bounds of an array or the length of a string. The bounds or length will be assigned to be the same as those for the argument supplied upon invocation. The DECLARE statement written in the ROWSUM procedure above could have been

DECLARE(A(*,*),B(*))FIXED;

This would allow arrays to be specified as arguments which varied with respect to their bounds.

12.33 A PL/1 PROGRAM FOR THE ROOTS OF A QUADRATIC

The time has come to apply our knowledge of PL/1 to the writing of a complete program. We shall develop the program to obtain the roots of a quadratic polynomial in this section and a program to process a payroll in the next section.

The roots of $AX^2 + BX + C$ can be obtained from the formulas

$$\text{ROOT\_1} = \frac{-B + \sqrt{B^2 - 4AC}}{2A}$$

and

$$\text{ROOT\_2} = \frac{-B - \sqrt{B^2 - 4AC}}{2A}$$

The input will be the coefficients A, B, and C, and the output should be the two roots, ROOT_1 and ROOT_2. In addition to providing the roots, we should format and label the output to make it easy to interpret and use the results. Because the volume of input and output is very small, self-labeling, DATA-directed I/O will be used. If the volume were large, some other approach would have been used. This would be done in order to make the preparation of inputs easier and to speed up the execution of the program. To simplify the interpretation of the results, the output will begin at the top of a new page and will look like the following (note the provision for several outputs):

ROOTS OF A*X*X+B*X+C=0

A = value of A	B = value of B	C = value of C
ROOT_1 = value of first root	ROOT_2 = value of second root	
A = value of A for second data	B = value of B for second data	C = value of C for second data
ROOT_1 = value of first root	ROOT_2 = value of second root	

. . . .

We shall also provide a special message, "ERROR IN INPUT, A=0," in lieu of the roots if A = 0.

Another critical consideration is that different things should be done depending on whether $B^2 - 4AC$ is positive, zero, or negative. Finally, as indicated in the output format, we wish to be able to handle several sets of input. The approach taken is to continue to read input cards until we have exhausted the supply of input data. The program would then raise the ENDFILE condition (see Sec. 12.30 and Table 12.8)

in reading the first control card following the data. This would serve to end the job.

Figure 12.3 contains an annotated listing of the program. The listing and the accompanying comments should be studied in order to develop a better understanding of the way the formulas, output specifications, and critical considerations are combined into the finished program.

Program listing	Corresponding comments
QUAD_ROOTS:PROCEDURE OPTIONS(MAIN)	"Quad-roots" is as good a name as any.
ON ENDFILE(SYSIN)GO TO RND;	What to do if a control card is read.
PUT LIST('ROOTS OF A*X*X+B*X+C = D)PAGE;	This takes care of both starting at the top of a new page and the header line in the output.
NULL:GET DATA(A,B,C);	So much for input.
IF(A*A+B*B+C*C) = 0 THEN GO TO RND;	Really, if all the coefficients are zero, let's just give up.
IF A = 0 THEN GO TO ONEROOT;	This will get us to the error message.
PUT DATA(A,B,C)SKIP(2);	This takes care of both leaving a one-line space and displaying A, B, and C.
Z = A+A;X = B*B−4.0*A*C;	Some necessary calculations.
IF X<0 THEN DO;CALL COMPLX;GO TO NULL; END;	What to do if the roots are complex; more details later.
X = SQRT(X);ROOT_1 = (−B+X)/Z;ROOT_2 = (−B−X)/Z;	We now have the roots, if they are real.
PUT DATA(ROOT_1,ROOT_2)SKIP(1);GO TO NULL;	Outputs roots on the next line and goes to the next set of data.
COMPLX:PROCEDURE;DECLARE(ROOT_1,ROOT_2,Y) COMPLEX FLOAT;Y = X;ROOT_2 = SQRT(Y);ROOT_1 = (−B+ROOT_2)/Z;ROOT_2 = (−B−ROOT_2)/Z; PUT DATA(ROOT_1, ROOT_2)SKIP(1); END COMPLX;	The messy details, including output, if the roots are complex.
ONE ROOT:PUT LIST('ERROR IN INPUT, A = 0') SKIP(2);	This will output the error message, after leaving a one-line space.
GO TO NULL;	To the next set of data.
RND:END QUAD_ROOTS	That's all, folks!

Fig. 12.3 A program for computing the roots of a quadratic, with comments.

12.34 A PL/1 PROGRAM FOR THE PAYROLL PROBLEM

Preparing a PL/1 program to process a payroll problem is more difficult than preparing a program to find the roots of a quadratic equation. This greater difficulty stems from the need to explicitly construct an algorithm, structure the files, analyze the application in order to determine the number of digits required in some of the operands, and provide for errors in input. The algorithm was first stated in Sec. 5.6 and then repeated in the form of flow charts in Sec. 6.5. The files were structured

and the operands laid out in Sec. 12.17. Provision for errors in input was made in developing the algorithms. Thus the extra effort has already been completed, and we can proceed to a statement of the program.

The PL/1 program is given in Figs. 12.4 to 12.6. One page of the printed listing of the program is given in each figure, so that this listing is $2\frac{1}{2}$ pages long.

In general, the listing of a PL/1 program begins with an options list, so that Fig. 12.4 was actually the second page of the listing as it came off the printer. The programmer has a number of options that he may exercise in programming and compiling a PL/1 program. The *options list* specifies those options that were actually exercised in a given compila-

```
PAYROLL:PROCEDURE OPTIONS (MAIN);

 1              PAYROLL:PROCEDURE OPTIONS (MAIN);
 2              DCL  1 MASTER,
                  2 MNO  FIXED,
                  2 NAME_M,
                    3 FIRSTM CHAR(14),
                    3 INITLM CHAR (1),
                    3 LASTM  CHAR(14),
                  2 HM      FIXED (2),
                  2 RATE    FIXED(4,2),
                  2 RWP     FIXED(5,2),
                  2 CGP     FIXED(7,2),
                  2 CFICA   FIXED(5,2),
                  2 D       FIXED (2),
                  2 CWT     FIXED(7,2),
                  2 WHD     FIXED(4,2),
                  2 RNP     FIXED(6,2);

 3              DCL  1 WEEKLY,
                  2 WNO  FIXED,
                  2 NAME_W,
                    3 FIRSTW CHAR(14),
                    3 INITLW CHAR (1),
                    3 LASTW  CHAR(14),
                  2 HW      FIXED (2);

 4              DCL (W,M,K) CHAR(1), L FIXED BIN;
 5              DCL (PFICA,AFICA) FIXED(5,2), (WT,NP,GP) FIXED(6,2), WTR FIXED(2,2);

 6              OPEN FILE (MASTR) RECORD UPDATE,
                  FILE (WKLY) RECORD INPUT,
                  FILE (ERR) OUTPUT,
                  FILE (WRITE) OUTPUT PRINT PAGESIZE(66);

 7              ON ENDFILE (WKLY) BEGIN; IF M='1' THEN GO TO STOP;
11                              W='1';
12                              GO TO ENDMSTR;
13                              END;

14              ON ENDFILE (MASTR) BEGIN; IF W='1' THEN GO TO STOP;
18                              M='1';
19                              GO TO INWK;
20                              END;

21              W,M='0';  NER=0;
23              INITZL: L=0;
24              PUT FILE (WRITE) PAGE;
25              L8_4: READ FILE (MASTR) INTO (MASTER);
26                    IF W='0' THEN GO TO INWK;
28              ENDMSTR: NER=NER+1;
29                       PUT FILE (ERR) EDIT (1,MNO,NAME_M) (F(1),R(FORM));
30                       GO TO L8_4;

31              INWK: READ FILE (WKLY)  INTO (WEEKLY);

32                    IF M='0' THEN GO TO L8_5;
34              L8_4_2: PUT FILE (ERR) EDIT (2,WNO,NAME_W) (F(1),R(FORM));
35                      FORM: FORMAT (F(5),2(A(14),A(1),A(14)));
```

Fig. 12.4 The first page of the listing of a PL/1 program to process a payroll.

points can appear only in the mantissa. The letter B is also used to conclude binary floating numbers. Examples are:

Binary floating	Decimal floating
1.01E2B	5E0
−1011E−3B	−1375E−3
1101E−1B	65E−1
1101E4B	2.08E2

Each of the four nonsterling types of arithmetic data can be used to represent complex numbers. The imaginary parts are written by concluding the representation with the letter I. Thus,

$$5E0+65E-1I$$

$$5+6.5I$$

$$101B+110.1BI$$

are all valid representations of the same complex number.

12.9 VARIABLES AND THEIR ATTRIBUTES

A *variable* is a quantity that can assume any one of a set of values. A *scalar variable* is a variable that denotes a single data item (as opposed to a variable that refers to an aggregate of data items). The specifications for the characteristics of variables are called *attributes*. Attributes are assigned to variables in a DECLARE statement (see Sec. 12.12).

Arithmetic-type variables refer to numbers rather than strings. They are given attributes with respect to base, scale, and mode. The *base* can be decimal or binary, the *scale* fixed or floating, and the *mode* real or complex.

In PL/1, every attribute of a variable has been given a *default* interpretation. If no alternative is selected by the programmer, the compiler will automatically assume one of the choices. This choice, which the compiler will make in lieu of specifications from the programmer, is called the *default condition* or *option*.

If the attributes of an arithmetic-type variable are not declared, then the default conditions are assigned as follows: If the first letter of the name is any of the letters I, J, K, L, M, or N, the default conditions are fixed, binary, and real. If the first letter is any other than those mentioned, the defaults are floating, decimal, and real.

If some, but not all, of the attributes of a variable are declared, then the remaining attributes are assigned as floating, decimal, and real. For example, the following statement declares the scale of TENSION as fixed:

DECLARE TENSION FIXED;

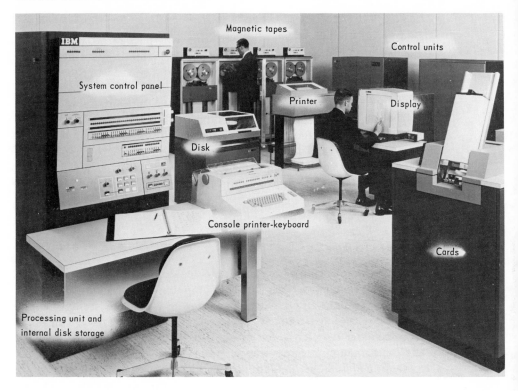

Fig. 14.1   An IBM System/360 in operation.

ferent models vary in speed, data-handling capacity, maximum allowable size of memory, and price.   Except for the model 20, the model 67 (which is designed especially for time-sharing applications), and the model 44 (which is designed especially for scientific computations), these computers were intended to be program-compatible.   This means that a program which runs on one model should run on any other model.   This compatibility, however, is limited by such things as the storage capacities and input/output devices of both machines.   Compatibility may turn out to be more nearly the exception than the rule.

The system is designed to operate with a supervisory program, supplied by the manufacturer, called the Operating System/360,† or more succinctly, OS/360.   The operating system has facilities for implementing storage protection, for relocating programs, for nonstop

---

† However, this operating system cannot be implemented on smaller models of the System/360.   The tape operating system (TOS) or disk operating system (DOS) is used on these models.   Reference [1] contains a description of the features of TOS and DOS.

operation, and for program interruption. (Program interruption was discussed in Sec. 13.2. The other terms will be defined in the next paragraph.) It also coordinates and executes all input and output instructions, handles exceptional conditions, and supervises the scheduling and execution of programs. OS/360 will be discussed in Chap. 15.

Storage protection refers to the protection of the contents of an area of core storage from being written over during the execution of a program; *relocating programs* refers to the movement of a program from one place in core storage to another while modifying the appropriate references to storage addresses so that the program can be executed in its new location. *Nonstop operation*, as the phrase implies, refers to the continuous operation of the computer.

14.3 MAIN STORAGE

The main-storage section of a computer contains the data that are to be processed, the instructions that the computer executes, and the results obtained. All data entering the computer go into main storage before they can be processed, and after processing, the results are held in main storage pending transfer to an output device. Magnetic cores (4.4) are used as the main-storage devices in the System/360.

Each model in the 360 family may have any one of several sizes of main storage. The following table shows both the smallest and the largest available memory sizes, in numbers of bytes, for each of several models.

Model	Smallest	Largest
20	4,096	16,384
30	8,192	65,536
40	16,384	262,144
44	32,768	262,144
50	65,536	524,288
65	131,072	1,048,576
67		1,048,576 (single processor)
		2,097,152 (multiprocessor)
75	262,144	1,048,576

14.4 STORAGE AND PROTECTION KEYS

Since a large computer is an expensive device, it should be kept as busy as possible. One problem in obtaining maximum efficiency is that the speed of the processor is much greater than the speed at which information can be moved to or from an input/output device. Even the high-speed I/O devices—magnetic tapes, disks, and drums (4.3)—transfer data at a much slower rate than that at which the processor operates. When, in executing calculations, it becomes necessary to move data into memory from an input device, the processor must initiate the movement of the data into the memory and then wait until the data transfer is completed before processing of the data can be continued.

One way to utilize this waiting time is to process some other data. If there were two programs in the memory at the same time, while one program was moving data in or out, the processor could be performing calculations in the other. During such operations, the System/360 storage-protection feature ensures that one program does not store information in those storage areas being used by the other.

Main storage can be protected by assigning a *storage key*, in the form of a four-bit number, to each block of 2,048 bytes. Before data are stored in a block, the storage key for that block is compared with a *protection key*, which is found either in the program-status word (PSW) or in the input channel. (The PSW will be discussed in Sec. 15.2, and channels in Sec. 14.11.) If storing is being done with a computer instruction, the key is in the PSW; if it is being done by reading information from an input device, the protection key is supplied by the input channel. If the storage key and the protection key are the same, the operation proceeds and the data are stored. If the keys do not match, the operation is terminated, the data are not stored, and the execution of the program is interrupted so as to transfer control to an error-handling program.

The storage key associated with each block of storage is not part of the addressable memory, so that no additional storage is required for this feature. The key can be changed by executing a machine instruction. The storage-protection check itself is made by circuits; i.e., it is hardware- rather than software-implemented. The only programs required are instructions to set the storage key and a program to handle any protection errors which may occur. This error-handling program is part of the operating system supplied by the manufacturer.

14.5 THE ARGUMENT FOR BASE ADDRESSING

Every byte in core may be individually addressable. This means that the number of bits reserved for the address portion of each instruction would have to be large enough to represent the highest-numbered address. For example, 20 bits would be required to address every byte of a 1,048,576-byte memory. Installations having a System/360 with a

65,536-byte memory, requiring only a 16-bit address, would have at least 4 unused bits in every address, thereby wasting space. Also, if the 20-bit address convention were universally adopted, it would be impossible to address some parts of those memories that contained more than 1,048,576 bytes. Some other scheme is required; base addressing is used.

Another, more important reason for base addressing is the need to keep the processor as busy as possible. Suppose, in order to gain greater utilization, there were two or more programs in memory, passing control back and forth between them whenever one program had to wait for some input/output function to be completed. This implies that:

1. There must be at least a part of the operating system stored in the memory at all times.† This part of the operating system is called the *in-core supervisor*.
2. The in-core supervisor must be able to call in and execute programs to perform the required input/output functions.
3. The operating system must be able to load the program into an area in memory that is not already being used by any other programs. Loading a program into any section of memory is called *relocating* the program, which was first discussed in Sec. 14.2. The relocation ability must be provided not only for the utility programs, such as the input/output functions, but for any other programs as well. The *linkage editor*, which is a part of the operating system, performs the loading operation for user programs.

The first requirement means that we must always give up some portion of the memory in order to contain the in-core supervisor. The second and third requirements have their greatest effect on the instruction format. The instructions should not occupy fixed positions in storage, nor should the data, which are referenced by the instructions, occupy fixed positions. Though we could still relocate the program if all addresses were fixed, this would require the program which relocates our program to look at each address of every instruction, determine the relocation increment to be added, perform this modification, and store the instruction at the appropriate place in memory. A very inefficient approach. Suppose instead of writing each address as an absolute number, the addresses were written such that large blocks of instructions could be loaded without inspecting each address in each instruction. Also, if just part of the address, instead of the entire address, could be stored, memory space would be saved. This is done by using base addressing.

† This requirement is not peculiar to this particular kind of operation. A part of the operating system must be kept in memory at all times in order to use the operating system.

14.6 BASE ADDRESSING

In order to obtain efficiency in space and also to reduce time in relocation, the System/360 employs a form of base addressing. (However, base addressing does have some disadvantages. The major one is the additional programming detail it introduces.) That is, only a part of the address is provided in the instruction, and the address is completed by adding a number from one of the registers to this part.

The central processing unit contains two types of *registers*, or *accumulators*. These registers are special storage capabilities contained within the processor that serve to expedite the execution of instructions. Nearly all computers have them. There are 16 general registers in the System/360, each 32 bits long, which are used as accumulators in fixed-point arithmetic and logical operations and to modify instructions and addresses. There are also four floating-point registers, used in executing floating-point instructions, that are 64 bits in length.

The number supplied by the register is called the *base address;* the number in the instruction is called the *displacement* or *relative address*. Programs may be written in sections, assuming that each section will be contained in one block of 4,096 bytes. The addresses used in the instructions would then be relative addresses and would take on the value 0 to 4095. The true address is the sum of this relative address and the base address that is supplied from a register. The instruction must therefore contain two pieces of information: the relative address within a 4,096-byte block and the number of the register which contains the base address.

This approach permits a whole block to be relocated merely by modifying the contents of the base register. Suppose, for example, we wished to relocate a block that is now stored in locations 5012 to 7016. The instructions relating to this block would refer to a base-address register that now contained the number 5012. If we modify the contents of this base-address register, we can relocate the block. For example, if we change the contents of this register to 10012, then we can relocate the block in locations 10012 to 12016.

14.7 ADDRESS MODIFICATION

Before continuing the discussion of the System/360, we pause to examine a concept, *address modification*, that is similar to base addressing.

Suppose that, in writing a program, a series of instructions are to be repeated many times and that some of the addresses used in the instructions are to be changed in each repetition. For example, suppose a series of 1,000 consecutive bytes are to be reset to zero. One way to do this would be to first set all 32 bits (four bytes) of one of the general registers to zero and then write an instruction to store the contents of this register in the first four bytes that are to be set to zero. Another instruction would then be written to store the contents of the register in the next four bytes, and so on, until a total of 250 instructions were written that would, finally, set zeros in all 1,000 bytes. This is obviously a very tedious procedure for the programmer and results in a lengthy program. (However, the execution time is quite fast.) Instead, a STORE REGISTER instruction is set up, and the address of the first byte that is to be set to zero is inserted as the storage address in this instruction. After each execution of the instruction, the storage address is increased by 4.† Finally, a check is made to ensure that this is done exactly 250 times. The flow chart for this procedure is given in Fig. 14.2. This is a much shorter program to write than one having 250 STORE instructions.

In carrying out a step in this procedure, the address portion of the instruction in memory is increased by 4. To do this, the instruction, or rather a part of it, is moved into a register, an addition is performed, and the instruction is returned to memory. This means that three instructions would be required to carry out the address modification. However, with indexing, only one instruction is needed.

14.8 INDEXING

In order to make address modification more efficient, the System/360 provides a feature, similar in many respects to base addressing, called

† Incrementing a storage address is slower than modifying a register because memory exchanges are slower than register exchanges.

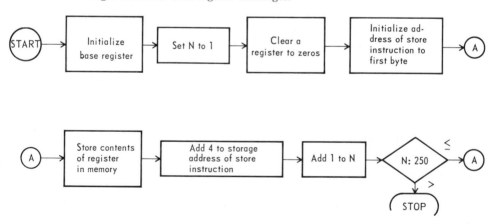

Fig. 14.2   Flow chart for setting 1,000 bytes to zero.

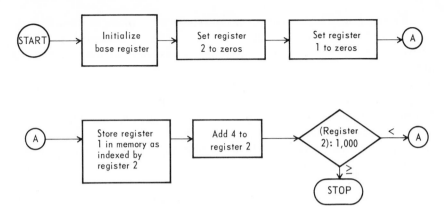

Fig. 14.3 Flow chart for setting 1,000 bytes to zero using index registers.

indexing. To implement this, certain instructions provide for a register, called an *index register*, to be specified other than the one used for base addressing. The computer, upon execution of the instruction, obtains the actual address to be used in memory by adding the relative address supplied as part of the instruction to the contents of the index register and the contents of the base register. To increment the address, an addition to a value in the index register rather than to a value in memory is required. This requires less machine time and permits address modification via a single instruction that modifies the value stored in the index register.

If we used register 1 to contain the four 0 bytes that are to be repeatedly loaded into core and register 2 as our index register, the flow chart for clearing 1,000 bytes to zero using indexing would be as shown in Fig. 14.3.

To review: Base addressing permits the relative address, given in an instruction, to be limited to the range 0 to 4095. The relative address is added to the base address, which is stored in a register, to obtain the actual address. Indexing expedites repeated modification of an address by allowing the contents of still another register, the index register, to be added to the relative and base addresses in order to obtain the actual address. Base addressing and indexing do not affect the contents of the address portion of the instruction.

14.9 THE CENTRAL PROCESSING UNIT

The central processing unit (CPU) is composed of two main sections: the control section and the arithmetic and logic section.

The *control section* governs the entire operation of the computer. It causes instructions to be brought from the memory, decoded, and executed, and it controls sequencing from one instruction to the next. It also governs the communication between storage and input/output devices and checks for storage protection. The control function is designed to operate in conjunction with a supervisor program which coordinates and issues all input/output instructions, loads programs and data, manages storage, and supervises scheduling of programs. As far as the programmer is concerned, the supervisor program and the control equipment cannot be distinguished, since they act together to perform a particular task.

The *arithmetic and logic section* contains the circuits necessary for executing each of the following types of operations:

1. Fixed-point binary arithmetic
2. Floating-point binary arithmetic
3. Fixed-point decimal arithmetic
4. Logical operations

These classes differ in the formats required for the data, the kinds of operations allowed, the ways in which the lengths of the data are specified, and the storage exchanges that take place in their execution. The formats were discussed in Chap. 13. The storage exchanges are discussed in the next section.

14.10 STORAGE EXCHANGES IN CARRYING OUT ARITHMETIC OPERATIONS

There are three basic methods for carrying out arithmetic in a computer. (This does not refer to the circuitry used but rather to the storage exchanges that take place.) These are the storage-to-register, the register-to-register, and the storage-to-storage methods.

The *storage-to-register method* obtains an operand from storage and performs an operation with it on some other operand located in a register. The result is placed in a register. The *storage-to-storage method* obtains both operands from storage and places the result in storage. The *register-to-register method* obtains both operands from registers and places the result in a register.

All three of these methods are used in the System/360. The register-to-register and storage-to-register approaches are used for fixed-length operations, and the storage-to-storage approach is used for variable-length operations.

We shall illustrate these exchanges by discussing the kinds of exchanges that take place in fixed-point, decimal, and floating-point arithmetic operations.

Fixed-point arithmetic operations use the storage-to-register method.

The operands are half-words, words, or double words.   The register used can be any of the 16 general registers numbered 0 to 15.   A general register, which is 32 bits long, stores a half-word operand in the 16 low-order bits (bits 16 to 31).   Since a double word is 64 bits long, one general register cannot contain a double word.   In an operation that requires an operand of this length (for example, the DIVIDE instruction), two adjacent registers are used and the pair must be an even-odd combination, such as 2, 3 or 8, 9.   In this case, the even register is addressed.   Addition, subtraction, multiplication, division, and comparison are performed upon one operand in a register and another operand which may be either in storage or in another register.

Decimal arithmetic operations use the storage-to-storage method and variable-length operands.   The length of the data for each operand is given as a part of each instruction and can be from 1 to 16 bytes. Addition, subtraction, multiplication, and division are performed on data in the packed format (13.7).   Instructions are also provided to change formats from packed to unpacked, and vice versa.   Since the storage-to-storage method is used, every instruction requires that two storage addresses be specified, with the result being stored in place of the data used as the first operand.

Floating-point arithmetic operations use the storage-to-register method.   The data are floating-point numbers in either the short or the long form.   Using the short form takes less space in storage and less time to execute each instruction than using the long form.   The long form, however, provides greater accuracy.   (Section 13.8 contains more specific information.   Roughly, the long form permits accuracy to about 16 decimal digits, and the short form to about 7.)   The registers used can be any of the four floating-point registers.   The registers are identified by the numbers 0, 2, 4, and 6 since they are each two words long. Instructions are provided to load and store registers, compare numbers, and perform addition, subtraction, multiplication, and division.   All the operations can be performed in either the long or the short form.

14.11   INPUT/OUTPUT IN THE SYSTEM/360—CHANNELS

The control of I/O devices is handled by a unit called a *channel* in the System/360.   Channels also provide a path along which data can be sent by the central processor from core to an I/O device or from the device to core.   The channel generates information that is used to control the flow along this path.   This information is used by the CPU to start and to monitor the channel; it is also used by the channel to notify the CPU that an operation has terminated.   The action taken upon receipt of these signals is performed under program control of the operating system.   That is, the hardware can recognize a particular signal and act upon the signal by transferring control to a program, but it is the program that decides what further action is required and initiates that action.

Input/output devices are attached to the channel by a connection called an *I/O interface*. Depending upon the I/O device, there may be another unit, called a *control unit*, connecting the actual I/O device to the interface. The control unit handles the transformation of the signals coming from the computer into the special signal configuration required by a particular I/O device. The computer can transmit the same kind of signals, no matter what the I/O device. Each different control unit functions only with the I/O device for which it was designed, and in many cases—for example, in the printer—the control unit is housed within the I/O device itself. The interface can have as many as eight control units attached to it, so that a separate interface for each control unit is unnecessary.

A schematic of the organization of the system for a single type of I/O device (magnetic tape) is shown in Fig. 14.4. Note that four tape drives are attached to the control unit. There could be as many as eight drives attached to a single control unit and, by using all eight control units to support magnetic-tape I/O, as many as 64 drives attached to a single channel.

The data rates of I/O devices, that is, the speeds at which a device can handle information, are such that we can group them into two classifications: high-speed devices (magnetic tapes, disks, and drums) and slower devices (printers, card readers and punches, paper-tape equipment, and the console typewriter). To provide greater efficiency, the two classifications of I/O devices are treated differently by the System/360. Large blocks of data are transferred directly to individual fast-output devices, but several slow devices are operated simultaneously by transferring small amounts of data to each device and cycling this transfer from device to device.

14.12 SELECTOR AND MULTIPLEXOR CHANNELS

The System/360 has two types of I/O channels, a selector channel

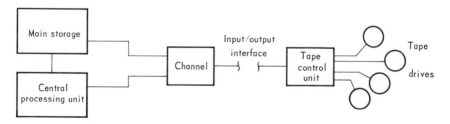

Fig. 14.4 Connections of magnetic-tape units to the computer.

to handle the high-speed I/O devices and a multiplexor channel to handle the slower devices. On a *selector channel*, an I/O device transmits one complete block of information over the interface. The transmission is performed serially, a byte at a time. While one device is transmitting over a selector channel, no other device may be transmitting over this same channel. This type of operation is called *burst mode*, and selector channels can operate in this mode only. The number of selector channels which can be attached varies according to the particular 360 model. For example, the model 40 can have two channels and the model 50 can have three.

Once the CPU begins transferring data, the actual transfer is controlled by the channel and the CPU is released to continue processing. This is done because the speed of the processor is greater than the speed at which even the fastest I/O devices can operate.

The *multiplexor channel* can operate in either burst mode or multiplexor mode. A single multiplexor channel may have several subchannels. A *subchannel* is defined to be the channel facility necessary to sustain an operation with a single I/O device.† The number of subchannels available varies according to the 360 model. Generally, there are at least 128 subchannels available on each multiplexor channel.

Even in the multiplexor mode of operation, the multiplexor channel is actually sending information to a single device at a time through the interface   However, while one device on a multiplexor channel handles the information passed to it, more information can be sent to another device. Thus, a number of devices can be operating simultaneously even though the channel is really sending information to one device at a time. Short sets of information can be transmitted in both the multiplexor and the burst modes of operation. The distinction is in the length of time required for the transmission. Whenever the transmission causes a device to be connected to a channel for more than approximately 100 microseconds, the channel is considered to be operating in the burst mode. A channel operating in burst mode will appear busy to a request for a new I/O instruction. A channel operating in the multiplexor mode is available anytime for initiating a new operation, providing the aggregate data rate does not exceed the capacity of the channel.

Figure 14.5 indicates how information is input in the multiplexor mode, assuming three input devices are reading data into memory. Note that the cycle order is A, B, C and that the last byte that was read into the channel was byte A2. Byte B2 will be read in next, followed by C2, A3, B3, etc. The I/O device will be working continuously because it is so much slower than the channel.

† This does not imply that only one I/O device can be connected to the subchannel; rather, only one device can be operated by each subchannel at a time.

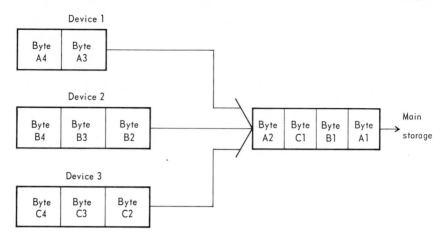

Fig. 14.5 Schematic of byte transfer when operating in the multiplexor mode.

PROBLEMS

14.1   How many general registers are there in the CPU and what is the length, in bits, of each? How many floating-point registers are there and what is the length of each?

14.2   Name the storage-exchange method used for each of the following types of operations:
    (a)   Fixed-binary arithmetic
    (b)   Fixed-point decimal arithmetic
    (c)   Floating-point binary arithmetic

14.3   A particular System/360 has, as its I/O units, a printer, four magnetic-tape drives, and a card reader. What would be the minimum number of control units, I/O interfaces, and channels necessary to operate this system?

14.4   Suppose a System/360 configuration has one selector channel, one multiplexor channel, and the I/O units described in Prob. 14.3. Indicate which devices should be connected to which channels in order to be able to operate at least one tape drive simultaneously with all the other devices.

14.5   Following are schematics of two different I/O configurations, each having two magnetic-tape units and two disks. Which configuration would permit the more efficient operation and why?

Configuration A

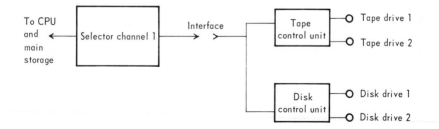

Configuration B

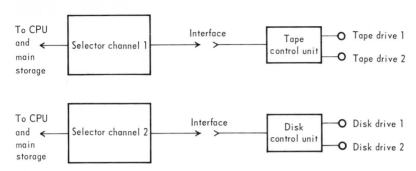

REFERENCE

1. Disk and Tape Operating System/360 Concepts and Facilities, *IBM Systems Ref. Library Form* C24-5030.

ANNOTATED SUPPLEMENTARY BIBLIOGRAPHY

The reader who is interested in more detailed information on those aspects of the System/360 discussed in this chapter is referred to:

1. IBM System/360 Principles of Operation, pp. 5–9, 19–21, 83–90, and 96–116, *IBM Systems Ref. Library Form* A22-6821. This is the basic user's manual on System/360 hardware.
2. The Structure of System/360, *IBM Systems J.*, vol. 3, no. 2, pp. 119–121 and 131–180, 1964.
3. Hopkins, M. E.: Programming 360-Class Machines, *Datamation*, pp. 47–50, April, 1965. An introductory, survey article that does, however, include a few brief details on instruction and data formats.
4. IBM Field Engineering Education, *Student Self-study Course Book 5*. A programmed instruction manual on input/output for the System/360, it is probably the best available detailed reference on input/output for the 360.
5. IBM's New System/360, *Datamation*, pp. 51–55, April, 1964. This somewhat dated reference includes a brief survey of peripheral devices available with the System/360.

chapter 15

THE PROGRAM-STATUS
WORD, INTERRUPTS, AND
THE OPERATING SYSTEM/360

15.1 INTRODUCTION

The emphasis in this last chapter on the System/360 will be on two distinct but related topics: interrupts and OS/360. Both of these topics have been mentioned repeatedly in our earlier discussions of the system, and it seems appropriate to conclude our sketchy overview of this family of computers with these two subjects. In addition, in order to better understand the processing of interrupts, the program-status word will be discussed before the discussion of interrupts begins. The chapter concludes with a broad description of OS/360 that is intended to provide an appreciation for the scope of this operating system and an understanding of its basic functions and capabilities.

15.2 THE PROGRAM-STATUS WORD

The *program-status word* (PSW) is a double word which is part of the computer circuitry and is not part of either the main storage or the registers. The 64 bits contained in it are used to indicate the status of the program being executed and to control the program. The exact meaning of all the bits in the PSW will not be discussed, but the most important functions will be covered. For a complete description of the PSW, see [1], pages 69 and 70.

The address of the next instruction is stored in bits 40 to 63 of the PSW. These 24 bits are called the *instruction address*. As each instruction is being analyzed by the CPU, its length is determined by the configuration of bits 0 and 1 of the instruction itself. The proper number of bytes (either 2, 4, or 6) are then added to the instruction-address portion of the PSW in order to obtain the address of the next instruction. For example, suppose an instruction is located in bytes 3004 to 3007; the instruction address of the PSW will be updated from 3004 to 3008. The PSW to which we are referring here is called the *current PSW* since it is the one that is currently being used. The need for this distinction will be evident as the discussion of the PSW continues. In executing a branch instruction, the contents of the instruction address of the current PSW are ignored; they are replaced by the address to which the instruction is to branch.

Bits 34 and 35 of the current PSW are called the *condition code* and are used to enable a program to determine something about the results of an arithmetic operation. It is often necessary, after performing some arithmetic, to make a decision about what to do next, depending upon whether the result was negative, positive, or zero. The condition code, along with a branch instruction to test the condition code, allows this procedure to be implemented. Since there are two bits available, the condition code can represent any one of four possible conditions corresponding to the bit combinations 00, 01, 10, and 11. The meaning of these codes is as follows:

Condition code	Arithmetic results
00	Zero
01	Negative
10	Positive
11	Overflow

The condition called *overflow* can result if a number is generated by some arithmetic operation whose representation exceeds the capacity of the space allotted for it. Overflow arithmetic conditions were discussed in Secs. 13.9 to 13.11.

A branch instruction, called a *branch on condition*, can be written to test the condition code and to branch if a result has a specified condition. If a result does not have the condition specified, no branch is executed and the next instruction is taken in the normal sequence. The condition code remains fixed until after the execution of an instruction which can change it (not all instructions affect this code).

15.3 THE NEED FOR INTERRUPT CAPABILITIES

Interrupts were first mentioned in the discussion of the flow of information in a computer servicing remote terminals (Sec. 13.2). It was pointed out there that a request for servicing from a remote terminal must be permitted to interrupt ongoing work. In addition, the initiation or termination of an input/output function may be permitted to interrupt ongoing work in order to keep the slower input/output units as busy as possible. An abnormal machine condition, such as a byte containing an even number of bits, may interrupt ongoing work in order to avoid wasting time in processing erroneous information. Also, an abnormal programming condition, such as a half-word operand being located on an odd byte address, could cause an interrupt.

The system must perform the following functions in servicing interrupts:

1. Recognize the condition
2. Store appropriate status information in order to return
3. Perform the particular housekeeping task dictated by the cause of the interrupt

The efficient way to handle the interrupt procedure is to allow the system hardware to perform as many of these functions as possible. Those functions that are not handled by the hardware must then be handled by instructions, i.e., by the software.

The System/360 hardware implements functions 1 and 2. Function 3 is implemented by providing a set of programs which are executed under control of the supervisor program. The actual steps involved are discussed in detail in Secs. 15.5 to 15.7.

15.4 CLASSES OF INTERRUPTS

The System/360 hardware recognizes the class of an interrupt. Recognition of specific conditions within each class is left to the supervisor program. The classes of interrupts are:

1. Input/output
2. Program
3. Supervisor-call
4. External
5. Machine-check

The *input/output interrupt* usually occurs at the termination of an I/O operation. This provides the supervisor with the means of determining when an I/O operation has been completed. The supervisor can then return to resume processing the program which called for the I/O function.

The *program interrupt* can occur when any one of a number of conditions, called *exceptions*, occurs.   Some of these exceptions are:

1. *Operation exception*   An attempt is made to execute an illegal operation code.
2. *Protection exception*   The storage key of a result location does not match the protection key.
3. *Addressing exception*   A specified address is outside the limits of the available storage.
4. *Specification exception*   Data or an instruction or control-word address does not specify the proper boundary for the information, for example, specifying a floating-point register address other than 0, 2, 4, or 6.
5. *Overflow exception*   A fixed-point, decimal, or floating-point operation causes an overflow.
6. *Divide exception*   A quotient exceeds the field specified to contain it, or an attempt is made to divide by zero.
7. *Privileged-operation exception*   A privileged instruction is encountered in the problem state.   The System/360 can operate in either of two states, the *problem state* or the *supervisor state*.   In the problem state, all the I/O, storage protection, and other instructions which can modify the PSW are treated as invalid.   These instructions are called *privileged instructions* and must be executed only in the supervisor state.

The third class of interrupt, called the *supervisor-call interrupt,* occurs as a result of executing the instruction SUPERVISOR CALL. The major purpose of this instruction is to switch from the problem state to the supervisor state.

The *external interrupt* provides the means by which the CPU can respond to signals from the built-in timer, from the interrupt key located on the control panel of the machine, or from some other external device.

The last class, the *machine-check interrupt*, provides the means for the recovery from, and location of, a machine malfunction.   This machine check can be caused only by machine malfunction and never by data or instructions.

15.5   INTERRUPT PROCEDURE—THE OLD, NEW, AND CURRENT PSW

An interrupt can occur only after an instruction has been executed and before another instruction has begun.   This means that no interrupt can ever occur while an instruction is being executed.   In general, upon interruption the current PSW is moved to a special place in main storage and is then called the *old PSW*.   Another PSW, called the *new PSW*, is brought from another particular place in main storage into the CPU, and this new PSW becomes the current PSW.   This is represented schematically below.

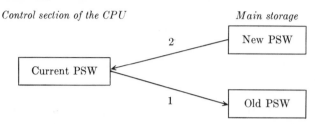

This general procedure then allows the operation of the computer to be altered and a new set of instructions to be executed.   By saving the old PSW, it is possible to return to the program which was interrupted and continue processing from the point at which it was interrupted.

There are still some problems to overcome.   Specifically, it is important to know the class of interrupt that occurred and, in some cases, the type of exception condition.   The class of interrupt can be distinguished because each of the five classes has its own distinct locations in main storage for the new and old PSW's.   The following table shows the locations assigned.   Since the PSW is a double word, the locations are all divisible by 8.

Interrupt	Old PSW	New PSW
External	0024	0088
Supervisor-call	0032	0096
Program	0040	0104
Machine-check	0048	0112
Input/output	0056	0120

A supervisor-call interrupt, for example, will automatically cause the current PSW to be stored beginning in byte 0032 and to bring in a new PSW from location 0096.

15.6 PROCESSING INTERRUPTS

It should now be clear that a program must be provided to process each of the five classes of interrupts.   This program will be a part of the supervisor program.   It will include provision for setting up an appropriate new PSW in each of the five special main-storage locations for them. Nothing will have to be put in the old PSW locations since the machine will take care of this when it executes an interrupt. These new PSW's contain the location of the first instruction to be executed after the interrupt takes place, which would be the location of some instruction in the supervisor program. The new PSW can be conceptualized as containing pointers† to a particular section of the supervisor that is the beginning of a program to process the interrupt. Since the instruction address of the old PSW contains the address of the instruction which would have been executed had the interrupt not occurred, the original program can be recalled and processing continued after the interrupt is serviced.

The five classes of interrupts tell the supervisor only the general reason for the interrupt. The determination of the exact reason is accomplished by examining the *interruption code* of the old PSW. When an interrupt occurs, a code is set in bits 16 to 31 which indicates the exact cause. For example, the fact that a new PSW was obtained from location 0104 tells the supervisor that the interrupt was caused by a program check. The program-check routine of the supervisor program can then tell what kind of exception occurred—whether operation, addressing, overflow, or some other type—by examining bits 16 to 31 of the old PSW. If, for example, an I/O interrupt occurred, the interruption code would specify which channel and which I/O unit caused the interrupt. For a description of the coding of the interruption code, see [1], page 148.

It is possible to have more than one interrupt occurring at the same time or occurring while another is being processed. Simultaneous interrupts are handled in a predetermined order. The machine-check interrupt has the highest priority. If no machine check occurs, the program or supervisor-call interrupt is taken first, the external next, and the I/O last.

As an example of the processing of interrupts, suppose two programs are being processed in main storage at the same time. One program (call it problem program 1) will be executed until some I/O function is called for. Then, while the I/O function is taking place, the second program (call it problem program 2) will be executed. When the I/O function is completed, execution of problem program 2 will be interrupted and control returned to problem program 1. Note that only the I/O operation of one program is being overlapped with the execution

† Pointers were defined and discussed in connection with list processing in Sec. 7.6. They are links that connect one element in a list to the next element in the list. They are a part of the first element. In this case, the pointer is a part of the new PSW and is an address in the supervisor. This permits the direct linking of the new PSW to the appropriate program in the supervisor for processing the interrupt.

of the other. The System/360 multiprograms (13.2) in only this sense. Simultaneous execution of two programs by the CPU is not really possible.

When problem program 1 reaches the point where it requires some I/O function, it will execute a SUPERVISOR CALL instruction (SVC). This will cause a supervisor-call interrupt to take place and the interruption code of the old PSW to be set to a value specified by the SVC instruction. The supervisor program will then take over, examine the interruption code, determine that some I/O function is to take place, and cause the function to begin. The supervisor program will then note that there is another program in main storage waiting to be executed, and control will be transferred to problem program 2. At this point, problem program 2 is being executed, and at the same time the I/O function requested by problem program 1 is taking place. For simplicity, assume that no interrupt takes place in problem program 2. Then, program 2 will continue to be executed until the I/O operation is terminated. When the I/O function is completed, an I/O interrupt will occur. The supervisor will note that this was the operation requested by problem program 1, and control will be returned to program 1 by reloading, into the current PSW, the old PSW from the supervisor-call interrupt. The old PSW and some other critical quantities were retained as a result of the housekeeping activities of the supervisor. The supervisor will find a place for it, note where it is, and see that it is retained when needed.

Though the method of interrupts allows very efficient utilization of the CPU, a supervisor program must be provided to handle all the internal bookkeeping and keep things moving. The example involving only two programs in memory at the same time is a very simple one, but it still requires a fairly sophisticated supervisor program. We assumed that we had available a supervisor program that handled the interrupts in just the right way. The operating system for the System/360 is discussed beginning in Sec. 15.8. It will be seen that only a small portion of the available operating support resources was used in this example.

15.7 MASKING OR PREVENTING INTERRUPTS

Suppose two interrupts of the same type occurred, one right after the other. (This could easily happen with an I/O interrupt since quite often I/O operations take place on two or more channels simultaneously.) Suppose that a problem program is running and an I/O interrupt occurs. This means that the current PSW is stored in the old PSW beginning at location 0056. The new PSW from location 0120 replaces the current PSW, and the supervisor takes over to process the interrupt. Suppose a second I/O interrupt takes place. The current PSW is again stored in the old PSW at location 0056, while the new PSW replaces the current PSW. But there is no way to get back to the original problem program because the PSW which would enable us to do this has been destroyed by the second interrupt. Some mechanism is required to prevent the second interrupt, and again, the PSW is the instrument. Bits 0 to 7, bit 13, and bits 36 to 39 of the PSW are called the *system mask*, the *machine-check mask*, and the *program mask*, respectively. Each bit corresponds to a particular interrupt condition, and when the mask bits are zero in the current PSW, the corresponding interrupts are prevented, i.e., masked. If a mask bit is set to 1, the interrupt is allowed. Neither the supervisor-call interrupt nor most of the program-check interrupts can be prevented by masking.† When the system mask contains zeros, I/O and external interrupts will be prevented. These two types of interrupts, however, will remain pending and will cause an interrupt just as soon as they are enabled (that is, when the current PSW contains some 1s in the program mask instead of 0s).

15.8 THE OPERATING SYSTEM/360—INTRODUCTION

It should be evident by now that the System/360 needs control programs in order to be able to operate. It is not realistic to expect each computer installation to write its own set of control programs, although some installations may want to provide a few of their own special control routines. The IBM Corporation, therefore, provides a set of control programs as well as other types of programs to facilitate the operation and programming of the computer. This collection of programs is called *Operating System*/360, or OS/360, or even more succinctly, OS. Only an overall view of OS and the general services that it will provide will be given here. The Annotated Supplementary Bibliography at the conclusion of this chapter contains several additional references to OS.

Every 360 computer installation does not have the same equipment. One installation may have a computer with six magnetic-tape units and two disks, another may have four tapes and no disks, another may have six tapes, two disks, and five remote terminals, and so on. Also, different installations have different requirements as to the kinds of jobs they must process and how they want to operate the system. To meet these different requirements in the most efficient way, OS is divided into a large number of sections, called *modules*. Each module performs a particular function. In some cases, several substitute modules are

† Why is it expected that this arrangement is workable? (*Hint:* Consider the purpose of masking in these cases and the fact that the supervisor is provided, after a great deal of testing, by the manufacturer.)

available, with the difference being that one module may take less main storage or less time to operate than another. In some substitute modules, the functions may differ slightly. Each installation can then select those modules that perform the functions they require. Also, as an installation adds to its equipment or increases its requirements, more modules can be added to the operating system without modifications to previously running programs. However, putting modules together is not a trivial process. Hours of computer time and a considerable amount of system talent are required.

15.9 THE CONTROL PROGRAM

Each operating system is composed of two general parts, the control program and a number of processing programs. The *control program* controls the processing of jobs and the input/output operations. The *processing programs* consist of a series of compilers and service programs which assist the user of the system by providing the ability to perform certain frequently used functions without having to write out these programs every time. The remainder of this section is devoted to a discussion of the control program. Processing programs will be discussed in the next section.

The control program has three major parts: the supervisor, the job scheduler, and the master scheduler. Certain parts of the control program always remain in main storage, while other parts are loaded into main storage only as they are needed to perform specific functions. The supervisor coordinates and controls the programming and physical resources of the system. In Sec. 15.6, we showed how the supervisor gains control as a result of the hardware interrupt feature. When an interrupt occurs, the supervisor must determine the cause of the interrupt and then take some action.

The services provided by the supervisor can be divided into two general classifications: (1) those functions that are required to keep the computer running and (2) those functions that provide information and assistance to the computer center in the administration of the facility. Among the services provided to ensure a smooth operation of the computer are:

1. Loading programs from some input device into main storage
2. Assigning the appropriate amounts of main-storage space required by the program
3. Providing standard procedures for handling exceptional conditions
4. Scheduling and controlling input/output functions
5. Controlling the concurrent execution of programs

In order to maintain the efficient operation of the computer center, there is certain information which the staff of the center would like to know and, in some cases, must know. For example, they might want to know the number of different types of errors which have occurred in order to determine whether additional service calls for the equipment are needed, or they might want to know the amount of time each program required in order to bill their users. The supervisor program satisfies these and other requirements by:

1. Keeping a cumulative log on errors which have occurred
2. Controlling the maximum amount of time a particular program may run without interruption
3. Providing data on the use of the facilities of the system

A few terms must be defined at this point. First, a *job* is an independent basic unit of work to be performed by the computer. A job is specified by control statements entered via control cards, that indicate to the operating system what is to be done. For example, a job could be a program and the data on which the program is to operate, or it could be just a set of data with the control statements indicating that the program desired is already stored as a part of the operating-system library. The most important distinction is that no job can affect any other job nor can the execution of any job depend on the successful completion of another job.

Jobs can be divided into a series of *job steps*. Only one job step can be performed at a time, and its execution may be conditional upon the successful completion of a previous step. An example of a job with more than one job step might be a program written in a language other than machine language. The first job step would be the translation of the program into a machine-language program, the second step would be the loading of the translated program into main storage, and the last step would be the execution of the program.

Job steps are specified by job-control statements, which are submitted in the form of a series of control cards. The preparation of these statements is the subject of an IBM manual [2]. We shall attempt to describe only the function of these statements. As the control program processes the job-control statements, it designates each job step as a *task*. In this way, in a sense, the control system can treat each task independently; that is, tasks can be executed concurrently, at least those tasks which arise from separate jobs. The control program arranges tasks from the same job within a priority structure so that a task which depends upon the successful completion of another task is not executed prematurely. A facility is also provided to abort a task if a task upon which it depends did not come to a successful completion. Tasks which are dependent upon other tasks are sometimes referred to as *subtasks.*

It should be kept in mind that the job-control statements are prepared by the individual submitting a job to be processed by the system. He must indicate with the control statement exactly what is to be done. The reading and processing of the job-control statements are handled by the *job-scheduler* section of the control program. When a computer center begins operation with OS, a particular input device, for example, a card reader, is designated as the standard source of control statements. The job scheduler then always reads the job definitions from this device.

After reading the control statements, the job scheduler allocates the appropriate input/output devices. If, for example, a job requires two tape units, two free units are located and a message is typed to the operator informing him which units have been selected. Also, if the appropriate number of devices is not available, the operator is so informed and the job will have to wait. At this point, each job step is designated as a task and is scheduled by the job scheduler. The job scheduler also initiates the execution of each job step at the appropriate time and handles the output from the job. There are several versions of the job scheduler available. The least versatile version allows only one job to be processed at a time. The remainder of the discussion concerns the most versatile version.

Jobs are not necessarily processed in the order in which they are submitted to the system. *Priority numbers* can be assigned to jobs, and the job scheduler will process the jobs in the order of their priority. Also, if a job requires resources that are not available, the job scheduler will hold it until it can be run. The OS will take care of saving the job by storing it on either magnetic tape or disk, so that the operator of the system need not take any action to have the job rescheduled.

The most versatile job scheduler performs three major functions. It can be thought of as containing three sections:

1. Reader/interpreter
2. Initiator/terminator
3. Output writer

The *reader/interpreter* reads input and identifies and interprets control statements. It then makes up, from the control statements, entries to control tables which serve to describe the job to the system. These entries, together with all the previous entries, make up an input queue, which is kept in a priority sequence. That is, jobs with higher priorities are arranged so that they will be processed first.

The *initiator/terminator* selects jobs to be processed from the input queue, makes sure that all the necessary input/output devices are allocated, and requests the supervisor to give control to the job step. When the job step is completed, it removes the appropriate entry from the control tables and releases the input/output units that were assigned. In order to minimize the time loss due to operator setup, the initiator/terminator gives messages to the operator several job steps in advance in terms of the volumes to be mounted. A *volume* is defined to be one of the following:

1. A reel of tape
2. A disk pack
3. A data cell
4. A drum†

Each volume has a unique label written on it by the computer in a standard location. Before the operator is notified to mount a particular volume, the initiator/terminator determines if the appropriate volume is already mounted. (There is a table in the initiator/terminator indicating, for each device, the name of the volume mounted.) If the required volume is already mounted, no message is sent to the operator and the processing of the job step will proceed.

If a job step cannot be executed because the operator has not completed mounting the volumes required for it, the initiator/terminator automatically searches the input queue to find and execute the highest-priority job that requires no setting up by the operator.

The third section of the job scheduler is the *output writer*. Most programs designate output to be written on the standard system output device, which is usually a printer. When a job is being executed which has designated that the output go to the system output device, the output is collected on a disk or drum. When the job is completed, control information is stored in a table called an *output work queue*. The output writer then obtains an entry from the output queue, locates the data, and processes the output. This output queue is also arranged in a priority sequence, so that the output with the highest priority is handled first.

The last section of the control program is called the *master scheduler*. It allows the operator to control the functions of the OS. It is through the master scheduler that the operator can specify which input unit, or units, are to be used as the standard device for the input of jobs and job-control statements. The operator can also issue commands to temporarily prevent a job from being scheduled for processing, can release

† Though this is defined to be a volume, drums cannot, in general, be mounted and dismounted.

a job that had been held from scheduling, and can request information from the system as to the jobs that have been run and the time on the machine taken by each. (There is more than one version of the master scheduler. The main difference among them is the number and types of commands which the operator can use.)

15.10 PROCESSING PROGRAMS

The second part of OS consists of a number of processing programs. They fall into two general classifications, language translators and service programs. The language translators, or compilers, allow a programmer to write instructions in problem-oriented languages.† Compilers for the following programming languages are provided by OS:

1. 360 Assembly Language of various levels
2. Report-program Generator
3. FORTRAN IV of various levels
4. COBOL
5. PL/1
6. ALGOL

There are also several service programs provided by OS. They are:

1. *Sort/merge program* This is a generalized program that can be used to sort records into either ascending or descending order. The sort/merge program can be used as an independent program, or it can be incorporated into programs written in COBOL or PL/1.
2. *Linkage editor* This is a program that can be used to combine two or more program segments which were written individually. The linkage editor can also be used to divide a program that is too large to be contained in main storage. In this way, one segment is brought into memory, and when it has been executed, the next segment is brought in for execution and overlaps the first.
3. *Utility programs* These are a set of programs, each designed to perform a particular function. Some of these are:
    a. Editing and moving data from one storage medium or input/output device to another
    b. Editing, rearranging, and modifying either programs or data that are stored as part of the system library
    c. Printing a list of the contents of the system library
    d. Modifying the indexing structure of the system-library catalog

† For a definition of this and a discussion of the computer as a translator, see Sec. 7.3.

The overall structure of OS/360 is summarized in the following diagram:

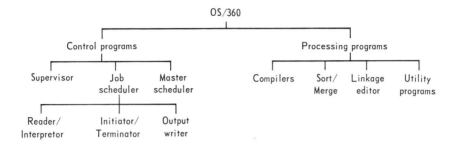

REFERENCES

1. IBM System/360, Principles of Operation, *IBM Systems Ref. Library Form* A22-6821.
2. IBM System/360, Operating System Job Control Language, *IBM Systems Ref. Library Form* C28-6539.

ANNOTATED SUPPLEMENTARY BIBLIOGRAPHY

The basic manual ([1] above) contains additional information relevant to the material in this chapter; pages 15 to 17 and 76 to 82 are pertinent. Also, pages 128 to 131 of the article on the structure of the System/360 (see Ref. 2 in the Annotated Supplementary Bibliography at the conclusion of Chap. 14) are pertinent.   In addition, a great deal of information on OS is available in the following.   (The title of the bibliographic reference pretty well delineates the aspects of OS discussed.)

1. The Functional Structure of OS 360, *IBM Systems J.*, vol. 5, no. 1, 1966.
2. IBM Operating System/360, Introduction, *IBM Systems Ref. Library Form* C28-6534.
3. IBM Operating System/360, Concepts and Facilities, *IBM Systems Ref. Library Form* C28-6535.
4. IBM Operating System/360, Data Management, *IBM Systems Ref. Library Form* C28-6537.

appendix A

POWERS OF 2
FROM THE FIRST
THROUGH THE NINETY-THIRD

POWER OF 2	EXPONENT
2.	1
4.	2
8.	3
16.	4
32.	5
64.	6
128.	7
256.	8
512.	9
1 024.	10
2 048.	11
4 096.	12
8 192.	13
16 384.	14
32 768.	15
65 536.	16
131 072.	17
262 144.	18
524 288.	19
1 048 576.	20
2 097 152.	21
4 194 304.	22
8 388 608.	23
16 777 216.	24
33 554 432.	25
67 108 864.	26
134 217 728.	27
268 435 456.	28
536 870 912.	29
1 073 741 824.	30
2 147 483 648.	31
4 294 967 296.	32
8 589 934 592.	33
17 179 869 184.	34
34 359 738 368.	35
68 719 476 736.	36
137 438 953 472.	37
274 877 906 944.	38
549 755 813 888.	39
1 099 511 627 776.	40
2 199 023 255 552.	41
4 398 046 511 104.	42
8 796 093 022 208.	43
17 592 186 044 416.	44
35 184 372 088 832.	45
70 368 744 177 664.	46
140 737 488 355 328.	47

POWER OF 2	EXPONENT
281 474 976 710 656.	48
562 949 953 421 312.	49
1 125 899 906 842 624.	50
2 251 799 813 685 248.	51
4 503 599 627 370 496.	52
9 007 199 254 740 992.	53
18 014 398 509 481 984.	54
36 028 797 018 963 968.	55
72 057 594 037 927 936.	56
144 115 188 075 855 872.	57
288 230 376 151 711 744.	58
576 460 752 303 423 488.	59
1 152 921 504 606 846 976.	60
2 305 843 009 213 693 952.	61
4 611 686 018 427 387 904.	62
9 223 372 036 854 775 808.	63
18 446 744 073 709 551 616.	64
36 893 488 147 419 103 232.	65
73 786 976 294 838 206 464.	66
147 573 952 589 676 412 928.	67
295 147 905 179 352 825 856.	68
590 295 810 358 705 651 712.	69
1 180 591 620 717 411 303 424.	70
2 361 183 241 434 822 606 848.	71
4 722 366 482 869 645 213 696.	72
9 444 732 965 739 290 427 392.	73
18 889 465 931 478 580 854 704.	74
37 778 931 862 957 161 709 568.	75
75 557 863 725 914 323 419 136.	76
151 115 727 451 828 646 838 272.	77
302 231 454 903 657 293 676 544.	78
604 462 909 807 314 587 353 088.	79
1 208 925 819 614 629 174 706 176.	80
2 417 851 639 229 258 349 412 352.	81
4 835 703 278 458 516 698 824 704.	82
9 671 406 556 917 033 397 649 408.	83
19 342 813 113 834 066 795 298 816.	84
38 685 626 227 668 135 590 597 632.	85
77 371 252 455 336 267 181 195 264.	86
154 742 504 910 672 534 362 390 528.	87
309 485 009 821 345 068 724 781 056.	88
618 970 019 642 690 137 449 562 112.	89
1 237 940 039 285 380 274 899 124 224.	90
2 475 880 078 570 760 549 798 248 448.	91
4 951 760 157 141 521 099 596 496 896.	92
9 903 520 314 283 042 199 192 993 792.	93

appendix B

USA STANDARD FLOWCHART SYMBOLS FOR INFORMATION PROCESSING

Reprinted with the permission of the American Standards Association, Inc.,† 10 East 40th Street, New York, New York 10016.

B.1. Purpose and Scope

B.1.1 *Purpose.* This standard established symbols for use in the preparation of flowcharts for information-processing systems, including automatic data-processing systems.

B.1.2 *Scope.* Symbols used on flowcharts are prescribed and defined to represent both the sequence of operations and the flow of data and paperwork of information-processing systems.

This standard does not cover: (1) identifying, descriptive, or explanatory information written inside or adjacent to a symbol; or (2) pictorial-type flowcharts that utilize pictures or drawings to depict a system.

B.2. Definitions

NOTE: The following terms and definitions have yet to be considered

† As of August 24, 1966, the American Standards Association was renamed the United States of America Standards Institute, and American Standards are now designated as USA Standards.

for standardization by ASA Sectional Committee X3 and are, therefore, subject to change.

Analysis. The investigation of a problem by a consistent method and its separation into related units for further detailed study.

Annotation. An added descriptive comment or explanatory note.

Automatic Data Processing. The manipulation of data within a machine to solve a problem by using stored-program techniques.

Auxiliary Operation. An operation performed on equipment not under direct control of the central processing unit.

Auxiliary Storage. Storage that supplements the primary storage.

Bidirectional Flow. Flow that can extend over the same lines in either or both directions.

Central Processing Unit. The component of a computing system that contains the arithmetic, logical, and control circuits of the basic system.

Communication Link. The means for automatically transmitting information from one location to another.

Connector. A means of representing on a flowchart the junction of two lines of flow or a break in a single line of flow.

Data. A representation of information in the form of words, symbols, numbers, letters, characters, digits, etc.

Decision. A processing operation to determine further action based upon the relationship of similar items of data.

Display. A visual representation of data.

Document. A medium on which information is recorded in a form for human usage, e.g., a report sheet, pages of a book.

Flow-direction Function. The indicating of the sequence of available information and executable operations.

Flowchart. A graphical representation of the definition, analysis, or solution of a problem where symbols are used to represent operations, data, flow, equipment, etc.

Flowline. A means of connecting flowchart symbols on a flowchart.

Function. A specific purpose or a characteristic action.

Information. The meaning assigned to data by the known conventions used in its representation.

Information Processing. The processing of data representing information and the determining of the meaning of the processed data.

Input/Output. A general term for the equipment, data, or media used in the entering or recording function, commonly abbreviated I/O.

Input/Output Function. The making available of information for processing and the recording of the processed information.

I/O. An abbreviation for input/output.

Magnetic Tape. A continuous medium coated with a magnetic substance on which data are recorded.

Manual Input.   The entry of data into a computer or system by direct manual manipulation of a device.

Manual Operation.   The processing of data in a system by direct manual techniques.

Medium.   The material on which data are recorded, e.g., tape, cards, paper.

Normal-direction Flow.   The direction of flow from left to right or top to bottom.

Offline Storage.   Storage not under control of the central processing unit.

Online Storage.   Storage under direct control of the central processing unit.

Operation.   The process of executing a defined action.

Predefined Process.   A named process consisting of one or more operations or program steps that are specified elsewhere, e.g., subroutine or logical unit.

Problem Description.   A term associated with both the statement and the solution phase of a problem and used to denote the transformations of data and the relationship of procedures, data, constraints, environments, etc.

Processing.   A term including any operation or combination of operations on data, where an operation is the execution of a defined action.

Processing Function.   The process of executing a defined operation or group of operations.

Punched Card.   A card that is punched with a combination of holes to represent letters, digits, or special characters.

Punched Tape.   A continuous recording medium in which data are punched.

Random Sequence.   A sequence not arranged according to any prescribed order.

Represent.   To use one or more characters or symbols to depict a well-defined concept.

Reverse-direction Flow.   The direction of flow other than left to right or top to bottom.

Symbol.   A unit representation for characteristics, relationships, transformations, graphics, etc.

System.   A collection of men, machines, and methods required to accomplish a specific objective.

Terminal.   A point in a system or communication network at which information can either enter or leave.

Transmit.   To transfer information from one location to another.

B.3.   Flowchart Symbols

B.3.1   *Symbols Represent Functions.*   Symbols are used on a flowchart to represent the functions of an information-processing system.   These functions are input/output, processing, flow direction, and annotation.

A basic symbol is established for each function and can always be used to represent that function.   Specialized symbols are established which may be used in place of a basic symbol to give additional information.

The size of each symbol may vary, but the dimensional ratio of each symbol shall be maintained.

B.3.2   *Basic Symbols*

B.3.2.1   *Input/Output Symbol.*   The symbol shown below represents the input/output function (I/O), i.e., the making available of information for processing (input) or the recording of processed information (output).

Dimensional Ratio
Width : Height = 1 : 2/3

B.3.2.2   *Processing Symbol.*   The symbol shown below represents the processing function, i.e., the process of executing a defined operation or group of operations resulting in a change in value, form, or location of information or in the determination of which of several flow directions are to be followed.

Dimensional Ratio
Width : Height = 1 : 2/3

B.3.2.3   *Flow-direction Symbol.*   The symbols shown below represent the flow-direction function, i.e., the indication of the sequence of available information and executable operations.   Flow direction is represented by lines drawn between symbols.   Normal-direction flow is from left to right or top to bottom.   When the flow direction is not left to right or top to bottom, open arrowheads shall be placed on reverse-direction flowlines.   When increased clarity is desired, open arrowheads can be placed on normal-direction flowlines. When flowlines are broken due to page limitation, connector symbols shall be used to indicate the break.   When flow is bidirectional, it can be shown by either single or double lines, but open arrowheads shall be used to indicate both normal-direction flow and reverse-direction flow.

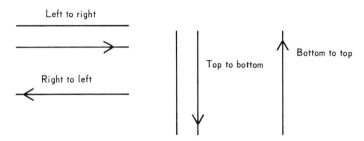

Left to right

Right to left

Top to bottom

Bottom to top

B.3.2.4   *Annotation Symbol.*   The symbol shown below represents the annotation function, i.e., the addition of descriptive comments or explanatory notes as clarification.   The broken line may be drawn either on the left as shown or on the right.   It is connected to the flowline at a point where the annotation is meaningful by extending the broken line in whatever fashion is appropriate.

Dimensional Ratio
Width:Height = 1:2/3

B.3.3   *Specialized Symbols*

B.3.3.1   *Input/Output Symbols.*   Specialized I/O symbols may represent the I/O function and, in addition, denote the medium on which the information is recorded or the manner of handling the information, or both.   If no specialized symbol exists, the basic I/O symbol is used.

B.3.3.1.1   *Punched-card Symbol.*   The symbol shown below represents an I/O function in which the medium is punched cards, including mark-sense cards, partial cards, stub cards.

Dimensional Ratio
Width:Height = 1:1/2

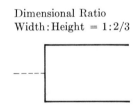

B.3.3.1.2   *Magnetic-tape Symbol.*   The symbol shown below represents an I/O function in which the medium is magnetic tape.

Dimensional Ratio
Width:Height = 1:1

B.3.3.1.3 *Punched-tape Symbol.* The symbol shown below represents an I/O function in which the medium is punched tape.

Dimensional Ratio
Width:Height = 1:1/2

B.3.3.1.4 *Document Symbol.* The symbol shown below represents an I/O function in which the medium is a document.

Dimensional Ratio
Width:Height = 1:2/3

B.3.3.1.5 *Manual-input Symbol.* The symbol shown below represents an I/O function in which the information is entered manually at the time of processing, by means of online keyboards, switch settings, push buttons, card readers, etc.

Dimensional Ratio
Width:Height = 1:1/2

B.3.3.1.6 *Display Symbol.* The symbol shown below represents an I/O function in which the information is displayed for human use at the time of processing, by means of online indicators, video devices, console printers, plotters, etc.

Dimensional Ratio
Width:Height = 1:2/3

B.3.3.1.7 *Communication-link Symbol.* The symbol shown below represents an I/O function in which information is transmitted automatically from one location to another.

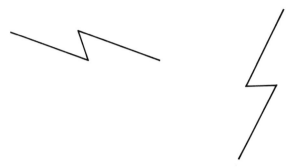

Unless otherwise indicated, the direction of flow is left to right, top to bottom. Open arrowheads are necessary on symbols for which the flow opposes the above convention. An open arrowhead may also be used on any line whenever increased clarity will result.

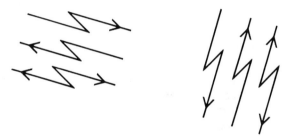

B.3.3.1.8 *Online-storage Symbol.* The symbol shown below represents an I/O function utilizing auxiliary mass storage of information that can be accessed online, e.g., magnetic drums, magnetic disks, magnetic-tape strips, automatic magnetic-card systems, or automatic microfilm chip or strip systems.

Dimensional Ratio
Width:Height = 1:2/3

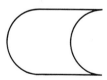

B.3.3.1.9 *Offline-storage Symbol.* The symbol shown below represents any offline storage of information, regardless of the medium on which the information is recorded.

Dimensional Ratio
Width : Height = 1 : 0.866

B.3.3.2 *Specialized Processing Symbols.* Specialized processing symbols may represent the processing function and, in addition, identify the specific type of operation to be performed on the information. If no specialized symbol exists, the basic processing symbol is used.

B.3.3.2.1 *Decision Symbol.* The symbol shown below represents a decision or switching-type operation that determines which of a number of alternate paths is to be followed.

Dimensional Ratio
Width : Height = 1 : 2/3

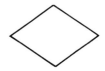

B.3.3.2.2 *Predefined-process Symbol.* The symbol shown below represents a named process consisting of one or more operations or program steps that are specified elsewhere, e.g., subroutine or logical unit.

Dimensional Ratio
Width : Height = 1 : 2/3

B.3.3.2.3 *Manual-operation Symbol.* The symbol shown below represents any offline process geared to the speed of a human being.

Dimensional Ratio
Width : Height = 1 : 2/3

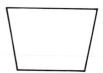

B.3.3.2.4 *Auxiliary-operation Symbol.* The symbol shown below represents an offline operation performed on equipment not under direct control of the central processing unit.

Dimensional Ratio
Width:Height = 1:1

B.3.4 *Additional Symbols*

B.3.4.1 *Connector Symbol.* The symbol shown below represents a junction in a line of flow. A set of two connectors is used to represent a continued flow direction when the flow is broken by any limitation of the flowchart. A set of two or more connectors is used to represent the junction of several flowlines with one flowline or the junction of several alternate flowlines.

Dimensional Ratio
Width:Height = 1:1

B.3.4.2 *Terminal Symbol.* The symbol shown below represents a terminal point in a system or communication network at which data can enter or leave, e.g., start, stop, halt, delay, or interrupt.

Dimensional Ratio
Width:Height = 1:3/8

B.4.   Presentation Techniques

B.4.1 *Symbol Orientation.* The orientation of each symbol on a flowchart should be the same as shown in 3, Flowchart Symbols.

B.4.2 *Symbol Size.* The size of each symbol may vary, but the dimensional ratio of each symbol shall be maintained as specified in 3, Flowchart Symbols.

B.4.3 *Flow Direction.* Flow direction is represented by lines drawn between symbols.

B.5. Summary of Flowchart Symbols

Basic Symbols

Input/Output	*Processing*	*Flow Direction*	*Annotation*

Specialized Input/Output Symbols   *Specialized Processing Symbols*

Punched card		Online storage	
Magnetic tape		Offline storage	
Punched tape		Decision	
Document		Predefined process	
Manual input		Auxiliary operation	
Display		Manual operation	
Communication link		*Additional Symbols*	
		Connector	
		Terminal	

appendix C

SOME FORTRAN-SUPPLIED LIBRARY FUNCTIONS

The table that follows contains descriptions of a few of the most important library functions supplied by the FORTRAN compiler. The first column contains a definition of each function. The second column contains the syntax for using the function. In every case, the function is used by naming it (using the indicated name, such as SQRT, DSQRT, or CLOG) and then enclosing an argument in parentheses. The argument may be any legitimate arithmetic expression, so that it may contain other library functions. For example, in

$$DSQRT(1 - DABS(1 - Z*Z))$$

the DABS library function is used in the argument for the DSQRT library function. Note that different names are used to indicate the type and length of both the arguments and the values returned for the function. A D before the name is used to indicate double precision, and C to indicate complex. CD is used to indicate double-precision, complex arguments and values.

Definition	Syntax	Argument		Function value	
		Type	Length, bytes	Type	Length, bytes
Square root of the	SQRT(argument)	Real	4	Real	4
argument	DSQRT(argument)	Real	8	Real	8
	CSQRT(argument)	Complex	8	Complex	8
	CDSQRT(argument)	Complex	16	Complex	16
Natural logarithm of	ALOG(argument)	Real	4	Real	4
the argument	DLOG(argument)	Real	8	Real	8
	CLOG(argument)	Complex	8	Complex	8
	CDLOG(argument)	Complex	16	Complex	16
Common logarithm,	ALOG10(argument)	Real	4	Real	4
that is, $\log_{10}$, of the	DLOG10(argument)	Real	8	Real	8
argument					
Exponential function,	EXP(argument)	Real	4	Real	4
that is, e raised to the	DEXP(argument)	Real	8	Real	8
power, of the argu-	CEXP(argument)	Complex	8	Complex	8
ment	CDEXP(argument)	Complex	16	Complex	16
The absolute value of	IABS(argument)	Integer	4	Integer	4
the argument	ABS(argument)	Real	4	Real	4
	DABS(argument)	Real	8	Real	8
Sine of an argument	SIN(argument)	Real	4	Real	4
that is given in	DSIN(argument)	Real	8	Real	8
radians	CSIN(argument)	Complex	8	Complex	8
	CDSIN(argument)	Complex	16	Complex	16
Cosine of an argument	COS(argument)	Real	4	Real	4
that is given in	DCOS(argument)	Real	8	Real	8
radians	CCOS(argument)	Complex	8	Complex	8
	CDCOS(argument)	Complex	16	Complex	16
Tangent of an argu-	TAN(argument)	Real	4	Real	4
ment that is given in	DTAN(argument)	Real	8	Real	8
radians					
The angle, in radians,	ARSIN(argument)	Real	4	Real	4
that has the given	DARSIN(argument)	Real	8	Real	8
argument as its sine					
The angle, in radians,	ARCOS(argument)	Real	4	Real	4
that has the given	DARCOS(argument)	Real	8	Real	8
argument as its cosine					
The angle, in radians,	ATAN(argument)	Real	4	Real	4
that has the given	DATAN(argument)	Real	8	Real	8
argument as its tangent					

appendix D

KEYWORDS IN PL/1

The information in these pages is based on data contained in "IBM System/360 Operating System PL/1 Language Specifications" File No. S360.29, Form C28-6571-4, and Technical Newsletter N28-0557.

Examples and other information

Notes:
1. *The numbers which appear in the columns on the left indicate pages in Form C28-6571-4.*
2. *Details on the built-in-functions and other computational subroutines are given in Form C28-6590.*
3. *References to page numbers are to C28-6571-4.*
4. *Keywords are not reserved words.*
5. *Lines changed in this revision are preceded by ●*

KEYWORD	Allowed abbreviation	built-in func. ①	condition ②	data attrib. ③	file attrib. ④	format ⑤	option ⑥	statement ⑦	Examples and other information
ABNORMAL	ABNL			50					DCL DOG ABNL FIXED(4,1); the variable DOG may be altered or accessed at unpredictable time.
ABS (x)		152							X=ABS(5−Y/2); calculates the absolute value of (x), e.g. of (5−Y/2).
ACTIVATE name	ACT							138	%LOOK:ACTIVATE TAX.DED; compile-time statement; makes explicitly deactivated (see page 135) identifiers replaceable.
ADD (x,y,w,d)		153							SUM=ADD(A,B,7,3); is equivalent to A+B in a field of 7 positions, with 3 positions to right of decimal point.
ADDR (name)		157							Q=ADDR(TABLE); gives a pointer value which identifies the location of the named variable in list-processing operations
ALIGNED				56					DCL 1 BOY ... ALIGNED; ... specifies start of each string data item of array or structure at storage boundary of implementation.
ALL (name)		156							K=ALL(TABLE); each item in the array TABLE is converted to bit string, left-aligned; result is logical AND, bit-by-bit.
ALLOCATE name								104	DCL A(N,N) CONTROLLED; ... IF ¬ALLOCATION(A) THEN ALLOCATE A; allocates storage for controlled data.
ALLOCATION (v)		158							A=ALLOCATION (TABLE); gives '1'B if storage has been allocated to (v), and '0'B if not.
ANY (name)		156							K=ANY(TABLE); See line 7. Items in the named array are converted to bit string, left-aligned; result is logical OR, bit-by-bit.
AREA			166	64					DCL Q AREA; specifies an area of storage into which several data items will be allocated; also a list-processing condition.
ATAN (x)		154							B=ATAN(Z**F); gives arctangent of (x) radians. For complex (x) see page 155.
ATAN (y,x)		154							B=ATAN(M,P+Q); gives arctangent of (y/x) radians; see page 154 for resulting values.
ATAND (x)		154							B=ATAND(Z**F); gives arctangent of (x) degrees.
ATAND (y,x)		154							B=ATAND(M,P+Q); gives arctangent of (y/x) degrees; see page 154 for resulting values.
ATANH (x)		154							B=ATANH(Z**Q); gives hyperbolic arctangent of (x). If ABS(x)>=1, error will result. For complex (x) see page 155.
AUTOMATIC	AUTO			75					DECLARE TABLE(10,12) AUTOMATIC; specifies that storage is allocated on each entry to the block, and released on leaving the block.
BACKWARDS					63			124	OPEN FILE(MASTER) SEQUENTIAL INPUT BACKWARDS; the named sequential input file is to be accessed from last to first.
BASED				TNL					DCL POP BASED; specifies based variable in list processing; DCL POP BASED (ZIP); associates pointer with based variable. TNL N28-0557.
BEGIN								111	ON OVERFLOW BEGIN; ... END; forms the heading statement of a begin block, which must terminate with END.
BINARY	BIN			44					DECLARE SCOP BINARY FIXED REAL(6,2); specifies (storage for) data in binary base.
BINARY (x,w,d)	BIN	153							A=BINARY((B*D)/(E+F),14,2); gives value of x in binary base, w-position field with d positions to right of point.
BIT (w)		155							A=BIT(C+D,10); converts x to bit string of length w. See also pages 33 and 90.
BIT (x,w)				47					DECLARE X BIT (8); specifies (storage for) data in bit-string form of length w.
BOOL (x,y,z)		156							AZ=BOOL(A,B,'0101'B); performs one (z) of the 16 possible logical operations between corresponding bits of bit strings x and y.
BUFFERED					63			124	OPEN FILE(SALES) BUFFERED INPUT; records from SEQUENTIAL RECORD file must pass through intermediate storage.
BUILTIN				53					DCL DATE BUILTIN; identifies DATE (or other name) as built-in-function, used when the name has had another use.
BY									separating ...; used in DO statement and BY NAME option (see lines 28 and 62).
BY NAME							70	111	TOTAL=FH+2*TAX.BY NAME; assigns to structure (e.g. TOTAL) elements with identical names in structures on right of =.
CALL entry-name								107	CALL #5ROUTN(A,B,C) TASK (T5) EVENT (E2) PRIORITY (+2); transfers control to called procedure.
CEIL (x)		153							C=CEIL(3*Y−1.4*D); value of C = smallest integer not exceeded by (x) (e.g. if Y=2.7 and D=3, C=−4). Complex (x) not allowed.
CELL				58					DCL 1 A,2 B CELL, 3 C FIXED(5),3 D FLOAT(9); gives storage equivalence (e.g. either C or D, but not both, may occupy B at one time).
CHAR (x,w)		155							A=CHAR ((B*C+D),6); converts (x) to character string of length w. See also pages 34 and 90.
CHARACTER (w)	CHAR			47					DCL NAME CHARACTER(50); specifies (storage for) data in character-string form of length w. (See also line 217.)
CHECK (name)			164						ON CHECK(A,JO) SYSTEM; prints new values of data (e.g. of A), and names of statements or entries executed (e.g. of JO).
CLOSE FILE (name)								112	CLOSE FILE(PAYROLL), FILE (MASTER); closes the named files and releases facilities allocated to them.
COLUMN (w)						96			PUT EDIT TAX (COLUMN (16), A); specifies absolute horizontal spacing in printed line; print next character in position w; may be used with PICTURE.
COMPLEX	CPLX			44					DCL VOLTS COMPLEX; specifies (storage for) complex data (e.g. a+ib) in numeric field; may be used with PICTURE.
COMPLEX (x,y)	CPLX	154							A=COMPLEX(B,C); is equivalent to z=x+iy; x and y are real.
CONDITION (name)			166						ON CONDITION(W) A=B; ... SIGNAL CONDITION (W); defined by programmer; SIGNAL interrupts, causes action specified.

Table 1

KEYWORD	Abbr.	①	②	③	④	⑤	⑥	⑦	Examples and other information
CONJG (x)		154							A=CONJG(B+4I); gives the conjugate of (x) (e.g. B−4I).
CONTROLLED	CTL			54					DCL TAX CONTROLLED; specifies storage class with control over storage allocation by ALLOCATE and FREE.
CONVERSION	CONV		162						ON CONVERSION GOTO #3S; raised by illegal conversion of character-string or bit-string data; std. sys. act.: ERROR + comment.
COPY FILE (name)								118	GET COPY FILE(MASTER); writes, without any change, the named file onto standard system print file SYSPRINT.
COS (x)		154							A=COS(SIN(D)**4.73); gives cosine of (x) radians. For complex (x) see page 155.
COSD (x)		154							A=COSD(SIND(D)**4.73); gives cosine of (x) degrees. For complex (x) see page 155.
COSH (x)		154							A=COSH(SINH(D)**4.73); gives hyperbolic cosine of (x) radians. For complex (x) see page 155.
COUNT (file name)		158							L=COUNT(PAYROLL); gives the number of data items transmitted during the last GET or PUT operation on the named file (e.g. PAYROLL).
DATA		157	157				90	90	GET DATA;PUT DATA(A,B,C); specifies data-directed transmission of data names and values.
DATAFIELD		158							A=DATAFIELD; gives the contents of the datafield which raised the last NAME condition interrupt.
DATE		158							PUT LIST PAGE(DATE, ...); prints the date supplied by the operator in a 6-position field as YYMMDD (for year, month, day).
DEACTIVATE name	DEACT							138	%DEACTIVATE TAX, DED; compile-time statement; retain identifier as found in source program.
DECIMAL	DEC			44					DECLARE Z DECIMAL FIXED REAL(7,2); specifies (storage for) data in decimal base.
DECIMAL (x,w,d)	DEC	153						39	A=DECIMAL((B*D)/(E+F),14,2); gives value of x in decimal base, w-position field with d positions to right of point.
DECLARE	DCL								DCL ((A FIXED B FLOAT) STATIC, C)EXTERNAL; specifies addresses and characteristics of contents of core storage areas.
DEFINED name	DEF			56					DCL A(20,20),B(10) DEFINED A(2*ISUB,2**ISUB); provides another name for the same data (e.g. B(3) is same as A(6,6)).
DELAY (n)								113	DELAY(15); execution of controlling task is stopped for (n) milliseconds.
DELETE								113	DELETE FILE(MASTER) KEY(COW); deletes record identified by the key (e.g. COW) from DIRECT UPDATE file named (e.g. MASTER).
DIM (x,s)		157							A=DIM(TABLE,5); gives the current extent of dimension s of the array x.
DIRECT					63			124	OPEN FILE(PAROLL) DIRECT; access attribute of RECORD file DIRECT files must be KEYED.
DISPLAY (x)								114	DISPLAY('NOB'||'BY!'); will display to operator the character string NOBBY!; processing continues; see REPLY.
DIVIDE (x,y,w,d)		154							A=DIVIDE(A,B,8,2); gives x divided by y, in w-position field with d positions to right of point.
DO								114	DO... END;DO 1=A*B BY 1.65 TO 1.89 WHILE ((C**D<EXP(3*Y/C))&(Q¬=P)); ... END; forms a group.
EDIT							92		GET EDIT(A,B,C)(F(3,2),X(2),B(5),A(4));PUT EDIT(A)(C(F(3),F(4))); specifies edit-directed transmission of data.
ELSE									separating keyword used in IF statement; IF A=B THEN G=C−D ELSE H=F;

Table 2

KEYWORD	Abbr.	①	②	③	④	⑤	⑥	⑦	Examples and other information
END								116	LAST:PROC... ; END LAST:BEGIN; ... END;DO; ... END; terminates blocks and groups.
ENDFILE			163						ON ENDFILE CALL #99; raised by attempt to read past end of file during GET or READ; std. sys. act.: ERROR + comment.
ENDPAGE			163						ON ENDPAGE SNAP GOTO #5ENTRY; raised by attempt to print past PAGESIZE; std. sys. act.: start new page, continue.
ENTRY					142			117	SPOT#7:ENTRY; specifies a secondary entry point to a procedure.
ENVIRONMENT	ENV					63			DCL LIST FILE STREAM ENV(list of options) the list of options is implementation-defined and specifies file characteristics not in PL/I.
ERF (x)		154							SUMX=ERF(3); gives $(2/\sqrt{\pi})$ times the integral from 0 to x of e^{-t^2}dt. The error function.
ERFC (x)		154							SUMX=ERFC(3); gives 1−ERF(3). See line 70 above.
ERROR			166						ON ERROR DISPLAY('GOOF'); always enabled, is raised by error forcing termination; std. sys. act.: raise FINISH condition.
EVENT		158							DCL #6 EVENT EXTERNAL; establishes identifier as name of event; used if WAIT is wanted. WAIT EVENT (#6);
EVENT (x)					48				A=EVENT (#6); returns value '1'B if event (x) is complete; '0'B if not complete.
EVENT								112	CALL PRINT(A,B) TASK (T2) EVENT(#6) PRIORITY(3); specifies that the called and calling procedures are asynchronous.
EXCLUSIVE					63			124	DCL MASTER#3 FILE EXCLUSIVE; prevents other tasks from gaining access to the same record in the DIRECT UPDATE file.
EXIT								117	EXIT; causes immediate termination of the task executing the statement and all other descendant tasks.
EXP (x)		154							Z=EXP(3*Y/C); gives e^x. For complex x see page 155.
EXTERNAL	EXT			54					DCL A CHARACTER (10) EXTERNAL; name (e.g. A) refers to same entry in all blocks where declared.
FILE			166						DCL INCOM FILE; OPEN FILE(INCOM); CLOSE FILE(INCOM); gives a name to a file of records.
FINISH			166		62				ON FINISH GOTO #5PUT; raised after STOP or EXIT statement; or ERROR condition; std. sys. act.: terminate major task.
FIXED				44					DCL X FIXED(3,1); describes scale of data item as being fixed decimal, (e.g. 12.6), or fixed binary (e.g. 10.1).
FIXED (x,w,d)		152				63			A=FIXED((D+C)/E,8,2); gives x in fixed-point scale, w-position field, with d positions to right of point.
FIXEDOVERFLOW	FOFL		162						ON FOFL D=D/20; truncates on left to maximum implementation field width; std. sys. act.: prints comment, then continues.
FLOAT			38						DCL X FLOAT(8); describes scale of data item as floating-point decimal (e.g. 1.5×10^9) or binary (e.g. 1.1×2^7).
FLOAT (x,w)		152							A=FLOAT((D+C)/E,8); gives x in floating-point scale, in w-position field.

KEYWORD	Abbr.	①	②	③	④	⑤	⑥	⑦	Examples and other information
FLOOR (x)		153							C=FLOOR((D+C)/E); gives largest integer not exceeding (x) Complex (x) not allowed
FORMAT format list							117		PUT FILE(MASTER) EDIT (Z)(R(FOR)); ... FOR.FORMAT (SKIP,COLUMN(2),A); specifies format list (which see on page 93).
FREE							118		FREE A,B,C; will release storage allocated to data items, e.g. scalar A, array B, and structure C.
FROM						130			WRITE FILE(MASTER) FROM (TAX); will write the value of TAX into the file MASTER.
GENERIC			52						DCL COMP GENERIC (A ENTRY(FIXED),B ENTRY(FLOAT)); defines a name as a family of entry names.
GET							119		GET DATA(A,B,C),GET LIST(A,B);GET FILE(JOB5) EDIT (X,Y,Z)(A(5),2 F(8,2)); used with STREAM transmission.
GO TO name	GOTO						119		GO TO PART5; will transfer control to the statement named PART5. GOTO X(1); identifier can be variable.
HBOUND (x,s)		157							A=HBOUND(TABLE,6); gives the current higher bound of dimension s of the array x.
HIGH (i)		155		113					M=HIGH(32); inserts the character highest in collating sequence (e.g. the ebcdic 1111 1111) into (i) positions of the field named (e.g. M).
IDENT (x)									CLOSE FILE(SLAVE) IDENT (JOE); makes (x) a trailer label; OPEN FILE(P) IDENT(Q); makes (x) a user label.
IF									IF (PAY=TAX)|(TODAY='SUNDAY') THEN GOTO FINISH;ELSE CALL #5JOB;
IGNORE (n)							120		READ FILE (INCO) IGNORE (15); the first 15 records in the sequential file INCO will be ignored.
IMAG (x)		154							A=IMAG((A+8I)*(C−5I)/(E−7.68I)); gives imaginary part of complex value.
IN (area-name)					104				ALLOCATE BILL SET (P2) IN (AREA#7); storage will be allocated in the area corresponding to, e.g., AREA#7.
INCLUDE name							139		%INCLUDE PAYRL; compile-time statement; incorporates strings of external text into next being formed.
INDEX (x,y)		155							I=INDEX (A,B); gives a binary integer (the index) which indicates the first character in string (x) of sub-string identical to (y).
INITIAL (x)	INIT			59					DCL TAB(10,10) INITIAL((63)0,(1)1,(36)8); will initialize first 63 elements to zero, next one to 1, last 36 to 8.
INPUT									DECLARE BILL FILE INPUT; specifies that the function of the file is to be an input file.
INTERNAL	INT				62				DCL A CHARACTER(10) INTERNAL; name refers to variable known only within block in which declared
INTO (variable)	INT			54					READ FILE (TAX) INTO (X); will read record from file TAX into variable X.
IRREDUCIBLE	IRRED			50					DCL QT ENTRY IRRED; overrides optimization by compiler; specifies that no. of references to (e.g. QT) cannot be reduced.
KEY (filename)			164						ON KEY (FILE1) DISPLAY('HOA!');raised by improper presence or absence of key in record;std. sys. act.: ERROR+comment.

KEYWORD	Abbr.	①	②	③	④	⑤	⑥	⑦	Examples and other information
KEY (x)								127	READ FILE (TAX) KEY (A93B) INTO (Z); identifies record to be read from the named file.
KEYED				63			124		DCL INV FILE KEYED; specifies that each record in the RECORD file has a key.
KEYFROM (x)							121		WRITE FILE(M2) FROM(U2) KEYFROM (C3); converts (x) to character string and attaches it as a key to the record.
KEYTO (c)								127	READ FILE (M3) INTO (PHT) KEYTO (JOHN); copies key of record into character-string variable (c).
LABEL (name)			47						DCL FOY LABEL (S1,S5,S5); specifies that, e.g., FOY is a label variable which will have as values only S1, S5, or S5.
LBOUND (x,s)		157							A=LBOUND (TABLE,5); gives the current lower bound of dimension s of the array x.
LENGTH (s)		155		61					A=LENGTH (NAME); gives current length of string (s) as fixed binary integer.
LIKE name					96				DCL 1 A EXTERNAL, 2 (B,C,D), 1 E LIKE A; specifies that the elements of structure E are identical to those of A.
LINE (n)							124		PUT DATA (A,B,C) LINE(5); will print on the n-th line of a page (current or next page, depending on current line no.). See line 185.
LINENO (file name)		158							M=LINENO (PAYROLL); gives the current line number of the named PRINT file (e.g. PAYROLL)
LINESIZE (n)							124	88	OPEN FILE (SALES) LINESIZE (99) ...; specifies the number of character positions in a line of a PRINT file.
LIST (names)							88	121	GET LIST (A,B,C); PUT LIST (X,Y,Z); specifies list-directed data transmission.
LOCATE name			154						LOCATE NAME SET (JOHN) FILE (PATIENT); applies to BUFFERED OUTPUT files; creates record in buffer storage.
LOG (x)		154							C=LOG (A+B/D); gives logarithm of x to base e. Error condition if x<=0. For complex if x<=0. see page 154.
LOG2 (x)		154							G=LOG2 (A+B/D); gives logarithm of x to base 2. Error condition if x<=0.
LOG10 (x)		154							G=LOG10 (A+B/D); gives logarithm of x to base 10. Error condition if x<=0.
LOW (i)		155							M=LOW (32); inserts the character lowest in collating sequence (e.g. the ebcdic 0000 0000) into (i) positions of the field named (e.g. M).
MAIN									FIRST:PROCEDURE OPTIONS (MAIN); not in PL/I; required by compiler to start compilation.
MAX (x,y,...,z)		152							IND=MAX (A,B,C); value of IND is that of A, B, or C, whichever is greater.
MIN (x,y,...,z)		152							IND=MIN (A,B,C); value of IND is that of A, B, or C, whichever is least.
MOD (x,y)		152							K=MOD (F,G); value of K is the positive remainder after division of F by G. Complex x or y not allowed.
MULTIPLY(x,y,w,d)		153							A=MULTIPLY(B,C,8,2); is equivalent to B*C in 8-position field with 2 positions to right of point.
NAME (file name)			164						ON NAME(NUSTOCK) GOTO ST3; std. sys. act.: prints comment and ignores the field of an unrecognizable identifier in GET DATA.
NO condition-name			18						(NOCONVERSION);JOB#5:PROC. ...; suppresses interrupt that would result from the condition named.
NOLOCK								127	READ FILE (#5CEL) INTO (JIL) KEY (JACK) NOLOCK; unlocks a record of EXCLUSIVE file so it may be read, updated, etc.

KEYWORD	Abbr.	①	②	③	④	⑤	⑥	⑦	Examples and other information
NORMAL			50						DCL A FIXED NORMAL; specifies that the variable (e.g. A) will not be accessed or modified abnormally.
NULL		158							P=NULL; a pointer function used, e.g. to mark end of chain of pointers. Used in list-processing. Implementation defined.
ON condition (name)								122	ON ENDFILE (MASTER) GO TO #7JOB; ON TRANSMIT (JOBFILE) DISPLAY ('TRIPPED'); specifies action after interrupt.
ONCHAR		157	157						A=ONCHAR; gives the character which caused the last conversion interrupt.
ONCODE		157	157						A=ONCODE; gives the value of the last interrupt in a code and for categories defined by the implementation.
ONFILE		157	157						A=ONFILE; gives the name of the file for which the last input/output operation was performed.
ONKEY		157	157						A=ONKEY; gives the value of the key for the record which caused the last transmission interrupt.
ONLOC		157	157						A=ONLOC; gives the name of the entry point in the procedure in which the last interrupt arose.
ONSOURCE		157	157						A=ONSOURCE; gives the contents of the field being processed when the last conversion interrupt occurred.
OPEN FILE (name)								124	OPEN INPUT FILE (#2REEL) TITLE ('SALES'), OUTPUT FILE ('STOCK), UPDATE FILE (MASTER);
OPTIONS (list)				125					PROGRAM: PROCEDURE OPTIONS (MAIN); specifies a list of options which are implementation-defined.
OUTPUT					62				OPEN OUTPUT FILE (REPORT); specifies that data will be transmitted to the newly-created file named
OVERFLOW	OFL		162						ON OFL GOTO ...; std. sys. act.: prints comment and raises ERROR when exponent of floating-point number exceeds permitted maximum.
PACKED			55						DCL 1 A(10) PACKED, 2 B ...; specifies that there is to be no unused storage between two adjacent string data items.
PAGE						96	126		PUT LIST (A,B,C) PAGE; causes a new current page to be defined within the data set starts printing on new page.
PAGESIZE (w)						124	124		OPEN FILE (REPORT) PRINT PAGESIZE (36); specifies the number of lines to be printed on a page of a STREAM PRINT file.
PICTURE	PIC					45			DECLARE Q PICTURE 'XAA9AA'; G PICTURE '(5)9V99'; defines format of data fields and specifies editing of data. See also C20-1651.
POINTER	PTR		64						DCL Q POINTER; used in list processing or to refer to data indirectly.
POLY (a,x)		156							if a (m:n) and x (p:g) are vectors, result is $a(m) + \Sigma$ (from $i=1$ to $i=n-m$) of $[a(m+i) * \text{II}$ (from $j=0$ to $i=j-1$) of $x(p+i)]$.
POSITION (i)	POS		56						DCL B CHARACTER (3) DEFINED C POSITION (6); if C is BILLYGOAT; then B will be GOA'.
PRECISION (x,w,d)	PREC	153							...A*PRECISION (B,26,5); a field of 26 positions with 5 to the right of point is given to B before multiplication by A.
PRINT					62				OPEN FILE (REPORT) PRINT; specifies that final disposition of data will be on printed page.
PRIORITY (x)		158							A=PRIORITY (#3TASK); gives the priority of task (x) relative to that of the task in which the statement is evaluated.
PRIORITY (x)							112		CALL PRINT (A,B) TASK (W) EVENT (L) PRIORITY (6); assigns priority x to the named task (e.g. W) relative to the calling task.
PROCEDURE	PROC							125	#6JOB:PROCEDURE OPTIONS (MAIN); identifies and defines primary entry point and attributes of procedure.

KEYWORD	Abbr.	①	②	③	④	⑤	⑥	⑦	Examples and other information
PROD (x)		156							PROD=PROD(TABLE); gives the real value after multiplying to each other all data elements of the array (x).
PUT								126	PUT DATA (A,B,C); PUT LIST (A,B,C/D); PUT FILE (#1R) EDIT (X,Y) (A(15)) PAGE LINE (4);
READ		154						127	READ FILE(#73) INTO (SALES); transfers a record from a RECORD INPUT or RECORD UPDATE file into storage.
REAL (x)				44					A=REAL ((A+B)*(C—D)/(E—F)); gives real part of complex value.
REAL		164							DCL A COMPLEX, B REAL; specifies that mode of data is real, e.g. B could be 395.67, 1001, etc.
RECORD					62		124	128	ON RECORD (SYSIN); raised if size of record $\neg=$ size of variable during READ or REWRITE; std. sys. act.; comment + ERROR.
RECURSIVE				125					DCL MASTER RECORD; specifies that data in a file is to be transmitted in RECORD-oriented mode.
REDUCIBLE	RED				50				#2SALE:PROC RECURSIVE OPTIONS (MAIN); specifies that this procedure may be invoked from within.
REPEAT (x,n)		156							DCL #2START ENTRY REDUCIBLE; specifies that the compiler may optimize by reducing no. of references to named block.
REPLY (c)							114		A=REPEAT ('CAT',3); gives 'CATCATCATCAT'; A=REPEAT ('01'/4); gives '010101010'.
RETURN								128	DISPLAY('T'+A) REPLY(PAT); message supplied by operator will be stored in character-variable (e.g. in PAT).
RETURNS (attribute)				53					RETURN; returns control to the point of invocation; RETURN(X**2+Z**5,6); may return value to function reference.
REVERT condition								129	DCL SEL ENTRY RETURNS (F(15,3)); specifies the data attributes of the value to be returned by the entry point.
REWRITE		156						130	REVERT ENDFILE; causes reversion to ON-unit for this condition saved by the encompassing block.
ROUND (x,n)		158							REWRITE FILE (DISK6) KEY(APT) FROM (LIST); replaces an existing record in an UPDATE file.
SECONDARY				49					A=ROUND(A/B,4); gives the value of (x) rounded on the n-th digit to the right (+n) or left (—n) of decimal point.
SEQUENTIAL				63			124		DCL F CHARACTER (6) SECONDARY; specifies that data does not require efficient storage.
SET (name)			104				121		DCL WASTE FILE SEQUENTIAL; access attribute of RECORD file, indicates access in physical order.
SETS (item,...)				51					ALLOCATE VAL SET (P); sets pointer variable to identify start of space allocated
SIGN (x)		152							DCL E ENTRY SETS (JOE); specifies that the named variables (e.g. JOE) may be changed by the named entry point.
SIGNAL condition								131	A=SIGN (B*C—D/F); A is binary 1 if (x)>0; 0 if (x) =0; —1 if (x)<0. Complex (x) not allowed. SIGNAL ENDFILE (SALES); SIGNAL CONDITION (OUT); simulates the occurrence of the named interrupt.

Table 1

KEYWORD	Abbr.	(1)	(2)	(3)	(4)	(5)	(6)	(7)	Examples and other information
SIN(x)		154							B=SIN(TAN(W—A)); gives sine of (x) radians. For complex (x) see page 155.
SIND(x)		154							B=SIND(TAND(W—A)); gives sine of (x) degrees.
SINH(x)		154							B=SINH(TANH(W—A)); gives hyperbolic sine of (x) radians. For complex (x) see page 155.
SIZE			163						ON SIZE EXIT: raised by conversions when a value is assigned to a data item which has been declared too few positions.
SKIP(x)						96	126		PUT FILE(REPORT) EDIT('ROOTS')(A(5)) SKIP(5); will cause x-1 blank lines to appear on printout. Will overprint if x <= 0.
SNAP								122	ON SIZE SNAP SYSTEM; a calling trace is listed when condition occurs.
SQRT(x)		154							A=SQRT(A+B); gives positive square root of (x). If X<0, error will result. For complex (x) see page 155.
STATIC				54					DCL TABLE(10,10) STATIC; specifies that storage is allocated at start of execution and is not released until completion.
STOP								131	STOP; causes immediate termination of major task and all sub-tasks.
STREAM									DCL MASTER STREAM; specifies that data in a file is to be transmitted in STREAM-oriented mode.
STRING(x)					62		124		A=STRING(TABLE); gives a string which is the concatenation of all elements of the packed string structure named x.
STRING(name)		158				119			GET STRING(HA)EDIT(FI,FI)(A(10),F(3,1)); data are to be taken from the named string (e.g. HA) in core.
iSUB				56					DCL Y(5)DEFINED M(1+FLOOR((1SUB—1)*2/3),1+MOD((1SUB—1)*2,3)); subscript dummy variable.
SUBSCRIPTRANGE	SUBRG		164						ON SUBRG EXIT; raised when subscript value is outside dimensions of array; std. sys. act.: ERROR and comment.
SUBSTR(x,i,j)		155							A=SUBSTR(U,3,2); gives a substring of length 1 starting with position i of string x (e.g. if U is '123456', then A=34).
SUM(x)		156							TOT=SUM(PAY); gives the total value after adding all data items which are part of the array (x).
SYSIN						100			GET FILE(SYSIN)...; specifies the standard system input file.
SYSPRINT						100			PUT FILE(SYSPRINT)...; specifies the standard system output file (printer).
SYSTEM								122	ON ZDIV SYSTEM; specifies standard system action when interrupt results from condition named.
TAN(x)		154							B=TAN(W—C*D); gives tangent of (x) radians.
TAND(x)		154							B=TAND(W—C*D); gives tangent of (x) degrees.
TANH(x)		154							B=TANH(W—C*D); gives hyperbolic tangent of (x) radians.

Table 2

KEYWORD	Abbr.	(1)	(2)	(3)	(4)	(5)	(6)	(7)	Examples and other information
TASK				48				48	DCL #3JOB TASK; CALL JANE; CALL JANE(A,B) TASK(NEL); specifies that associated identifier is the name of a task.
THEN									IF A=B THEN C=D; clause used in IF statement to begin the block which is to be executed if the comparison gives "true".
TIME		158							PUT LIST(TIME)...; prints clock time in 9-position field as HHMMSSTTT (for hours, minutes, seconds, milliseconds).
TITLE(x)							124		OPEN FILE(FILE) TITLE(NUT); converts x to character string which identifies the data set to be associated with the file.
TO									DO I=9 TO —67 BY —1.5,—71 TO —90 BY —1, 5 TO 15 BY 0.5; separating keyword used in DO statement.
TRANSMIT(name)			163						ON TRANSMIT(PAYROLL) WAIT(Z4); raised by permanent transmission error on file named; std. sys. act.: ERROR + comment.
TRUNC(x)		153							A=TRUNC(X); value is FLOOR(X) if X>=0; CEIL(X) if X<0. See lines 87 and 30. Complex (x) not allowed.
UNBUFFERED					63		124		DCL CASH FILE UPDATE UNBUFFERED; specifies that records will not pass through intermediate storage.
UNDEFINEDFILE	UNDF		164						ON UFL(MASTER) STOP; raised if the file named cannot be opened; standard system action: ERROR + comment.
UNDERFLOW	UFL		163					131	ON UFL GOTO #3STEP; raised when exponent of floating-point number is smaller than permitted minimum; std. sys. act.: continue.
UNLOCK								131	UNLOCK FILE(DISK8) KEY(JOHN); makes the specified locked record of named UPDATE, DIRECT, EXCLUSIVE file available.
UNSPEC(x)		156							A=UNSPEC(COD); gives a bit string which is the internal coded representation of the arithmetic, string, or pointer variable (x).
UPDATE					62		124		DCL LEE FILE UPDATE; specifies that the file named is to be used for both input and output.
USES(item,...)				51					DCL #9 ENTRY USES(IT); is referred to in the named entry block.
VARYING	VAR			47					DCL FILE CHARACTER(50)VARYING; specifies storage for data in character-string form of varying (maximum must be given) length.
WAIT(event name)								132	WAIT(EVENT3); suspends operations in the task where it appears, until the named event(s) are completed.
WHILE(e)									DO I=6 TO 15 WHILE(A<B);... END; before execution, e is evaluated; if false, loop is terminated.
WRITE								132	WRITE FILE(SALES) FROM(TODAY) KEYFROM(#198); transfers a record from core to RECORD OUTPUT or UPDATE file.
ZERODIVIDE	ZDIV	163							ON ZDIV A=B+C; raised by attempt to divide by zero; standard system action: ERROR + comment.

BUILT-IN ARITHMETIC
FUNCTIONS IN PL/1

1. GENERAL ARITHMETIC FUNCTIONS

The arguments may, unless otherwise specified, be any arithmetic expressions. The formulas used in specifying the precision of the results are explained in Sec. 12.36.

Name	Arguments and function value
ABS	*Argument:* One is given. *Function value* = absolute value of argument, i.e., positive value of real argument, positive magnitude of complex argument. The magnitude of the complex number $x + yi$ is defined to be $\sqrt{x^2 + y^2}$. The mode is REAL. Base, scale, and precision are those of the argument unless the argument is FIXED COMPLEX, in which case the precision is $(\mathrm{MIN}(N, p + 1), q)$ for an argument of precision (p,q).
MAX	*Arguments:* Two or more are given. Complex arguments are not permitted. *Function value* = value of maximum argument, converted to highest characteristics of all arguments specified. If the arguments are FIXED of precisions (p_1, q_1), (p_2, q_2), ..., (p_n, q_n), the resulting precision is $(\mathrm{MIN}(N, \mathrm{MAX}(p_1 - q_1, \ldots, p_n - q_n) + \mathrm{MAX}(q_1, \ldots, q_n)), \mathrm{MAX}(q_1, \ldots, q_n))$.

Name	Arguments and function value
MIN	*Arguments:* Two or more are given. Complex arguments are not permitted. *Function value* = value of minimum argument, converted to highest characteristics of all arguments specified. If the arguments are FIXED of precisions $(p_1,q_1),(p_2,q_2), \ldots ,(p_n,q_n)$, the resulting precision is $(\text{MIN}(N,\text{MAX}(p_1-q_1, \ldots ,p_n-q_n)+ \text{MAX}(q_1, \ldots ,q_n)),\text{MAX}(q_1, \ldots ,q_n))$.
MOD	*Arguments:* Two are given, x and y. Base and scale of the arguments are converted to the higher characteristics of the pair. Complex arguments are not permitted. *Function value* = positive remainder after division of x by y to yield an integer quotient. The mode is REAL; base and scale are those of the converted arguments. Precision for FLOAT is the higher of the precisions of the arguments. Precision for FIXED is defined as follows: Let the precision of x be (p,q) and the precision of y be (r,s). The resulting precision is $(\text{MIN}(N,r-s+\text{MAX}(q,s)),\text{MAX}(q,s))$.
SIGN	*Argument:* One is given. Complex arguments are not permitted. *Function value* = integer 1 if argument >0; $= 0$ if argument $= 0$; $= -1$ if argument <0. The result is fixed binary with default precision.
FLOOR	*Argument:* One is given, x. A complex argument is not permitted. *Function value* = largest integer not exceeding x. Base, scale, and mode are those of the converted argument. Precision of result for x FIXED (p,q) is $(\text{MIN}(N,\text{MAX}(p-q+1,1)),0)$.
CEIL	*Argument:* One is given, x. A complex argument is not permitted. *Function value* = smallest integer not exceeded by x. Base, scale, and mode are those of the converted argument. Precision of result for x FIXED (p,q) is $(\text{MIN}(N,\text{MAX}(p-q+1,1)),0)$.
TRUNC	*Argument:* One is given, x. A complex argument is not permitted. *Function value* = FLOOR(x) if $x \geq 0$, = CEIL(x) if $x < 0$. Base, scale, and mode are those of the converted argument. Precision of result for x FIXED (p,q) is $(\text{MIN}(N,\text{MAX}(p-q+1,1)),0)$.
COMPLEX	*Arguments:* Two real arguments are given. The first is the real part; the second is the imaginary part. *Function value* = complex number formed from the two arguments. Base, scale, and precision of result are the highest characteristics of those of the arguments.
REAL	*Argument:* One is given, complex value. *Function value* = real part of argument. Base, scale, and precision are unchanged.
IMAG	*Argument:* One is given, complex value. *Function value* = conjugate of the argument. Base, scale, mode, and precision are unchanged.

2. FLOATING-POINT ARITHMETIC FUNCTIONS

The arguments of the following functions may be any expression. The argument is converted to floating point before the function is invoked. However, the functions

LOG2	ATAND	SIND	ERF	ATAN
LOG10	TAND	COSP	ERFC	

are defined only for real arguments.

Name (arguments)	Function value
EXP(x)	exp (x); i.e., e^x
LOG(x)	ln (x); error if $x \leq 0$
LOG10(x)	$\log_{10}$ (x); error if $x \leq 0$
LOG2(x)	$\log_2$ (x); error if $x \leq 0$
ATAND(x)	arctan (x) in degrees
ATAN(x)	arctan (x) in radians ABS (arctan (x)) $<$ pi/2
TAND(x)degree argument	tan (x)
TAN(x)radian argument	tan (x)
SIND(x)degree argument	sin (x)
SIN(x)radian argument	sin (x)
COSD(x)degree argument	cos (x)
COS(x)radian argument	cos (x)
TANH(x)radian argument	tanh (x)
ERF(x)	2 divided by square root of pi, multiplied by the integral from 0 to x of EXP($-t^2$) with respect to t.
SQRT(x)	The positive square root of x; error if $x < 0$
ERFC(x)	$1 - \text{ERF}(x)$
COSH(x)radian argument	cosh (x)
SINH(x)radian argument	sinh (x)
ATANH(x)	arctanh (x); error if ABS(x) ≥ 1

Name (arguments)	Function value

ATAN(y,x)   The arguments are converted to the highest characteristics of the pair. The value is:

$\arctan(y/x)$	if $x > 0$
$pi/2$	if $x = 0, y > 0$
error	if $x = 0, y = 0$
$-pi/2$	if $x = 0, y < 0$
$pi+\arctan(y/x)$	if $x < 0, y \geq 0$
$-pi+\arctan(y/x)$	if $x < 0, y < 0$

ATAND(y,x)   ATAN(y,x) in degrees; i.e., $(180/pi)*ATAN(y,x)$

If the arguments are complex, some of these functions are multiple-valued. The following table defines which value is actually retained. $z = x + yi$ is used to refer to the argument, and $w = u + vi$ is used to refer to the value retained by the function.

Name (arguments)	Function value
EXP(z)	exp (z)
LOG(z)	log (z), where $-pi < v \leq pi$; error if $z = 0$
ATAN(z)	$(LOG((1+z)/(1-z)))/2$; error if $z = +1$ or -1
ATANH(z)	iATANH(iz); error if $z = +1i$ or $-1i$
SIN(z)	sin (z) = sin (x) cosh (y) + icos (x) sinh (y)
COS(z)	cos (z) = cos (x) cosh (y) − isin (x) sinh (y)
SQRT(z)	$z**(\frac{1}{2})$; either $u > 0$, or $u = 0$ and $v \geq 0$
COSH(z)	cosh (z) = cosh (x) cos (y) + isinh (x) sin (y)
SINH(z)	sinh (z) = sinh (x) cos (y) + icosh (x) sin (y).

3. MANIPULATING ARRAYS AND STRUCTURES

All the built-in general arithmetic functions listed in Sec. 1 of this appendix may have array or structure expressions as arguments. They yield an array or structure of the same dimension bounds or structure architecture as the argument. The result is an array or structure whose elements are the named function of the corresponding elements of the argument.

4. FUNCTIONS ESPECIALLY FOR MANIPULATING ARRAYS

Two functions are listed below which may have only array expressions as arguments. The result is a scalar value that is a single number, with the precision, mode, and base (see Sec. 12.12 for a discussion of these terms) identical to those of the elements in the arrays that appear in the argument. Each element of the array is converted to FLOAT before being summed with or multiplied by the previous sum or product. The result is always in floating-point scale.

Function reference	*Function value*
SUM(X)	A scalar value equal to the sum of all the elements of X
PROD(X)	A scalar value equal to the product of all the elements of X

index

Page references in **boldface** indicate definition.

393